Sport in a Changing World

This book shows how the dynamic interplay of a powerful "golden triangle" of sports, media, and business interests with social, cultural, economic, and political forces shapes sport in a changing world. This edition is a condensed and updated version of the first edition, with an emphasis on current social issues in sport. It also has more global content. The golden triangle concept is more developed and applied more extensively. Other key themes of the first edition—power, status, and inequality—are also more developed. New "Stop and Think Questions" have been added to challenge students to think about the meaning of what they have read. The book is now divided into five sections. The new sections highlight sociology and the sociology of sport; inequality and diversity; globalization and social deviance; major social contexts of sport, including the high school, college, and professional levels; and power, political economy, and global sports.

Howard L. Nixon II is Professor Emeritus of Sociology at Towson University near Baltimore. Having studied and taught sport for thirty-five years, he is the author of several books and book chapters and many articles on sport sociology.

Sport in a Changing World

Second Edition

Howard L. Nixon II

Routledge
Taylor & Francis Group

NEW YORK AND LONDON

Second edition published 2016
by Routledge
711 Third Avenue, New York, NY 10017

and by Routledge
2 Park Square, Milton Park, Abingdon, Oxon, OX14 4RN

Routledge is an imprint of the Taylor & Francis Group, an informa business

First edition published 2008 by Paradigm Publishers

Library of Congress Cataloging-in-Publication Data
Nixon, Howard L., 1944–
  Sport in a changing world / Howard L. Nixon II. — Second Edition.
    pages cm
  Includes bibliographical references and index.
  1. Sports—Sociological aspects.   2. Sports—Social aspects. I. Title.
  GV706.5.N593 2015
  306.4′83—dc23
  2014043051

ISBN: 978-1-61205-856-6 (hbk)
ISBN: 978-1-61205-857-3 (pbk)
ISBN: 978-1-315-67597-8 (ebk)

Typeset in Bookman
by Apex CoVantage, LLC

Printed and bound in the United States of America by
Edwards Brothers Malloy on sustainably sourced paper

To Sara

Contents in Brief

Contents

Part III Building, Spreading, and Disrupting Sport in the Golden Triangle

4 Globalization, Mass Media, and Sports Culture   99

5 Sport, Social Deviance, and Social Problems   129

Part IV Social Contexts of Sport

6 Youth and High School Sports   167

7 College Athletics   199

8 Professional Sports   233

Part V   Power, Political Economy, and Global Sports

9 Politics, Economics, and Sport in a Changing World   273

Special Features

Acknowledgments

I would like first to thank Dean Birkenkamp, who allowed me to do the serious and extensive revision I had in mind, and his outstanding editorial, production, marketing, and support staff at Paradigm, especially Megan McClure. I would also like to thank the staff at Kinetic Publishing Services, as well as the staff at Routledge. All of you have consistently displayed professionalism, dedication, responsiveness, and a commitment to quality that I have very much appreciated. Forgive me if I have forgotten anyone. I am fortunate to be married to the most resourceful, knowledgeable, and helpful reference librarian anywhere, Sara Nixon. The extent of my scholarship for this book would have been substantially diminished without her help. In addition, her questions and suggestions clarified my thinking and pointed me in more fruitful directions, and her support was an important source of encouragement. Finally, I would like to acknowledge my former colleagues at Towson University who regularly offered good ideas and support, my colleagues in sport sociology who have made the knowledge in our still relatively young field much richer, deeper, and wider over the years, and, of course, sport sociology students at Towson University and elsewhere, who inspired me to write and revise this book.

Introduction to the Second Edition

Building on the framework of the first edition, this edition is condensed and fully updated and has more global content. The aim, as in the first edition, is to show how sociological perspectives can enable us to see important social and cultural dimensions of sport and understand how they shape the social organization of sport and its relationship to society. The central idea remains the golden triangle, and it is more developed and applied more extensively to explain the influence of commercial factors on sports around the world. Other key themes of the first edition—power, status, and inequality—remain important and are also more developed. Special research and topical content are no longer separated from the text, but instead are fully integrated, with coverage of new research and more recent topical issues. However, fifty "Probe" segments have been added. Since they are embedded but highlighted in Chapters 2–9, they provide an opportunity to pause and reflect on interesting and provocative ideas and issues raised by the text in these chapters. They could also be the basis for class discussions or debates. In addition, seven "Stop and Think Questions" appear at the end of each chapter. They could be used for reviewing and thinking more deeply about important ideas in each chapter. They could also be essay questions on exams or study questions to prepare for class discussion.

The text was thoroughly rewritten to reflect feedback from students to the first edition. It has the sociological foundation and general organizational framework of the first edition. But it is truly a new book. It addresses many of the major issues of sport that have surfaced or gained greater significance over the past decade. The new content has made the book topical. But as in the first edition, core sociological ideas and perspectives give meaning to the assorted behaviors, events, issues, and problems that characterize commercialized sports in the United States, North America, and around the world. The book is now divided into five parts to add clarity and coherence, and the original chapters were reduced in number and slightly reorganized. The new sections highlight sociology and the sociology of sport; the social organization of sport focusing on inequality and diversity; building, spreading, and disrupting sport in the golden triangle, with major emphases on globalization and social deviance; major social contexts of sport, including the high school, college, and professional levels; and power, political economy, and global sports. Much has happened in the various realms of sport since the first edition was written. This new edition captures both the enduring social and cultural patterns and how they are or may be changing. This illumination of sport should make much of what is important about the larger society clearer as well.

Part I

Sociology and the Sociology of Sport

1

A Sport Sociologist's Perspective of Sport

Sport sociologists look at sports differently than most people do. People who follow sports as fans or even casual observers often focus on the scores, team standings, and athletic accomplishments of individual athletes and teams. Increasingly, though, these aspects of sport seem to be overshadowed in the sports news by what happens off the field. Reports of these extracurricular activities can be very distracting and annoying to those who only want the sports news to be about what happens on the field. These reports can be especially disconcerting when they raise serious questions about the conduct or character of those who play, coach, or run popular sports.

For a sociologist of sport, the action outside the lines is of primary interest because it places sport in the larger context of society. Sport is interesting to sociologists because it gives us important insights about what society and culture are like. Although people act in distinctive ways when they play and watch sports, they are nevertheless participating in a sector of society that bears the imprint of the larger society and its culture. It may be easy to dismiss sport as unworthy of the serious attention of scholars. However, even casual observers understand that sport is often taken very seriously by a large number of people in society. People pursue careers in sport, take various kinds of risks with their bodies and careers when they play sports, and organize their lives around sports as fans. People who genuinely care about sports, as well as many who do not, have used sports events, teams, and stars to advance their purposes in realms as diverse as education, business, religion, and politics. This widespread interest in sport and the serious commitment it can create are reasons why sociologists should study sport and why it is important to understand what sociologists learn about sport.

Sport sociologists often draw from the facts, observations, and insights of journalists and expert sports commentators, and learn from what athletes, coaches, and fans do and say. However, unlike these other people, sport sociologists understand sport on the basis of theories and research. Sport sociology is a way of talking about and understanding sport and society that relies on critical thinking, careful theoretical analysis, and systematically gathered evidence.

Sport sociologists challenge assumptions that other people often take for granted, and in doing so, they open windows on sport and society through which you may never have looked or have purposely ignored or avoided. Sport sociology could create an experience of *culture shock* for those not used to looking critically at this realm (Berger 1963). Culture shock occurs when we realize that the world we have taken for granted is different, more complex, and less innocent than we had previously assumed. It can be unsettling for the familiar to become unfamiliar.

Since there are so many ostensibly simple and obvious truths about sport that we learn as children and are reinforced as we get older, it is easy to understand why applying a critical sociological perspective to sport could create culture shock. It is also easy to understand why an unsettling sense of culture shock could result in a refusal to believe that sport is not what we always thought it was. Tainted heroes often remain on their pedestals long after their images have been besmirched because their devoted fans refuse to accept the realities that undermine their heroic status. After all, sports heroes inspire devotion, and sport is an anchor giving meaning to the lives of many ordinary people. Making sports heroes more human and embedding sports in the messiness of real life can be too disorienting for people to accept. Although the purpose of sport sociology is to create understanding, helping people understand the world as it really is can create discomfort. This discomfort of culture shock has to be overcome in order to see the insights and knowledge about sport that can come from the sociological perspective and sociological research. Sociologists are not in the business of preaching values, but one value statement that characterizes the sociological study of sport is that understanding the realities of sport is better than being uninformed about them or misunderstanding them. Being armed with such insights and knowledge offers some insulation from the discomfort of culture shock.

When the news seems to contain too many stories of war, terrorist threats, environmental dangers, and risks to our health and well-being, along with a multitude of social problems from family violence and divorce to a variety of crimes on the street and in the corporate suite, we can easily understand why people seek refuge in or escape to the world of play and games. Philosopher Michael Novak (1976) wrote about the special joy that could be found in sport as a diversion from everyday stresses and concerns. Some have even attributed a religious meaning to sport. For example, Novak and others have written about the religious qualities of sport as a source of inspiration and fulfillment, capable of inspiring devotion and dedication that more traditional religion often seems incapable of inspiring in contemporary society. Still others have written about sport as a symbolic refuge, offering a safe haven of fantasy in a world often filled with too many stresses, strains, frustrations, disappointments, and problems (e.g., see Nixon 1984:207–211; Nixon and Frey 1996:55–56).

Much as we might want sport to be a fantasyland or refuge, it is embedded in the same society that we may idealize or try to escape when we follow sports. Athletes are real people, as are the coaches, managers, owners, investors, officials, commentators, reporters, and spectators whom we also associate with the world of popular sports today. The games athletes play are real, too. They incite real passions, even violent ones at times. People spend large sums of money on the games, media, and assorted paraphernalia sold in the sports marketplace. Newspaper publishers and radio and television producers create sports sections and sports programming because they realize that a lot of people follow sports, and many do so faithfully and passionately. Politicians and world leaders sometimes use sports to further their careers and their political or national interests. Major corporations use athletes and the games they play to increase their market and their bottom line.

The challenge for sport sociologists should be clear. It is to document and explain the realities of sport in a way that is compelling for the audience. This is challenging because the myths of sports are themselves highly compelling, and demystifying sport can create culture shock and make people dismissive. After all, myths and illusions may be far more reassuring, gratifying, and meaningful than reality.

Documenting and explaining major social and cultural patterns in sport will necessarily involve an analysis of change, since powerful forces of social and cultural change are leaving their imprint on society and sport. We will examine contemporary forces of social demographic, organizational, economic, political, and technological change as well as changes in social institutions and in the patterns of social interaction and social relationships linking networks of people, groups, and organizations to each other. We are ultimately interested in how these various kinds of social factors influence sport and cause it to change. We will also see how various inequalities weave their way through sport in different contexts and at different levels of sport. Sport itself will be understood in terms of a dominant network of powerful and intertwined people and organizations in highly commercialized sports, the media, and the corporate world, which we will call the golden triangle. Since we cannot understand change today without seeing it from a global perspective, we will look at sport in a changing world and try to understand how the most visible and commercially successful sports are being shaped by forces and patterns of change occurring in a global context.

Sociology and the Sociological Imagination

Although this book draws from the insights and evidence of scholars in many related fields, sociology is the foundation for the analysis that is presented in these pages. As sport sociology, this analysis utilizes sociological concepts, theories, and evidence to describe and explain the relationship between sport and society. This analysis of sport in society will reveal important ideas about how people interact with each other, how society is organized, and how it changes.

Sociologists look for patterns in social connections linking people in social interactions, relationships, and networks. These patterns form social structures, which are the recurrent or enduring characteristics of social interactions, relationships, and networks. Sociologists are interested in how social structures form, what they look like, how they influence people interacting in society or social actors, and how they change. In contrast, psychologists are more interested in the qualities of social actors as individuals, including the brain and cognition, consciousness, memory, sensation, emotions, learning, motivation, personality, and mental health problems. Thus, while sport sociologists may focus on how interactions in sports groups and organizations are structured by social and cultural forces in society, sport psychologists are more likely to be interested in how the cognitions, perceptions, motivations, and social adjustment of individuals in sport shape their performance and the performance of their teams.

The idea of social structure can seem fairly abstract. It may be clearer if we think of it as similar to the basic framework of a house, which includes the basement, walls, windows, door frames, floors, ceilings, and roof. It is what endures in the face of strong winds; new coats of paint; changes in furniture, appliances, floor and wall coverings, and heating and cooling systems; and new homeowners. The framework of a house may warp, rot, or even collapse over time, and it may be seriously damaged or leveled by extreme weather or fire. However, these kinds of changes take time or are relatively unusual. Thus, social structures are like the framework of most houses because they endure over time.

Unlike the framework of a house, though, the basic elements of social structure are abstract and cannot be directly observed. These basic elements include social norms, statuses, roles, relationships, and networks. Social norms are the expectations or rules we have for how we will interact with each other. Norms vary from informal to very formal, and some may be enacted as laws. However, informal norms, called folkways by sociologists, should not be mistaken as inconsequential. For example, the informal rules that teammates have about the secrecy of hazing rituals can lead to shunning or more serious social penalties if they are ignored. Violating some norms has significant moral implications, such as when athletes are publicly blamed for intentionally and seriously injuring teammates in practice or opposing players in competition.

Statuses are the positions we occupy in society, such as occupations and places in the family, other social groups, and organizations. Statuses are defined by the expectations we associate with them. We expect certain kinds of behavior from people in distinctive places in the social structure in relation to others with whom they interact in these positions. For example, mothers and fathers are expected to act in certain ways toward children, teachers are expected to fulfill certain responsibilities toward students, and coaches are expected to treat athletes in certain ways. These status expectations are defined reciprocally, which means that just as coaches are expected to inter-act in certain ways with the athletes on their team, athletes are expected to interact in certain ways with their coaches. It should be evident that status expectations may be broad and also could be very narrowly defined in relation to particular social contexts, such as the locker room, the coach's office, the playing field, or public settings for coaches and athletes.

While we occupy social statuses, we perform social roles. For example, there are athletes who diligently try to do all the things that coaches ask of them, and there are athletes who display much less diligence or even defy their coach. In a sense, then, roles are the ways people interpret and respond to status expectations. Since the expectations of different statuses that people occupy can clash, people can experience stress or discomfort when they perform their roles. This stress or discomfort is called role conflict, such as when a woman who is a coach and mother is pulled in different directions by the competing expectations of these two statuses. Role strain occurs when people have to deal with competing expectations in different roles associated with the same status, such as when a public high school coach must tell players who want team prayers before games that school administrators expect the coach to discontinue this practice. Role conflicts and role strain are called social structural issues because they result from clashing expectations related to different statuses, norms, or role relations in the social structure rather than from the personalities or desires or motivations of individuals.

Social relationships are established when our interactions with others persist over time. Social relationships link us directly or indirectly to others in social networks. Social networks can be as simple as a small group or as complex as the relationships between national bodies and teams in the Olympics. We may be connected to others in a variety of ways, such as talking to them, e-mailing them, communicating through social media, engaging in economic transactions or exchanges with them, or trying to influence them. Sometimes we have direct or face-to-face interactions with others in a group or organization, and at other times, we are indirectly linked to them because they are friends of our friends or members of the same large group or organization who are tied to others in the group or organization but are not directly tied to us. For example, professional athletes in different sports who have no direct contact with each other may nevertheless have an indirect tie to each other because they are represented by the same agent or marketing firm. Both will be affected by how well their agent and marketing firm represents them and all the others in their business networks.

We refer to the enduring patterns of social arrangements of norms, statuses, roles, relationships, and networks that serve larger purposes in society as societal institutions. These institutions are an essential aspect of social order since their existence contributes to the persistence of society by making it possible to meet the needs of everyday life in expected or predictable ways. For example, organized societies have some form of family life to prepare children for their membership in society, of religion to provide spiritual meaning for people's lives, of economy to enable people to produce and exchange the goods and services needed to sustain life in their society, of government to order or organize collective lives and decisions of people in a society, and of mass media to enable people to communicate in and across social networks in modern mass societies. Sport is also a societal institution since it is part of the structure of societies. As part of popular culture in modern societies, it serves as a diversion or form of entertainment. The nature of sport will be made clearer later in the chapter when the concept of sport is more formally defined.

The *sociological imagination* is a perspective introduced by C. Wright Mills ([1959] 2000) that helps us see the distinctive way that sociologists understand human behavior, and it shows us how to interpret sport from a sociological perspective. The sociological imagination pushes our perspective beyond seeing the uniqueness of each individual's behavior to seeing human behavior in a broader social, cultural, and historical context, where the behavior of people in one context can be compared and contrasted with the behavior of people in other contexts. Thus, the serious injury you sustained when you were training for a marathon becomes more than something that disrupted your training or prevented you from competing in the marathon. It is one of many similar cases in a statistical pattern of training injuries sustained by runners or recreational athletes in a particular year, age group, and region or country. By looking at statistics about rates of training injuries over time for different types of athletes in different types of sports, we begin to see that human behavior is not merely a collection of unique random events or experiences that happen only to particular individuals. We also see that certain kinds of behavior form patterns where the same kinds of things happen repeatedly to the same kinds of people under the same social or cultural circumstances or conditions.

Mills proposed that cultural influences combine with social structural influences and our historical understandings to shape our experiences in society. These combined influences make us similar to some people in society and different from others. Sharing a culture is one of the important reasons we are like other people. The word "culture" is sometimes casually used interchangeably with the word "society," but sociologists distinguish these ideas. *Culture* refers to our way of life and beliefs we have in common or share with other people in a society or sector of society. It includes shared patterns or practices of everyday life, such as our work and family life routines, our politics, and our cuisine, housing, music, and recreation. It also includes shared values, beliefs, behavior, and material objects or artifacts the people in a society create and pass on to later generations. We interact as a cultural group in society when we are influenced by shared cultural ideas and traditions. *Society* refers to social networks among people in a specific area, and it reflects how we organize our social interactions and relationships. The substance or meaning of relationships in social networks reflects cultural influences.

The sociological imagination enables us to see beyond the things that make us unique to patterns of social behavior that tend to characterize groups or categories of people and tend to recur when the same causal factors are present in the contexts of our experience. To return to the case of sports injuries, we may find, for example, that in contact sports that are played at high levels of competitive intensity by big, strong, and well-conditioned athletes, there are fairly predictable rates of certain types of injuries over time. The fact that athletes continue to compete in dangerous sports despite the risk of injury may be understood with sociological imagination as a result of the influence of status expectations for serious athletes to "play hurt" and of a culture in sport that glorifies "playing hurt" and minimizes the seriousness of injuries. This contrasts with the view that athletes independently make decisions to keep playing despite the risk, pain, and damage of injuries. Rather than seeing these athletes as irrational or masochistic individuals, we are able with sociological imagination to see their behavior as a product of larger forces of society, culture, and history in serious or highly competitive sports. This is the sociological analysis I have proposed in my own research about pain and injury in sport (Nixon 1993).

The sociological imagination implies a type of clear and precise thinking and generalizing about the social world, which is often different from the ways we think and talk about our experiences in our everyday lives. However, what people think and say about sport in their everyday interactions is important to sport sociologists as data that inform their own sociological imaginations and help them make sense of sport and society. One of the purposes of this book is to use sport sociology to convey an understanding of sport and society that enriches and broadens your sociological imagination and helps you see the social world of sport with new eyes and new insights.

Sport Sociology

Sport sociology is the application of sociology and the sociological imagination to the study of sport. Its purpose is to produce knowledge to help us interpret, understand, and predict patterns of social interaction and organization in sport. For sociologists, sport is a useful lens for understanding social patterns, problems, and issues found in other parts of society, but sport itself is important to study because it is part of the established institutional structure of society and because many people take it very seriously, invest a great deal of their identities and resources in it, and organize much of their lives and the structures of society around it. Thus, the sociological study of sport helps us understand an important part of society, and the sociology of sport enables us to see significant and recurring patterns, problems, and issues of social life and societies. Sport sociology also can have useful applications in helping sports policymakers, sports officials, and others with responsibility for making decisions about sport and sports participants to be more informed in their policies, plans, and actions.

Sport sociology, like the systematic study of sport in general, has a relatively short history, with most of the scholarly work in the field produced over the past forty to forty-five years. It may be an indication of the significance we attribute to sport in society and in our individual lives and of the complexity of sport that it is now studied from many different disciplinary perspectives. Scholars now study sport from psychological, anthropological, political and policy science, business, economic and financial, management, legal, biomedical and human performance, nutritional, cultural studies, literary, aesthetic, media, geographic, and philosophical perspectives as well as from sociological perspectives. Sport sociology is the broadest of the social and behavioral science perspectives.

In the United States and other societies with capitalist economies, there are strong beliefs in the power of individualism and the ability of individuals to shape their own destinies. These beliefs make people more inclined to explain their own sports experiences and the things they observe or think they know about sport in terms of individualistic perspectives, which is why sports teams are more likely to hire sport psychologists than sport sociologists to deal with team problems and improve team performance. There are limits, however, to what personality profiles or psychological assessments can tell us about the dynamics of team relationships or team performance. We sometimes fail to grasp that acknowledged influences such as peer pressure or team cohesion are social forces and not qualities of individuals. Smart coaches understand that players who work effectively together are more likely to make their team successful than are players who seek individual success. Consider, for example, the success of underdogs that defeat star-studded opponents and the struggles of "dream teams" of superstars in the Olympics and other international competitions in recent years.

Thus, sport sociologists have important insights to teach us, insights that complement the insights derived from psychological and other perspectives of sport. In a society emphasizing individual more than social influences, sport sociology can lead us to insights and knowledge that may surprise us and challenge our more casual everyday ways of understanding sport and society. The critical perspective that is a central element of sociological thinking should make us question the things we are sure we know about sport because we assume they are "common sense." We have already considered how teams with more physical talent or superstars than their opponent may lose to their less talented foes. This may seem counterintuitive, but sport sociology focuses our attention on the influence of social forces on team performance, which could minimize the influence of factors such as individual talent.

Sport sociology also compels us to look at theoretical ideas and concrete research evidence before we draw conclusions or make predictions about matters such as the types of teams that are most likely to win. Being pushed to look at the realities of sport may be uncomfortable. If we are passionate about sport, have committed a great deal of our lives to playing, coaching, administering, or following sport, have depended on sport for a major part of our identity or our livelihood, and have been taught that sport is inherently virtuous and beneficial, we are unlikely to accept or want to see that sport has the same kinds of warts or problems we find elsewhere in society. For those who are devoted to sport and who seek in sport a refuge from the problems and pressures of everyday life, sport sociology can represent a very unappealing way of looking at sport. It is difficult for us to acknowledge that the assumptions we take for granted may not be true, especially if they cast sport in a less positive light than we want to see or accept.

Looking for facts about sport by probing beneath the surface and beyond the obvious can lead sociologists of sport to unexpected and disillusioning kinds of evidence. On the surface is the heroic and glamorous image of sport presented by the sports media. Sometimes beneath the surface or out of plain sight is an uglier side of sport involving sexism, racism, exploitation, homophobia, abuse of the body, and various forms of social deviance, such as drug use, violence, and other crimes. It is not the purpose of this book to emphasize the ugly and unattractive qualities of sport to make it less appealing and seem less worthy of commitment, investment, or interest. In trying to reveal and understand the realities of sport, we will see a realm of society that has the complexities, contradictions, diversity, richness, excitement, and challenges that we find in society's other realms. We will also see how sport is related to these other realms of society. In providing this kind of picture of sport and society, sport sociology should be as exciting and interesting as sport itself. Looking at sport through the eyes of a sociologist, with an open and objective mind, sociological imagination, and a critical perspective, will lead to discoveries about sport that are exciting and interesting.

The Concept of Sport

Sport is the central concept in sport sociology and in this book. Most of us have informal or intuitive conceptions of what sport is and we are not particularly concerned about being precise or consistent in talking about sport. Sociologists try to be precise and systematic in defining and using concepts so that the focus of their analysis is clearly understood. A general sociological definition of *sport* is institutionalized physical competition occurring in formally organized or corporate structures (Nixon and Frey 1996:3–4). The most basic component of the definition of sport is that it is physical competition. That is, sport is about individuals and groups using their physical skills to try to defeat their opponents in interaction that has winners and losers. In sport sociology, however, we are interested not only in the social aspects of the competition itself, but also in the broader organizational context in which the competition is embedded. Thus, sport is defined here in terms of both the physical competition and its larger organizational context.

The organizational context of sport is formally structured, which means that it has official rules, official enforcement of the rules by regulatory bodies, a hierarchical arrangement of positions or statuses, and, usually, a bureaucratic form. *Bureaucracy* is a type of administrative organization based on rational-legal authority in which people are supposed to interact with each other in terms of their competence, their productivity, the rules and goals of the organization, and the positions they hold rather than in terms of their personalities and how much they like each other. The idea of bureaucracy today generally implies hierarchical organizations run by "officials," "executives," or "management." Getting things done efficiently and effectively is more important in bureaucracies than is making sure everyone feels good or is personally happy. Presumably, organizational success or profitability makes people feel happy in a bureaucracy.

The formal organization of sport is corporate as well as bureaucratic. The *corporate* organization of sport implies that it is a legally defined entity that has a formal legal existence that is distinct from the legal status of its individual members. As such, sports organizations can enter into formal legal agreements with individuals or other organizations; can make their own rules and policies; can have boards, officials, and employees who run them and do their work; can sell tickets, merchandise, and media broadcast rights; and can make money that can be used to pay employees, make investments, build and maintain facilities, and market their business. If they are for-profit corporations, they pay taxes and earn profits for their private owners or dividends for stockholders. The corporate organization of many sports clubs, leagues, and governing bodies involves business operations that are intended to generate revenue or financial profits. The businesslike corporate organization of contemporary sport is one of its most distinctive characteristics, which means that it often is difficult to separate what happens on the field from the influence of money or the behavior of people trying to make money from sport.

The idea that sport is *institutionalized* implies that its social structure is established and relatively stable. The institutional character of sport further implies that it has a predictable form that is familiar to us because people in sport repeatedly do the same kinds of things and interact with others in the same kinds of statuses, roles, and relationships in the same kinds of settings over time. These structures tend to be relatively stable over time because they exist in formal or corporate organizations or networks that have officials, executives, or managers responsible for making and articulating rules and policies and for making sure that people follow the rules and conform to formal expectations for their roles and relationships.

It should be evident that whether an activity is or is not a sport may not be immediately obvious. For example, people competing against each other in volleyball may look as though they are playing a sport, but we need to look more closely to determine whether their activity is actually sport. Are the players representatives of formal teams? Do they have a formal coach? Is their competition part of a formal schedule devised and monitored by the officials in a formal league? Are the length of the game, who plays, how many play at one time, how points are scored, and how games and matches are won determined by formal rules? Is the game formally refereed? Is this match part of a championship or does it have a bearing on whether the teams are eligible for a championship with trophies and other formal rewards? Do the players receive some type of subsidy or compensation or special privileges for competing? Does the game receive media attention? Are there spectators and do they pay to watch? These questions suggest the kinds of activities we are interested in studying as sport. If we do not carefully distinguish between casual pickup games of volleyball and volleyball played as part of interscholastic or intercollegiate athletics or professional leagues, we might make incorrect generalizations about the players, how they interact, and what happens to them as a result of their participation in this game.

Impromptu or informal games of volleyball are sociologically interesting, but they are different from the institutionalized and formally organized corporate behavior we are defining here as sport, and they have different social implications. What is especially interesting from a sociological perspective about the conception of sport we have presented here is that by virtue of its type of organization, it is connected to many aspects of the major institutional structures of society as well as to significant contemporary global social patterns and forces of social change. We should recognize, though, that sport is complex, is played in many different venues, has many different forms, and exists at different levels, from local sports leagues and tournaments for very young children to professional and Olympic competition at the global level. We know, too, that even for young children, sport can be organized at an international level, as in the case of Little League Baseball, Inc.

Although the corporate character of sport generally implies that it is commercialized and may involve paid professionals, sport may not be commercial or professional. A number of activities that begin as informally organized recreational physical activities evolve into formally organized sports and ultimately become commercialized and professionalized. For example, as a result of corporate and commercial influences, activities such as snowboarding have been transformed from leisure pastimes pursued by a relatively small segment of society into "big-time" sports on a global scale. Sport sociologists are interested in how sport contrasts with more informally organized recreation, play, and games, how certain kinds of activities evolve into sports, and the different implications of sport and more informal physical activities.

I assume that sport is *serious* competition, which means that the results are not known or fixed in advance. This assumption is important because people who watch and play sport expect it to have integrity. The appeal of sport depends in part on the assumption that "anything is possible" when even badly mismatched individuals or teams take the floor, court, or field. Sport would lose its integrity and appeal if the results were fixed in advance. This fact is what distinguishes professional wrestling as a theatrical performance and differentiates it from the sport of high school, college, and Olympic wrestling.

The evolution and complexity of sport are seen in the historical development of track and field events that originated in ancient Greek and Roman times and in sports today that use modern technology, such as automobiles, snowboards, and skateboards. Some sports have evolved as informal "extreme sports" and ultimately have become part of the established order of corporate sport. Sports events have been very exclusive, limited only to the elite members of society, but democratization has made more sports accessible to more people. Indeed, we have seen sports evolve to accommodate societal outsiders or special interests, including sports for people with disabilities, such as the Special Olympics and Paralympics, and sports for people who are gay, such as the Gay Games.

Historian Allen Guttmann (1978) identified a number of characteristics of the social organization of modern sport that distinguish it from forms in earlier eras. For example, he proposed that modern sport is organized as a *secular* rather than a sacred activity. That is, even though a number of athletes, especially winners, say that they are dedicating their performance to the glory of their god or that they are thankful to God for enabling them to win, the *purpose* of sport today is not religious or sacred. Sport is not organized to satisfy, appease, or glorify deities. It is a form of secular entertainment, and it is played by people who are very much interested in rewards such as trophies, money, fame, or influence that they can enjoy or use in this world. In fact, devout athletes, coaches, and fans often experience conflicts between sport and religion today because so many sports events are scheduled on holy days, when believers are not supposed to be focused on secular or worldly activities.

Guttmann also proposed that the organization of modern sport emphasizes equality of opportunity, quantification or counting, and records and is bureaucratic, rational, and specialized. These characteristics are generally consistent with the definition of sport presented earlier. For example, the *bureaucratic* organization of modern sport implies that it is *rational, specialized,* and focused on the *measurement* of performance and formal *record keeping.* The *rationality* of modern sport is related to its planned, intentional, purposeful, and formal mission and goal-seeking behavior and to its corporate legal and commercial structure. Sport has become increasingly *specialized* in the modern era as sports officials, coaches, and athletes have performed more and more narrowly defined roles. For example, in US football, players rarely play both offensive and defensive positions, and some who play a defensive position such as linebacker may enter the game only for anticipated passing or running plays.

In the modern period, the computer and similar devices have made it much easier to *measure* and *record performances*; and with more precise measuring instruments, records have become more precise. For example, swimming and other sports that time their competitors rank them by hundredths of a second. Our increased capacity and desire to measure things has produced a plethora of categories of performance and records.

Bureaucracies are hierarchical, with people in higher positions having more authority than people in lower positions. This kind of inequality in the organized world of modern sport is accompanied by inequalities that are created by the outcomes of competition. That is, we generally give winners more rewards than we give losers, from publicity and fame to cash prizes and salaries. In earlier historical periods, sport was unequal in another way. Access to sport or at least certain kinds of sport favored by the elite was limited to people in the higher social classes or in dominant ethnic or racial groups. Democratization, which is the opening of sports to people from more diverse social class or status backgrounds, is a characteristic of the modern era of sports, and it has meant that more people from middle and working classes, more racial and ethnic minorities, more people with disabilities, and more women have been able to participate in a wide range of sports in a variety of roles, from athlete to spectator. Democratization implies equality of opportunity, which means that even though competitors are unequal—as winners and losers—at the end of the competition, those who want to and are able to compete are all supposed to have a chance to be at the starting line at the beginning of the competition, regardless of their social background.

A number of modern sports have some degree of stratification or inequality in their opportunity structures, but even the formerly elite sports such as golf and tennis espouse the *principle of equality of opportunity* and talk about trying to attract minority and less advantaged people. Thus, when we refer to equality of opportunity as a characteristic of the organization of modern sport, we would be more precise in referring to the *principle or goal* of equality of opportunity. In some sports, the cost of training, access to facilities, travel, clothing, and equipment is so high that the idea of equal access is more myth than reality.

Summarizing Guttmann, the major characteristics of the modern social organization of sport are (1) secularism, (2) bureaucracy, (3) rationality, (4) specialization, (5) quantification, (6) records, and (7) the principle or goal of equality of opportunity. Two other characteristics also seem worthy of inclusion in the definition of contemporary sports: the influence of mass media and the influence of economic forces of commercialism and capitalism. The mediated character of contemporary sports is especially evident when we consider the imprint of television and now increasingly the Internet, digital technology, and new electronic media. The value of television and these other contemporary mass media to sport can be attributed to their capacity to convey sharp, intense, and compelling messages and images to people around the world in real time (see Smart 2005:8). It is difficult to think of contemporary sport without thinking of mass mediated sports messages and images, and it is difficult to understand the organization of contemporary sport without recognizing the powerful influence of the mass media on it. Sport would not have developed as a corporate and commercial enterprise in the modern era or have become as globally popular as it is today without the publicity and financial investment of the mass media. Before television began to influence sport in the mid-twentieth century, print media played a critical role in the development of sport in the nineteenth century and then radio played a key part in the early twentieth century.

The rise of industrial capitalism in the nineteenth and twentieth centuries also had a significant impact on the growth of sport. That is, sport became more associated with the business of making money. Sport became a form of capitalist production when entrepreneurs and owners tried to make a financial profit from their sports investments. Although there are realms of sport, from the youth club level to high schools and colleges, that are not strictly capitalistic, they are commercialized and try to emulate the business models embedded in the capitalistic professional sports industry. The commercialized sports industry in general involves manufacturing, marketing, and selling sports events and merchandise to make money. Sport has become an important vehicle for the global expansion of capitalism today. In his book *Michael Jordan and*

Boy manages street store selling national team jerseys during World Cup in Brazil in 2014.
(© Marcos Brindicci/Reuters/Corbis)

the New Global Capitalism, LaFeber (2002) argued that the construction and selling of Michael Jordan as a global sports icon illustrated how transnational capitalist corporations used sport and high-tech telecommunications technology to sell their products around the world.

With this discussion of the defining characteristics of modern sport, we are ready for a more refined definition of sport than the general one proposed at the beginning of this section. This refined definition builds on the earlier definition and conceptualizes *contemporary sport* as a mediated capitalist enterprise with defining elements of modern rational bureaucratic and corporate commercial organization. Thus, contemporary sport is associated with the evolving characteristics of modern societies, including most prominently rationality, bureaucracy, corporate commercialism, consumer capitalism, and the mass media. Not surprisingly, Guttmann (2000:258) observed that modern sports are least popular in the Islamic world, where religious fundamentalism prevails and an aversion to the products of modern scientific rationality and consumer capitalism is strongest—that is, where powerful and pervasive traditional cultural elements contrast sharply with the dominant characteristics of the modern social organization of sport.

Sociological Theory and Sport Sociology

Both theories and research are essential for producing sociological knowledge. Sociologists use theories to construct understandings of society that explain its major social patterns, problems, and issues. Different theories are like different sets of glasses that give us different pictures of the social patterns that constitute society and how and why these patterns emerge, persist, and change. Theories that focus on the *micro* level emphasize how individuals interact with each other, develop a sense of self in their interactions, and derive meanings for the social patterns, problems, and issues they observe and experience. Thus, micro-level theories give us pictures of life at the street level, where we can see the individual social actors. Theories that focus on the *macro* level give us understandings of more abstract institutional and societal patterns. Thus, they provide views of society from 40,000 feet, where only the broader shapes of social structures are observable. At this level, we can see structures of inequality, corporate and community organization, population trends, and various societal institutions.

Theoretical ideas and knowledge are important and useful because they can guide policymaking, decisions, and actions. Theoretical thinking about cause and effect may lead us to predict particular outcomes of particular factors or conditions, such as the expansion or contraction of athletic programs or new rules to make certain types of sports less dangerous, and may lead us to act in ways to create the conditions we think will lead to predicted desired outcomes. In the simplest sense, we cannot understand society sociologically without applying the coherent framework embedded in a theory. However, theoretical understandings are only speculations or hypotheses and do not become knowledge until they are substantiated with evidence from careful research.

Sociology does not have a single theoretical perspective that explains everything sociologists study or that enables us to predict all types of social behavior, nor does it have a single research method that all sociologists use to collect social data. My aim here is not to present all the theories and research methods sport sociologists have used. It is instead to provide a brief and general summary of some prominent theoretical perspectives and research methods sport sociologists have used to understand sport.

We will look at theoretical perspectives in this section and research methods in the next. *Structural functionalist* theories help us understand sport as a societal institution because they focus on the purposes or functions established or institutionalized social patterns serve in sport and society. The structural functionalist perspective can be traced to the work of French sociologist Emile Durkheim in the nineteenth century. A basic structural functional assumption is that social structures of norms, statuses, roles, and relationships arise in social networks because people need certain things to happen in order for their groups, organizations, or the larger society to survive and be effective. For example, for social order in society to exist, people need to be socialized so that they understand what society expects of them. A function of sports participation in society might be to socialize us by teaching us how to conform to established social norms or expectations for our behavior, such as team or group loyalty, or how to act in socially acceptable ways in social roles in society. Another example of a structural functional analysis of sport might be an explanation of the contribution to society and social stability that comes from excluding girls from more aggressive forms of team sports. This practice teaches a socialization lesson about appropriate gender roles, which reinforces traditional ideas about gender and gender roles and helps maintain established gender-differentiated structures in society. Thus, social structures do not merely exist. They have *functions* or purposes and consequences. Societal institutions such as sport have the broad function of contributing to the life, vitality, and orderly organization of the society. This kind of analysis suggests what some critics have called a "conservative bias" in structural functionalism because it seems to legitimate enduring or traditional practices that maintain the stability of society.

Social conflict and critical theorists often have a macro perspective and focus on broad patterns of inequality in society and how dominant groups or classes exploit or oppress less powerful and privileged people to benefit themselves and other people of high status. These kinds of perspectives derive from the work of Karl Marx in the nineteenth century. We can see the roots of critical perspectives of modern scientific rationality and bureaucracy in Max Weber's nineteenth-century ideas about how the formal constraints of bureaucratic rules and roles create an "iron cage" for those who work in bureaucracies or have to deal with them.

Neo-Marxist critical theorists focus on how contemporary bureaucracies and patterns of scientific, legal, and organizational rationality exploit and dehumanize human beings. This happens in sport when scientific training methods and medicine are used unethically and illegally to enhance athletic performance and turn athletes into what John Hoberman (1992) called "mortal engines." According to Hoberman, mortal engines are a product of the values of industrial technology and how they have shaped the evolution of "scientific sport." Thus, an appropriate metaphor for neo-Marxist critical theory might be of robots, and particularly athletes as robots.

Closely related to Hoberman's critique of scientific rationality is George Ritzer's critical analysis of rationality in modern versions of bureaucracy, which he called "McDonaldization." This kind of organization drew its inspiration from the McDonald's restaurant chain and became the model for many other businesses and organizations. Ritzer (2011) referred to the "irrationality of rationality" in his critique of McDonaldization. He argued that the ostensibly rational organizational structures of McDonaldization become irrational when they suppress human individualism, creativity, choice, and freedom. Thus, both the iron cage and the irrationality of rationality deprive people of a sense of control over their roles in organizations.

More classical *Marxist theorists* focus their critical eyes on economic inequality and its consequences in modern capitalist industrial societies. Marxists draw attention to the divide between the owners or people who control capitalist enterprises and the people who work for them. Marx assumed that owners had an interest as a class in trying to generate as much profit as possible from their businesses. He argued that owners believed that they could maximize their profits by investing as little as possible in their workers. The resulting exploitation and oppression of workers was the primary target of Marx's critique of capitalism. Sociologists of sport with a Marxist perspective might study how wealthy capitalist owners have historically exploited athletes in professional sports and how professional athletes have engaged in union activity as a collective or class response to the exploitative and oppressive power of owners.

Feminist theorists concentrate on structures of patriarchy or male domination and see sexist ideology and historical patterns of gender inequality as the basis for continuing patriarchy and male privilege. Sport has been a logical target of feminist critiques because it has historically been so biased toward males. *Critical race and ethnic theorists* have a perspective similar to the feminist perspective but focus more on racial and ethnic inequalities and racism.

Like sexism and gender inequality, racism and racial and ethnic inequality have been prominent aspects of the history of many sports.

A variety of Marxist, neo-Marxist, feminist, racial, ethnic, and other critical perspectives have been applied to the study of sport (Giulianotti 2005). While not necessarily explicitly rooted in classic Marxism, contemporary critical theories incorporate elements of Marxist conflict theory in their emphases on conflicts or struggles over ideology, status, power, or economic advantage involving minorities and women. It is easy to see the contrasts between structural functionalists and social conflict and critical theorists. Structural functionalists see existing social and cultural patterns in terms of their functional value to an entire group, organization, society, or other social system. Social conflict and critical theorists tend to see these patterns in terms of how they advantage certain social classes, strata, races, or ethnic groups over others or advantage men over women. They also focus on the conditions under which the disadvantages, exploitation, or oppression associated with economic, political, and social inequalities can be challenged and changed and society can be made more fair or just. Thus, sport sociologists influenced by structural functionalism focus on the things that bring people together in society and serve society's interests, while social conflict and critical theorists focus on the things that divide people and serve the particular economic, social, or political interests of the dominant class or elite.

Interactionist theories present a third, and significantly different, type of theoretical perspective for understanding social behavior. Unlike structural functionalism and various social conflict and critical theories, they focus on the *micro* level of society, where individuals and groups directly interact with one another. *Symbolic interactionists* tend to be less concerned with uncovering the causes that predict patterns of large-scale social behavior than they are with providing rich and detailed descriptions of the patterns of everyday social life. Symbolic interaction refers to the construction and exchange of meanings in social interaction through which we define ourselves, our roles, and our experiences in society. This emphasis on symbolic interaction derives from the work of Charles Horton Cooley at the turn of the twentieth century and the work of George Herbert Mead a few decades later. This perspective focuses on how we form ideas about ourselves, understand others' expectations for us that are embedded in social roles, and perceive the expectations of society that are incorporated in social norms, ranging from informal everyday rules for interaction to highly formalized regulations and laws.

We are able to think about ourselves, others, and the larger society in terms of the symbols represented in language, and we use talk and other forms of communication to develop or negotiate mutually acceptable ways of referring to each other and interacting with each other. Of course, people with higher status and more power can exert more influence on how they and other people are labeled and treated in society. Higher-status and more powerful people may react to others they like or respect with recognition, admiration, affection, or other positive forms of attention, sentiment, or status, which can help these others become more accepted or successful in established social circles. For example, consider the value to a high school soccer player of being blessed as a "future star" by a prominent college or professional coach. On the other hand, people with high status and considerable power also can impose negative or deviant labels on those they do not like or respect, who threaten them, or who disagree with them. Imagine being a college football star who is criticized as having a "bad attitude" or being lazy by a major scouting service or by prominent sports columnists prior to the draft by the National Football League (NFL). Negative or deviant labels can be difficult to shed when those who are labeled have less status and power than those imposing the label, and like positive labels, they can have significant effects on how we are treated, the opportunities we have in society, and even how we think of ourselves.

A prominent example of a contemporary interactionist perspective is Erving Goffman's (1959, 1967) *dramaturgical* approach to the study of everyday life, which conceptualizes social life as theater. On the stage of this theater of life, we perform roles as if we were actors playing roles. Goffman assumed that we actively and intentionally create and negotiate "scripts" for our interactions that are meant to make positive impressions on others and make social relations go as smoothly as possible, as in a well-scripted and well-performed play. An important conceptual distinction in Goffman's perspective is the difference between "front-stage" and "back-stage" behavior. For example, professional athletes perform on the front stage of athletic fields and sports arenas where they are observed in action by spectators, television viewers, sports reporters, and many others who form impressions of these athletes as competitors. These athletes also interact with boosters, fans, and the press in assorted other public venues off the field. What makes these settings front-stage settings is the wide visibility of the athletes' performances and the careful construction and management of impressions by the athletes who play their roles as sports stars and role models.

We expect these athletes to conform to our expectations of what professional athletes are, and these athletes often try to follow this script. Their behavior is not restricted to the front stage, however. They also act more informally, and sometimes "out of character," in the back stages of the closed locker room, their homes, and other private venues, where they do not expect the public to see them. At times, we learn things about athletes that reveal substantial discrepancies between their public selves seen only in front-stage areas and their private selves played out in the back stages of these athletes' lives. For example, those who saw cyclist Lance Armstrong as a sports hero and embodiment of the American Dream were disillusioned to hear him admit to doping during his ascent to the top of his sport. Fans of NFL star Ray Rice were shocked and appalled to see a video of him punching and knocking out his girlfriend (who became his wife) during an altercation at a casino hotel. We can understand in this context why professional athletes might be wary of the close scrutiny of the public and especially probing sports reporters, who are interested in learning more about the back stage of athletes' lives.

Sport sociologists have used a symbolic interactionist approach to study many aspects of sport. For example, in a classic study of failure in sport, Donald Ball (1976) observed how athletes interpret and cope with being cut in different professional sports and how the person who delivers the news (called the "grim reaper" on some teams) interacts with the person targeted to be cut. He found that in sports such as baseball, in which players cut from Major League rosters are "sent down" to a minor league team, players were likely to experience this failure as a form of degradation or embarrassment as a "deadman" or "nonperson." Teammates, especially those who felt insecure about their own status and wanted to maintain their confidence, often avoided them as if they were social outcasts or lepers. In contrast, players who were cut in sports without a lower tier or minor league to send players who have been cut, such as professional football, did not experience as much humiliation or embarrassment as players in two-tiered sports because they typically were out of the public eye after being cut. They tended to be treated with relatively more sympathy by teammates than their counterparts in baseball were.

Ball's study is distinctive in its focus on the micro level of social interaction and on how social or cultural contexts shape people's experiences and how they think about, evaluate, and label them. In general, interactionists share the basic approach of all interpretive sociologists in their primary focus on "human agency," or how we actively construct and reconstruct social reality in an ongoing process of social negotiation (Donnelly 2002). This perspective contrasts with more structural approaches, such as structural functionalism and some forms of conflict and critical theory, which place more emphasis on how established social structures of social norms, roles, relationships, and networks constrain or limit our perceived choices for action in society.

Some social theorists have argued that we have moved to a post-structural or postmodern era of widespread skepticism about the social processes that created modern society. *Postmodern critical theory* points to problems of modern societies and sport associated with structural and cultural emphases on order, individualism, rationality, objectivity, scientific progress, democracy, meritocracy, and violence. Focusing on the failure of modernism to create a more understandable and just world in which people live more meaningful and fulfilling lives, post-structural and postmodern analyses have constructed very different lenses for seeing society and sport than previously established social theories offered. Andrews (2000) proposed that these critical perspectives represented a new way of thinking about sport and doing sport sociology. He suggested that they shift our attention away from the structural analyses of both functionalism and Marxism and away from neo-Marxist and other structural critiques of modern society that focus on the intertwining of the political and the economic in political economy, the dominance of large-scale rational organizations of the modern state and economy, the influence of modern culture, and the various political, economic, and social inequalities of the postmodern era. Postmodernism shifts our attention to issues of the body, sexuality, identity, consumerism, and humanistic concerns in medicine, science, and technology in a world in which meaning is often ambiguous and little is certain. Furthermore, postmodern perspectives in the sociology of sport draw our attention to the declining influence of history as we are bombarded with a steady stream of new images and stories produced by the mass media, which sometimes create confusion about what is real and what is fantasy. In this context, subjectivity has a powerful influence over language and social relations in society and sport.

The lens of postmodernism presents us with a picture of a highly diverse and complex world where there seems to be little agreement about the direction we are heading. This is a picture of a world where we engage in ongoing and intense cultural debates or struggles over whose values or interests should prevail, and it is a picture of a world where the meanings we construct come from a continuing stream of ideas and images manufactured by mass media interested primarily in their own profits. Thus, contrary to the materialist thrust of Marxist theory and other structural critiques of modern capitalist society and their assumed centrality of the economic conditions of society, postmodernists tend to focus more on the importance of ideas and images in the modern world. Where this mediated world has become dominated by the new technologies of the Internet, we seem to respond more to fantasy or "virtual" constructions than to concrete things and real people. In sports, for example, there has been an increasing interest in fantasy leagues, and sometimes it is difficult to separate fantasy from reality.

Despite the criticisms of modernism and structural thinking advanced by postmodernism, we will focus on the structural patterns and social and cultural meanings and practices associated with contemporary sport. We will rely on a mix of structural functional, conflict, critical, and interactionist perspectives that help us see and understand these aspects of sport. We will not ignore the postmodernist criticisms, however. These perspectives will be especially useful in helping us to see and understand the major forces of change that are shaping and reshaping sport and society. In combination, they will enable us to focus on sport and society from the micro level of social relationships to the macro levels of interactions between and among leagues, sports, and even nations. We will view sport as a global corporate structure dominated by the golden triangle, whose primary social actors compete on a variety of stages, from the local level to international venues such as the Olympics and the World Cup. A critical factor we will examine in the big-time contexts of contemporary sport is the mass media. A major player in the golden triangle, the mass media both shape and use sport. The golden triangle is the network of money, prestige, and power that dominates sport. Sociological imagination will enable us to see how the mass media and golden triangle operate in sport and influence it in the various historical, social, and cultural contexts in which sport is embedded.

Social Research Methods and Sport Sociology

We observed earlier that social research methods exist alongside social theories as core elements of sociology. In the early years of sport sociology in the 1960s, systematic research about sport and society tended to be limited and scattered in focus. Since then, a fairly substantial body of research has been produced by self-identified sport sociologists and by others with a sociological interest in sport. In some areas, such as gender studies, there has been a substantial amount of research, which has made sport sociologists more confident about what they can say about sport. However, there remain many gaps in the literature about important social aspects and issues of sport, which means that there are many things we do not know or understand about these aspects and issues. The theoretical perspectives we considered earlier will enable us to make sense of the meaning of the social patterns that researchers have uncovered. Important data have come from a number of sources, including investigative journalists and news and sports organizations as well as social scientists.

Sport sociologists often face the challenge of convincing students and the public that what they know about sport from their personal experiences may not be true or at least may need some qualification. At the same time, sport sociologists must acknowledge that there is much we do not know about sport and there is much more to learn. Students of sport sociology often seem more skeptical of what sport sociologists have learned than about what they have been taught about sport by coaches, teammates, or sports announcers, especially when their entrenched beliefs are challenged. People with a lot of experience in sport or a lot of information about the facts and trivia of sport often have difficulty thinking objectively about sport. Their passion may make them biased, or they may find it easier or more comfortable to accept myths, opinions, or unsubstantiated assertions rather than the careful systematic research of sport sociologists who may challenge these beliefs. Thus, sport sociologists must convince students and the broader public that carefully formulated theories are a more systematic way of trying to understand and explain the realities of sport and society and that these realities are best understood on the basis of systematic social research.

This section will briefly summarize various types of social research methods for collecting facts about sport and society. This summary is intended to raise questions and point to limitations of our ordinary ways of knowing and to show that the gathering of facts about social patterns in sport requires careful procedures that conform to well-defined rules of research methodology. Sport sociologists can be fairly confident that we know the things we say we know when a number of different studies find similar results. Some research methods allow us to talk about cause and effect, which means that differences or changes in one factor, the cause (such as the type of reward structure of sports teams), lead to differences or changes in another factor, the effect (such as the amount of interpersonal attraction or friendship among team members, or the level of competitive success of the team). Other research methods are less oriented to cause and effect and focus more on describing what social experiences or interactions mean to people. This section will focus on four major types of research methods used in sport sociology to collect data: (1) experiments, (2) social surveys, (3) field studies, and (4) secondary data analysis.

Experiments are a type of controlled observation in which hypotheses about cause and effect relationships are tested. Experimenters manipulate the independent or causal variable to determine whether it actually has the effects it was hypothesized to have. If the results do not support the hypothesis, the researcher must think about whether the experiment had flaws, such as a poor measure of one or more variables or a failure to control other possible causal factors that might have influenced the results. Or, if there were no major flaws in the design of the experiment, its execution, or its measures, the researcher would conclude that the hypothesis was not supported by the evidence. The researcher might consider revising the hypothesis or doing additional research to retest it.

Researchers sometimes are able to take advantage of events in real-life settings to do experimental research. These studies are called natural or field experiments. There have been a few examples in sport sociology of experimental research in lab and field settings, such as studies of the relationship of team cohesiveness to team success (Martens and Peterson 1971; Nixon 1976, 1977) and of the effects of viewing aggressive sports on the hostility levels of spectators (Arms, Russell, and Sandilands 1987). In general, though, sport sociologists seldom do laboratory or natural experiments because it is difficult to simulate the full complexity of the social settings that interest them theoretically, especially when they are studying large social networks. It also is difficult and possibly even unethical to manipulate hypothetical causal factors in many cases. For example, one could not and would not want to create experimental conditions that tempt players to cheat to see if they actually cheat, that encourage racism to see if players or coaches display racism, or that promote violence to see if athletes or fans act violently. Sport sociologists are much more likely to rely on other social research methods to collect data. One of these methods is the social survey.

Social surveys enable researchers to make generalizations about large populations of people, organizations, or other social networks on the basis of information collected from only a portion of those people, organizations, or networks. According to probability theory, as long as researchers rely on *random samples* of members of the population of interest to them, which give all the members of these populations an equal chance of being included in the sample, they can expect that the major characteristics of the population of interest will be represented in their sample. Thus, randomly drawn representative samples of 3,000 members of the US population allow us to make generalizations about the entire population of nearly 300 million people or major segments of it. Survey researchers use interviews or mailed questionnaires to collect standardized information about the social characteristics, attitudes, beliefs, or behavior of various types of people or about the characteristics of social relations in groups, organizations, or other social networks.

We are generally familiar with the methodology of survey research because so many organizations, including news departments of newspapers and television networks, political campaign organizations, and marketing departments of businesses, conduct surveys or polls of our attitudes, opinions, tastes, buying habits, and a variety of other things. When a Major League Baseball player or world champion bicycle racer is accused of using illegal performance-enhancing drugs, public attitudes are surveyed by news organizations. Online technology makes possible instant surveys of our opinions, even about the outcome of a sports contest that is in progress.

Serious news organizations tend to be careful about relying on *scientific* surveys, which use random sampling methods, so that they can make accurate generalizations about what we think, feel, or do. Organizations interested more in using surveys for entertainment purposes or to attract viewers or customers pay less attention to generating representative samples. We should be wary of generalizations based on nonrepresentative samples because the results may not accurately represent what all women or all men or all sports fans or all athletes or all sports executives or all members of a particular racial or ethnic group in a particular population think, feel, or do. We can judge the scientific value of a survey with certain crucial facts, such as how the sample was generated, how many were sampled, and how well the sample represents the population of interest.

In survey research, statistical analysis, rather than the manipulation of the research setting, is the basis for drawing conclusions about cause and effect. Survey researchers may administer their questionnaires in a variety of ways, including the mail, the telephone, in-person interviews, or the Internet. They also sample in particular ways to ensure that they get sufficient representation of minority groups and other categories of people or organizations that are relatively less numerous. In addition, it is standard procedure in surveys to ask for background information about factors such as gender, age, race, ethnicity, education, type of job, income, and where the respondent lives, because they could influence the dependent variables more than the hypothesized independent variables.

Surveys may be designed with great care and survey researchers may use highly sophisticated statistics, but survey research, like experiments, may have limitations or flaws. For example, respondents may not answer questions openly or accurately. They may not understand or be informed about the questions, care about them, or want to respond in terms of the standardized fixed-choice questions presented by the researcher. Or, respondents may not answer at all. Scientifically designed procedures meant to produce representative samples lose their value when large numbers of people or organizations do not respond. For example, if a survey of the US sports public only reaches people under thirty years old, the generalizability of its results will be substantially limited. Furthermore, preparing, administering, and analyzing the results of surveys, as well as identifying the sample and following up to increase the response rate, can be expensive. Despite these possible problems and the failure to measure factors that could have significant effects on the dependent variables of interest, survey research is an efficient way of gathering large amounts of data about large populations.

Researchers who wish to collect rich and detailed information about social interaction are likely to rely on nonexperimental *observational or field studies*. They may use their own careful observations or largely unstructured interviews to gather data. Ball's study of failure in sport cited earlier is an example of this type of research. Researchers guided by interactionist perspectives typically rely on this type of method because their aim is detailed description rather than causes, effects, and predictions.

In some observational studies, the researcher is a participant in the setting she or he is studying, and in others, the researcher is a detached observer. While experimenters and survey researchers typically are interested in testing hypotheses, finding causes and effects, and predicting social behavior, researchers conducting field studies generally are more interested in the description of major patterns of social interaction or organization. The *case study* is a major type of observational or field study. It describes prominent and recurring social patterns and processes in groups, organizations, or wider social networks. The scope of the description and analysis tends to be limited to what the researcher can directly observe or learn from those she or he directly observes or interviews. Since researchers are able to use this method to uncover the complex and subtle meanings of social interaction in everyday life, we can understand why symbolic interactionists are especially inclined to rely on field studies or observational research to collect data.

While field studies can provide insights about important principles underlying social interaction and rich details about patterns of social interaction and what they mean to social actors, they also have limitations as a method of collecting data. First, the quality of the research is substantially related to the observational or interviewing skills of the researcher and his or her subjective interpretation. Second, with research typically requiring informed consent of participants or subjects in most settings, it can be awkward or difficult to get prospective participants to agree to be studied. Third, researchers who observe the same people for extended periods of time could become close to their subjects and lose their objectivity. Fourth, the advantage of obtaining a great depth of knowledge from concentrating on a single case, social setting, or set of social actors may be offset by the disadvantages of potentially limited generalizability and difficulties in replication of the results. Despite these limitations, the accumulation of systematically conducted field studies contributes substantially to what we know about social life.

Along with experiments, social surveys, and field studies, sport sociologists may use *secondary data analysis* to collect data. This method involves the analysis of data collected by someone else for other purposes than those of the researcher's own study. It could involve data collected by another individual researcher or data collected by an organization, such as survey data produced by a large research organization or institute, demographic data collected by the Census Bureau, crime data collected by a law enforcement organization, or graduation data provided by colleges and universities to the National Collegiate Athletic Association (NCAA). It also could rely on existing documents or texts produced by historians, journalists, authors, and others who create mass media content or culture. Thus, secondary data could be shared between researchers, or it could be official records, historical documents, or the content of mass media, such as books, newspapers, magazines, and websites. Studies of mass media texts or audio and video files might involve a *content analysis*, which is an interpretation of the meaning of the sounds, images, or words in these data sources.

Secondary analysis can be used to identify social trends, correlations, or even causes, depending on the nature of the data available to the researcher. Sport sociologists also may use historical documents or studies to do comparative analyses of social history to reveal similarities and differences in social patterns of sport in different cultures or nations. Examples are the series of studies conducted by Michael Messner and his colleagues about sexism in televised sports coverage (e.g., Cooky, Messner, and Hextrum 2013; Messner, Cooky, and Hextrum 2010) and my own research about how major print media such as *Sports Illustrated* have covered pain and injury in sport (e.g., Nixon 1993).

Content analysis and other types of secondary data analysis benefit from the time, effort, and money invested by others in collecting or publishing data or possible research content. Secondary data analysis also has limitations related to the fact that the data were not collected by the researcher for his or her research purposes. For this reason, these data may not directly or fully address important research questions. They also may have problems of *validity* in not accurately representing the concepts or variables of interest to the researcher or of *reliability* in not being easily reproducible in the same form by other researchers. Despite their shortcomings, content analysis and other forms of secondary data analysis can be very valuable in providing evidence revealing important social patterns or bearing upon important theoretical questions or social issues.

Over time, many of the shortcomings of individual research projects are offset by the critical scrutiny of the community of sociological researchers and scholars, refinement of past studies by new research, and the accumulation of similar research results from different studies. The accumulation of sociological evidence about sport and society, in combination with theoretical analysis of its meaning, represents the body of knowledge in sport sociology. This body of knowledge is the focus of this book.

Structural Analysis of Social Networks in Sport Sociology

Sociologists who see society from different theoretical perspectives and utilize different research methods to collect data about society often share an interest in studying the social connections or ties that link people, the positions they occupy, and the groups, organizations, and larger social bodies to which they belong. They may be interested in how these connections form and endure as *social structures* or how dynamic forms of social interaction or *social processes* such as power, competition, exploitation, conflict, or deviance attenuate, disrupt, or destroy existing social connections. We can learn a lot about society and sport by uncovering the basic social connections that define them, the characteristics of these connections, and how these connections change. *Social network analysis* is an approach for studying social connections or social ties (see Nixon 2002). It is not really a theory, but rather an analytic framework that reveals the basic structural "skeleton" of society.

Social networks are webs of social ties that link people through various types of social relations. Tracing the connections that directly and indirectly link people, positions, groups, organizations, and other social bodies helps us see the social ties that affect our social experiences. People may be linked in social networks through ties of sentiments such as friendships or intimacy, through exchanges of resources such as money, goods, or property, or through the exercise of influence such as interpersonal power or authority. Social network analysts measure the relative strength or weakness of social ties, which is the amount of commitment to social ties and the value we place on them. They also measure relative density, which is how concentrated network ties are or the extent to which possible links in a network actually exist, and the amount of openness of networks, which is the tendency or willingness to connect to outsiders. Thus, social networks could be linked by strong or weak social ties among members, be more or less densely connected, or be relatively open or closed to outsiders.

The idea of *social capital* implies that social connections or relationships can be a useful or valuable resource for exerting influence, conferring prestige, and pursuing economic opportunities. We know the importance of being connected. The number of social contacts or Facebook friends we have is a measure of how connected we are. Our social connections are our social capital. Social networks may provide more or less social capital, depending on the status, wealth, and power of our social contacts. For example, professional athletes who are associated with teams in big cities that are big media centers can use their connections to obtain major commercial endorsement contracts, even though they or their team may not be as successful as those in smaller media markets. Knowing the "right people" can also help fired coaches get new jobs, even though there may be others who are more qualified but also less "connected." Sometimes social connections can be a liability rather than an asset. For example, professional athletes may get into trouble with drugs or violent crimes because they are unable or do not want to cut their ties to their old crime-ridden neighborhoods and friends who have been in trouble with the law. Or athletes with gambling problems may find themselves involved with criminal networks when they cannot repay their debts, and this involvement could lead athletes to share inside information with gamblers or shave points or purposely lose games to help criminal "fixers."

At this stage of history, many people who study sport are especially interested in how sport and society are linked through the mass media (Raney and Bryant 2006). We have seen the growing influence of the Internet and various social media, as well as older mass media and other global communication systems, on people and organizations in sport. These media provide valuable resources such as visibility, information, and money to support the popular and commercial growth of modern sports. They facilitate the growth of many sports as global enterprises, as people are able to follow athletes and teams competing many thousands of miles away.

Network analysis enables us to trace global linkages and influences and the flow of resources through sports networks. For example, young men who play basketball in African villages may become connected through local coaches or teachers to recruiters for college teams in the United States and, as a result, move to the United States to become part of the social world of NCAA college basketball. This process of global migration, which connects the United States and American basketball to other countries through processes of cultural diffusion and competitive or commercial growth, indicates how extensive networks can be in sport and society. We are especially interested in considering how powerful social forces in contemporary societies, such as globalization, are creating, sustaining, expanding, and otherwise changing the major sports networks of our time and how people interact with each other in these sports networks. The social network of primary interest throughout this book is the golden triangle. It consists of social, economic, and political relations linking powerful individuals and organizations in corporate commercialized sport to the sports media and the corporate sponsors and other businesses that invest in sport or sell sports merchandise.

The Golden Triangle

The term "golden triangle" was proposed by Smart (2005) in his book *The Sport Star* and was inspired by Aris's (1990) conception of the "Sportsbiz." According to Aris, the "twin props" of the business of sports were television and sponsors (p. xi). In my conception of the golden triangle, I emphasize links among the three sectors of commercialized sports, television and other major sports media, and other businesses that make money from and for sports. This dominant sports network shapes the global sports culture and makes prominent athletes global sports stars. The concept of the golden triangle is defined essentially the same way that Messner, Dunbar, and Hunt (2000) defined the "sports/media/commercial complex" and is similar to Maguire's (1999) conception of the "global media-sport complex." The golden triangle is a product of global capitalism and is oriented primarily to expanding commercial markets and generating profits.

"The" golden triangle is actually many different golden triangles associated with different sports in different local, regional, or national domains, and these different golden triangles may be loosely or tightly linked to one another and may cooperate or compete, depending on social, economic, political, or sports circumstances. I use "the golden triangle" many times in a generic sense to refer generally to patterns or influences associated with the dominant network of power, money, and prestige in sport, and other times I refer to a particular golden triangle associated with a specific sport or sports context. In the broadest sense, the generic golden triangle refers to the high-level or macro-level networks of power in sport that operate on a global scale, such as in the Olympics. At the local level, golden triangles may involve local television and radio stations that have agreements with local commercial sponsors to broadcast games of local teams. Thus, the "golden triangle" term may be used in various ways, but in all cases it refers to a dominant power structure within the global cultural economy of capitalism operating in some commercialized domain of sport. The term may seem to be an abstraction when it is applied to vast global networks of power, but there should be no mistaking the fact that there are macro-level networks of power in sport that exert substantial influence over sport at all levels. For example, Little League, Inc., influences how young boys and girls participate in baseball in communities throughout the United States and many other countries.

Smaller and more localized or regionalized golden triangles may compete economically with other golden triangles that are operating in their markets and perhaps on a larger scale as well, and they are often formally affiliated with larger corporate organizations that are part of larger-scale golden triangles. Whatever the connections or competition between different golden triangles, they are all likely to be controlled by the same kinds of people and organizations, which embrace the same kinds of cultural values and general economic interests. Thus, despite their differences, they will typically have the same kind of influence on sport, on people in the sports world, and on sports consumers.

For these reasons, we can assume there is one loosely integrated golden triangle network that includes an array of commercial sports, media operations, and corporate sponsors and business investors and has common values and interests. This is why I frequently refer to "the" golden triangle. Whatever the specific manifestation of the golden triangle in a particular sport or sports context, it is likely to share the same basic purpose as other golden triangles or the golden triangle in general, which is to make money. Rooted in the global cultural economy and consumer capitalism, sports enterprises, sport media, and other businesses are primarily interested in using sport to make money. Related to this aim is the desire to build brand recognition, which is a matter of prestige, and increase power and economic status in the marketplace. Thus, when we think of sport throughout this book, it is important to remember that the games, the athletes, the coaches, and the spectators are less important than the people and practices that make money, contribute to prestige, and enhance power for the organizations that control sports in the golden triangle.

Looking Ahead: Sport in a Changing World

Armed with a general understanding of sociology, the sociological imagination, the concepts of sport and the golden triangle, sport sociology, and major social theories, research methods, and analytical tools used by sport sociologists, we are now ready to explore sport and society in more depth. Major social themes that will appear throughout the book are the *commercial and bureaucratic structure* of sport; the amount of *social and cultural diversity* of those who participate in sports; the *inequalities* that give some people and groups more economic advantages, prestige, and access to power than others; *globalization and the global cultural economy* in which sport has an important and pervasive role; and the influence of the *golden triangle*. The concept of the golden triangle highlights the powerful influence on all realms of commercialized sports of the networks linking sport to the mass media and capitalist businesses. These sports realms are the focus of the analysis in this book, and this is reflected in the refined definition of contemporary sport presented earlier in this chapter.

The theoretical perspectives and analytical frameworks in this chapter will be explicitly or implicitly incorporated into the interpretation of sport in the ensuing chapters. Evidence will be cited that was gathered by the types of systematic procedures described in the section on research methods. The book is organized into five main parts, beginning with this section on sociology and the sociology of sport. Part II is about the social organization of sport. It includes a chapter concerning social stratification, class, and mobility in sport and a chapter regarding diversity and inequalities in sport. Part III concerns building, spreading, and disrupting sport in the golden triangle. It has a chapter about globalization, mass media, and sports culture and a chapter concerning sport, social deviance, and social problems. Part IV is about major social contexts of sport and has chapters on youth and high school sports; college athletics; and professional sports. Part V concerns power, political economy, and global sports and includes the final chapter, about politics, economics, and sport in a changing world.

The global growth of sport has expanded the reach of the golden triangle around the world. For this reason, this book about contemporary sport must be about growth and change from a global perspective, reflected in the title *Sport in a Changing World*. Although much of the research in sport sociology is about sport in the United States and other higher-income countries, increasing attention is being paid to sport in developing nations. Some of the ideas and evidence I will present are from this recent research. With its sweep across the global terrain of contemporary sports and with its focus on fundamental social structures and processes of sport and society, this book will help you understand both the enduring structural and cultural aspects of contemporary sports and the ways sport has been changing in recent years. Seeing the world through the lens of sport sociology and with sociological imagination should bring into focus things you never saw before and make a number of those things that were familiar and that you assumed you understood appear in a new, clearer, and sharper light.

Stop and Think Questions

1. How is the sociological imagination different from our everyday ways of looking at sport?
2. How is your definition of sport different from the way sport sociologists define it?

3. Why do you think that sports vary in popularity across nations?

4. How does the sociology of sport differ from your personal opinions about sport?

5. Can you think of a social issue or social problem in sport that you would see differently from different theoretical perspectives, and how would your interpretations differ?

6. Why do sport sociologists rely on research?

7. In what sense is the golden triangle a social network, and why are sport sociologists interested in social networks?

Part II

Social Organization of Sport

2

Stratification, Social Class, and Social Mobility in Sport

One of the basic truths about the social organization of society and sport is that things are not equal. People generally realize this fact fairly early in life. We learn that some people make more money and are wealthier than others, some people are respected a lot more than others, and some people have more authority and power than others. These are things we value in society, and *social stratification* refers to the persisting patterns of unequal or hierarchical distribution of these valued things to different types or categories of people. The social stratification system is a set of ladders with the steps representing categories of people with differing amounts of the valued resources in a society. More stratified societies have more distance between the top and bottom steps or strata of their stratification ladders. For example, a society in which the difference in average annual incomes between the richest 10 percent and the poorest 10 percent is $150,000 is more stratified than one in which this gap is $75,000. Professional sports leagues that have more salary stratification may have the same base starting salaries for players as others but pay their top players much more than the others.

Winning and losing are often the basis for major differences in rewards from the golden triangle of commercialized sports, sports media, and sports business. These differences are generally built into the structure of more and less commercialized sports. Winning teams and their star athletes and coaches tend to earn more money and other material rewards, get more media attention, and have more influence in their sport and in the larger society. The relative amount of each of these rewards depends on how big a part the golden triangle plays in the sport and the size of media and consumer markets in which leagues and teams play.

Social Class and Mobility

A *social class* is a category of people sharing the same relative economic status in modern societies, and the fact that there are different social classes in a society means that there is social class inequality in that society. All known societies have had some type of social inequality, such as slavery, feudal estates, castes, and classes. *Capitalism* is the economic system that has spawned social class hierarchies as societies have industrialized. Under capitalism, individuals have been allowed to engage in free enterprise in their economic activities and amass private property and wealth. The basis of class distinction in modern capitalist societies is between those who own or control the means of production such as factories, equipment, and financial resources and those who work for these owners and do not share in the ownership or control of the productive process or the goods they produce through their labor.

The class structure of capitalist societies has evolved and become more complex over the past 150 years. Managers have gained more control over industrial and other types of corporations in the most productive nations, such as the United States. In addition, jobs have changed in the shift from an industrial society based on heavy manufacturing to a postindustrial society in which services and electronic and information technologies have played increasing roles in the economy. The financial sector of the economy has also become increasingly prominent. So we now see classes of sophisticated technology entrepreneurs, financial investors and money managers, and consultants who sell various kinds of expertise. Ideas, knowledge, and entertainment are now important commodities in the new postindustrial cultural economy. In a sense, athletes in the golden triangle are part of the social class of entertainment workers in this new economy. Although athletes may make a lot of money, their sports are still run by classes of owners and managers who control who plays, how the games are played, and how much the players are paid.

As in musical chairs, some individuals may change positions with each other, move from one step to another, or displace others on higher or lower steps in the class hierarchy. But the *structure* of this hierarchy generally remains pretty much the same over time, with each social class having the same relative size and generally occupying the same relative position on the ladder of class inequality. The idea of class stratification as an element of the social structure of society implies this relative stability. The dynamic element in stratification systems is *social mobility*.

Mobility involves movement up or down the stratification hierarchy. For example, individuals may climb to a higher social class or sink to a lower social class than that of their parents or rise and fall in status during their careers. *Structural mobility* occurs when categories of people move up or down the social hierarchy largely as a result of structural changes in the economy. For example, the expansion of the high-tech sector and, on a more modest scale, the growth and increasing commercial success of professional sports leagues have added a number of high-paying jobs to the economy. Of course, the reverse can happen. The deindustrialization of the US economy over the past few decades has resulted in the elimination of many relatively high-paying blue collar factory jobs and their replacement by jobs in the service sector that pay much less. The fact that this kind of mobility is structural means that individuals' chances of success may be affected more by forces of society over which they have little personal control than by their own efforts.

The class system in the United States is considered an *open stratification system* because individuals can move up or down the social hierarchy as a result of their personal achievements. Many individuals have risen above their social origins as a result of their talent, hard work, and achievements. The fact that many who aspire to move up are more or less frustrated in their pursuit of success does not negate the reality of mobility in the United States. It merely means that the American Dream of unlimited success is exaggerated. Open stratification systems contrast with *closed systems*, such as those based on slavery, estates, or castes. In these closed systems, people generally do not move above the status level into which they were born, no matter how talented or hardworking they are. Even in open systems such as that in the United States, people may spend their lives either taking advantage of the high-class status into which they were born or trying to overcome the disadvantages of that class background. The dynamic nature of mobility in class society is illustrated by athletes who grow up in poor inner-city neighborhoods or in rural poverty, use their athletic talent to propel them into college sports and a professional sports career, and then struggle to find a good job and earn a good income after their sports career ends. In a number of cases, the fortune they earned as professional athletes dwindles and their fame fades, suggesting a *mobility roller coaster*.

Structures of inequality can be weakened or changed by intentional or unintentional efforts to transform the stratification system. For example, Karl Marx argued for a revolution of industrial workers in capitalist societies to rid these societies of structures of economic inequality that exploit and oppress working-class people (Marx and Engels 1978). Changes in class systems could also result from efforts at reform or from behavior less explicitly directed at societal change. Reformers in legislatures could change tax systems by taxing richer people and businesses more and redistributing this money to welfare and income enhancement programs for less affluent members of society. They could also create government jobs or subsidize better-paying jobs for lower-class people to lift them up the economic ladder. This would decrease the

(© jtyler)

The America's Cup, with its expensive yachts (see page 35), is a striking contrast to the poverty seen in youth soccer in the Brazilian favelas or slums. This chapter is about the inequalities of social stratification in sport and society. (© EduLeite)

gap between more and less affluent classes and make the society less stratified. Economic booms in industrializing societies that have raised the standard of living have had the same effect. This is the case of structural upward mobility.

Marx's conception of stratification in capitalist societies focuses on the antagonistic relationship between the economic classes of owners and workers as the driving force of historical change in these societies. In the work of another classical sociologist, Max Weber, social and political dimensions of stratification are also seen as consequential factors affecting structure and change in societies (Weber 1978). Weber's perspective includes a broader conception of *economic or class inequalities* than in Marx's theory. Weber's conception of class refers to the relative amount of marketable skills, qualifications, and property that people possess, along with their material wealth, and he assumed that class differences are associated with different *life chances* of people. Weber also focused on *social inequalities* of prestige, deference, social worth, or social honor associated with different positions or occupations and *political inequalities* of access to authority and the opportunities or resources for exercising power. Weber's multidimensional view has led to the study of *socioeconomic status*—or *SES*—which is a composite ranking of standing in society based on various dimensions of social inequality. In studies of social class in contemporary sociology, SES measures represent social class as a composite of various status factors such as educational attainment, income, occupational status or prestige, and residential type and location.

Although various factors could make a society more or less stratified, even extensive social mobility does not necessarily change the general contour of the stratification system. Past patterns of inequality persist over time even though small mobility bumps or dips happen and people of higher and lower status play musical chairs and switch positions in the class hierarchy. The rich may get richer, but the shape of the system of inequality remains largely the same as in the past if the less affluent also increase their occupational income and prestige.

The rich in the United States have actually gotten much richer over the past several decades, and this has brought about a change in the stratification system, creating more inequality. That is, the structure of inequality has changed, with an increased gap between the rich and everyone else. The gains in income by the middle and working classes resulting from the post–World War II industrial boom have largely been canceled out by deindustrialization, corporation downsizing, and a stagnation in middle-class and lower-middle-class salaries. Although some wealthy people initially suffered from the financial collapse in 2008, they recovered very well and continued to enrich themselves by huge gains in their salaries and investment income. Thus, the rich have become richer and other people have become relatively or absolutely poorer. In 2013, the income gap in the United States was reported to be the largest since 1928 (DeSilver 2013).

Social Stratification and Sport

Much of the rest of this chapter will focus on how social stratification, class, and mobility are related to sport. Focusing first on stratification, it is important to point out that money, media exposure, and influence from an array of golden triangles in the United States and across the world—which I typically refer to as "*the* golden triangle"—have played an important role in the commercial development of modern sport. The power of the golden triangle in many societies has elevated the most commercialized sports to a prominent position in the popular culture of those societies. Since there may be substantial inequality in the way golden triangles typically allocate resources, sport tends to be highly stratified. Specific sports differ in their popularity, the quality of their facilities, the amount of revenue they generate, the amount they pay athletes and coaches, and their place in popular culture.

US college sports demonstrate the complexity of sports stratification. The National Collegiate Athletic Association (NCAA) has historically been the dominant organization in the intercollegiate golden triangle, and it has organized its members into different divisions of different ranks. The NCAA today has over one thousand member institutions, and they are stratified into three main divisions. Division I is generally seen as the "big time" of college sports because it is the most commercialized level, and in regard to football, the Football Bowl Subdivision (FBS) is a higher or more elite level than the Football Championship Subdivision (FCS). The schools at the top or most commercialized level of Division I are usually referred to as "the majors," and those at the lower level of Division I are usually called "mid-majors." The different divisions are generally distinguished by the scope of their athletic mission, their program size and level of competition, and the types of rules governing competition. These divisions reflect the major stratification hierarchy of college athletics in the United States because, in addition to being differentiated organizationally, they differ in the relative amount and quality of resources they have. The higher levels have more athletic talent, financial support for programs, financial and academic support for athletes, commercialization, visibility, and economic and political power in the NCAA. They also generally have bigger and more expensive facilities, and pay coaches and administrators higher salaries. The rank of athletic programs in the NCAA hierarchy is associated with the number and strength of ties to the intercollegiate golden triangle.

There is substantial inequality of financial resources between the top athletic programs at the highest level of the NCAA and programs at different levels of the NCAA. For example, in the 2010–2011 academic year, the athletic department of the University of Texas spent nearly $134 million and produced a surplus of over $16.5 million. Meanwhile there were historically black institutions that spent less than $5 million competing at the Division I level. The athletic departments of these latter institutions relied on institutional subsidies that were over half of their budgets (Nixon 2014:ch. 2). Better-funded programs tend to be more successful in competition because they are able to recruit more talented athletes. They can recruit better athletes because they can afford better and bigger coaching staffs and more extravagant facilities and because they have more visibility in the intercollegiate golden triangle. As long as they remain successful, they will reap more of the rewards offered by the golden triangle, which increases the likelihood of future success. This is the dynamic nature of stratification in big-time college athletics: past success produces the resources needed for future success. Institutions with fewer resources have more difficulty moving up the college sports hierarchy and staying there.

Like the different programs in the NCAA divisions and conferences, professional sports leagues have a *wealth gap* between the franchises that produce the most revenue and those that produce the least. Although wealth is not a perfect predictor of competitive success, wealthier professional teams have the luxury of spending more than their less wealthy competitors on the most talented athletes and coaches. Sports leagues differ in their wealth gaps because they vary in their efforts to share league revenue from the golden triangle and to cap the amount of spending by individual teams. Sports with more economic competition tend to have bigger wealth gaps, reflecting a common pattern produced by capitalism. The more restrictions on competition (i.e., the more "socialistic" sports or leagues are), the less economic inequality exists among teams. Since the National Football League (NFL) has had a strong commitment to revenue sharing and competitive parity, it should not be surprising that it has had a smaller wealth gap than those of sports leagues such as the National Hockey League (NHL), National Basketball Association (NBA), Major League Baseball (MLB), and European soccer, which have been less committed to revenue sharing and parity (Nixon 2008:302–303).

While economic inequalities among athletic programs, teams, and leagues are important elements of the stratification of sports, the public is often much more interested in the incomes of individual athletes and coaches, perhaps because it is easier to identify with these people than with organizations and the people who own or run them. Income figures reveal a clear economic class structure among athletes, with the richest athletes making substantially more money than their more modestly compensated teammates and competitors.

Also, athletes in the wealthiest sports make far more than their counterparts in less wealthy sports. Various media annually compile lists of the top-paid professional athletes and college coaches. They reveal some interesting patterns.

Sports Illustrated compiled a list of the best-compensated athletes in the United States in 2013 (Roberts 2013a), who were either US citizens or competitors in a US-based league. Compensation was from salary or winnings, endorsements, and bonuses. At the top of the list was boxer Floyd Mayweather Jr., who earned an estimated $90 million. Number fifty on the list was MLB player Alfonso Soriano, who made $18.2 million. Overall, there were twenty-six MLB players, twelve NBA players, eight NFL players, two golfers, and a NAS-CAR driver along with boxer Mayweather. Salaries are affected by the popularity and wealth of the sport, the number of players per team, and the revenue and media coverage each year from the golden triangle. They are also affected by the effectiveness of athletes during collective bargaining in negotiating salary caps and league minimums and by how well agents negotiate with management on behalf of their athlete clients. Floyd Mayweather benefited from the unusual promotional and pay-per-view media revenue opportunities for popular boxers in championship fights, which is why he earned nearly $33.5 million more than the second athlete on the list, NBA star LeBron James.

Sports Illustrated also published a list of the twenty best-paid international athletes in 2013 (Roberts 2013b). The range was from $15.2 million for Ivory Coast soccer star Didier Drogba to $48.3 million for British soccer icon David Beckham. Of the twenty athletes, ten were soccer players, five were tennis players, three were auto racers, one was a golfer, and one was a boxer. Beckham earned $3 million less than the fourth-ranked athlete on the US list, basketball player Kobe Bryant of the NBA Los Angeles Lakers (who earned $46.9 million), but $2.5 million more than golfer Tiger Woods, who made $40.8 million and was number five on the US list. Two women, tennis players Maria Sharapova from Russia and Li Na from China, were on the international list but none were on the US list.

Other news sources have published similar types of lists of athletes. For example, *Forbes* magazine compiled its own list of the world's one hundred highest-paid athletes in 2013 (Forbes 2013). Although the figures and the rankings of the athletes differ in these lists (due to the use of different time frames and sources), it is evident from all these lists that the best-compensated athletes in the most commercialized sports in the golden triangle earn huge sums of money in salaries or winnings, endorsements, and bonuses and appearance fees. They convey a picture of a very privileged class of elite athletes. Increasing numbers of college football and men's basketball coaches at the highest level of their sports also make millions of dollars and are part of the privileged class. However, the compensation of these athletes and coaches is not representative of how much other athletes and coaches in their sports are compensated. Professional athletes and coaches in the most commercialized college sports generally make significantly more than the median family income in the United States of slightly more than $51,000 in 2012 (Lowrey 2013). But they make much less than the stars in their sports.

In the US class system, professional athletes and coaches in the most commercialized realms of sport sit near the top of the class hierarchy, but in the class system in their sports, they may be members of more or less privileged classes. According to 2013 data from the professional leagues and associations, the average salary in the NBA was $5.2 million, in MLB $2.5 million, in the NFL $1.75 million, and in the NHL $1.3 million. Similar data from mid-2013 revealed that male professional golfers in the Professional Golfers' Association (PGA) averaged slightly less than $1 million in annual tournament winnings, but female golfers made much less, an average of $162,000. In tennis, the gender disparity was reversed, with women making an average of $345,000, while men averaged $260,000 (Statistical Brain 2013). According to the collective bargaining agreements negotiated by players unions, the 2013 minimum salaries were $525,000 in the NHL, $500,000 in MLB, $490,180 in the NBA, and $405,000 in the NFL. The differences reflect the relative negotiating skills of labor and management in these leagues and the year when the collective bargaining agreements were negotiated.

To put these numbers in perspective, the best-paid NBA player in 2013 was Miami Heat forward LeBron James, who earned $17.5 million in salary and another $39 million in endorsements. That year, New Orleans quarterback Drew Brees was the best-compensated NFL player, earning $40 million in salary and $7.8 million in endorsements. New York Yankees third baseman Alex Rodriguez was paid the most in MLB, earning a salary of $29 million and $900,000 in endorsements. All these players made the *Sports Illustrated* list of the "fortunate 50." Pittsburgh Penguin center Sidney Crosby did not make the list, but according to *Forbes* magazine, he was the best-paid player in the NHL in 2013, earning $12 million in salary and $4.5 million in endorsements.

Coaches and athletic directors at universities with the most commercialized programs also earn big salaries and substantial compensation packages. *USA Today* salary databases showed that in 2011, six athletic directors earned over $1 million dollars, with the best paid earning $2.6 million at Vanderbilt University; seventy head coaches in football earned over $1 million in 2013, with the best paid earning $5.5 million at the University of Alabama; and coaches of over half of the sixty-eight teams that competed in the 2013 NCAA men's basketball tournament earned over $1 million, with the coach of Duke the best compensated at $7.2 million. These levels of compensation are part of a stratification system in college sports in which head coaches and athletic directors at schools with more modestly funded athletic programs are paid far less than their elite counterparts. In NCAA Divisions I and II, athletes may receive "educational grants" or athletic scholarships to pay for their education. But since they are viewed as amateurs, they technically receive no compensation. We will see in the chapter on college sports that this conception of college athletes and their right to actual compensation seems to be changing. At this point, though, they are at the bottom of the economic hierarchy in college sports. The stratification of college athletes reflects whether they receive full athletic scholarships, partial scholarships, or no scholarship at all.

In professional sports, there can be huge discrepancies in the compensation of star players, average players, and unproven rookies making the league minimum. In winnings-based sports, there may be even bigger discrepancies, since those who compete in these sports seldom have the contractual guarantees of players in salary-based sports. In addition, they have to pay their expenses of travel, equipment, coaches and training, and fees. The weaker players in these sports may go home with little in their pockets after a poor performance. We can understand how the sports marketplace and golden triangle can affect the more modest compensation of athletes in less popular and minor-league sports, but the reasons for the amount of stratification in the more popular and commercialized sports may be less obvious. After all, all of these sports with more money and media coverage from the golden triangle depend on large numbers of talented and motivated athletes to fill team rosters or the brackets in tournaments. In the next section, structural-functional and conflict perspectives will be used to provide two very different explanations of social stratification in sport.

Explaining Social Stratification in Sport

Structural functionalism emphasizes the motivational value of unequal economic and social rewards in the productive process. According to Kingsley Davis and Wilbert Moore's (1945) classic structural-functional analysis of stratification, society needs people to do the functionally important jobs. Some jobs are easy and can be done by almost anyone. Others are demanding or difficult and require people with unusual talents or extensive training. Thus, economic and social stratification, especially in income and occupational prestige, is a motivational device that society uses to ensure that the right people, with the appropriate talents, skills, and training, are in the functionally important and demanding jobs and are productive in them. One could argue in this vein that the stress-filled and sometimes deadening jobs of modern society require the distraction and excitement that popular entertainment such as sport can provide. We could further argue from this perspective that sport needs inequalities in pay and recognition between winners and losers, between stars and more ordinary athletes, and between more and less successful coaches to be able to attract talented people to play, coach, and invest in sport and to encourage athletes and coaches to make the sacrifices needed to create the exciting competitions that draw fans and allow sports as we know them today to flourish.

One could fault structural functionalists for seeming to ignore the dysfunctional consequences of excessive inequalities in sport and society. We could also question whether the compensation and fame earned by the best-paid and most popular athletes and coaches in sport today are excessive and necessary for motivational purposes, especially when we consider them in the context of the larger society. However, structural functionalists are likely to counter that societies having relatively small differences or lacking sufficient differences in rewards between more and less productive members will be much less productive than societies that offer the chance for some to do much better than others. The American Dream is a set of cultural beliefs that legitimizes this kind of perspective, in promising big rewards and a better life to those willing to make the effort.

In the special feature "Sport Needs Losers," the role of losers in sport is explored in a sociological way that may seem surprising or counterintuitive. This feature is the first of the brief "Probe" sections that appear in this and ensuing chapters. Probes bring attention to interesting and provocative ideas and issues about sport and society that may escape our usual scrutiny. They are meant to raise questions and stimulate discussion and further exploration.

Probe 2.1: Sport Needs Losers

A logical extension of the structural-functional perspective could be that sport *needs* losers, minor leaguers, and bench warmers. They are needed because they reinforce a belief in the importance of sacrificing and winning by showing the adverse consequences to reputation and economic status and the influence of not trying hard enough to win. This view of the functions of having a "lower class" of losers and also-rans in sport is similar to Gans's analysis of the functions of the "undeserving poor" for US society, particularly those who are more advantaged. In his creative use of the functionalist perspective, Gans (1972) suggested that more advantaged people want and need us to believe that poor people deserve their poverty. They hold an enduring stereotype of poor people as undeserving of help and a better life because, among other things, they are perceived as irresponsible and lazy. This kind of stereotype of the undeserving poor allows advantaged members of society to blame the poor as scapegoats for the ills of society, stigmatize them as perpetual losers, and ignore or dismiss them. This stereotype also reinforces the idea that not being serious about the pursuit of the American Dream can have very negative consequences, and it obscures the facts that many disadvantaged people actually share the same aspirations and work just as hard as those who are more advantaged.

A structural-functional explanation of stratification in sport may make intuitive sense to many people in societies that value the pursuit of success in all realms of society, the achievement of success based on hard work, and the right of achievers to be rich and famous. However, critics of this type of explanation have pointed to the questionable nature of the huge amounts of money and fame that some athletes and coaches receive, when others in sport and in the rest of society who perform essential, demanding, and risky jobs are rewarded much less for their efforts and sacrifices. They have also observed a kind of circularity in structural-functional reasoning in general. It is the idea that if inequality is part of the social structure in sport or some other domain of society, it must be functional or necessary because it would not persist if it was not. That is, structures become institutionalized because society needs them, and evidence that society needs them is the fact that they are institutionalized in the social structure.

Conflict and critical theorists challenge structural-functional explanations. From a Marxist conflict perspective, patterns of inequality in pay and recognition in sport do not exist to meet the broader needs of sport and society, but instead reflect the domination and exploitation of sports workers by owners and management. Owners, management, and coaches push athletes to sacrifice their bodies and commit themselves to performing at as high a level as possible because they make more money and gain more recognition for themselves when athletes do these things. In professional sports leagues, owners and management are willing to pay some athletes relatively large sums of money and let them enjoy substantial media attention because the prospect of a big future salary, a big bump in a contract extension or new contract, or more fame motivates athletes on their team to make the physical sacrifices needed for their teams to be entertaining and successful. They are also willing to pay head coaches relatively large sums of money for their single-minded dedication to fielding winning teams, even at the expense of lost time with their families, chronic stress, and job insecurity. In return, owners and management are able to retain control over their teams and sports, make money, and bask in the reflected glory of their teams' accomplishments.

Inequalities among athletes related to pay and fame in professional sports and to scholarship status and media attention in college sports could be seen as functional. These class systems could provide incentives for athletes to play harder and make more sacrifices of their bodies to move up the class ladder in their sport. From a Marxist perspective, though, these inequalities are more likely to be seen as a form of exploitation that ultimately benefits the people who run and make money from sports more than the athletes who play them.

So, which of these theoretical perspectives is more valid? The answer is neither simple nor straightforward. Both offer insights and help us see inequalities in sport in different ways, and neither offers a single definitive explanation of the stratification of sport. Economic and social inequalities can motivate performance in open stratification systems, but excessive and enduring gaps between classes can cause envy and anger and provoke powerful reactions and conflicts. Job insecurity could be an important motivator, but lavish and secure long-term contracts could make athletes complacent. Furthermore, too much job insecurity could make athletes too nervous to be able to compete effectively, and paychecks perceived as too small could make them too frustrated to care about playing better. Thus, we must be careful not to make sweeping generalizations about the implications of social stratification for sports or the people who participate in them.

Social Class and the Democratization of Sport

Although sports are stratified and have their own class systems, it is widely believed that sport is a meritocracy in which talent and hard work trump social background in the attainment of status. After all, it is not difficult to think of star athletes who rose from poverty or overcame racial or ethnic prejudice and discrimination to achieve prominence in modern sports. Thus, despite the stratification of sport, social class does not *appear* to affect who gets to play and succeed, whether we are talking about budding basketball stars from the inner cities of the United States or budding soccer stars from the grinding poverty of the favelas of Brazil. In fact, class origins mattered in the past in many sports, and even though social class may have less effect than in the past on access to sport, it generally continues to matter today. This is despite a trend toward *democratization*, which is the leveling of class differences among those who participate in sports.

Recent research by White and McTeer (2012) in Canada showed that low SES had an adverse effect on access to community sports programs among younger children who could not afford the cost or did not live in neighborhoods with nearby sports facilities. However, as children grew older, they tended to find more and less expensive sports opportunities, which seemed to diminish the influence of SES background. In the United States, public school athletic programs could be an intervening factor that mitigates the influence of SES on participation in these sports. But many schools and community recreation programs in less affluent neighborhoods have been pinched by the public fiscal crisis of the past decade, which has squeezed budgets. "Pay-to-play" fees have been introduced to help fund athletic programs in schools and in the community.

Probe 2.2: Paying to Play High School Sports

In one public school district in Ohio, for example, fees varied by sport, costing $521 for cross country, $715 for golf, $783 for football, and $933 for tennis (Cook 2012). In Utah, district-imposed fees to play high school football may be much more modest than in this Ohio school district, but the cost of playing this sport in Utah may be inflated by optional fees determined by coaches (Donaldson 2013). These optional fees ranged from zero to over $800, and some schools that claimed to have no additional fees expected athletes and families to participate in fund-raisers to cover the cost of summer camps, weekly team meals, weight training in the summer, highlight videos, and "spirit clothes" such as T-shirts and shorts. Although there were efforts to help finance students whose families struggled financially and legal restrictions on making optional fees mandatory, a number of these financially struggling families perceived the costs to be an obligation and did not let their children try out. In general, it appears that unless aspiring young athletes are fortunate enough to be from affluent families that can afford the fees, are good enough to be subsidized or sponsored, or live in communities that offset fees with sponsorships from generous local businesses, playing school sports may not be afford-able. Less advantaged youths who want to compete in club sports outside the school generally find the costs of registration, coaches, equipment and clothing, tournaments, and travel quite expensive. Only those talented enough to be sponsored are likely to participate.

Even in less expensive sports that appeal to poor inner-city youths, such as basketball, the chance for talented teenagers to play at a high level may depend on being located in a school district with a strong high school program or being discovered by recruiters for a competitive club or Amateur Athletic Union (AAU) program. In either case, having a team or individual sponsor will enable these youths to make a serious commitment to their sport, one that could lead to a college scholarship and possibly a professional career.

If athletes from modest backgrounds are able to participate in high school sports, they are likely to get a mobility boost from their participation. Research has shown that when compared with nonathletes eight years after they were slated to graduate from high school, former high school athletes were more likely to have gone to college and graduated, to have a full-time job, and to make more money (see Sage and Eitzen 2013:283). Graduating from high school and espe-cially graduating from college are important because educational attainment is a significant predictor of social status and the chances of mobility (Supiano 2014). Education can help overcome the drag of growing up in a less affluent family or provide a further boost to those who are from a more affluent and educated family (Greenstone, Looney, Patashnik, and Yu 2013). Thus, even though the chances of significant upward mobility and becoming a professional athlete or coach in the United States are relatively slim, high school athletes from lower-income families can be propelled into a higher class through sport. This is because it keeps them in school and may make them more likely to attend and graduate from college.

The Golden Triangle and the Evolution of Elite Sports

Sports can serve as a vehicle for upward mobility only if they are democratized enough to allow athletes from lower classes to participate at the highest levels and take advantage of educational and professional sports opportunities. Some sports historically resisted democratizing influences because they were wed to the elite and their country clubs or were very expensive to pursue. Golf, tennis, polo, and yachting quickly come to mind. However, even these traditionally elite sports have opened up so that talented athletes from more modest social backgrounds have been able to pursue them seriously or professionally. Money and exposure from the golden triangle have played a role in this democratization. Yachting is a good example of how the golden triangle has influenced the evolution of an exclusive sport of the upper classes into a sport with a more commercialized and somewhat more democratic profile.

From its start in 1851 until the twenty-first century, the elite America's Cup yachting competition took place in Cowes, England; New York; Newport, Rhode Island; Fremantle, Australia; San Diego; and Auckland, New Zealand (Mellgren 2006; Phillips 2006). In 2007, the America's Cup competition was in the waters of a non-English-speaking host, Valencia, Spain. This location was distinctive because it was not the home of the club defending the prize given to the winner, the Auld Mug trophy. Location became an issue because the victor in the 2003 race was from a landlocked nation, Switzerland. Valencia was also the location in 2010, when the Swiss boat once again defended the Cup. The competition moved to San Francisco in 2013 because this was the home of the 2010 winner, *USA-17*, and its owner syndicate BMW Oracle.

Named for the first winner, the US yacht *America*, the America's Cup trophy officially has represented "a perpetual challenge cup for friendly competition between nations" (Mellgren 2006). In fact, the America's Cup has been a highly competitive and increasingly intense competition between nations, wealthy yacht owners, and exclusive yacht clubs. For example, 2003 and 2007 Cup winner *Alinghi* was often characterized as a Swiss boat, but it actually represented Société Nautique de Genève, a Geneva yacht club. America's Cup winners *USA-17* (BMW Oracle) in 2010 and *Oracle USA-17* (Oracle Team USA) in 2013 represented the San Francisco Golden Gate Yacht Club. Thus, the race has become more than a contest among yacht clubs, nations, or wealthy yacht owners.

According to Mellgren (2006), the America's Cup has become a "high-tech battle among wealthy global syndicates." For example, the 2013 Cup winner, *Oracle USA-17*,was funded by billionaire Oracle Corporation founder Larry Ellison, who was ranked by *Forbes* magazine as the third-wealthiest person in the United States in 2013. Two of the three challengers were also funded by individual billionaires, one a Swedish oil trader and the other the CEO of fashion house Prada. The fourth team, the most formidable of the challengers, was Emirates Team New Zealand (ETNZ). Its funding came from both the Dubai-based airline Emirates and the New Zealand government. In the most recent races, teams typically got an average of 40 percent of their funding from wealthy individuals and 60 percent from commercial sponsors (Onishi 2013).

The America's Cup today occurs whenever organized syndicates can raise enough money, usually between $50 million and $150 million, to mount an enticing challenge to the defending Cup holder. A series of elimination rounds among challengers determines the winner of the Louis Vuitton Cup and the right to challenge for the America's Cup. The club in possession of the Cup may hold a series of defender races to determine who will represent it. A number of format changes may occur from race to race, and for the first time in 2013, the Cup was won with nine victories in the match races. In addition, the winner has the right to decide the location of the race and can specify the type of boat design.

Larry Ellison's stipulation of very fast and very expensive high-tech seventy-two-foot wing-sailed catamarans significantly inflated the cost of competing. As a result, there were only three challengers to his Oracle Team USA boat, the smallest number of entrants in the modern history of the America's Cup. The high cost may have scared away corporate investors, while it also created a public controversy in New Zealand (ONE News 2011). The New Zealand syndicate that sponsored the winning boat ETNZ in the Louis Vuitton series and Cup challenge had to turn to the national government for an investment of $36 million in public tax money to be able to afford to compete. In response to critics, the managing director of ETNZ, Grant Dalton, argued that the government's investment enabled his team to be competitive on the world stage. He said, "We take pride in showcasing the New Zealand brand, skills and expertise across the major yachting regattas of the world today" (ONE News 2011).

The imprint of the golden triangle on the evolving America's Cup can be seen in the increasing influence of outside investors and the role of the media, including the reemergence in 2013 of television among the media covering the races. The competition between the sporting elements even took a strange twist leading up to the 2010 Cup. Wealthy yachtsman Larry Ellison negotiated with contending clubs to sponsor his boat and ultimately chose a club that countered the traditional elite stereotype associated with the Cup. The Golden Gate Yacht Club (GGYC) in San Francisco sponsored Ellison's Oracle entries in 2010 and 2013, but it was not in the mold of the upper-class clubs of the past (Branch 2013).

Fitting the stereotype was the nearby St. Francis Yacht Club, with its members including wealthy corporate magnates and Olympic sailors and its long history of sailing success in every important regatta except the America's Cup. Ellison was a member who was both very wealthy and experienced in financing and occasionally captaining boats in major sailing races. He hoped that his club would sponsor his quest to have a boat in the America's Cup. When negotiations broke down, he turned to the more modest and debt-ridden GGYC, which gladly accepted his overtures. He now had a sponsoring club, and it had a wealthy new member who was willing to make investments to save the club from bankruptcy and elevate its reputation on the world stage of sailing. Even though the GGYC had grown to 425 members and had annual revenues of about $662,000 in 2011, these numbers were a fraction of the 2,300 members and $12.9 million in revenue of the St. Francis Yacht Club. However, the GGYC had a billionaire member who would twice win the America's Cup.

Ellison hoped to broaden the appeal of the America's Cup and sport of sailing, but the America's Cup had been unable to attract television interest for the previous twenty years because the sport lacked the popularity that Ellison wanted to create. With the race taking place in San Francisco in 2013 and having Ellison's backing, it was ultimately able to attract network television coverage (Sandomir 2013). But in an arrangement that reverted to the early days of radio broadcasts of major sports in the United States in the 1930s (Smart 2005:83), the NBC Sports Group paid nothing for the rights to televise the Cup races. Instead, the America's Cup Event Authority bought time on NBC and NBCSN and sold advertising slots to sponsors. It also utilized the race production hosted by the America's Cup. NBC got more than it expected, though, since the race featured a remarkable comeback by Oracle Team USA, which came back from an 8–1 deficit to win 9–8 over ETNZ.

The distinctive golden triangle of wealthy individual investors, corporate interests, government funders, and renewed television interest contributed to the continued viability of the Cup. Golden triangle influences had also led to some democratization and diversification of crews and elevated a struggling club on the verge of bankruptcy into prominence and financial viability. Yet there were critics who said that the event essentially was "a vanity race for the super-rich." A disgruntled city supervisor complained of the cost to San Francisco and remarked that the Cup was a "yacht race for billionaires" and "a stupefying spectacle of how this city works for the top 1 percent on everyone else's dime" (Coté 2013). His remarks were made at a time when the projected city deficit for hosting the race was only half of later estimates of over $11 million (Coté 2014). He preferred that the money be used for more critical city services for his constituents.

Thus, despite some changes that are at odds with the upper-class image of the America's Cup, the race and the sport in general are still perceived as elite. They survive as global sports events because very wealthy sailing enthusiasts have continued to invest in them. As the small number of entrants in the 2013 America's Cup demonstrated, though, even the wealthy may be put off by the rising costs. Furthermore, the undeniable excitement of *Oracle USA-17*'s comeback victory was not likely to elevate the event and sport above the minor status they occupy in the ranks of the broader golden triangles of North American and global sports.

From a structural-functional perspective, expensive sports such as sailing are functional for the upper classes precisely because they are so expensive. Their cost makes them more exclusive, and this exclusivity burnishes the status of those who can afford to invest in the sport. The fact that teams race for the Auld Mug and win no prize money reinforces the status value of the sport. Surely there are commercial investors in America's Cup defenders and challengers and cities that host the races that want to see a financial as well as status return on their investment. There is also little doubt that the GGYC was pleased by the good fortune of gaining a billionaire member whose Cup victories saved the club from financial ruin. Yet the race arguably is ultimately about prestige for the primary investors whose boats compete in the Cup. The race survives only because there are sailing enthusiasts and investors who care about the prestige and have the resources needed to compete for it.

Probe 2.3: Conspicuous Leisure and Conspicuous Consumption in Sports of the Wealthy

The idea of prestige as a motivator in sport is consistent with Thorstein Veblen's (1899) classic notions of "conspicuous leisure" and "conspicuous consumption." He theorized that the wealthiest classes in capitalist societies were driven by a deeply rooted need for approval or respect or by status envy. Since capitalist societies value money and possessions, being able to show off one's financial worth can convey one's status. Thus, Veblen's perspective suggests that the wealthy engage in conspicuous displays of their wealth by pursuing expensive leisure and spending extravagantly on sporting events. Critics have faulted Veblen for overestimating interest in such conspicuous displays among the upper classes and underestimating its importance among those trying to climb the socioeconomic ladder and make a name for themselves. His perspective also fails to account adequately for the seriousness of the wealthy competitors in elite activities such as the America's Cup (Nixon and Frey 1996:211). Notwithstanding these criticisms, spending $50 million to $150 million on a very exclusive race that involves only four competitors from around the world and offers no monetary prize is the kind of status display that conforms to Veblen's ideas of conspicuous leisure and consumption.

Although it is largely a competition for prestige, the America's Cup is also an opportunity for major or upwardly mobile transnational corporations to advertise themselves among the wealthiest segments of competing nations. For them, branding considerations are definitely important in trying to expand their business. Thus, we can see that contemporary elite sports may retain their exclusivity in many respects, but also reflect the increasing influence of money and commercialism on sporting events that want to be truly international in their competition and appeal. Sports such as the America's Cup mix traditional elements of amateur sports, such as exclusivity and the quest for a prestigious trophy, with very modern elements of professionalism, commercial investment, and an intense commitment to winning, which reflect the imprint of the golden triangle.

The American Sports Dream and the Sports Opportunity Pyramid

Not many people are able to marshal the resources needed to create a syndicate to race in the America's Cup. Dreams of winning the America's Cup or owning the winner of the Kentucky Derby are not likely to be part of the popular imagination. These kinds of experiences are a long distance from the lives of people from modest backgrounds. Dreams of sports success are more likely to involve popular sports in the golden triangle. After all, opportunities to play these kinds of sports are available in public schools and community recreation programs where talented athletes can develop their skills and move up to more competitive levels. For some, dreaming of careers and stardom in sport is realistic; for most, this success is a pipedream; and for a number of others who "make it," success is a relatively short ride on the mobility roller coaster.

Achieving upward mobility and material success *through* sport is an example of the fulfillment of the *American Dream*. The American Dream happens in this way when athletes use sport as a springboard to success elsewhere in society. For example, talented young athletes from families with limited means are able to earn an athletic scholarship to attend college, then graduate from college, and use their degree to pursue a career outside sport that elevates them above their parents on the socioeconomic ladder and brings them material comfort. The *American Sports Dream* is about achieving mobility and success *in* sport, for example, as a professional athlete, coach, or athletic director or in some other desirable and rewarding job in sport. One does not have to remain mired in poverty or stuck on the same rung on the socioeconomic ladder where they started. Sport offers hope.

Recall the widespread belief in the principle of equality of opportunity in modern sport that was discussed in the first chapter. This is consistent with the American Sports Dream. This dream implies that everyone who is talented enough, tries hard enough, and wants success enough has a chance to be successful, regardless of where they start in life. There is some truth to the ideas that sport and American society are open stratification systems and that merit matters in the climb up the ladder of success. The ideas of equal opportunity and meritocracy seem to be borne out by the many individual cases of athletes climbing or clawing their way to success by overcoming significant social and economic deficits. Thus, there is much that seems to validate the American Sports Dream.

The most commercialized sports have propelled many of their players and coaches into the upper classes of society. They are not as rich as the wealthiest owners and investors in sport, but the lowest-paid players in the most commercialized sports earn many times more than the average worker does in a year, and veterans in these sports who are not among the best paid still earn more in one year than most people earn in a lifetime. With the promise of these financial rewards as well as fame, it is little wonder that young athletes nurture American Sports Dreams of careers in professional sports. When they achieve their sports dreams, they may engage in conspicuous consumption and extravagant lifestyles. This is the kind of behavior Veblen assumed would happen among those with status insecurities who feel the need to show off their status. Others may make bad investment decisions ironically intended to give them long-term financial security. In either case, the results cast a dark shadow over their dreams of success.

The infusion of increasing amounts of media money into sports created structural mobility for the past few generations of athletes and coaches in the most popular sports. But unlike the experience of those born into the more established upper classes in society, many star athletes have found it difficult to retain their newly earned affluent or upper-class status. They have experienced a genuine mobility roller coaster, with steep ascents and descents. Some prominent examples include former heavyweight boxing champion Mike Tyson, who went through $300 million in prize money and declared bankruptcy in 2003; Allen Iverson, who earned between $180 million and $200 million in his pro basketball career and told the court just two years after retiring from the NBA that he had no money to pay his debts; Curt Schilling reported that he lost all $50 million that he had earned as an MLB pitcher as a result of his investment in an unsuccessful video game company; linebacker Lawrence Taylor also reported being broke after making more than $50 million in the NFL; and Sheryl Swoopes reported more than $1 million in debts when she became the first prominent WNBA star to declare bankruptcy (Corben 2012; Warner 2012).

These are not isolated cases. In a widely cited article about how and why athletes go broke, *Sports Illustrated* reported that within two years of retirement, 78 percent of former NFL players were broke or were suffering from severe financial strain as a result of unemployment or divorce (Torre 2009). In addition, within five years of retirement, an estimated 60 percent of former NBA players had run out of money. Bad investments also depleted the assets of many one-time rich star athletes. A number who had achieved prominence in NFL football and other major sports in the United States were brought down by gambling debts, criminal activities, or other self-destructive or disreputable behaviors (Warner 2012). The problems of the radically diminished status of former professional athletes are exacerbated by the fact that many did not take advantage of their educational opportunities in college and many did not even graduate. Evidence from 2009 indicates that NFL players were the most educated among the athletes in the big-money North American sports leagues. But only 53 percent earned college degrees, despite the fact that they typically had athletic scholarships that paid for their college education during their years of athletic eligibility. The numbers were significantly worse in the other major professional sports leagues in North America: 20 percent for the NBA and less than 10 percent for professional baseball and the NHL (see Sage and Eitzen 2013:284).

These stories and statistics provide important insights about the American Sports Dream. We see that sports can provide opportunities to ascend the class ladder and achieve big rewards of education, money, fame, and social influence. At the same time, the shape of the opportunity structure in sport is a pyramid with a broad base of aspirants and a tiny peak of those who make it. The slope of this *Sports Opportunity Pyramid* is slippery. It is difficult to keep climbing, more difficult to reach the top, and with the relatively brief careers of many professional athletes, even more difficult to remain there very long. Thus, the American Sports Dream is real for some, out of reach for most, and a diving roller-coaster ride for many of those who get to the top.

Recent NCAA statistics clearly show what this pyramid looks like. The NCAA (2012) estimated that 535,289 played men's high school basketball, and of the 152,940 high school seniors who played this sport, an estimated 3.3 percent were likely to make NCAA college teams and 1.3 percent were likely to make it from college to the professional level. This means that seniors playing men's high school basketball had a 0.03 percent (3 in 10,000) chance of being drafted by an NBA team. Some undoubtedly would be able to sign contracts to play in other leagues or in other countries, but the pay, prestige, and playing and living conditions were not likely to measure up to those of the NBA. The number of young women identified in this study as high school basketball players was estimated to be 435,885, with 124,539 of them seniors. The odds of the high school seniors making it to the NCAA level were 3.7 percent and of college players making it to the pro level were 0.9 percent, which meant that seniors playing women's high school basketball had a 0.02 percent (2 in 10,000) chance of being drafted by a WNBA team. The female undrafted college players had many fewer and much less lucrative opportunities than their male counterparts to play outside the major league in North America. In addition, those who played in the WNBA earned far more modest rewards than their male counterparts in the NBA.

Relatively large numbers of males played football (1,095,993), baseball (474,219), soccer (411,757), or ice hockey (35,732) at the high school level. Of these athletes, 313,141 football players, 135,491 baseball players, 117,645 soccer players, and 10,209 hockey players were seniors. Although these athletes had a better chance of playing at the college level than their counterparts in basketball, only the high school seniors playing baseball had a significantly better chance of becoming professionals in their sport. The odds of making it from high school to college and from college to the pro level were 6.7 percent and 9.7 percent, respectively, in baseball, 6.4 percent and 1.6 percent in football, 10.9 percent and 1.2 percent in ice hockey, and 5.6 percent and 0.7 percent in soccer. Thus, 0.51 percent of the high school seniors playing baseball, 0.08 percent of the seniors playing football, 0.10 percent of the seniors playing hockey, and 0.03 percent of the seniors playing soccer were likely to become professional athletes in their sport.

Statistics about the average length of careers in the most commercialized professional sports leagues in North America show exactly how slippery this pyramid is for those trying to stay at the top. According to the RAM Financial Group (2014), a financial services company with many professional athletes as clients, the average length of careers in the first decade of the twenty-first century was 3.5 years in the NFL, 4.8 years in the NBA, 5.6 years in MLB, and 5.5 years in the NHL. Unlike careers in other realms of society, athletic careers remain highly demanding from beginning to end. There are no desk jobs for athletes, and only those who continue to compete or are among the elite with long-term contracts survive. Since most NFL, NBA, MLB, and NHL players as well as athletes in other physically demanding and collision sports are cut, forced out by injuries, or retire as relatively young men, they face starting new careers years after others of their age have already begun pursuing their careers. Many of these former pro athletes cannot fall back on their education, because they did not earn their degree or pursue their studies seriously enough, as previously cited statistics showed.

Thus, while inspiring, the American Sports Dream, like the American Dream, is not true as a generalization, since many who strive for upward mobility face significant structural obstacles such as limited opportunities. Furthermore, those who achieve mobility often achieve less than they desire, despite their hard work. Various kinds of discrimination have also blocked the path to success. Coming from the lower classes, having ethnic or racial minority status, or being a female or gay has historically restricted the pursuit of the American Dream in general and the American Sports Dream in the United States and other countries. Athletically talented people with permanent physical disabilities have rarely entered the conversation about sport and mobility, until recently. We look more closely at the experiences of these people beginning in the next chapter. The purpose of noting their frustrated pursuit of sports success here is to underscore the exaggerated belief in the American Sports Dream that many lower-class and minority males and even some females are socialized to believe.

We might wonder why the American Sports Dream continues to inspire people in the United States and other countries. A critical theorist's answer is in the paradox that the American Dream and American Sports Dream in particular do not have to be true for people to believe in them and for them to affect their behavior. We need to see these kinds of belief systems as cultural ideologies to understand this paradox. A *cultural ideology* is an argument or set of claims about society that is accepted as true because powerful people assert its validity and because it is learned as an indisputable truth during socialization. Thus, although the American Sports Dream is more of an ideology than a scientifically valid set of factual statements, its inspirational quality makes it difficult to refute, even with systematic evidence. This is because many less advantaged and upward striving people *want* it to be true and because it serves the interests of advantaged and powerful people in implying that they deserve to be where they are and deserve the rewards and power of their status.

As an ideology, the American Sports Dream obscures the structural obstacles that prevent or discourage people from challenging the elite or questioning the fairness of the opportunity structure in sport. Two key underlying beliefs of the ideology of the American Sports Dream explain how it justifies the existing opportunity structure and resulting hierarchy in the major sports. First is that success is assumed to be earned by all those who work hard enough and are willing to make sacrifices and take risks to achieve it. The second belief follows from the first. It is that successful people must deserve their success because they earned it as a reward for their responsible and virtuous behavior of hard work, sacrifice, and risk taking. With this reasoning, we would conclude that the American Sports Dream is true, the Sports Opportunity Pyramid is fair, and those at the top of this pyramid deserve to be there. Another implication is that those who do not succeed are responsible for their failure because everyone has a chance to succeed and not making it implies that they did not try hard enough, sacrifice enough, or risk enough. That is, it is their "fault." Embracing this ideology is functional in the sense that it legitimizes the status quo and helps keep the organization of sport relatively stable over time.

Golden Triangles and the Power Elite

The American Sports Dream has been fueled by the golden triangle, or more specifically, by the various golden triangles that are critical sources of revenue and popularity for each of the major commercialized sports. At the top levels of golden triangles are the people who run sports, invest in them, produce and promote them for public consumption, negotiate the business of sports, and sell endorsed and branded sports products that connect us to our favorite athletes and teams. Being a sports executive, owner, producer, promoter, agent, or entrepreneur may not seem as exciting as being a star athlete or coach for those who dream of sports success. However, the leaders of the sport, media, and business sectors of golden triangles shape the kinds of dreams that can actually be achieved in sport. These dominant figures in sport constitute a network of power or influence, which can be called a "power elite."

Sociologist C. Wright Mills (1956) used the power elite concept to characterize the network of the wealthiest and most powerful people in the major institutional sectors in the United States. An important insight from Mills is that wealthy and powerful people and organizations in power elites are generally more committed to their own interests and the maintenance of the institutions they dominate than to the interests of more ordinary people. This is the perspective of a critical theorist. In sport, these more ordinary people include the general public, fans, and even athletes and coaches. The ties in golden triangles may not be as strong as those that Mills hypothesized for the societal power elite. Despite looser and sometimes conflicting ties, the members of the power elite of sport work together to ensure that their mutual interest in making money is served by the production of popular sports entertainment.

Being involved with a winning or championship team may be an important motivation for investing in a sports team. However, those who own sports teams typically share a broader interest in commercial success with others in the sport sector. This commercial motivation is what motivated their partners in the media and business sectors to get involved in their sport. Since golden triangles are embedded in societies with capitalist economies, we should not be surprised that the shared interest of the elite members of golden triangles revolves around selling things, making money, and generating profits or surpluses. Sometimes this can mean that athletes, coaches, and the integrity of the game itself are relegated to a position of less importance than the production of a lucrative entertainment spectacle that appeals to a mass audience. This audience will likely include people with varying degrees of interest in the sport.

Although there is an array of golden triangles at the local, national, and global levels of different sports, they are all characterized by networks of ties among sport, media, and business interests. Star athletes and coaches rarely reach the upper echelons of the golden triangle of their sport during their active careers or afterward. The most successful athletes and coaches are paid well but are rarely wealthy enough to own professional sports teams. They do not become sports commissioners or NCAA presidents. They do not run media corporations. While some are successful business entrepreneurs or agents, few make the jump from success in sport to success in a business that becomes a prominent player in a golden triangle.

Wealth can help people gain entry into the power elite of sport, and being in this elite can make people wealthy. However, although wealth is typically associated with membership in the power elite of the golden triangle, amount of wealth is not perfectly correlated with ranking in this elite. That is, wealth does not necessarily buy a corresponding amount of power in the golden triangle. Those who are most able to exploit their status and resources to get what they want are the most powerful. Sometimes people who are not rich or part of the established power structure of sport, such as judges, legislators, or government officials, can influence the power elite of a sport because they have the authority to alter the rules, resources, or profitability of a sport. There are also people who attract the interest of the elite of a sport because they are tied to an issue or cause that threatens the status quo in a sport. For example, the issues of doping, the rights of college athletes to unionize or share in revenue from the commercial use of their images, the serious effects of concussions, and domestic violence have thrust advocates of these causes into the spotlight and, in some cases, into direct or indirect interactions with members of the power elite of sport.

The status of some people or organizations in the power structure of golden triangles may fluctuate with the rise and fall of the salience of the issues to which they are connected or the strategic value of the resources they command. Thus, the specific composition of the power elite of a sport may shift over time. A number of factors affect who is in the power elite of a golden triangle and who is considered important or influential enough from outside the usual circles of power in a sport to be included in its list of the most powerful at a particular time. Important factors affecting membership in the more powerful and prominent elites of national and international golden triangles might include the size of a sport, its rank in the global sports hierarchy, and proximity to the major decision-making processes in the golden triangle.

The major players in the golden triangle certainly are not faceless, but they are not as well known to the public as are the athletes and coaches in the games people watch. Who are the most prominent members of the power elite in the merged golden triangle of the richest and most popular North American and global sports? Two leading publications in the popular sports world, *Sports Illustrated* (*SI*) (Rushin 2013) and the *Sports Business Journal* (*SBJ*) (Madkour 2013), offer a glimpse into who these people are. Both focused on the fifty most powerful or influential people in the sports industry. They are the people who make the deals that shape what happens in their sports and how popular and financially successful their sports are. While specific names change over time, the jobs these people occupy and the types of interests they represent tend to be more stable. The *SI* and *SBJ* rankings reflect the biases of these publications toward North American sports, but they include some major players in the global sports arena. In addition, their rankings include some figures who are not in the inner circles of the power elite of sport but were included because they have had a significant impact on the status and actions of the elite in recent years. The two lists are relatively similar in their basic compositions.

At the top of *SI*'s "Power 50" list for 2013 was Roger Goodell, the National Football League commissioner. His strong hold over the most popular sport in North America—with the most popular event in US sports, the Super Bowl—earned him this status. His salary of $44.2 million in 2012 reflected both the wealth of his sport and his stature in the golden triangle of US sports (Belson 2014a). Goodell was ranked second on the *SBJ*'s list of the fifty most influential people in the sports business in 2013. The top spot was shared by two people, Randy Freer and Eric Shanks. Freer is president and COO of Fox Networks Group, and Shanks is president and COO of Fox Sports. The editorial staff of *SBJ* ranked them first on the list because they were behind the launch of Fox Sports 1 and Fox Sports 2. *SBJ* saw media rights contracts as critical factors driving the dynamics of the North American sports marketplace and these men as key players in the recent history of this realm. With these new sports channels, Fox was now able to expand its sports offerings, increase its potential for advertising revenue, and bid seriously for the rights to broadcast a number of major sports and sports events. All of this contributed to the continuing importance of the media and media money in the growth of the golden triangle, and also caused media competitors to react with moves such as hiring new talent.

Fifty-eight percent of the fifty members of the *SI* elite and 54 percent of the fifty members of the *SBJ* elite are in the sport sector of the golden triangle. They include professional sports team owners, professional and college sports commissioners, executive officers and top officials in league offices, players association directors, the NCAA president, and Olympic officials at the international level (IOC) and in the United States (USOC). The president of the international soccer governing body (FIFA), Sepp Blatter, was on both lists because soccer is the most popular sport in the world. However, reflecting the North American bias of these lists, he was ranked sixteenth on the *SI* list and twentieth on the *SBJ* list. Retired NBA star Michael Jordan was on the SI list as an owner.

Former college basketball star Ed O'Bannon was on both lists, as an outsider. He made the lists as the lead plaintiff in a lawsuit against the NCAA concerning the use of athletes' images for commercial uses without permission or compensation. Highly paid one-time baseball superstar Alex Rodriguez of the New York Yankees was another outsider on the *SBJ* list. He served a season-long suspension for use of performance-enhancing drugs. He made the *SBJ* list because of the amount of attention generated by his stature in his sport, the charges against him, his suspension, and his very public legal battle with the league to be reinstated. The chief arbitrator in his grievance case, Fred Horowitz, was also on this list.

SI's inclusion of the head of the US Anti-Doping Agency, Travis Tygart, on its list reflected its perception of the importance of the fight against doping in the United States. He might seem to be an outsider, but the ongoing impact of doping on sport and the established status of the World and US Anti-Doping

Agencies in the sport sector of the golden triangle would seem to qualify Tygart as an insider in elite circles. His power and effectiveness in the golden triangle undoubtedly have made members of the power elite wary in a number of sports. His relentless investigation of Lance Armstrong helped lead to the toppling of a US sports icon. Armstrong had to forfeit his victories in the Tour de France, and after years of claiming innocence, he finally admitted to illegal substance abuse, which effectively ended his big-time cycling career. This kind of influence warrants a place in the top ranks of the power structure of sport.

Media executives were 18 percent of the *SI* list and 22 percent of the *SBJ* list, and members of the sports business sector were 22 percent of both lists. In view of the strong influence of the media on the continuing expansion of the golden triangle, the percentage representation of the media in the golden triangle's elite underestimates the power of this sector. The reason for this is that there are many more people and organizations in the sport sector than in the media sector, but sports depend more on the media for their growth than the media depend on sports. This is why sports media can often influence when, where, how often, and even how sports are played.

Sports businesses also have an important role in the sports power elite. They buy the advertising spots that enable the media to invest in sports. They manufacture and sell clothing and equipment to athletic teams and use sports branding by athletes and teams to sell these things to the public. They are involved in the promotion and marketing of teams, sports, and sports events, and they represent athletes' and coaches' interests as their agents. They also invent or utilize new technologies to make money for and from sport. One member of the *SI* list was vaguely defined as "hedge-fund (investors)." Although this category includes owners who are in the sport sector, I included it in the business sector because it represents a purely business interest in owning a team. There is a long history of these kinds of investors in sport who value the profit potential or tax advantages more than the sport itself (see Nixon 1984:157–159). Although the golden triangle is generally and primarily motivated by an interest in making money, the hedge-fund approach has so little to do with an interest in sport it seemed to fit more in the business sector than in the sport sector of the golden triangle.

Government was also represented on the two lists. President Barack Obama was listed by *SI* because the prestige of his office gave his personal opinions about sports extra weight in the sports world. Vladimir Putin, the president of Russia, was on the *SBJ* list for using the power of his office to influence the choice of Sochi as the site of the 2014 Winter Olympic Games. He also played a major role in the preparations of Sochi for the Games by pressuring developers to invest in resorts and hotels for Olympic visitors and by firing a member of the Russian Olympic Committee as a result of excessive spending on the Games.

Being in a pivotal position may trump wealth in the power elite, but wealth remains important to buy entry, attention, or influence. Wealth in the power elite is evidenced most clearly among the owners in the sport sector. Thirty-two of the 122 teams in MLB and the NBA, NFL, and NHL were owned in 2013 by individuals on the *Forbes* list of the four hundred richest Americans (Rovell 2013). Looking backward, we can see that the golden triangle has been attracting more wealthy owners. The thirty-two super-wealthy owners in 2013 represented a 3.5 times increase over the nine owners on the first *Forbes* 400 list in

1982 (Rushin 2013:46). The wealthiest in 2013 was Microsoft cofounder Paul Allen, owner of the 2013 Super Bowl champion Seattle Seahawks and the NBA's Portland Trail Blazers. He was the twenty-sixth-richest American and reportedly worth $15.8 billion. Fourteen of these super-rich owners were in the NFL. The NBA had thirteen owners on the list, the NHL four, and MLB two. Wealthier than anyone in the sport sector of the golden triangle of North American sports was Phil Knight, the dominant figure in the business sector. He was twenty-fourth on the *Forbes* list with an estimated worth of $16.3 billion. He made his wealth from sports as Nike founder and chairman. The wealthiest actor in the media sector of this golden triangle was Fox Sports owner Rupert Murdoch, worth an estimated $13.4 billion. His enterprising Fox executives, Randy Freer and Eric Shanks, were extremely effective in representing Murdoch's corporate and financial interests. While the owners in the sport sector came to sport with their wealth, major actors in the other sectors often used sport to create their wealth or make themselves much wealthier. It is easy to lose sight of the games when we consider how much money and power flow through the social networks linking members of the power elite in the golden triangle.

Global Sports Hierarchies

With all the power and wealth from North America in the *SI* and *SBJ* lists, one could get the impression that North American sports dominate the top ranks of the sports hierarchy in the global golden triangle. But this is not true. There is evidence from various sources that the most popular and commercially successful spectator sports in North America are not equally popular in other parts of the world (e.g., see Brown 2014b; Dixon 2013; Doley 2009; Economist 2011; FIFA 2011; McLaughlin 2010; Nielsen 2013; Ozanian 2013; TNS Global 2010; Weinstein 2013). The rankings of specific sports in national, regional, and global golden triangles vary according to historical factors, cultural tastes, and annual economic fluctuations in the marketplaces of sport and society.

Nielsen ratings showed that NFL games were nine of the top ten individual program telecasts in the United States in 2013, led by the Super Bowl. NBC Sunday Night Football was the top-rated regularly scheduled primetime TV program in 2013, and the 2014 Super Bowl game was seen by more viewers than any other television event in history, with 111.5 million viewers. However, only a few million of these viewers were outside the United States, Canada, and Mexico. Even with its huge North American TV audience, the Super Bowl does not match the audience attracted by soccer's mega-event, the FIFA World Cup. FIFA claimed on its website that the 2010 World Cup was shown in every country and territory in the world and reached 3.2 billion people, which was over 46 percent of the world's population. Even though the World Cup spans one month and the FIFA numbers are likely overestimated, there is no question about the global popularity of the sport. The European soccer (UEFA) championship also draws huge live crowds and TV audiences, with about as many people watching this game as watch the Super Bowl. The size and geographic diversity of the soccer fan base bolster arguments that soccer is the most popular sport in the world and *the* truly global sport.

People in many countries outside the United States watch sports that are popular among Americans such as golf, tennis, basketball, baseball, hockey, and auto racing as well as NFL football. In addition, the Summer and Winter Olympics appeal to viewers from around the globe. However, many sports, such as soccer, are far more popular outside the United States than they are in the United States. For example, Americans are avid followers of stock car racing and NASCAR, but European racing fans are interested in Formula One racing. Rugby and cricket are played and watched by large numbers of people in Europe and other parts of the world, but are scarcely noticed in the United States. Cycling is a very big sport in Europe, but its premier event, the Tour de France, tends to attract a US audience only when Americans are contenders. Of course, its reputation among sports fans in the United States was blemished by the publicity about doping that Lance Armstrong brought to the sport.

Perhaps the best or most appropriate measure of the rank of sports in the global golden triangle is the value of their commercial brand or cachet in the global marketplace of sport. Each year, *Forbes* magazine compiles a list of forty of the world's most valuable sports brands. Its 2013 list of the top ten athlete brand names included two golfers and two NBA players from the United States, and two soccer players, two cricket players, a tennis player, and a track athlete from outside the United States (Ozanian 2013). US golfer Tiger Woods and Swiss tennis player Roger Federer were tied for first. The ten most valuable sports business brands included six media companies and four apparel manufacturers, with Nike at the top. Among the ten most valuable sports event brands were the Super Bowl, followed by the Summer Olympics, the FIFA World Cup, the NCAA Men's Basketball Final Four, the MLB World Series, the Winter Olympics, the UEFA Champions League, the Daytona 500, the Kentucky Derby, and the MLB All-Star Week. The list of the ten most valuable team brands comprised five European soccer teams, three MLB teams, and two NFL teams. The individuals and corporations on these lists earned their place because of their prominence, endorsement value, impact, or profitability in the marketplace of world sports commerce. That is, their names were widely recognized and commanded respect from sports fans, consumers, and investors around the world.

From a commercial standpoint, the game of US football, with its many built-in breaks in action, has a structural advantage over games such as soccer that have a continuous flow to the action. Breaks are opportunities to insert advertising, which means that US football is better suited to the commercial television medium. In addition, the United States is one of the most lucrative advertising markets in the world. This is why, according to *Advertising Age*, Fox Sports billed advertisers an average of $4 million for a thirty-second ad during the 2014 Super Bowl, but a thirty-second ad cost an estimated $250,000 during the ABC broadcast of the 2010 World Cup Final, according to the *Wall Street Journal*. These differences may help explain why *Forbes* valued the Super Bowl event brand as worth $464 million and the FIFA World Cup event brand at $160 million in 2013. Along with the second-ranked Summer Olympics, valued at $348 million, these were the three most valuable event brands on the *Forbes* list.

The lofty position of soccer in the global stratification hierarchy suggests that other sports that are played by a lot of people should also rank high in global or national sports hierarchies and receive a lot of attention from the commercial media and corporate sponsors. However, the rank of a sport in these hierarchies is affected by financial and commercial performance in the sports marketplace of the golden triangle and thus reflects more than popularity alone. For example, in the United States, many more people bowl and play soccer than play golf and tennis, but golf and tennis receive more television coverage and attract more commercial sponsorship money. The answer to this apparent paradox lies in the influence of social class. The golden triangle is generally more strongly influenced by the tastes and purchasing power of more affluent members of society than less affluent ones. More affluent people can buy more, and more expensive, consumer goods. Golf is played and watched by more affluent audiences than bowling is, which makes golf more attractive to television executives and corporate sponsors. In the case of soccer in the United States, the audience seems to be growing, but it cannot yet compete with the more established sports for coverage. The US golden triangle is already very crowded. Thus, it is a combination of the size and the social class composition of the audience, called *demographics*, that shapes the relative interest and investment of the golden triangle in sports. What puts soccer at the top of the global sports hierarchy—beyond North America—and makes it so appealing to corporate investors and the golden triangle is the combination of the ethnic diversity of its huge global audience and its appeal to affluent consumers as well as poor.

Conclusion

We have examined various ways of thinking about stratification, class, and mobility throughout this chapter. We have seen that the American Sports Dream is a set of beliefs that emphasizes the value of success and the process of striving to attain it. The successful are seen as worthy because it is assumed that success is achieved by those who make the effort, whatever the obstacles in their path. The pictures and stories we get from the sports media in the golden triangle, and particularly television, tend to obscure how formidable these obstacles can be, even for the very talented, ambitious, and hardworking. This is understandable because the golden triangle represents the established institutional structure of sport, and it is in the interest of the power elite of sport to be biased toward its preservation. It is a structure in which the power elite sits at the top of the hierarchies of money, prestige, and power.

By embracing the American Sports Dream and assuming that talent, ambition, and hard work can overcome any obstacle, the power elite holds a conception of sport as fair to all. This means that anyone who is successful in sport deserves success and those who fail similarly deserve their failure. This justifies their own status as well as the stratification system in the golden triangle in general. It also enables them to overlook the effects of inequalities in society on opportunities and the pursuit of success in sport. Stories of individuals who climb the ladder of success in sport reinforce the American Sports Dream and the perception of sport and society as fair. When the media in the golden triangle tell these stories, they convey the message that inequalities are obstacles that are overcome by worthy competitors. At the same time, they distract from the enduring and deeply entrenched structural obstacles of stratification in society that unfairly restrict access and opportunities for success in sport. Thus, we are much more likely to be exposed to heroic stories of determined and successful striving than to stories of talented people who cannot achieve success or even get to compete despite their best efforts. When female and minority athletes and coaches complain about the unfairness of sport, their complaints are typically dismissed both by the sports public and by the power elite of sport. This is because the golden triangle has done such an effective job selling the American Sports Dream to itself as well as to the public.

In reality, class background still matters in the pursuit of success in sport. So do gender, sexual orientation, race, ethnicity, and physical disability. However, patterns of access and opportunity in the golden triangle have been changing for women, gays, people of color, and people with physical disabilities. Although the American Sports Dream remains out of reach for many people, it nevertheless is true that people who once found the door of opportunity in the most popular sports in the golden triangle closed now find opportunities to play, coach, and excel. As these people made it to the highest realms of their sport, there was a lag in coverage and respect they received from the media. However, as the face of sport has continued to change along with parallel changes in the larger society, it has become difficult for even the more conservative mainstream sports media to ignore these changes. In the next chapter, we will turn from a focus on social class inequalities in sport to other dimensions of diversity and inequality in sport.

Stop and Think Questions

1. What are social stratification and social mobility, and how do these terms apply to sport and the American Dream?

2. How do structural functionalists and conflict or critical theorists differ in how they interpret salary inequalities in sport?

3. Why do you think that aspiring athletes believe in the American Sports Dream despite the reality of the Sports Opportunity Pyramid?

4. Why is the Sports Opportunity Pyramid a slippery slope for athletes climbing up *and* for those who "make it"?

5. Why is the involvement of the golden triangle in the America's Cup inconsistent with its history as a sport of the elite?

6. What does the power elite look like in the golden triangle, and why is it important in sports?

7. How does the sports hierarchy of the United States differ from the global sports hierarchy?

3

Diversity and Inequalities in Sport

The golden triangle has fueled commercial expansion of sport that has opened up opportunities for many from less advantaged backgrounds. This democratization has even affected some of the most elite sports, such as yachting. Of course, as we saw in the last chapter, this democratization has been largely confined to those who play or coach the games, and has had relatively little effect on the composition of the elites who control sports. The public face of sport today nevertheless is much more diverse than in the past in terms of social class and in a number of other ways, too. This is because the American Sports Dream is true for at least some of those from less advantaged and minority backgrounds and women. We considered the myths and realities of social class and mobility and sport in the last chapter. In this chapter, we will look at how factors such as gender, sexual orientation, race, ethnicity, and physical disability have influenced participation in the sports of the golden triangle.

As in the case of social class, sports have erected structural barriers of discrimination that have restricted access, mobility, and rewards for people of lower-status backgrounds. Similarly, they have also created hurdles of prejudice that have made success in sport more difficult to attain or enjoy for those from lower-class and minority backgrounds and females who have broken through the barriers of discrimination. Consider what the terms "prejudice," "discrimination," and "minority status" imply. *Prejudice* is an inflexible and irrational generalization about an entire category of people. It is irrational or arbitrary because people hold on to attitudes supported by little or no concrete evidence and dismiss contradictory evidence as wrong or irrelevant. While prejudice is attitudinal, discrimination is behavioral and may be built into the social structure as "the way things are." *Discrimination* is the unequal treatment of an entire category of people, and like prejudice, it is irrational or arbitrary and thus unfair. Both prejudice and discrimination may be positive or negative, but we will focus on the types that are biased *against* people because they unfairly limit their chances of seeking and attaining the American Sports Dream. *Minority groups* are categories of people who are perceived as physically or culturally different and inferior in a society and as a result are relegated as a category to a subordinate status by the majority or the most powerful people in the society. Women have shared the minority status of people of color, gays, and people with permanent physical disabilities in sport.

As with social class, other barriers of discrimination in sport have fallen as the golden triangle has expanded opportunities. Hurdles of prejudice have kept these barriers from disappearing. Discrimination and prejudice may be less blatant than in the past in most contemporary sports, but their persistence is the reason we cannot talk about sport being completely fair to females and minority-group members of various types. *Fairness* is an important theme in sport because the integrity of serious competition depends on the rules of the game being applied in the same way to all participants. It is also an important theme because the American Sports Dream presumes that everyone has the same chance to participate and succeed.

In this chapter, we will see how social inequalities of gender, sexual orientation, race and ethnicity, and physical disability have affected the kinds of opportunities participants have been able to pursue in sport and how much they have been rewarded for their accomplishments. Although separate chapters could be devoted to each of these dimensions of diversity and inequality, we will address all of them in an integrated fashion in a single chapter. Females, people of color of different races and ethnicities, gay people, and people with physical disabilities have had distinctive experiences related to their particular minority status. We will consider these distinctive experiences, but we will also focus on the similar experiences that represent what it means to be socially or culturally different and unequal in sport. Since diversity and inequalities have been such prominent elements of sport at all levels, we will encounter these themes in future chapters about the major social and cultural contexts of sport in which the golden triangle has been involved.

Dealing with Difference in Sport

Difference has been a pervasive social theme in all societies, and struggles over difference have also been a common theme. Groups try to elevate themselves above others perceived as different from them, and to the extent possible those who have been relegated to minority status have tried to resist or overcome their subordination. The idea of cultural pluralism has become popular as a central aim of multiculturalism programs in many public schools in the United States in recent years. It implies respect for social and cultural differences as people try to live together with people who are different. However, it has been controversial as opponents argue that respecting too many differences or emphasizing differences too strongly can fragment a society. Opponents of cultural pluralism often prefer a melting pot in which people who come from different cultural backgrounds all try to be like the dominant cultural group in its lifestyles and beliefs.

It has been a long struggle for females and minorities to break through the barriers and overcome the hurdles in sport preventing or limiting their access and opportunities. With barriers and hurdles falling and sports in the golden triangle becoming more diverse, team and league officials, the sports media, and sports businesses have been able to construct a compelling narrative about the progressive character of the sports they run and invest in. This is a narrative about sports teams as great integrators of teammates from diverse backgrounds who come together in pursuit of a common goal of winning. This narrative could also be construed as a validation of the American Sports Dream. A story line of diversity and integration serves the commercial purposes of the golden triangle because it enables sports, the media, and sports businesses to connect with more diverse fans and consumers.

The idea that sport is meritocratic and has become more diverse and more committed to integration suggests that it stands apart from other realms of society that continue to struggle with issues of prejudice, discrimination, diversity, and integration. However, even if sports are sometimes more open, diverse, and integrated than some other segments of society, the institution of sport and the golden triangle are still intertwined with the rest of society. This means that they continue to reflect social and cultural patterns such as discrimination and prejudice elsewhere in society. One example is the sexism in televised sports coverage that was found in research by Messner and his colleagues and was cited in the first chapter.

Although prejudice and discrimination have generally lessened in intensity, remnants of the past continue to influence how women and minorities are treated in the golden triangle. The history of diversity in the golden triangle has been marked by ideologies and practices that have excluded or marginalized women and minorities or made their pursuit of success very challenging. Thus, along with recognizing breakthroughs and changes in diversity, this chapter will look at the sexism females have experienced, the homophobia gays have faced, the racism that people of color have suffered, and the ableism people with physical disabilities have gone through in trying to pursue many of the major sports of the golden triangle.

Gender and Sport

Sexism has been the historically dominant gender ideology in the United States and other nations around the world. The core belief of this ideology is that males are naturally superior to females due to their greater physical prowess and that, as a result, males deserve more respect, authority, and privilege than females. Sexism has been the ideological justification for structures of *patriarchy* in which males dominate females. Structured inequalities of gender have been as entrenched and consequential as any status inequalities in sport. When gender inequalities and patriarchy are so embedded in the social structure that most people assume they are normal, natural, or to be expected and accepted, we refer to *institutional sexism*.

Because we are born with certain biological or *sex* differences as males and females, people typically have assumed that differences in *gender* identities, statuses, and roles traditionally associated with sex differences are natural. This helps explain the persistence of institutional sexism over history. In fact, while sex differences are natural, gender differences are socially and culturally constructed. This construction of gender has traditionally made females feel inferior to males and relegated females to subordinate and less valued and rewarded statuses than males. In addition, cultural ideologies of gender have traditionally justified other sexist beliefs and the unequal and unfair treatment of women. These ideologies have shaped personal and societal conceptions of masculinity and femininity and reinforced structures of gender inequality. They have conveyed a broad justification for male privilege in relations with women and encouraged men to think of women as sexual objects rather than in terms of what women are capable of doing with their bodies and minds.

The roots of sexism and patriarchy can be traced to ancient times. For example, in ancient Greece, women participated in the Heraean Games, while men participated in the Olympics, but women were obligated to adhere to a dual ideal of "fertility and femininity" (Nixon and Frey 1996:18–19). This ideal implied that women could participate in athletic activities to help them prepare for the rigors of childbirth and defense of the state in case of war, but they also had to display culturally defined qualities such as dependence and passivity in relations with men. The general historical pattern was for women to be excluded or segregated or to receive little recognition or support for their sports participation. On the brink of Title IX in 1972, when the law redefined the opportunity structure for females in US high school and college sports, sport was viewed as a "male preserve" where males participated to establish their masculinity and women sat on the sidelines to ensure their femininity (Nixon and Frey 1996:252–254). The law and pressure from a global women's movement in the 1970s began a fundamental restructuring of the opportunity structure of sport in the United States and other countries.

Pressures from earlier women's rights movements in the twentieth century had increased opportunities for women to participate in global competitions, such as the Olympics, with the percentages increasing from 0 percent women in 1896 to over 44 percent in the 2012 London Summer Games and over 40 percent in the 2014 Sochi Winter Games. In 2012, women participated in 46.3 percent of the Olympic events, and in 2014, the participation level reached 50 percent for the first time, including mixed-gender events (FIS-SKI 2014; IOC 2013). Furthermore, women could be found throughout the twentieth century in more "feminine sports," such as tennis, swimming, golf, figure skating, and gymnastics, which seemed more graceful and less reliant on physical strength, aggression, or physical contact. However, support for women's team sports historically was minimal, and girls and women generally had few chances to participate compared with boys and men. The door opened wide for all kinds of sports participation in the United States in the 1970s following the passage of Title IX of the Higher Education Act, which outlawed sex discrimination in all educational programs and activities receiving federal financial assistance. While sports participation has significantly increased for girls and women in many sports since the 1970s, there have also been a number of areas of sport where progress has lagged in the United States and in other countries. Let us examine the progress first.

Before Title IX, fewer than 300,000 girls in US high schools, or one in twenty-seven, participated in athletics, and fewer than 32,000 women participated in college athletics. By 1974, only two years after Title IX became law, there were 1.3 million females in high school athletic programs, and by 2012, this number reached 3 million, or one in two females, at the high school level and 200,000 at the college level (Acosta and Carpenter 2012; Armour 2012). Playing sports appears to provide short-term educational and long-term economic and health benefits for females (Kaestner and Xu 2010; Parker-Pope 2010; Stevenson 2009).

Probe 3.1: Sports Are Good for Girls and Women

Stevenson (2009) studied the educational and economic effects of expanded female high school athletic participation following Title IX. Using state-level educational and census data, she found that the rise in female athletic participation during the 1970s resulting from Title IX produced increases in educational attainment and employment among females who were in high school during this period. Specifically, each 10 percent increase in state-level female sports participation produced a 1 percent increase in college attendance among females and a 1–2 percent gain in female participation in the labor force. In addition, expanded sports participation among females led to more females in previously male-dominated occupations, especially highly skilled ones. These facts are even more compelling when we consider how much high school athletic participation increased among females after the passage of Title IX. Along with getting more involved in the labor force, girls and women who participate in athletics may learn to compete more successfully in their careers. A 2002 Oppenheimer Funds survey showed that 82 percent of female business executives were involved in athletics after elementary school (Armour 2012). Women who were involved in high school sports after Title IX also experienced at least modest long-term health benefits. Kaestner and Xu (2010) found that adult women who had a chance to participate in athletics twenty to twenty-five years earlier as a result of Title IX were more physically active, had a lower body mass index (BMI), and had a lower rate of obesity than their counterparts who did not have a chance to participate in athletics. Although the health benefits they found may have been modest, even small weight reductions can have important health benefits. Other health benefits associated with school sports participation for females were lower rates of smoking and drug use (Armour 2012). Taken together, all these effects show that sports participation resulting from Title IX have been good for girls and women.

Recent research has revealed that after a huge reduction in the *gender gap* in sports participation in the decade following the passage of Title IX, the gap has stabilized or even gotten bigger in more recent years. The Women's Sports Foundation has been involved with the University of Michigan in a cooperative venture called the Sport, Health and Activity Research and Policy (SHARP) Center to sponsor interdisciplinary research about women's sports and gender issues. This research has sharpened our knowledge and understanding of the gender gap in sports participation.

Two important products of the SHARP Center have focused on trends in gender and high school athletic participation in the United States since the 1990s. Both the first study, *Progress without Equity* (Sabo and Veliz 2011), and the second study, *The Decade of Decline* (Sabo and Veliz 2012), utilized high school data from the Office of Civil Rights and the National Center for Education Statistics covering a seventeen-year period from 1993 to 2010. The titles of the two reports clearly convey their main conclusions. These studies showed that high school girls increased their participation in athletics between 1993 and 2000 and achieved greater gender equity during this period, reducing the gender gap from 14 percent to 11 percent. However, this trend essentially came to a halt between 1999 and 2006, and then the gender gap increased to 13 percent by 2010. This pattern characterized all types of communities and geographic regions and schools with a wide range of economic resources. Although the number of sports and of sports teams for boys and girls increased in the first decade of the twenty-first century, the gender gap continued or got worse. Boys had an average half-sport advantage over girls during this period, and they started and finished the decade with an average advantage of one to two teams over girls. Although schools with more economic resources offered more athletic opportunities than did schools with fewer resources, boys consistently had more sports and teams than girls across all types of schools.

A study using national data from 2002 found that high school students in the United States were generally supportive of increased opportunities for females in sport, with girls more supportive than boys (Brown, Ruel, and Medley-Rath 2011). Comparing males and females and athletes and nonathletes, the male athletes had the most negative attitudes. This might reflect more conservative attitudes in general about female roles. If these attitudes persist into adulthood, they may affect how sports administrators and executives in the golden triangle view girls and women in sport. This helps explain the persistence of patterns of institutional sexism in sport and the golden triangle.

Sabo and Veliz (2012:35) called the period from 2000 to 2010 "an era of lost opportunity." It was a chance to reduce the gender gap in high school sports, but instead the reverse happened. This is despite the fact that Americans generally approved of the idea of equal opportunity for boys and girls in sport (Mellman Group 2007) and that parents wanted both their daughters and sons to receive fair treatment in all realms of education (Sabo and Veliz 2008). Sabo and Veliz (2012:35) also referred to an "illusion of equality" that affected the American public's perception of equity in sport, which is similar to its belief in the American Dream and American Sports Dream. It is the belief that since females have made so much progress in sport (and elsewhere in society), there must be equality and equity or fairness in school sports. There may remain some questions about college athletics, but the illusion is that surely there must be a level playing field for girls and boys at the high school level. Sabo and Veliz's research points to a different reality, and what is curious, they point out, is that many parents might not realize that Title IX applies to both the high school and college levels. As a result, they may not press school officials to provide more or better opportunities for their daughters.

The first decade of the twenty-first century was a period of lost opportunities in another and perhaps more literal sense. The percentage of schools without interscholastic athletic programs rose from 8.2 percent in 2000 to 15 percent ten years later. Athletic programs were more likely to be dropped in urban schools (9.6 percent) than in schools in rural (7.7 percent), town (6.6 percent), or suburban (5.8 percent) areas. Sabo and Veliz (2012) found that the poorest schools with the most racial and ethnic minority students were most likely to close athletic programs. This helps us understand why poor and especially poor minority females have had a harder time benefiting from efforts to achieve gender equity than their more affluent and white counterparts. A study using national data in the United States showed that high schools that African American females attended did not provide the same range of sports opportunities as did the schools that white females attended (Pickett, Dawkins, and Braddock 2012). African American females typically attended high schools that did not offer many of the sports that provided pathways to college athletic scholarships, for example, soccer, volleyball, crew, and softball. As a result, African American females tended to be highly concentrated in a few college sports, in particular, bowling, basketball, and track. They were sparsely represented in most others.

Probe 3.2: The Racial Gap and the Limits of Title IX

Title IX has provoked many court cases and judicial decisions about its justification and enforcement. These cases generally have focused on unfairness in opportunities, the elimination of teams, women on men's teams, and men on women's teams, but the issue of racial disparity has been virtually ignored. Thus, while gender inequalities have been pronounced enough to make the elimination of gender discrimination in schools a matter for legislative redress, racial inequalities among females have not seemed to warrant similar attention. As a result, the gender gap in participation in interscholastic and intercollegiate sports has been significantly reduced by Title IX, but the *racial gap* for minority females has gotten worse at both levels since 1972. In 1972, African American females had a higher rate of high school athletic participation than their white counterparts, but this gap was reversed by the 1990s and continues to exist today. At the college level, white females have consistently participated in athletics at a higher rate than African American females. This gap got bigger during the first decade of the 2000s.

The experiences of female coaches and athletic administrators have been similar to or even worse than the experiences of minority female athletes. After the passage of Title IX, women formed their own athletic organization, the Association for Intercollegiate Athletics for Women (AIAW), to administer women's intercollegiate athletics. It grew rapidly, and by 1981 it had 950 member institutions. However, fearing a threat to its dominance of commercialized college sports, the National Collegiate Athletic Association (NCAA) began offering championships in women's sports at the beginning of the 1980s. This led to a flood of new NCAA members from the AIAW, and by 1982 the AIAW was essentially out of business (Sage and Eitzen 2013:329). The effect of this organizational shift was that women no longer ran women's intercollegiate sports. For example, in 1972, 90 percent of the coaches in women's college sports were female (Halkidis 2012). However, according to The Institute for Diversity and Ethics in Sport (TIDES), the percentage of women coaching women's college teams had declined to 38 percent by 2012 (Lapchick, with Agusta, Kinkopf, and McPhee 2013). It went up at the Division I Football Bowl Subdivision (FBS) level to 40.2 percent in 2012–2013, but fell to 39.6 percent in 2013–2014 (LaVoi 2014).

TIDES has produced annual report cards indicating the status of minorities and women in college and professional sports. TIDES found that the coaches of women's college teams were not only disproportionately male but also overwhelmingly white: 84.5 percent of coaches in Division I were white males and 92 percent in Division III were white males. TIDES also found that in 2012, only 8.2 percent of the athletic directors at the NCAA Division I were women. There were more chances to administer athletics at the Division II (17.5 percent) and Division III (28 percent) levels, but there were also significant gender gaps. There were more chances for women at the associate athletic director level, with near gender parity at the Division III level, but at the Division I level 30 percent of associate athletic directors were women. Male and female African Americans held less than 10 percent of athletic director and associate athletic director positions at any NCAA level. One of the most powerful positions in the sport sector of the golden triangle is commissioner of an FBS conference. In 2012, 100 percent of these eleven positions were held by white men. A similar pattern of limited opportunities for women in leadership positions in college sports also was found in Canada (Donnelly, Norman, and Kidd 2013).

Even though women once had more control over their own sports, the dominance of men in women's sports reflects a kind of institutional sexism in which male dominance seems to be accepted and even acceptable when men and women coexist in organizations. Claringbould and Knoppers (2012) proposed that the institutional sexism they found in persisting patterns of skewed gender ratios in leadership positions in sports organizations was sustained by paradoxical practices of gender. They came to this conclusion on the basis of their interviews with sport journalists working for national newspapers or television and interviews with members of national governing boards of Olympic sports organizations. Two-thirds of the journalists they interviewed were males, and twelve of the thirty-two board members they interviewed were male.

The researchers explained the persistence of skewed gender ratios in leadership in terms of the practices of gender neutrality, normalcy, and passivity, which they saw as paradoxical in the way they sustained and challenged this institutional sexism. *Gender neutrality* refers to the paradoxical practice of recognizing the need to change the skewed gender ratio in leadership but failing to acknowledge that gender or sexism had anything to do with it. By trying to be "gender neutral" in this way, the journalists and board members were actually contributing to the persistence of institutional sexism in leadership. The women in these positions felt pressure to exhibit gender neutrality in order to be taken seriously in the male-dominated sports world.

Paradoxical practices of *gender normalcy* happened when gender inequality in leadership was seen and accepted as normal despite the fact that women possessed qualifications that should have enabled them to be equally represented in leadership positions. For instance, women may have viewed it as normal for there to be only one or two women among journalists and board members in sports settings, and men may have thought that it was normal for males to be in the majority. The perceived normalcy of the skewed gender ratio may be attributed to the beliefs that sport was something that men pursued and that it was normal or understandable that relatively few women would want to seek leadership positions in this man's world. Being a sports journalist or sports board member might be acceptable for a woman if her focus was on women's issues or women's sports. Thus, the normalcy of institutional sexism in these realms tended to be reinforced by gender stereotypes.

Gender passivity was another paradoxical practice that the researchers saw as contributing to the persistence of institutional sexism in sports leadership positions. The sports journalists and board members in Claringbould and Knoppers's study engaged in gender passivity when they acknowledged that they did not feel responsible for the gender imbalance in sports journalism or the governance of sports and did little to change the inequality. Although they said they wanted to see an increase of women in their areas, they were generally opposed to affirmative action. They paradoxically did not think such policies were effective or needed, despite the persistence of gender inequality.

Claringbould and Knoppers did not think their findings were limited to the Netherlands, where they conducted their research, and cited similar results in studies of Danish and Norwegian sports organizations. In fact, their findings and analysis seemed to apply even more broadly to sports organizations in other parts of the world and to all three sectors of the golden triangle. It is not that patterns such as gender segregation and the glass ceiling are invisible in sport or the larger society. Yet in spite of efforts by feminists and other activists to challenge them, the paradoxical practices of gender neutrality, normalcy, and passivity seem to be powerful enough to deflect these challenges and maintain established patterns of inequality in sports leadership in the golden triangle. These practices are also likely to have played a role in maintaining the imbalance in the gender ratio among sports participants in recent years. The paradoxical thinking that applies here is that even though girls and women have clearly shown a serious interest in a wide variety of sports and have substantially increased their numbers and achieved much success in sports when given a chance, the continuing gender gap may be interpreted as a reflection of the normal or natural state of affairs in a world intended mainly for males.

Probe 3.3: Invisibility of Women's Sports in the Media

Part of gender normalcy in US sports is the limited visibility of women's sports in media coverage. Certain sports are almost totally invisible. Research has pointed to women's baseball as an example of this invisibility (Ring 2013). Even though the US Women's National Team earned a medal in a highly competitive Women's World Cup in Venezuela in 2010, this success was largely unreported by the US media and largely unknown to the US public. The irony is that Team USA received an enthusiastic welcome in Caracas and played in packed stadiums and drew large television audiences. Their lack of attention and financial support at home may have reflected the popular cultural belief that men play baseball and women play softball in the United States. This kind of thinking is what institutional sexism means.

As long as sports in general or specific kinds of sports are viewed as male preserves, chances for females to participate or receive respect and media coverage in certain sports will be limited, and females who participate in these sports are likely to be viewed as strange or unfeminine. For example, studies of women boxers and their coaches (Mennesson 2000) and of women bodybuilders (Lowe 1998) showed that the women in these sports had to face sexist stereotypes in forming their identities. Whereas the women boxers had to deal with identity issues in a highly combative sport, the women bodybuilders had to face questions about the appearance of their bodies. A more recent study of female bodybuilders found that individual competitors generally spoke out against feminine stereotypes and took pleasure in being "different" (McGrath and Chananie-Hill 2009). However, at the same time, the women did not identify with excessive muscularity and did not want to appear too "manly." Women will continue to have to deal with contradictory feelings about being female and looking like an athlete as long as narrow conceptions of *gendered sports* are embedded in culture. The idea of gendered sports implies that some sports are seen as more appropriate for one gender than the other. The problem for women is that the traditional gendering of sports has identified sports in general as more appropriate for males. Gender boundaries are especially high in sports with highly visible displays of strength, muscularity, and aggression. Despite the substantial progress women have made in breaking down traditional barriers in sport, women who transgress the boundaries of the more manly sports are likely to continue to have to deal with the issues of identity and gender expression found by researchers.

Traditional gender stereotypes explain why team sports involving physical contact or confrontation have typically been gendered and defined as masculine. Women have challenged the idea that team sports are for men, and over the past several decades, female participation in team sports has gradually increased, with the Olympics adding women's volleyball in 1964, basketball in 1976, and field hockey in 1980. The timing of the addition of field hockey is interesting because it had been the rare example of a female team sport since the 1930s, and girls and women had competed in it from the high school level to the international level since that time. The first women's team sport to be added to the Winter Olympics was ice hockey in 1998, and this sport provided an opportunity to study how women have challenged traditional ideas about masculinity when playing a masculinized sport.

Theberge (2000) studied elite women ice hockey players in Canada. These women faced ambivalence or resistance to playing the game, but persisted because they loved the game and developed a sense of community as a team. They played the same game as the men, except for one noteworthy difference. The women's rules prohibited intentional body checking but did not eliminate the extensive body contact from efforts to gain control of the puck and the game. The fact that the women's rules were more likely than the men's rules to limit injuries did not increase appreciation of their game, since the elements of physical aggression and risk probably contributed to the popularity of the men's game among hockey fans. While men generally play a more aggressive style of hockey, the two best women's ice hockey teams in international competition, Team Canada and Team USA, have been distinguished by their aggressive styles. This demonstrates that women are more successful when they play the "men's game." It also shows that women are able to play the men's game quite successfully.

Probe 3.4: Women on Men's Turf (or Ice)

The women's game of ice hockey reached a new level of respect after the Sochi Olympic Games in 2014. Shannon Szabados, the gold-medal-winning goalkeeper for the Canadian women's national team, became the first female player in the Southern Professional Hockey League in March 2014 shortly after her Olympic success. She lost her first game, 4–3, but fans greeted her with cheers when she skated onto the ice of her home rink (Gierer 2014). This is significant because it implies that (very talented) women may be gaining respect among fans of masculinized sports when they play with the men. Race car driver Danica Patrick has seen a mixed reaction among fans and fellow drivers, with critics suggesting her opportunities on the track have had more to do with her appearance than her driving skills (Pockrass 2014a). There have been a few female referees in the National Basketball Association (NBA), but their chances have been limited by perceptions that the first woman referee in 1997 was not as qualified as the men referees (Dwyer 2012). Women can be expected to try to break into a few other men's sports or sports roles. However, we are not likely to find a significant transformation of the gender demographics in major male sports. For serious women athletes, though, the point is to have equivalent kinds of opportunities to play and equal rewards for the same kinds of success. This is what Billie Jean King fought for in women's tennis nearly four decades ago. They also want a chance to show that they have the ability to take their place on the sidelines and in the front office.

It is easy to see why women with the talent to perform various kinds of sports roles in women's sports or in men's sports or in sports organizations for both sexes have been frustrated by the barriers and obstacles they have faced. The damaging consequences of male dominance in sport for males may be less obvious. Much research and writing in sport sociology has examined how sport socializes men to be masculine and how males often struggle with the masculine expectations imposed on them by sport. Messner (1990, 1992) has done extensive research about sport and the "problem of masculinity" for males, and he has shown how social class affects the dependence of males on sport for their masculine identity and self-respect. Poorer boys and young men have fewer options for defining themselves as successful, which is especially important to males in a culture where males are supposed to be dominant and successful. Thus, the importance of success in sport is inversely related to a male's social class: the lower the class, the more important is sports success.

Messner's (1990) research has shown that sports not only are gendered but also play a *gendering* role in socialization. As a gendered institution, sport exhibits many of the dominant patterns of gender differentiation, segregation, and inequality we find in other institutions in society. At the same time, sport reinforces these patterns by teaching males sexist ideas of what it means to be masculine. In doing so, masculinized sports also convey the message that girls and women do not belong because being feminine means not playing these sports. The more females transgress traditional gender boundaries in sport, the less gendered sport is as an institution and the less effective it is in its gendering function. It is clear, though, that there continue to be gendered sports that are perceived as more manly, which still serve a gendering function. Females who participate in these sports may put their stereotypical femininity at risk and be seen as lesbian. Perhaps less obvious is that certain sports are gendered to be more feminine, which can make males who participate in them seem less masculine and perhaps gay. Thus, the gendering of sports can create challenges of gender expression that give salience to issues of sexual orientation and homophobia in sport.

Sexual Orientation and Sport

The corporate world of the golden triangle has generally seemed reluctant to embrace openly homosexual or gay athletes because it is more reactive than proactive in relation to social change. This reluctance derives from the traditional conception of sport as a male preserve dominated by strong, aggressive, heterosexual males. This conception of sport has cast doubt on the femininity and heterosexual orientation of women in more masculinized sports. It also calls into question the masculinity of gay male athletes and makes it difficult for them to be open about their sexual orientation when they participate in highly masculinized sports. In addition, it can discourage heterosexual males from participating in more feminized sports or lead people to assume that males who participate in these kinds of sports must be homosexual. Figure skating embodies these issues.

Probe 3.5: Men in "Girls' Sports"

Adams (2011) analyzed how male singles figure skaters have adapted to the gendering of their sport that began over fifty years ago. She raised an important question about why males have chosen to participate in a sport that has become increasingly gendered as a "girls' sport." She dismissed the idea that figure skating is a "gay sport" that attracts only gay men as athletes, coaches, and officials. At the same time, she argued that no other sport has subjected male participants to more questions about their sexual orientation. The fact that the aesthetic beauty of movement in this sport is associated more with femininity than masculinity contributes to the feminization of the sport and the suspicions about the sexual orientation of male skaters. Adams observed that as a result of this gendering, a number of male skaters over the past two decades have gone to great lengths to try to appear more masculine. We can see this in the costuming, the programming, the insertion of increasingly physically demanding quadruple jumps, and off-ice involvement in "macho" activities such as riding motorcycles and doing martial arts. Like any constraining construction of gender, though, the gendering of this kind of sport for males and of the masculinized conception of certain sports played by females robs participants in both types of sports of the freedom to pursue the sports they love most in the ways they most want to compete in them. The stigmatization of gay males and lesbians often deprives them of the freedom of open gender expression, full enjoyment of their sports, and the respect and other rewards their talents and accomplishments deserve.

In an age of ostensibly increasing tolerance and acceptance of homosexuality and gay marriage, prejudice and discrimination toward gays in sport would seem anachronistic. We have to be careful, though, not to overstate the amount of acceptance. A 2013 Pew Research Center global survey of attitudes toward homosexuality found more acceptance in more secular and affluent nations (Kohut 2013). However, the amount of acceptance in the United States was far less than in many other secular and affluent countries. While 60 percent of US respondents agreed in 2013 that homosexuality should be accepted—an increase of 11 percent over the 2007 figure—the United States was far behind Spain (88 percent), Germany (87 percent), Canada and the Czech Republic (80 percent), France (77 percent), Great Britain (76 percent), and Argentina and Italy (74 percent). Most of these countries were more accepting in 2013 than in 2007. Younger people tended to be the most accepting, and in countries with a gender gap, such as the United States, women tended to be more accepting than men. The United States may be less accepting than other affluent nations because the issues of homosexuality and gay marriage, in particular, have been made moral issues by powerful socially conservative interest groups. The increased acceptance of homosexuality in the United States between 2007 and 2013 reflects the inroads made in recent years by advocates for gay marriage and for the rights of members of the lesbian, gay, bisexual, and transgender (LGBT) community.

The fact that 49 percent of US respondents in the 2007 Pew survey expressed acceptance of homosexuality provides a context for interpreting the results of a 2005 survey of attitudes in the United States toward homosexuals in sport (SI. com 2005; Wertheim 2005). There were 979 people from the general population interviewed for the NBC/USA Network study. The results were published by *Sports Illustrated*. The study found that 86 percent thought it was acceptable for male homosexual athletes to play sports, even if they were open about their homosexuality. In addition, 78 percent expressed the same attitude about female homosexual athletes. The survey also found that 61 percent believed that homosexuality was a way of life that should be accepted by society, 67 percent said that the private life of athletes was their own business, and 48 percent said they admired athletes who were openly homosexual. These and other findings suggested fairly widespread public acceptance of homosexuals in sport and society.

However, there were other responses indicating that even those who seemed to accept homosexuality may have had reservations or may have held conflicting beliefs. For example, 68 percent said it would hurt an athlete's career to be openly homosexual, 44 percent thought it was a sin to be homosexual, 40 percent said it was OK for homosexuals to be in sports as long as they were *not* open about their sexual orientation, 52 percent thought the public would react negatively to more emphasis on homosexual athletes in *Sports Illustrated*, and 42 percent thought viewers would be "enraged" if ESPN did a special on the achievements of homosexual athletes. These findings explain why the subtitle of the article in *Sports Illustrated* accompanying these poll results was "Americans Believe They Have Become More Accepting—but Have They?" It should be remembered that at the time of this study, no gay athlete in a major team sport had revealed his sexual orientation. Wertheim (2005) observed that of the 3,500 men who were playing professional basketball, baseball, football, and hockey in North America at that time, none admitted to being gay. Gay athletes who had acknowledged their sexual orientation at that time were retired from sport or played minor or individual sports. While there were openly lesbian athletes and some concern about homophobia on women's sports teams, the issues of sexual orientation and homophobia in women's sports did not receive the media attention that was later given to gay men who came out of the closet while still active in their sport.

It can be difficult to assess the validity of survey responses to questions about sensitive issues, and people often are able to rationalize inconsistent attitudes. It may be that many respondents in this survey did not see themselves as homophobic but still believed that a number of other people were homophobic, despite the expressed perception by many of increasing tolerance in society. Whether subtle or overt, homophobia is damaging to people who are not heterosexual, just as sexism is damaging to women, racism is damaging to racial and ethnic minorities, and ableism is damaging to people with disabilities. *Homophobia* refers to a pattern of irrational hostile or negative feelings toward people with a nonheterosexual orientation and to a fear of homosexuality, and often results in discriminatory or unfair treatment of homosexuals and others with a bisexual or transgender orientation.

It seems clear that homosexual participants in sport have not trusted public tolerance expressed in attitude surveys. Perhaps they recall the reaction when retired NBA player John Amaechi revealed that he was gay at the time of the publication of a book about his life and career. Most notable were the comments by a former NBA star, Tim Hardaway, who said that he "hated gay people," he did not like being around them, and gay players should not be in the same locker room as heterosexual players (MSNBC 2007). There have also been a number of instances since then of prominent athletes using homophobic slurs (e.g., Zillgitt 2011). An unscientific ESPN survey in 2014 of fifty-one National Football League (NFL) players following the announcement by prominent draft prospect Michael Sam that he was gay revealed that NFL locker rooms are not entirely devoid of homophobia (Mascaro 2014). An overwhelming forty-four of the fifty-one respondents said that a player's sexual orientation did not matter to them, and thirty-nine said they would shower around a gay teammate. However, only twenty-five of the fifty-one believed that an openly gay player would be comfortable in an NFL locker room, and thirty-two said that they had teammates or coaches who had used homophobic slurs in the past season.

At the college level, homophobia seems to be declining in the athletic culture, as it has been on the campus in general. But it still exists, especially among male athletes (e.g., Ganucheau 2013; Southall, Nagel, Anderson, Polite, and Southall 2009). A study of seven hundred male and female athletes at four universities conducted by Southall and his colleagues found that 1.6 percent of the male athletes identified themselves as gay and 3.8 percent of the female athletes identified themselves as either lesbian or bisexual (Southall et al. 2009). The male–female difference may reflect differences in their willingness to acknowledge being gay rather than actual differences in prevalence. This could be explained by the strong heterosexually masculine emphasis in many sports settings. Results from another study suggested that athletes who had more contact with openly gay or lesbian athletes had more positive attitudes toward gay men and lesbians (Roper and Halloran 2007). The problem is that with so few athletes privately admitting to being gay, lesbian, or bisexual in the survey, and with even fewer likely to publicly acknowledge their sexual orientation, the chances of "straight" athletes interacting with openly gay athletes is relatively limited. The perception of homophobia tends to stifle the disclosure of a gay or lesbian sexual orientation among athletes and especially males.

With acceptance of homosexuality limited in many countries of the world, it would not be surprising to find homophobic displays involving sports and athletes in these countries. The Pew Research Center global survey found that in Russia, for example, acceptance of homosexuality dropped from 20 percent in 2007 to 16 percent in 2013. This explains the passage of an antigay law in June 2013 in Russia that forbids "propaganda" in favor of "nontraditional" sexual orientations. It was part of President Putin's conservative social agenda. The timing of the passage of this law was awkward because it occurred less than a year before Russia was set to host the Sochi Winter Olympic Games. This law was in conflict with the Olympic charter, which opposes "discrimination of any kind." However, with a long-standing policy of trying to minimize the intrusion of politics into the Olympic arena, International Olympic Committee (IOC) officials made a statement condemning any move that would jeopardize its human rights principle (Longman 2013).

After IOC officials got assurances the law would not be enforced during the Games, they made no further comments and essentially dropped the issue. Although NBC Olympics anchor Bob Costas strongly criticized Russian policies, including those hostile to gay rights, in a commentary toward the end of the Games, his network did little to draw attention to homophobic anti-LGBT displays that had been occurring in Russia (Farhi 2014). In the golden triangle, letting the Games go on trumps concerns about human rights. This was also true of sponsors of the Games. This kind of environment might have been the reason why there were only seven openly homosexual athletes competing in the Sochi Games, and all were women (Quinn 2014).

Organizations and corporations in the golden triangle may not actively or intentionally abet those promoting intolerance or oppression in sport and society. However, they obviously are reluctant to take any kind of stand that might disrupt the organization or operation of the games and sports they run or sponsor. This means that change in sport is more likely to come from outside than inside the golden triangle. Change has been happening in sport regarding various kinds of prejudices and institutional discrimination. Sexual orientation has been especially resistant to change because sport has historically been about expressing stereotypical heterosexual masculinity in many cases. This traditional orientation has brought clarity to the meaning of gender difference in and out of sport. But women and especially LGBT people playing sport have disrupted established ideas about who deserves priority in sport and society. Although the golden triangle has not taken the lead in spearheading these changes, it has slowly, perhaps begrudgingly, accommodated them.

A moral compass has not guided the golden triangle in its approach to sexual orientation. It has been guided more by its interest in keeping in tune with the changing attitudes of its fan and consumer base. On the other hand, individual athletes have begun to take the courageous step of making public their own homosexuality or they have spoken out in support of others who are homosexual. We have also seen athletes who were outspoken opponents of gays in sport recant and express public support for LGBT rights in sport and society. Tim Hardaway is an example of one of these outspoken opponents who have reversed their position and joined others advocating for same-sex marriage (Highkin 2013). This action made more credible his earlier apology for his intemperate homophobic remarks about John Amaechi.

We can readily understand the preference of gay athletes for individual sports, in which athletes find it easier to protect their identity and avoid homophobic teammates (Pronger 2005). Yet gay athletes in team sports are beginning to come out. While not yet a flood, a number of gay athletes still active in traditionally masculinized and commercially popular team sports have been transgressing the boundaries of homophobia in their sport by disclosing their sexual orientation. In late 2009 when Welsh rugby star Gareth Thomas announced that he was gay, he was the only openly gay athlete playing a major men's team sport (Smith 2010). An Australian rugby player and an English soccer player had come out in the 1990s, and their disclosures had prompted cruel and ugly reactions from crowds during games and even from family members. However, years later, Thomas received largely positive responses to his announcement as an act of courage.

NBA player Jason Collins became the first openly gay athlete in a major team sport in the United States in 2013. He experienced largely positive reactions (Collins, with Lidz 2013), although it took him several months before an NBA team signed him to a contract and he played in a game (Araton 2014). Collins was not a star, but defensive end Michael Sam had the potential to become a star in the NFL when he announced he was gay prior to the NFL draft in 2014 (Price 2014). Sam was on the brink of becoming the first openly gay player in the league. He had already told his University of Missouri teammates, but his sexual orientation was not widely known before his public announcement. He was cut by the team that had drafted him and then was released by the Dallas Cowboys after a brief stint on their practice squad. Soccer star Robbie Rogers had won championships at the University of Maryland and with the Major League Soccer (MLS) Columbus Crew and had kept his sexual orientation secret. In 2013, at age twenty-five, he revealed that he was gay and also decided to step away from his sport. However, he changed his mind about retirement and signed with the MLS Los Angeles Galaxy so that he could serve as a role model as a soccer player and an avowed gay athlete and Christian (Foss and Brady 2013).

While lesbian athletes have also been reluctant to acknowledge their sexual orientation while they were still active, there have been some notable cases of openly lesbian athletes who were actively playing their sport, such as tennis player Martina Navratilova. Navratilova came out in 1981. She was a trailblazer, although she disavowed this label (Wertheim 2013). A dominant player in her sport, she made her announcement at great personal risk. She went against the wishes of the governing body of her sport. She also gave up millions of dollars in lost commercial endorsements and stood alone as other athletes in her sport and others she knew were homosexual but chose not to stand with her.

Like gay men, lesbians in women's team sports have been reluctant to come out. Sue Wicks was the first lesbian player in the WNBA to reveal her sexual orientation while still active, and she did so in a rather perfunctory way shortly before her retirement in 2002. This was more than twenty years after Martina Navratilova's announcement. Three years later, when WNBA star Sheryl Swoopes came out, she was the only openly gay or lesbian athlete active in a major professional team sport in North America (Seattle PI 2005). The fact that the LGBT community had become more visible and a potentially lucrative market by 2005 contributed to more acceptance and more commercial opportunities for lesbian athletes. However, the commercial opportunities were still limited. Swoopes and lesbian golfer Rosie Jones became endorsers of a lesbian cruise line, Olivia Cruises.

It is not uncommon today to read about lesbian women in the team sports of soccer, softball, and ice hockey as well as basketball and in a number of individual professional sports including tennis and golf. Although a tiny minority of the female athletes at recent Summer and Winter Olympic Games, openly lesbian athletes competed in a range of sports (Buzinski 2012; Quinn 2014). The relatively small number of openly lesbian athletes in sports in the golden triangle very likely reflects concerns about homophobic reactions in their sports.

Probe 3.6: Social Pressures and the Problem of Being Openly Homosexual in Sport

Lesbian basketball star Brittney Griner publicly announced her sexual orientation in 2013, but she waited until after she had completed her career at Baylor University. She explained that this was because her coaches were uncomfortable with her being open about her sexual orientation. She was even asked to remove a tweet revealing her homosexuality. Her coaches feared that such openness could imply that they accepted homosexuality and that this could cost them potential recruits (Morgan 2013). This kind of pressure from club officials and agents also explains why gay male players have been reluctant to come out in association football (soccer) in Europe. In their study of these athletes, Cashmore and Cleland (2011) observed that this pressure was the main reason for a "culture of secrecy" regarding sexual orientation that allowed or encouraged homophobia in the sport.

Although gay and lesbian athletes have been exposed to various forms of homophobia, *transgender athletes* have had additional challenges owing to the perceived ambiguity of their gender as well as sexual orientation. From the time in the second half of the 1970s when Renée Richards (née Richard Raskin) fought for the right to compete in the US Open tennis tournament, transgender athletes have had to sue for the right to compete in the golden triangle. They have not been embraced by officials in women's professional sports. It took a New York State Supreme Court ruling for Richards to overcome the opposition of officials in the US Tennis Association. She went on to a four-year career in women's professional tennis while also continuing her career as an ophthalmologist. In 2005, former police officer Lana Lawless fought the ban of transgender players in women's professional golf. Renée Richards observed that three decades after her own battle, transgender issues remain "largely unsettled" in sport (Robson 2010; also see Torre and Epstein 2012).

These issues were more complicated than other forms of sexual orientation because they involved the surgical reassignment of sex as well as a change in gender or sexual identification. Women's sports officials in the golden triangle were especially sensitive about these issues because they feared that having openly transgender athletes would undermine the respect for their sport they had worked hard to achieve. This is why we have seen cases where sports officials have required some very big or strong-looking women athletes to undergo so-called sex or gender verification tests to prove they are biologically female. A highly publicized case in the past decade involved star South African runner Caster Semenya, who earned a gold medal in a women's 800-meter race in 2009. As in the case of transgender athletes in women's sport, *sex testing* reflects concerns that women who are too manly or are too much like men have an unfair advantage in competition (Cooky and Dworkin 2013). This resurrects arguments about whether females are good enough in sports to warrant the same opportunities as males and whether they deserve the respect males receive in many sports because they cannot defeat males in these sports. These were the kinds of arguments made in the 1960s and in the early 1970s to keep women out of sport (Gilbert and Williamson 1973). This is why Title IX is so relevant to athletics. LGBT athletes have arguably had to contend with even more deeply rooted opposition because their involvement raises issues of sex and biology as well as gender.

Just as sexism limits opportunities in sports management and coaching, homophobia seems to have a similar effect on these kinds of opportunities for LGBT persons. As in the case of athletes, openly LGBT sports executives and coaches have been rare. Rick Welts broke new ground in 2002 when he became the first gay top executive in a major professional sport in North America as the president and CEO of the NBA Phoenix Suns (Weir 2011). He waited until months before he resigned in 2011 to reveal he was gay. He subsequently became president of the NBA Golden State Warriors. Welts's reluctance to come out reflected the perception among LGBT sports administrators of continuing homophobia in their workplaces. However, Welts's success in finding a new high-level job in his sport indicated that in his workplace, homophobia was muted by his demonstrated competence. A study of ten gay men employed by professional, collegiate, and club sports showed that their experiences varied widely (Cavalier 2011). Some were like Welts in having a positive experience, but others' experiences were quite negative. Although the sample was small, these results suggest that homophobia is not universal in sport and that other factors may mitigate the effects of homophobia and open up opportunities for homosexual men and women in sport. The experiences of lesbians in the sports workplace are less known than those of their male counterparts, though.

Despite recent breakthroughs, the representation of openly LGBT athletes, coaches, and administrators in the sport sector of the golden triangle remains limited, certainly much more limited than the representation of women and racial and ethnic minorities. A study of NCAA Division III athletic administrators indicated that athletic departments that had more racial and gender diversity also were likely to be somewhat more accepting of sexual orientation diversity (Cunningham 2010). Thus, a broad commitment to diversity could be part of the organizational or administrative culture of athletic departments, and it may be multifaceted. In addition, when officials promote antidiscrimination policies and recruit openly gay and lesbian athletes and hire openly LGBT employees, the environment is likely to be conducive to more openness about sexual orientation and attract others who are LGBT. At this point, relatively more progress has been made in struggles to reduce inequalities of social class, gender, race, and ethnicity than in efforts to reduce inequalities of sexual orientation and disability in sport because society in general has lagged in the latter types of efforts. In the next two sections, we will look at patterns and implications of inequalities of race and ethnicity and of physical disability in sport.

People of Color in US Sports

Notions that people of color and particularly African Americans have become dominant in the golden triangle and have erased the legacy of segregation, inequality, and racism are exaggerated in some sports and completely untrue in others. *Racism* is like sexism and homophobia in embodying an ideology and practices that are used by dominant groups in society to devalue and disadvantage minorities. Racism may be so integrated into the structure of everyday life that we accept it as normal and do not notice it. This *institutional racism* was found in US sport in the patterns of bias and discrimination that kept blacks out of many major sports for many years, denied them opportunities to play certain prestigious and central positions in certain sports such as quarterback in football, denied them chances to coach or manage, gave them less respect and pay than their white teammates for comparable or better performances, and gave them less access to commercial endorsement opportunities than their white teammates. During the long period of *racial segregation* that lasted without many exceptions until around the middle of the twentieth century in many major US sports, black athletes in these sports competed in segregated sports leagues or at historically black colleges and universities. When they broke the color barrier in the 1940s and 1950s in Major League Baseball (MLB), the NBA, and the NFL, black players had to stay in segregated hotels and eat at segregated restaurants apart from their white teammates when they traveled to southern cities where these practices were still in place.

Despite the well-documented history of racial and ethnic discrimination in sport, it has sometimes been heralded as a great social experiment in integration or as a means of uniting people of different racial and ethnic backgrounds who have difficulty interacting with each other elsewhere in society. Waves of new immigrants and blacks found opportunities in certain less reputable or "lower-class" sports, such as boxing, throughout the nineteenth and twentieth centuries. When Jesse Owens triumphed in track and field events at the 1936 "Nazi" Olympics, and the "Brown Bomber" Joe Louis won the heavyweight championship of the world over German Max Schmeling just before World War II, their nationalities became more important than their race for some Americans. When Jackie Robinson broke the color barrier in MLB, sport very visibly stood as a counterexample to lingering patterns of racial segregation and discrimination in the larger US society. Some saw his entry into the previously segregated MLB world as an example for the rest of society, potentially leading the way toward change. At least in sport, Jackie Robinson opened the door in Major League Baseball to other black players, just as black athletes opened the door to racial integration in other professional, college, and Olympic sports before and after him. Outside North America, the racially and ethnically diverse French national soccer teams led by superstar Zinedine Zidane, of Algerian descent, were considered a unifying force in a French society with significant racial and ethnic tensions.

The picture of sport, race, and ethnicity is more complicated than this image of unity amid diversity, as we have seen. For example, the proud and controversial black boxing champion in the early part of the twentieth century, Jack Johnson, provoked so much antagonism by his defiance of racial conventions, such as dating white women, that he inspired a search for a "Great White Hope" to challenge him as heavyweight champion. The search for other Great White Hopes in boxing and other sports endured long after his career ended in exile. A variation of this search occurred in the twenty-first century as white ethnic boxing fans sought a reaffirmation of their ethnic identity and masculinity in bouts between white ethnic fighters, called "vanilla thrillas" (Cooley 2010). Enthusiasm for these fights and fighters could be interpreted as evidence of lingering racial resentment of the domination of the sport by boxers of color. Rooting for white ethnic fighters reflected a nostalgic longing for a return of the sport to the days long past when "their people" dominated the sport. Promoters cynically used these racist themes to increase interest.

Probe 3.7: Limits of Social Integration through Sport

Jackie Robinson faced racist reactions from his own teammates as well as from fans around the league. His status as an MLB star did little to change the racial segregation in society when he played the game, and did not prevent the racial tensions that turned into riots in the late 1960s or the more recent patterns of intensifying racial segregation of US cities. Putting aside his disreputable act of head butting in the final game of the 2006 World Cup, Zinedine Zidane was a cultural hero, but he and his teammates did not eradicate racial and ethnic tensions in France. Even popular Latino, Asian, and other foreign players in MLB and the NBA today have not eliminated strong anti-immigrant feelings directed toward illegal, and legal, foreign workers in the United States.

New York Times sports columnist William Rhoden (2012) has suggested that native-born minorities from different racial and ethnic backgrounds in the

United States may not be perceived the same way by the public. In sport, we see this when we compare public and press reactions to African Americans and people of color from other ethnic backgrounds when they suddenly rise to prominence. He argued that the gushing of adulatory "Linsanity" that Asian American Jeremy Lin experienced with his burst of stardom with the NBA New York Knicks in 2012 was unlikely to happen for sudden stars who were African American. Rhoden argued that Lin ironically benefited from stereotypes of Asian Americans as smart but not particularly athletic. This stereotype was partially validated because he played basketball for Harvard. His success was a pleasant surprise for Asian Americans and the US public. On the other hand, Rhoden proposed, African American males are stereotyped as athletic, not particularly smart, and having character flaws. Thus, they are deemed less worthy of adulation.

Overall, though, as in the larger society, there has been a great deal of progress over the past half-century for African Americans as well as other people of color in reducing the amount of racial and ethnic inequality in sport. However, this progress has been uneven, more so in some sports than in others and more so in some areas of specific sports than in others. The NBA illustrates how far people of color and especially African Americans have come in US sport but also how much further they still have to go to achieve equal opportunity and success. TIDES director Richard Lapchick wrote in 2013 that the NBA continues to be "the industry leader among the men's sports (in North America) for racial and gender hiring practices" (Lapchick, with Hippert, Rivera, and Robinson 2013). Yet his institute's 2013 diversity report card for the NBA showed that the players were overwhelmingly people of color and white internationals, while the league was run by white American men. In the 2012–2013 season, 76.3 percent of players were African Americans, and a total of 81 percent were people of color. Twenty-three minority owners were people of color—twelve African Americans, seven Asians, and four Latinos. But one majority owner, former NBA superstar Michael Jordan, was a person of color. Only four of the CEOs and presidents were African American, and none of the others had ethnic minority status. The percentage of general managers who were people of color declined to 23.3 percent from 25.8 percent the previous year. An especially bright spot in the report was that 43.3 percent of coaches were African American, the second-highest percentage in league history. In addition, one of the coaches was partially Asian American. However, even among coaches, people of color remained a minority in a sport dominated on the court by people of color. Furthermore, revelations about racist comments by owners in the league showed racism persisted at the top level of sports, even in socially progressive sports leagues dominated by players of color such as the NBA.

Probe 3.8: Racist Owners in Minority-Dominated Sports

In the first major test of his tenure as NBA commissioner, Adam Silver had to deal with racist remarks made by longtime Los Angeles Clippers owner Donald Sterling. Media reports of a tape of these remarks provoked widespread anger and outrage in and out of the league. Facing media criticism and the departure of a number of sponsors, Silver acted swiftly and dramatically to minimize damage to his league's reputation and brand. He imposed a lifetime ban on Sterling and a maximum $2.5 million fine and pressured him into selling his team. However, Sterling's comments resurrected concerns about vestiges of a plantation mentality in this and other professional sports leagues dominated by players of color but with a number of older owners who were rich white men out of touch with the players (Branch 2014; Golliver 2014b). Further evidence came from another NBA owner. Perhaps chastened by the public reaction to the Donald Sterling case, Atlanta Hawks' majority owner Bruce Levenson sold his interest in the franchise after his racist comments in an e-mail became public (Keh 2014).

Among athletes of color in the North American golden triangle, African Americans continue to garner the most attention as a result of their longtime exclusion, their breakthroughs, and their impact on the marquee sports of basketball and football over the past half century. The statistical representation of African American players in the NBA, the WNBA, Division I of the NCAA, and the NFL today is quite impressive. Along with being over 76 percent of NBA players and 73 percent of WNBA players in 2013, and over 57 percent of Division I men's basketball players and nearly 48 percent of women's Division I basketball players in 2012, African Americans were 66.3 percent of NFL players and 51.6 percent of Division I football players at the FBS level in 2012 (Lapchick, with Agusta, and Kinkopf 2013; Lapchick, with Agusta, Kinkopf, and McPhee 2013; Lapchick, with Beahm, Nunes, and Rivera-Casiano 2013; Lapchick, with Hippert, Rivera, and Robinson 2013). MLB presents a very different picture of African American players. The league that famously dropped its color bar in 1947 so that Jackie Robinson could play has been trying to figure out how to halt the steady decline of African American players over the past few decades (Lapchick, with Bernstine, Nunes, Okolo, Snively, and Walker 2013).

Klis (2003) cited statistics showing that between 1989–1990 and 2002–2003, the percentage of black players increased in the NBA from 75 percent to 78 percent and in the NFL from 60 percent to 66 percent, while decreasing in MLB from 17 percent to 10 percent. The percentage in MLB had peaked in the late 1970s at 27 percent, and in 2002–2003 it was at the same level as it was in 1960. TIDES reported that by Opening Day in 2013, the percentage had dropped even more, to 8.3 percent (Lapchick, with Bernstine et al. 2013). Klis explained the decline in African American Major Leaguers in terms of the increase in Latino players, up from 13 percent in 1989–1990 to 28 percent in 2002–2003, which took roster spots from black players; the inspiring examples of black stars in the NBA; poor facilities in inner cities; perceptions of racism in MLB management and among owners; and the expense of playing youth baseball. The decline is important because there remain relatively few avenues to professional sport for African Americans, and lost opportunities affect the overall number of blacks in sports careers. While international players who are white and people of color may be edging out white American players in sports such as the NBA, they appear to be among the reasons today why African American numbers in baseball remain low. Of course, the story in baseball has been the continuing influence of foreign-born and especially Latino players, who were still about 28 percent of MLB in 2013. Although only 2.1 percent of MLB players were Asian in 2013, they were attracting attention because a number of them were established stars overseas before playing in MLB, where many of them excelled.

When we look at the entire picture of the representation of racial and ethnic minorities in the North American golden triangle, we see evidence of both accomplishment and ongoing challenges. We have seen African Americans and a few other people of color become sports superstars in North America and overseas. Indeed, Michael Jordan and Tiger Woods became global sports icons whose influence stretched beyond their sports of basketball and golf, and Latina golfer Nancy Lopez became an instant media star when she was dominating her sport in the late 1970s and 1980s. One of the major criticisms of MLB and the NFL was that a kind of segregation continued to characterize them even after the color bar was lowered. They practiced *racial stacking*—or racial segregation by position. It was a form of institutional racism to assume that racial minorities in particular were less suited than whites for certain kinds of positions. Into the 1990s, it was the most researched form of racism in US sports (Nixon and Frey 1996:242). It meant that African Americans were underrepresented in central positions or ones that required leadership or decision-making skills. Thus, for example, black players were underrepresented at catcher, pitcher, shortstop, and second base in baseball and at quarterback, center, and middle linebacker in football.

Gradually this pattern changed, and in week one of the 2013 NFL season, there were a record nine African American starting quarterbacks. This number dropped after one week, but at the end of the season, the quarterback for the winning Super Bowl team was an African American, Russell Wilson. All of this seemed to convey the powerful message that the most popular sport in the North American golden triangle had seemed to overcome its racist past. Baseball is a different story, if only because so few African Americans play the sport now. In addition, it is still unusual to see African American catchers. However, even in the NFL there were hints of lingering racism, albeit of a more subtle kind. While some observers referred to the emerging "golden era" of black quarterbacks, others were not so sure. Rhoden (2013), for example, suggested that the old racial stereotypes had not completely died. They were the ideas that white quarterbacks relied relatively more on their brains while black quarterbacks relied relatively more on their natural physical gifts. Nevertheless, it is evident that at least in football, African Americans are getting chances to play positions that formerly were inaccessible.

African American activist and sport sociologist Harry Edwards once voiced concerns about the unrealistic preoccupation with sport among young black males dreaming of professional sports careers. However, in recent years, his message has changed somewhat as his concerns have become more complex in the context of increasing black urban poverty and the intensifying social problems of young black males (Anderson 1999; Eckholm 2006; Wilson 1996, 2011). These problems were exacerbated by the financial crash in 2008 and the ensuing recession that hit inner-city neighborhoods especially hard. The problems included high dropout rates from school and high rates of unemployment, gang violence, crime, incarceration, and early death. While these problems have increased, sports interest and participation in school and community sports and recreation programs have declined for these young men, as public funding and facilities also declined. Thus, the reality and the dream of mobility through sport both seem to be eroding in African American families.

In this context, Edwards (1998) welcomed any legitimate road out of the life of despair in the urban ghetto for young black men (also see Wiggins 2011).

He proposed that deepening problems of the black urban poor required the reinvigoration of black communities with stronger institutions and more opportunities for young black men in the larger society. Wilson (1996) argued that the institutional revitalization of black families, schools, and other institutions needed to begin with better employment opportunities. Edwards agreed, but proposed that building more and better community and school sports programs could be part of the solution. He thought that black youths who had turned away from legitimate institutions or who were at risk of doing so could be brought back to the mainstream and more promising paths to the future by getting involved in respectable activities such as sports, which involved community leaders and represented alternative values and roles to those learned on the streets or in gangs. Thus, he argued that black youths and their parents should dream about sport as a means to stay in school, go to college, and even earn a living because, for some, sport was a realistic vehicle of mobility.

But being realistic also meant "dreaming with their eyes open" and recognizing that books and school were ultimately the most likely route to success for most. The rise or fall of the symbolic and practical significance of sport that has existed among African Americans will be a useful lens for interpreting the future of race in US society. Past history suggests that the best chance for blacks to improve their life chances through sport depends on learning to play by the rules of the dominant white power structure in the golden triangle and making gradual advances in access to positions of authority and power. Thus, attracting young black males to sport implies challenging the countercultural values and roles of the culture of the streets and the gangs with the more conventional values and roles of the dominant sports culture.

African Americans have generally been attracted to sports that have had lower entry barriers for minorities and lower classes; that depend less on expensive equipment, facilities, and coaching; and that resonate with their everyday life experiences. Black females and other women of color have had to contend with the limited professional opportunities in affordable and accessible sports and the dual barriers of color and gender. A study of a small sample of African American female athletes suggested that the intersection of race and gender seems to prompt complex reactions. On the one hand, these athletes wanted to view their experiences from a "colorblind" lens. But on the other, they also were very motivated to prove themselves on and off the court (Withycombe 2011), perhaps somewhat as a result of being women of color.

The experiences of American Indians in sport are distinctive because they have been relatively invisible in the racial and ethnic mix of major sports in the United States, reflecting the highly disadvantaged status of American Indians in general in US society. American Indians were rarely mentioned in the TIDES racial and gender report cards of US sports because they were relatively invisible. There is no special category for American Indians in any of the report cards for the professional sports leagues for which there were data—that is, the NFL, the NBA, the WNBA, MLB, and MLS. There was a category of "American Indian/Native Alaskan" in the college report card. The data for Division I showed that 0.1 percent of male basketball players and 0.6 percent of female basketball players, 0.5 percent of football players, 0.4 percent of baseball players, 0.5 percent of female track athletes, and 0.8 percent of female softball players were in this category. While Jim Thorpe has been recognized as one of the greatest athletes of the past century, most Americans would have difficulty naming other outstanding American Indian athletes. However, there have been some stars, including Boston Red Sox outfielder Jacoby Ellsbury, New York Yankees pitcher Joba Chamberlain, St. Louis Rams quarterback Sam Bradford, golfer Notay Begay III, and the Schimmel sisters of the University of Louisville women's basketball team (Martel 2013). In general, though, like the poor black urban ghetto, the poverty and poor equipment and facilities of the typical Indian reservation have made it difficult for Indian youths with athletic talent to participate seriously and become stars in sport and attract recognition in the larger society and sports culture. In addition, a lack of cross-cultural understanding and a long history of insensitivity in exploiting American Indian imagery with team names and mascots have contributed to the difficulties of American Indians gaining acceptance and respect in mainstream sports in the golden triangle (Zirin 2007). A study of adolescent aboriginal athletes in Canada showed that their experiences with special adaptive challenges, limited support, and racism in mainstream sports off the reservation were similar to those of their counterparts in the United States (Schinke, Blodgett, Yungblut, Eys, Battochio, Wabano, Peltier, Ritchie, Pickard, and Recollet-Saikonnen 2010).

We do not want to be dismissive of the accomplishments and struggles of other racial and ethnic minority groups in the golden triangle of US sports. However, African Americans and American Indians have been the main focus so far in this section because they have had especially difficult struggles with racism in the United States. The dominant classes in the United States have largely ignored concerns about the treatment of American Indians over the past century, but they have been unable to suppress the issue of racial equality for African Americans. The struggles of African Americans have had a powerful influence on the American conscience. In the words of Swedish sociologist Gunnar Myrdal (1944), their prolonged experience with virulent racism in a nation publicly committed to ideals of fairness and equality for all has made this racism "an American Dilemma." A small percentage of African Americans, mostly males, has overcome racism as athletes and achieved the American Sports Dream in a few sports. At the same time, the climb up the ladder of success in other US sports and in other realms of the golden triangle in the United States involving authority or control has been more limited for African Americans and other people of color from the United States.

The strong international imprint on MLS might lead to the impression of greater racial and ethnic diversity in professional soccer in the United States than in other sports in the North American golden triangle. This was partially true in the 2013 season. Overall, 52.3 percent of the players were people of color, including Latinos at 24.1 percent and African Americans at 10.6 percent. Internationals were 42.8 percent of the players. The 14.7 percent of the majority owners who were ethnic minorities outpaced the percentages of other major sports in the North American golden triangle, but it was still not a high percentage. In addition, only 10.5 percent of the head coaches were people of color. Both were Latinos, and one had replaced the single African American coach the year before. Only 5.9 percent of the CEOs and presidents and 6.3 percent of the general managers were people of color, and in both of these positions the trend from the previous year was downward (Lapchick, with Hippert and Bernstine 2013).

Diversity and Racism in Sports outside North America

If we look outside North America to Great Britain and Europe, for example, we see more blatant cases of racism in soccer and in a number of other sports in recent years (Murphy 2013; Schaerlaeckens 2013; Thompson 2013). Soccer is called "the beautiful game" by many of its ardent fans. It is unrivaled in popularity in the global golden triangle and is played by people from a diverse assortment of backgrounds around the world. However, rather than being a poster sport for diversity, it has an ugly side. Along with unruly hooliganism by fans, there has also been a history of racism among spectators. Despite a series of antidiscrimination programs sponsored by the sport's global governing body FIFA, including the "Say No to Racism" campaign begun prior to the 2006 World Cup, racist incidents have continued. FIFA vice president Jeffrey Webb headed an antiracism task force that was announced a year before the 2014 World Cup. He acknowledged that harsh penalties including steep fines had not been enough to curb racist and anti-Semitic taunts and other displays against people of color, ethnic minorities, and immigrants on the field (FIFA 2013).

In recent years, soccer has been a site of significant and growing racial and ethnic tensions, and these tensions have crossed a number of national borders in Europe. Fans have had difficulty accepting the waves of immigrants and multiracial people entering their countries, and they have demonstrated their intolerance and unhappiness in their treatment of immigrant and racial and ethnic minority soccer players. This has been happening since black and

FIFA #Say No to Racism; players display anti-racism banner during 2014 World Cup quarterfinals in Brazil. (© Marcelo Machado de Melo/Fotoarena/Corbis)

mixed-race players began to establish themselves in the game in the 1960s and 1970s (Schaerlaeckens 2013). The players were visible and easily targeted victims of fans' racial and ethnic hatred and xenophobia, and they felt the sting of these racist displays, which have included taunts, slurs, and monkey noises from opposing fans.

A survey conducted by Kick It Out, an antidiscrimination group in soccer, showed the reach of these displays on the players (Daily Telegraph 2014). The survey polled two hundred players from the top two levels of soccer in the United Kingdom, the Premier League and the Football League. Approximately one-third of the players in these leagues were from black or minority backgrounds. Fifty-seven percent of the respondents said they witnessed racist abuse in stadiums, and 24 percent said they were victimized themselves. Furthermore, 20 percent said they witnessed racist abuse during training or in the locker room, and 7 percent responded that they were victims of such abuse in these contexts. Not surprisingly, racism and homophobia overlapped, with 39 percent saying they saw homophobic abuse in stadiums and during training or in the locker room. Sixty-two percent of the players, including both whites and blacks, who responded to the poll favored mandatory shortlisting for black and minority ethnic applicants for coaching and administrative jobs in their sport.

Despite the pervasiveness of racism (and homophobia) in elite soccer in the United Kingdom indicated by these survey results, racism among fans in soccer has actually been worse in other European countries. Some of the worst displays have been among white soccer fans in Italy and Eastern Europe (Schaerlaeckens 2013). Their hatred has historical roots and has been associated with waves of neo-fascism and neo-Nazism after World War II. This extremism has found expression in hostility and intolerance toward immigrants and racial and ethnic minorities in society and in the soccer stadium (Thompson 2013). These racist displays show the complexity of the politics of diversity, since it was noted earlier that a number of European countries including Italy expressed high levels of tolerance toward gay people. However, racism may be more openly expressed because of its historical and economic roots.

In the 1960s and 1970s, racist displays in European soccer were spawned by a trend of increasing diversity from the recruitment of immigrants from African and Arab countries into a previously all-white game on the continent. Racism has been fanned in recent years by unemployment, financial stresses, and insecurities following the severe economic downturn that began in 2008. FIFA, like other governing bodies in the golden triangle, faces a difficult reality in trying to remove or reduce racism from its game. What happens in popular sports cannot be easily separated from what happens in society, especially since sport in the golden triangle ultimately depends on the support of fans who reflect their society.

It is challenging for minorities and immigrants to integrate into sports when there are few others like them. It is even more difficult to integrate into society when their skills on the field do not give them entrée into mainstream social circles and their stature in sport does not convert into equivalent status outside the sport. When their racial or ethnic status is under suspicion or attack in the larger society, their integration into sport and society are further complicated. This is the case of Muslim athletes in English cricket. They have had few other outlets for their athletic talents in England, but they have played cricket in England since the beginning of the twentieth century (Burdsey 2010). English research about Muslim cricketers has generally focused on their play for other countries. For example, it has revealed a history of rancorous relations between opposing English and Pakistani teams. There have been displays of national-ism, xenophobia, and racism in the English cricket establishment as well as anti-Muslim reporting, including allegations of cheating by Pakistani players and biased refereeing. In addition, Pakistani spectators have been subjected to racist and Islamaphobic taunts by rival English fans. These kinds of atti-tudes contributed to the virtual absence of British Muslim cricketers from the first-class level in England despite the long history of South Asian and espe-cially Pakistani Muslims in the country and of their playing English cricket.

Things began to change for British Muslim cricket players late in the twen-tieth century, which led to the first Asian British Muslim cricket player at the first-class level, Ajmal Shahzad, in 2004. By the end of the 2009 season, there were an estimated thirty Muslims in English first-class cricket, with about one-third foreign and two-thirds British citizens. Their adjustment was assumed to be complicated by the events of the 9/11 bombings in the United States and the 7/7 London transport bombings, which brought forth consider-able anti-Islamic sentiment in Western countries. For example, British press coverage of the death of the Pakistani coach at the 2007 Cricket World Cup demonstrated negative stereotypes of Islam and Muslims (Malcolm, Bairner, and Curry 2010). Displays of racism may be less widespread and less intense in cricket than in soccer in England and Europe (Burdsey 2010). Yet cricket players still may have little space to openly express their racial and ethnic identities without fear of reprisal when faced with pockets of chauvinistic, xenophobic, and racist fans (Fletcher 2012).

Disabilities, Disability Sport, and the Mainstream

Athletes in disability sports historically have had relatively few experiences with the vicious or even milder prejudice experienced by many other minority athletes in the golden triangle. This is because athletes with disabilities have had so few opportunities to participate in mainstream or any other kinds of sports. Having to deal with stereotypes of dependency and helplessness in the ideology of *ableism* helps explain their past invisibility. People with permanent disabilities have long had to deal with negative stereotypes and discomfort from able-bodied people. Ableism is an ideology that has paralleled class elitism, sexism, homophobia, and racism in viewing people with disabilities as inher-ently *un*able and physically, socially, and morally inferior to those perceived as able-bodied in society. The term "disabled" is typically used in mainstream sports to refer to athletes who are out of action, sidelined by an injury. We must distinguish between *temporary disabilities*, which keep athletes out of action for a few games or even for a season or more and can be healed with surgery, rehabilitation, and rest, and *permanent disabilities*, which result from a disease, an accident, or a genetic condition and cannot be reversed. People are *physically disabled* when impairment from these causes restricts their physical abilities or skills. Physical disabilities are especially relevant to sport because sport involves physical competition.

Although sports for people with disabilities have existed for over one hun-dred years, the structural barriers and attitudinal hurdles of ableism have been formidable for much of that history. Since the mid-1970s in the United States, legislation has created new rights and opportunities for children with disabilities in public schools and for adult with disabilities in the workplace. This kind of legislation has reflected pressures in society, the economy, and politics to reduce the huge inequalities between people with disabilities and the rest of society. Not surprisingly, we began to see more interest and involvement in athletics among people with disabilities in the United States during this period. However, the participation gap between young people and adults with disabilities and their able-bodied counterparts remains fairly large in the United States and in other countries (Nixon 2011).

The sports participation gap between people with disabilities and able-bodied people is large because participation rates for people of all ages with disabilities are relatively low. This is especially true in organized sports. With relatively few young people participating in highly competitive sports programs, there is not much of a pipeline into big-time disability sports in the golden triangle. Without a lot of participation or public awareness of disability sports or their stars, there is not likely to be a lot of investment by the golden triangle in individual disability sports.

One of the few national surveys of sports participation among people with disabilities in the United States was conducted by the Harris Interactive polling organization in 2008. It produced data from a sample of 704 adults with disabilities and from samples of about 200 participants in Disabled Sports USA and 200 military service members who were disabled and participated in Wounded Warriors sports rehabilitation programs supported by Disabled Sports USA. Since its founding in 1967, Disabled Sports USA has existed to help wounded warriors, young people, and adults with disabilities enhance their lives through sports and recreation programs. The survey was part of this effort. It showed that approximately 22 percent of the general sample of adults with disabilities reported that they currently were involved in a sport or physical activity or exercised more than four times a month. The clear implication is that relatively few were regular participants and even fewer were serious sports participants (Nixon 2011). There is no evidence showing significantly higher participation patterns in other countries. Indeed, there is very little research about sports participation patterns among people with disabilities anywhere in the world.

The numbers and effects are difficult to document. However, it appears that efforts by organizations such as Disabled Sports USA and Special Olympics and others dedicated to promoting particular disability sports or sports opportunities for people with particular types of disabilities are beginning to pay off. The Harris poll found that many adults with disabilities in the sample were aware of a number of organizations sponsoring disability sports opportunities, with Special Olympics being the most well known, by 86 percent of the sample. Other organizations, such as Wheelchair Sports USA and US Paralympics, were known by more than 25 percent of respondents (Nixon 2011). We can assume the number aware of the Paralympics has increased in recent years with the increased media exposure it has received. In fact, the growth of the Paralympics may be the most compelling evidence that disability sports organizations and their advocates have been expanding their reach and influence.

Governments are also playing a growing role in supporting disability sports. A number of countries, including Great Britain, Canada, Australia, and New Zealand, now provide federal funding to their Paralympic organizations. The

United States generally does not directly fund Paralympic—or Olympic—organizations, except in the case of special funding for disabled military veterans or active military involved in Paralympics programs. However, the US federal government and a few states are beginning to mandate that public schools and colleges provide athletic opportunities for students with disabilities. For example, as part of its enforcement responsibilities, the US Department of Education Office for Civil Rights (OCR) in 2013 clarified the responsibilities regarding athletics of public educational institutions under the Rehabilitation Act of 1973.

The OCR stipulated that it was the schools' responsibility to provide qualified students with disabilities equal opportunities for participation in appropriate extracurricular activities, including athletics. This generally meant that schools had to provide reasonable accommodations and adaptive services to make this possible. They were cautioned to avoid prejudice and stereotypes about disabilities in creating opportunities for students with disabilities. They also were directed to avoid "unnecessarily separate or different services," since that would be discriminatory (Office for Civil Rights 2013). The State of Maryland was already moving in this direction at the time of the OCR directive. In 2008, its state legislature passed a law, the Fitness and Athletics Equity for Students with Disabilities Act, requiring the provision of opportunities and accommodations for public school students enabling them to participate in physical education and athletic programs. By 2013, eleven other states had similar laws (Pathe 2013).

As with other types of institutional discrimination, legal pressure and political pressure have been important elements in counteracting institutional ableism. However, the challenge has been the implementation because it can be expensive for schools to provide appropriate programs and accommodations with already strapped budgets. The OCR stated that modifications of sports to increase inclusion had to be "reasonable," but modifications were not required if they involved a "fundamental alteration" of the extracurricular athletic activity. In addition, alterations could not give players with disabilities "an unfair advantage over others." With some vagueness in this language and with questions about who qualifies as disabled, what it means to be "qualified for participation," and what discrimination looks like, it is easy to see why the implementation of antidiscrimination laws can take a long time. Furthermore, we have seen foot-dragging and inappropriate or inadequate accommodations and adaptations influenced by ableist beliefs.

The OCR wanted to see as much inclusion as possible of athletes with disabilities in mainstream programs, but stipulated that adapted programs should be created when necessary. One estimate from the American Collegiate Society for Adapted Athletics database in 2014 was that there were fewer than twenty-five colleges and universities offering adapted athletic programs for students with disabilities. It was not clear how extensive opportunities for intercollegiate competition were for the athletes in these programs. The lack of national or even more local coverage of these sports reflects their marginal status in the college sports world, their absence from the intercollegiate golden triangle, and their limited access to the resources that could develop these sports. Thus, the legacy of institutional ableism in education and in the golden triangle remains a formidable barrier to establishing a wide range of athletic opportunities for students with disabilities at the high school and college levels.

Although policymakers may emphasize the value of inclusion and trying to get students and adults into integrated sports settings, this can be difficult on a large scale for a variety of reasons. It can be difficult to figure out how to achieve full, appropriate, and meaningful integration within the structure of most existing sports. Beyond resistance fueled by ableist ideas and restrictive policies and structures, there are economic and practical factors making real integration difficult or impossible. For example, people who are blind cannot play sports requiring the use of vision, and we cannot expect sighted athletes to give up their sports for beep baseball, goal ball, or other sports created for people who are blind. This is why athletes with disabilities are more likely to pursue their American Sports Dreams in segregated disabled sports settings than in fully integrated settings.

The International Paralympic Committee (IPC) and the Summer and Winter Paralympic Games organized by the IPC have been major factors in advancing high-level disability sports opportunities around the world. Among the many organizations committed to providing sports opportunities for people with disabilities, the IPC is foremost in providing access to the golden triangle for elite athletes with a wide range of disabilities. The precursor of the Paralympics was a competition among wheelchair athletes called the Stoke Mandeville Games, which began in 1948. The Stoke Mandeville Games evolved into the much more elaborate Paralympic Games, which were first staged in Rome in 1960 with four hundred athletes from twenty-three countries and became a quadrennial event (IPC 2014). The Winter Paralympics first took place in Sweden in 1976. The IPC was established as the governing body of the Paralympic Movement in 1989, and it cemented a relationship between the IPC and the IOC that was established in 1988 to stage the Paralympics after the Olympics in the same location and venue. This cooperative arrangement between the IPC and the IOC was an important step in generating serious media and commercial interest in disability sports in the golden triangle.

The Paralympics still lags far behind the Olympics in commercial development, media exposure, and popularity. For example, there were 1,539 hours of NBC Universal network, cable, and digital streaming coverage of the Winter Olympics in Sochi. In contrast, there were 52 hours of selected television coverage and live streaming of all events of the 2014 Sochi Winter Paralympics presented by NBC Sports and the United States Olympic Committee (NBC Sports 2013; USOC 2014). However, it was the most extensive media coverage ever of the Paralympics and disability sports and demonstrated a pattern of growing interest of the golden triangle in these sports events. Most importantly for para-athletes, the Summer and Winter Paralympic Games were their major stages to demonstrate their prowess.

Some countries provide generous subsidies to para-athletes, but there is still a huge gap in the amount of corporate investment in them and their sports. The 2014 Sochi Winter Paralympic Games set a record in generating $95 million in corporate sponsorships. However, this was still a stark contrast to the $100 million that each of the top-tier Olympic sponsors paid for its four-year contract. In addition, a second level of Olympic sponsors each paid about $50 million (Hildebrandt 2014). The golden triangle of disability sports will generate more revenue as the visibility of its star athletes increases.

Some of the stars of disability sports have had modest corporate sponsorship deals and a few have had fairly lucrative ones (Topping 2013). Tatyana

McFadden received substantial attention in the United States because she was adopted from a Russian orphanage at age six with congenital spina bifida, fought for the right to participate with able-bodied track teammates in high school (McFadden 2014), and went on to win multiple medals in the Summer Paralympic Games and even one in the Winter Games in Sochi. She also completed two consecutive grand slams of wheelchair racing in 2013 and 2014 by winning the marathons in Boston, London, Chicago, and New York each year. Her sports success brought her endorsement deals along with international publicity (Whiteside 2013; Williams 2008), but her compensation and exposure were modest compared with what able-bodied stars in the golden triangle typically get.

Probe 3.9: Controversy, Stardom, and Disgrace for a Disability Sports Star

The biggest star of disability sports in recent years was South African sprinter Oscar Pistorius, and he was able to convert his success in sport into international fame and big commercial endorsement deals in the golden triangle. Controversy about the carbon filter prosthetic blades he used to compete added to his celebrity. Known as "the blade runner," he was a double below-the-knee amputee. He was very successful in the Paralympics and other disability sport competitions, and then set his sights on able-bodied competition and the Olympics. The international governing body for track and field saw his blades as an unfair advantage and created a rule prohibiting his participation in its events. He eventually overcame the ban and became the first double-amputee runner in the Olympics in 2012, finishing in eighth place in the 400-meter semifinal and running the anchor leg for the eighth-place South African team in the 4×400 meter relay (CNN 2014a). Oscar Pistorius's story of struggle and success made him a hero and earned him an estimated $2 million per year in commercial endorsements. However, his star turn came crashing down with his shocking arrest in February 2013 and subsequent conviction for culpable homicide in the murder of his girlfriend, model Reeva Steenkamp. His image quickly deflated and his commercial value in the golden triangle plummeted (Davis 2013) as his sponsors distanced themselves from him. His loss of commercial endorsements is not surprising, since corporate sponsors have little interest in being associated with controversial or disgraced athletes.

Although the Paralympics and other disability sports have provided challenging and fulfilling sports opportunities for elite athletes with disabilities, the Paralympic model is not the only one that provides competitive opportunities for athletes with disabilities. In some cases, these athletes have been able to participate in fully integrated mainstream sports settings, as in the cases of MLB players who were deaf or had one hand, athletes at Gallaudet College who were deaf, athletes who played golf using a cart because they were unable to walk the course, and wrestlers who were blind. In other cases, wheelchair racers have competed in marathons with able-bodied runners, but have participated in a parallel competition started prior to the race for able-bodied runners.

In my own writing, I have addressed the issue of how to provide appropriate sports opportunities to people with varying disabilities and sports abilities, interests, and motivations (Nixon 2007). I proposed that models of sports opportunities for people with disabilities should reflect considerations of choice, fairness, and structure. *Choice* implies having a range of sports options in the mainstream and in segregated disability sports settings, from more casual and less competitive recreational sports to more organized and intensely competitive sports. *Fairness* implies that people can choose the sports that they wish to pursue. The *structure* issue is a matter of organizing sports so that they match sports roles and interaction requirements with the capabilities and interests of participants. This is a general principle that actually applies to all kinds of sports settings in disability sports and in the mainstream.

My model of diverse opportunities for people with disabilities distinguishes seven types of opportunities in terms of five organizing principles or structural features. These types are "ideal types" and are not meant to be perfect representations of actual sports. They are instead intended to serve as useful models for comparing and contrasting the elements of different types of sports settings that can accommodate the range of sports abilities and interests of people with disabilities. The five basic structural elements in these models are (1) type of classification, which specifies who is eligible to participate in terms of type or degree of disability; (2) segregated or integrated access and the amount of selectivity based on athletic skill; (3) amount of adaptation or accommodation for disability; (4) level of competitive intensity or seriousness; and (5) amount of direct competitive interaction between able-bodied athletes and athletes with disabilities. The seven types of sports settings form a continuum from relatively less and more intense segregated disability sports with appropriate accommodations for people with a particular type of disability modeled on the *Special Olympics* on one end to *Fully Integrated Sports in the Mainstream* having different levels of competitive intensity with no accommodations for people with disabilities on the other end. In between are five types of disability sports settings: (1) ones modeled on the *Paralympics*, with competitors having the same type of disability; (2) settings modeled on a *Mixed Paralympics* format, with competitors having different types of disabilities but equivalent performance capabilities; (3) *Reverse Integration* settings, in which able-bodied people compete with and against people with disabilities using artificial adaptations such as wheelchairs or blindfolds; (4) *Parallel Competitions* for competitors with and without disabilities, as in marathon road races; and (5) *Minimally Adapted Integrated* settings, as when a constant contact rule allows wrestlers who are blind to compete directly against able-bodied opponents. This continuum represents a range of choices for the diverse range of abilities and interests of people with disabilities. Since my argument is that sports experiences are most stimulating, enjoyable, and productive when the sport and athlete are appropriately matched, some models are more appropriate than others for certain people, and none of these models is an appropriate match for everyone. My model is an attempt to get beyond rigid, narrow, oversimplified, and either-or conceptions of sports opportunities to a continuum of possible choices.

The likelihood that people with disabilities will become involved in some form of sport and then rise to an elite level in the golden triangle will depend on early and constant encouragement and support. Even when structural barriers fall and laws mandate the availability of opportunities, they will need to overcome ableism among key people in their social networks. Parents, physical educators, rehabilitation specialists, sports organizers, coaches, teachers, and friends may not recognize or respect their sports potential or interests and may not do much to foster their serious sports involvement. When this lack of encouragement and support is combined with low socioeconomic status, inadequate funding of school and community programs, and inappropriate or inadequate adaptations and accommodations, students and adults with disabilities are unlikely to progress far in sport, if they get involved at all (Nixon 2011).

We often think of the mass media as a source of potentially influential role models. However, media portrayals of athletes with disabilities vary. For example, athletes with visible impairments who do not meet the normal aesthetic standards embraced by mainstream media are likely to be ignored or, if not, treated as strange or "freaky" (Peers 2012; Schell and Duncan 1999; Silva and Howe 2012). On the other hand, the media sometimes characterize athletes with disabilities as exceptional or as "supercrips." Supercrip images would seem to be a source of inspiration and an effective way to overcome ableist stereotypes held by the public. Their effects are a bit more complex than this. On the one hand, stereotyping could lead the media to portray ordinary feats by athletes with disabilities as extraordinary and thus perpetuate the idea that most people with disabilities cannot do ordinary things. This is an underestimation fallacy. On the other hand, when the media portray elite athletes with disabilities as supercrips with rare talents, they may put pressure on aspiring athletes in disability sports to measure up to overinflated and unrealistic standards. This is the problem of overestimation. Neither underestimating nor overestimating the achievements of athletes with disabilities contributes to accurate assessments of the capabilities and achievements of athletes or other people with disabilities (Silva and Howe 2012). Part of ableism is making invalid generalizations about people with disabilities. Until the media portray athletes with disabilities more accurately, it will be difficult for the general public and people with disabilities to develop valid ideas about the capabilities, talents, and achievements of athletes and others with disabilities. It also will be difficult for people with disabilities to form realistic ideas about how they can participate in sport.

Exposure to disability sports can be very important for young people growing up disabled. For example, a study of adolescent girls with disabilities showed that participating in wheelchair sports helped them develop an identity as an athlete, which made them proud, enhanced their self-esteem and social adjustment, and made them feel more competent (Anderson 2009). These can be important factors in creating aspirations to not only become serious athletes but also be successful in other kinds of roles as adults. These effects of sports participation may be especially important for females because disability can add to the common problems young women have in dealing with sexism in socialization. Even among young males with disabilities, playing disability sports can help them become more comfortable in their bodies and perhaps, ironically, make them more confident about their chances of being successful in the mainstream of society (Nixon 2011).

Conclusion

Despite pervasive media stories that reinforce the American Sports Dream, the stratification of sport has meant that access to sport and movement up the sports hierarchy have been very unequal for lower-class people, women, and various types of minority groups. More affluent heterosexual able-bodied white men in the ethnic majority have had an advantage just because of who they are. The stereotypical structures and culture of sport represented by the golden triangle have been dominated by people like them with their values. Those who control these networks of power have tended to make decisions, provide opportunities, and give rewards in ways that favor other people like themselves. Despite pervasive ideologies that convey elitist, sexist, homophobic, racist, and ableist ideas and reinforce patterns of inequality through subtle or more overt prejudices and discrimination, people from less advantaged backgrounds, women, and minorities have broken through structural barriers and overcome attitudinal hurdles to become successful in sport.

The forces of change in the larger society, along with intentional efforts to bring about change, have contributed to the gradual erosion of entrenched forms of inequality in sport. Sport has been affected by the increasing socio-demographic diversity of society; the increasing number of women graduating from college, earning professional degrees, and attaining influential positions in business and politics; the social and economic decline of black urban communities; and increasing political pressure to make sport more accessible to women and minorities. The organizational expansion of certain sports, such as soccer in the United States, has provided women and ethnic minorities with new avenues of sports opportunities and enjoyment as athletes and fans. In addition, new technologies have enabled the golden triangle to reach more people around the world, which has increased the diversity of the sports market and exposed more young people from diverse racial and ethnic backgrounds with athletic talent to the possibilities of sports careers. Technological advances have also increased the sophistication and effectiveness of assistive devices, such as wheelchairs and artificial limbs, used by athletes with disabilities. Advocates of change have also sometimes been able to influence the media to promote new conceptions of sport, such as sport for gay and lesbian people and sport for people with disabilities. But they have had to confront media images that have often reinforced damaging or demeaning stereotypes.

Patterns of inequality have been among the most intractable aspects of social structure in society and sport. Yet, established patterns of inequality in sport have been eroding in recent decades. Change can be slow, and high-status people do not readily yield their power or privilege in the golden triangle. However, the golden triangle offers the powerful incentives of money, fame, and the chance to compete and succeed at the highest levels of sport. These incentives motivate talented athletes, coaches, and others from diverse backgrounds to push hard against the institutional structures of discrimination and discredit the prejudice that has stood in the way of making sport and the golden triangle more diverse, equal, and fair.

Stop and Think Questions

1. How has sport been influenced by the ideologies of sexism, homophobia, racism, and ableism, and do these ideologies seem more prevalent in the major sports of North America or other countries?

2. How has Title IX affected high school, college, and professional sports in the United States?

3. What does "black dominance" of sports in North America mean, and why is it an overgeneralization?

4. What does Edwards's idea of "dreaming with eyes open" imply for aspiring female and minority athletes?

5. What have surveys shown about attitudes toward homosexuals in sport, and how have these attitudes and other social and cultural factors influenced the willingness of gay and lesbian athletes to disclose their sexual orientation?

6. How does the typical usage of the term "disability" in mainstream sports misrepresent the capabilities of athletes with disabilities?

7. Which minority groups have had the most and least success in men's and women's sports in the golden triangle, and what kinds of social and cultural factors explain the differences in success?

Part III

Building, Spreading, and Disrupting Sport in the Golden Triangle

4

Globalization, Mass Media, and Sports Culture

The chapters in Part III are about building, spreading, and disrupting sport in the golden triangle. This chapter focuses on how the golden triangle shapes and disseminates sports culture within nations and through globalization. The influence of the media will be given special attention. The role of the media will be particularly evident in the examination of how sports stars are made global celebrities and cultural icons and how they sometimes dramatically fall from their pedestals. An example of this process is the case of Oscar Pistorius, whom we considered in the last chapter. In addition, we will consider how the dominant US sports culture has changed and how sport could be interpreted as a secular religion in the United States and elsewhere. This chapter will conclude with a discussion of how the golden triangle has adapted to pressures to change by featuring new sports, including ones that emerged in alternative sports subcultures. The next chapter will focus on how social deviance and social problems can disrupt sports by threatening established cultural and social patterns in sport and society.

Globalization generally involves the diffusion, spreading, or flow of cultural, social, economic, and political capital, resources, or influences around the world. We are mainly interested in cultural globalization in this chapter, but it is difficult to disentangle its influence from the spread of organizational influences such as McDonaldization, the expansion of capitalism, or efforts to replace more authoritarian regimes with democracy. In the *cultural globalization* associated with the golden triangle, new cultural values, products, and practices of modern commercialized sports are introduced into countries and markets with little or no prior experience with them. Like social deviance and social problems, globalization can be a disruptive influence as people try to deal with influences that may clash with their ordinary understandings and experiences.

The global expansion of capitalism has transformed more traditional economies, cultures, societies, and political systems around the world. According to world systems theory (e.g., Wallerstein 1974), the global spread of capitalism created a world system with its center or core initially located in industrializing Europe and especially Great Britain. This core was surrounded by concentric circles of economically developing nations in the semi-periphery of the system and the least developed and poorest nations in the peripheral outer region.

Along with its other effects, the globalization of capitalism in the world system in the nineteenth and twentieth centuries and into the twenty-first century has transformed how people have thought about the world and its influence on their lives. It has increased awareness of the world as a whole, made the world seem smaller, increased interactions at the global level, and connected the local level in many nations to global influences (Harvey, Rail, and Thibault 1996). World systems theorists and critical dependency theorists (e.g., Frank 1979) have also argued that global interactions in the world system have enriched imperial nations in the core, and more recently large multinational corporations, at the expense of developing and poor nations on the semi-periphery and periphery of this system.

Markovits (2010) has argued that one of the most compelling validations of world systems theory has been sports. In its first major phase of globalization from 1860 to 1914, British influence transformed locally and informally organized games in other nations into new forms of sport. Its major export of Association football, or soccer, led to the creation of various forms of the kicking sport in countries such as Australia, New Zealand, the United States, and Canada. These countries played the purer form of the British version of football, but new sports of "football" were created that bore the imprint of the indigenous local or national culture.

Australia and New Zealand developed different types of rugby with varying combinations of kicking, running, and passing, while in the United States elements of soccer and rugby were combined to create American football. Canadians play this type of football, but with its own distinctive rules. This reshaping of imported sports by local or national cultural influences is called "glocalization" by globalization scholars (Giulianotti and Robertson 2012). Although the term implies a number of different kinds of influences and relationships, it generally refers to the ways people and groups at the local level interpret, modify, and adapt to global influences in their everyday lives. Glocalization is an important concept because it challenges the assumption rooted in dependency theory that globalization necessarily means that local social patterns and cultural ideas and practices are dominated and replaced by global imports.

Although global-local interactions often involve global concessions, these kinds of interactions can be tilted largely toward global interests at times. Ritzer (2011) proposed the concept of "grobalization" to refer to the process of globalization in which global influences overpower local and national social, cultural, economic, and political patterns through social and cultural corruption, economic exploitation, and political domination. Ritzer used the concept in relation to the spread of McDonaldization in the world. This process has transformed the nature and operation of businesses and institutions around the world to make them more modern and rational. McDonaldization has placed more emphasis on efficiency, standardization, accountability, automation, and, ultimately, profitability in the business world. Ritzer saw the globalization of McDonaldization as problematic for a number of reasons. But he was especially concerned about how this globalization process involved grobalization, in which nations, transnational corporations, and global organizations were motivated by the aim of domination to enhance their power or profits (Ritzer 2011:169–172). The spread of modern cultural, social, economic, and political influences around the world is sometimes characterized as *Americanization*, which represents a form of grobalization. However, this globalization process encompasses more than American influence, and its critics have characterized it more broadly as a form of modern imperialism. This kind of foreign domination has reflected the combined influence of the global capitalist growth imperative, McDonaldization, and the increasing power of multinational corporations.

Grobalization clearly implies a unidirectional process of globalization in which powerful external forces impose their will on weaker nations and localities and can create patterns of dependency. Glocalization implies something quite different. It implies the interplay and integration of global and local cultural influences. We will see the importance of glocalization in the second phase of globalization of sport conceptualized by Markovits. It is the period beginning in 1990 when the golden triangle was fully established as the dominant structure of power in sport.

Globalization and the Golden Triangle

In the second phase of globalization of sport, two cores emerged, according to Markovits (2010). One was European and revolved around soccer, and the other was North American and revolved around the "Big Four" sports leagues of the National Football League (NFL), the National Basketball Association (NBA), the National Hockey League (NHL), and Major League Baseball (MLB). The second core was essentially US-centric because most of the power and money in these leagues was in the United States. In the golden triangle organized around European soccer, the United States has been relegated to the semi-periphery region. It has its own soccer system with various levels from youth to professional, but its most talented players have had to play in Europe to reach the highest level of their sport and make the most money. Even Latin America remained in the semi-periphery of the Eurocentric system because it lacked the financial and economic capital to compete with the European leagues. As a result, its most talented players have also migrated to Europe. The same can be said about other areas of the world, even though Asia and parts of Africa have been rapidly developing in soccer.

In the golden triangles organized around each of the Big Four sports, the roles of Europe and the United States have been reversed, with Europe and other nations in the semi-periphery and peripheral regions. As in the Eurocentric soccer world, nations on other continents have been challenging the dominance of the United States and North America in professional basketball, hockey, and baseball. North American football is a special case because, despite the aggressive efforts by the NFL to market the league overseas, so far it has not significantly taken hold elsewhere in the world. For this reason, it has represented the limits of Americanization.

We can see how Americanization is tempered by glocalization in the current stage of the globalization of sport in the case of a Big Four North American sport trying to move into a market dominated by sports popular in the Eurocentric golden triangle. Research by Falcous and Maguire (2006) looked at efforts to expand the reach of the NBA to television audiences in the United Kingdom. Their study found that globalization involved concessions to the local. More specifically, their results showed that even powerful global actors such as the NBA, with broadcasts in over two hundred countries and over forty languages and a global audience of 750 million households, had to negotiate with the local. This may have been especially true because the local in this case was once a superpower in the world and had an established media industry and highly popular sports of its own. Global/NBA concessions to local influences in the UK included such things as giving up some control over the media production process and the presentation of the NBA brand image. On the other hand, local viewers in the UK were exposed to somewhat stereotypical views of US cultural values and practices. They were given the impression that consuming NBA basketball had a prominent place in the United States, which was intended to elevate its brand status in the UK sports culture.

Efforts to spread the influence of sports leagues and their brands around the world during the second phase of the globalization of sports has had significant global economic implications. These efforts have infused new economic capital into sports in many countries. In addition, the growth of these sports has contributed to the growth of business activities and consumption associated with these sports in countries around the world. Despite the significance of these economic consequences, Markovits (2010) has argued that the cultural, social, and political forms of capital produced by this globalization have been more important than the economic capital it has generated.

Being exposed to the glamor and excitement of global sports and its stars can open windows to modern culture and social life and create new aspirations as people identify with modern sports stars of the Eurocentric and US-centric golden triangles and their lifestyles. However, especially when globalization is perceived as grobalization, the possibility or threat of change may cause people to resist or reject global influences. Even glocalization can imply significant changes as people try to meld local and national cultures and social relations to global influences. Globalization may be most threatening to leaders in the cultural, religious, economic, and political spheres who are morally or politically committed to the status quo or have a vested interest in it. One of the most publicized clashes incited by the second phase of the globalization of sport and the golden triangle has been the conflict between modern and traditional conceptions of the proper status and roles of women.

Women in modern secular societies have fought for the right to participate in sports and have demanded gender equity. Progress toward gender equity has been a bumpy road in these societies, but it has been much slower in traditional Islamic societies with entrenched patriarchal systems (Dorsey 2014a, 2014b; Springer 2012). However, the globalization of Eurocentric and US-centric sports of the golden triangle has made it difficult for governments in these societies to keep aspiring female Muslim athletes completely away from sport or keep the stadium gates closed to female Muslim spectators. Despite government bans and harassment from males who do not believe women belong in sport or in sports arenas with men, women have gradually overcome prejudice and broken down barriers in a number of conservative Islamic countries (Gohir 2012). Advocates of change are getting help from the golden triangle. For example, in 2013, FIFA president Sepp Blatter met with Iranian officials to urge them to end their nation's ban of female soccer spectators in the stadium (Al Jazeera 2013). The ban had been in place since the Islamic revolution in Iran more than thirty years earlier.

**Probe 4.1: Muslim Women in Sports and the Culture Wars
in the Middle East**

Middle Eastern nations may have felt more pressure to alter their patriarchal practices after Qatar was chosen to host the 2022 soccer World Cup. Qatar had its first female Olympic athletes in 2012 and promised it would allow women spectators in the stadium for its Olympic Games. The 2012 London Olympics was a watershed event for Muslim women athletes. It was the first Olympics in which all participating nations sent women athletes. Along with Qatar, Brunei and Saudi Arabia also sent women for the first time. A number of these women expressed their hope that their participation would help create new opportunities in sport and elsewhere in society for other women in their nations (Springer 2012). A survey in one of the most conservative nations, Saudi Arabia, indicated that a large majority of the public, 73 percent, unconditionally supported giving women the right to participate in sports (Dorsey 2014a). However, the Saudi government and the governments of other very traditional and patriarchal nations have not been in tune with public opinion. In 2014, Iranian women were still protesting for the right to attend men's sports events. Protesters were arrested when they tried to enter a stadium where their men's national volleyball team was playing Italy in June of that year. They were especially piqued by the fact that Brazilian women had earlier been permitted to watch their national team play the Iranian men (Dorsey 2014b). Being banned from athletic fields and the stadium has been only one type of restriction women have faced in Iran and other conservative nations in the Middle East. These protests have placed the women and sport at the center of the "culture wars" in these nations.

In some countries in the midst of major social, cultural, economic, and political changes, the globalization of the golden triangle has proceeded unevenly across different sports. For example, in Turkey, women's professional basketball and volleyball leagues have flourished, but women have had difficulty breaking into soccer, the country's most popular sport (Erhart 2013; Schleifer 2009). Yet even soccer has played a modernizing role in this country, as Turkish Super League matches have become events watched by women and families as well as the traditional male fan base. Turkey has wrestled with the tensions between its historical roots in the Ottoman Empire and its modern desire to be more like European democracies. These tensions are found in soccer, where struggles over gender equality and multiculturalism have played out. As one analyst pointed out, sexism, racism, and homophobia continue to exist in Turkey, but their expression in soccer is less flagrant than in other European nations (Amani 2013).

The FIFA president's effort to get Iran to open the soccer stadium to women and concern expressed by Olympic officials about an antigay law in Russia prior to the Sochi Olympics might give the impression of an ideological commitment in the golden triangle to human rights or political freedom. This would not be a correct assessment, though. The interest of the golden triangle is in cultural, social, and economic globalization that fosters the growth of sport around the world. But sports officials, the media, and sponsors in the golden triangle have been willing to tolerate various forms of cultural, social, and political oppression. China was chosen to host the Olympics despite its lack of political freedom and its human rights violations. Qatar had a long history of suppressing women's rights before being chosen to host the soccer World Cup. Russia was allowed to host the Sochi Olympic Games after passing its antigay law, with Olympic officials making only a tepid public statement of their commitment to human rights principles. On the other hand, all of these nations embraced the capitalist economics that was the foundation of the growth of the golden triangle. Thus, we see that economics takes precedence over politics and human rights in the golden triangle.

In grobalization, the thrust of globalization is toward uniformity, with pressures aimed at making nations and localities conform to the powerful influence of foreign or global forces of change. This kind of globalization of sport in its second phase seeks to make sports in other countries develop in ways that conform to European or US models of dominant sports in the golden triangle. Glocalization, on the other hand, produces new and diverse forms of sport and sporting practices as nations and localities resist, accommodate, and adapt as they respond to global influences. Not surprisingly, as nations build their economic and political capital, they are more able to respond to global influences with glocalization and are less compelled to yield to grobalization. That is, they are able to put their own imprint on modern sports in their countries. In fact, in 2012 an entire issue of a major sport sociology journal was devoted to glocalization and sports in Asia (Cho, Leary, and Jackson 2012). Asia has become the rising giant in the global economy. It has also been playing a bigger role in the global golden triangle as Asian countries have sought more prominence in and through sport.

One of the ways the ascension and glocalization of sports in Asia have played out in the golden triangle has been the increasing frequency of *sports mega-events* (see Horne and Manzenreiter 2006). Since 2000, we have seen the 2002 FIFA World Cup cohosted by South Korea and Japan; the 2008 Beijing Olympics; the 2010 Commonwealth Games in India; the 2011 Cricket World Cup cohosted by Bangladesh, India, and Sri Lanka; the annual Grand Prix Formula One race in Singapore and 2014 races in Malaysia, China, and Japan; and IAAF World Track and Field Championships in South Korea in Japan in 2007, South Korea in 2011, and Beijing in 2015. These sports events are global cultural productions that enable these hosts to utilize the resources of the golden triangle to market themselves as well as the sports in the global cultural economy. That is, they have been able to sell themselves as brands in this economy as people identify the host cities and nations as part of the global sports world. Thus, these cities and nations trade the often substantial investment, the foreign influence, and the marketing of global products that come with hosting these events for more visibility in the world and increased stature in the global economy.

We see glocalization in the appeals to nationalism and local tastes by the NBA, MLB, and English Premier League (EPL) of soccer as they have tried to globalize their fan bases in Asia. This glocalization has also involved partnerships between local and national governments and transnational corporate sponsors. As local fans develop ties to global sports teams and leagues, they may also express pride in local stars exported to Europe or the United States. However, their support for foreign teams and their consumption of products associated with foreign teams and leagues contribute to the commercial growth of Eurocentric and US-centric golden triangles. In some cases, as in soccer in

Malaysia, there is evidence of grobalization as support for the Asian Cup and local football leagues pales in comparison with interest in the EPL (Gilmour and Rowe 2012). The EPL is readily available on television, and the consumer products promoted by the league blanket local markets.

North Korea provides an example of a largely isolated nation that counts sports among its relatively few ties to the outside world (Merkel 2012). There is some glocalization, but strict government control over sport in North Korea limits the influence of globalization. Sport and sport culture are generally used by the government to reinforce nationalism and support for the regime and its policy of self-sufficiency and independence from global influences. Its use of sport is similar to how communist countries used sport during the era of the Soviet empire, but the extent of its isolation distinguishes it from the earlier era of communism and from its Asian neighbors. While North Korea is an anachronism, other countries in Asia and other parts of the world display diverse responses to globalization in their forms of glocalization. As we have seen, there is also some evidence of grobalization as nations have difficulty resisting the lure of global sporting and commercial influences of the golden triangle.

China is an interesting case of a nation that has jumped aggressively into the global capitalist economy and the golden triangle, while still trying to hold on to its political past of communism. It has tried to glocalize sports to serve its political and economic purposes. However, it has found it a difficult balancing act at times when it has had to face global media scrutiny for its suppression of dissent, human rights abuses, pollution, and other social and political issues as it has tried to burnish its global image by hosting sports mega-events such as the Olympics. We will revisit North Korea and China in the last chapter in our discussion of different communist approaches to sport and the golden triangle.

Media Influence in Globalization and the Golden Triangle

Along with showing the diverse ways that individual countries adapt to the globalization of the golden triangle, the glocalization of sports in Asia also has highlighted the importance of the role of the media in these globalization processes. The powerful communication technologies and substantial financial capital in the media sector of the golden triangle have transformed sports events into global mega-events. These events generate huge investments from corporate sponsors, are broadcast around the world, and attract large audiences. Much cultural significance is attributed to these kinds of events as they become special dates on the sports calendar.

Sage (2010:147–149) has argued that a "global media/sport production complex" has become an increasingly powerful force in global sports and has had a significant impact on consumers around the world. This complex is the foundation of the media sector of the golden triangle. It has so much power in sport because it has the capacity to construct, transmit, finance, and sell sports events and turn them into global mega-events. Sport has been a major factor in the global expansion of mass media because many sports appeal to audiences that cross cultural lines. On the other hand, major contemporary sports and sports events could not have achieved their current levels of popular and commercial success without the exposure and money provided by the media sector of the golden triangle (Falcous and Maguire 2006). The media link corporate sponsors to the sports sector. By playing a critical role in making sports, sports events, and sports figures popular and commercial successes, the media create the building blocks for making sport a valuable consumer good in the cultural economy. The processes of globalization that rely on the media make the cultural economy of sport a global entity. In this *global cultural economy of sport*, sports, sports events, and sports celebrities and heroes become commodified as cultural products to be manufactured, marketed, sold, and consumed. They are like the merchandise advertised by the sports media that sports stars endorse.

Newspapers and radio played a major role in the commercial development of sports in North America in the nineteenth and early twentieth centuries. However, for much of the twentieth century and into the twenty-first century, television and the new media that have been outgrowths of the Internet have been the key media in the golden triangle and its globalization. All of these media have shaped what we know about sports. Television, the Internet, and social media have shaped how we experience sports of the golden triangle in more recent times. Although it has had to share the stage with the emerging media in the Internet era, television—in its various over-the-air, cable, satellite, and Internet forms—continues to be the most powerful of the modern sports media, both in its reach and in its financial impact.

Television has connected local cultures to the global cultural economy of sport. Although its effects on local sports cultures, perceptions, and experiences may vary, television helps embed the consumer culture of the global golden triangle in local cultures by using sports and sports stars to carry the powerful commercial messages of its corporate sponsors. It has also made individual athletes and coaches global celebrities and even icons or heroes—and it has turned stars into former stars, and icons and heroes into villains. Fading sports and falling stars learn that the sports media and their sponsors are ultimately less interested in the success of specific sports and stars than they are in sports brands that make money for them and burnish their own brands.

Television broadcasts construct events and provide us with interpretations of their meaning that reflect television production values (Lipsyte 1996; Silk 1999). Television executives and producers make choices about the events they cover, how and when they cover them, and whom they choose to give special attention. The images, storylines, and profiles they present in their coverage of sports are meant to attract more viewers and sell more, and more expensive, advertising minutes. Television sports broadcasts emphasize particular cultural values, such as talent, opportunity, achievement, courage, sacrifice, overcoming odds, success, and the American Dream. These values reflect the modern values and interests of sport and its corporate sponsors. Furthermore, their commercial advertisements do more than expose their audiences to the products their sponsors sell. They also convey the message that we should embrace the cultural practices of consumer capitalism associated with acquisition and accumulation. Thus, watching television sports broadcasts subtly but powerfully influences the tastes, interests, values, and identities of viewers. They are encouraged by these broadcasts, and particularly by the advertisements on them, to buy the various products and live the lifestyles that sports stars and cultural icons endorse or display. We also learn from watching sports on television—and the accompanying commercial advertisements—that the products of companies such as Nike, adidas, Under Armour, McDonald's, Coca-Cola, Pepsi, Anheuser-Busch, and General Motors have special value because they are endorsed by star athletes.

Television sports play a role in economic globalization through cultural globalization and the spread of the consumer culture of capitalism. These are the kinds of influences that have created cultural resistance in countries with traditional Islamic cultures or autocratic communist regimes that are not interested in emulating the United States or modern Western or capitalist cultures. However, as we have seen, it has been difficult to distract people in these countries from the powerful globalizing influences of the golden triangle. Television and newer media have transmitted compelling images of modern sports and their stars and the array of products they endorse. Glocalization is interesting because it represents how people at the local level interpret and respond to these global media influences in their everyday lives.

Probe 4.2: The Cultural and Economic Power of Televised Sports

In making sports more important in more places around the world, television has given its transnational corporate sponsors the chance to use sports to build their brand recognition and make their products more familiar and more appealing. Especially where there has been disposable income, some leisure time, and the desire and opportunity to consume the products of popular culture, sport has become a popular product of consumption as both a form of entertainment and a source of meaning for people who are drawn by the perceived authenticity of the competition, their favorite teams and athletes, and their stories. Buying things that are endorsed by their favorite teams and athletes gives these sports fans a chance to identify with something bigger than themselves, with broad cultural significance. By watching sports, they are reflecting and reinforcing the power of television. By ardently following sports and sports stars and buying the merchandise endorsed by sports and athletes and advertised on television and in other mass media, they are demonstrating the cultural significance and power of sport and contributing to the legitimacy and profitability of consumer capitalism.

Television has increasingly had to share the media sector of the golden triangle with the Internet and the new media it has spawned. Together these media have constructed "mediascapes" (Appadurai 1996). Sports mediascapes are images, perceptions, and understandings of sport that are shaped by the sports media. They are related to Lipsyte's (1996) idea of *sportainment*, which refers to how our sports experiences are mediated by television. Since we cannot directly experience most sports events or personally interact with the personalities we see in these events, television gives us eyes to see. But we see what television wants us to see. Television in the golden triangle wants us to see an exciting broadcast that will reinforce our sports interest, make us want to keep watching, and especially draw our attention to the commercial ads. Ad revenue is how the media make money, which is spent in part to buy media rights from sports organizations but is also their profit from sports broadcasts.

In the past, for many people around the world, the only images of sport that they had were what television gave them. This is changing, as the media sector of the golden triangle has become more crowded and in some ways more

Production control room at NBC Sports Network studios in Stamford, CT during live broadcast of English Premier League games in 2013. (© Tim Clayton/30148116A/Corbis)

competitive. We now have multiple mediascapes with conflicting images and interpretations of sport. New media are reshaping the global sporting culture (Leonard 2009; Sage 2010:168–175; Sociology of Sport Journal 2009). There are live streaming broadcasts on the Internet, online reports and blogs, Wikipedia entries, and various other forms of user-generated content that may challenge the authoritativeness or authenticity of media images and stories from the older established mainstream media of television, radio, and print. Social networking sites such as Facebook, blogs and microblogs such as Twitter, and video-sharing websites such as YouTube can instantly circulate opinions and images around the world, which might provide alternative or contradictory interpretations of sports and sports figures. Athletes themselves have been active on these social media. In addition, there are video games and fantasy sports worlds that occupy the commercial media space of the golden triangle.

A number of these media are turning passive sports spectators into active participants. Furthermore, fantasy sports and emerging professional sports video game leagues are new, competitive venues for serious sports fans. They compete with the mainstream sports media for the attention of these fans. Research has revealed a paradox of fantasy sports participation (Dwyer 2011). Participants in fantasy football expressed the typical NFL fan's strong loyalty to a particular team, but the more involved they got in fantasy football, they less likely they were to restrict their viewing of actual NFL games to their favorite team. Thus, fantasy sports participation may dilute tangible and traditional commitments to the real sport. All of these media amount to a dizzying array of ways to access sports. Yet despite the complexity and variety of sports media and efforts to merge them, television continues to be dominant because of the exposure and revenue it can provide.

US Exceptionalism in Global Sports Culture

In the Eurocentric global golden triangle dominated by soccer and the EPL, the United States has been relegated to a minor status. Although it is above those on the periphery or fringes of the sport, it has not been able to penetrate the core. In part, this is a result of prior glocalization in which the United States largely rejected soccer (and rugby) in favor of a homegrown product that fused elements of these two sports into "American football." Even though the NFL version of this sport became the premier sport in popularity and revenue among the Big Four by the late twentieth century, it has stumbled in its efforts to globalize.

Some, including Markovits and Hellerman (2001), have argued that the sports preferences in the United States, particularly the obsession with American football and lukewarm interest in soccer, reflect US peculiarity or *exceptionalism*. That is, the US passion for its version of football and its limited interest in soccer made it different from most other countries and sports cultures in the world. The United States made a choice in the nineteenth century to invent its own sport of football rather than play the foreign sports of soccer and rugby. This choice may have reflected a broader desire at the time to carve out a distinctive American cultural identity in the world of nations. The addition of baseball, basketball, and hockey to the dominant sports culture in the United States further distinguished the United States and its sports culture from other countries in the world.

By the time football, baseball, basketball, and hockey had embedded themselves in the dominant sports culture of the United States, there was little room left for soccer. American sports fans were already too attached to one or more of these other sports and their stars. Hosting the men's World Cup in 1994 did not seem to change the status of soccer in the US sports hierarchy (Sugden and Tomlinson 1996). Nor did the international success of the US women's team or hosting the women's World Cup in 1999 and 2003. Efforts to build on the popularity of these mega-events, especially when the US women won in 1999 on home soil, did not lead to a successful women's professional soccer league in the United States. The United States remained distinctive or exceptional in its passion for its Big Four, especially football, and its lack of serious interest in soccer. Or so it seemed.

Buffington (2012) questioned the idea of US exceptionalism in attitudes toward soccer and the World Cup. He tested this idea by analyzing coverage of the men's World Cup in 2002 and 2006 by five major US newspapers. He found that this media coverage presented a picture of US attitudes toward soccer that was more complex than often presumed by the media. The United States may not be so exceptional in its attitudes toward soccer after all. Other countries have fluctuating interest in soccer, and soccer fans in the United States may be more numerous and passionate than the media often presume. He saw media coverage of US soccer attitudes as mythmaking.

Buffington proposed that the media were engaging in "boundary work," in which sport was being used to construct symbolic national boundaries around the United States to make it appear culturally distinct when in fact it was not nearly as distinct as suggested. While soccer passion might symbolically unite other countries, soccer indifference and a preference for a form of football that excited little interest elsewhere might be a way of uniting the US population and make it appear unique.

The emergence of a growing soccer fan base can be explained away by suggesting that this interest has marginal significance for national identity. According to Buffington, this marginalization of soccer is reflected in its characterization as a sport largely of immigrants, females, and adolescents. That is, soccer's biggest stars are foreigners, US women have had far more success in the sport than their male counterparts, and adolescents play the game but are expected to turn their attention to activities that are more distinctively American when they become adults. All of this may be an oversimplification of the reality of soccer in the United States. But perpetuating misconceptions and myths of US exceptionalism in attitudes about sports avoids potentially confusing questions about national identity and the actual cultural complexity of American society and its sports.

Probe 4.3: Putting Down Soccer to Protect the Big Four and Their Golden Triangle

Downplaying or denigrating soccer implicitly helps sustain the elevated status of the Big Four and North American golden triangle over a competing golden triangle dominated by soccer. Many more Americans than we usually assume may enjoy soccer and the World Cup. But from Buffington's perspective, the media are inclined to minimize this passion and question how authentic it is in America. By doing this kind of boundary work, US media may be implying that there are other sports that are more authentically American, such as the Big Four. In contrast, media in Europe and elsewhere in the world are likely to characterize soccer as "the world's game," which conveniently ignores the more limited passion for the sport in the United States. This kind of nationalistic or global language ultimately serves the interests of the particular media and golden triangle using it because it helps sell the sport or sports it features to the national, continental, or global audience it has targeted. Media interpretations of the uniqueness of US attitudes toward soccer may not be accurate. However, even if not true, these kinds of characterizations have symbolic functions and serve the needs of the sports and golden triangle the media are promoting.

In the current phase of the globalization of sport, with its varied and far-reaching effects, it is difficult for nations to claim they have been untouched by the influence of sports that are popular elsewhere in the world. Although sports of the North American golden triangle have spread their influence around the world, globalization is not synonymous with Americanization. Today the most prominent golden triangles are centered in North America and Europe, and their sports compete for attention and revenue across and within these golden triangles. They grow through grobalization in some countries and glocalization in others.

The Construction and Globalization of Sports Heroes and Villains in the Golden Triangle

The role of the media in globalizing sports has involved turning sports figures into stars. Some have become global celebrities, and the most admired have become cultural heroes or icons. The biggest sports stars are powerful vehicles for selling cultural values and assorted products of the golden triangle. Some of these products are sports related, such as TV spectacles and running shoes, but others become associated with sports through the investment of sponsors and endorsements by athletes and coaches. They can include products as diverse as underwear, milk, automobiles, and Disney World vacations.

NBA star Michael Jordan was one of the earliest global icons created during the second stage of the globalization of sports. He was not the first African American athlete to become a major celebrity or hero in US sports or to be recognized outside the United States. For example, world champion heavyweight boxers Joe Louis and Muhammad Ali and Olympic track star Jesse Owens had achieved this distinction. Racial prejudice toward Joe Louis and Jesse Owens was minimized by the national pride they engendered in America and hostility in the world toward opponents competing under the banner of Nazism. Muhammad Ali was a controversial figure in the United States because he was very talented, outspoken, a Muslim convert, and an opponent of US involvement in the Vietnam War. These things made him wildly popular in a number of other countries. Michael Jordan was different. Like the others, he was extremely talented, exciting, and successful in his sport, but he was also apolitical and marketed by the golden triangle as essentially without color. He became a brand in the sports marketplace with whom both whites and people of color could identify. As a result, the global reach of Michael Jordan's celebrity and his brand recognition and selling power around the world were unprecedented for African American and US athletes during the peak of his stardom in the 1990s (Andrews, Carrington, Jackson, and Mazur 1996; LaFeber 2002; Snider 1996). Michael Jordan was not the only athlete to achieve global iconic status. For example, soccer stars Pelé of Brazil and David Beckham of Great Britain also achieved this status. In addition, golfer Tiger Woods may have surpassed the popularity of Jordan in the global cultural economy of sport in the twenty-first century (Tucker 2006). However, Michael Jordan made his mark as the first African American athlete to be successfully marketed by the US-centric golden triangle as an athlete without color.

Michael Jordan was more than a popular American sports star. *USA Today* referred to him as "bigger than basketball" and a "pop icon" (Snider 1996). He was a global star, recognized by billions of people around the world. Part of his legend is that he went from being cut from his high school varsity basketball team as a sophomore to sinking the winning shot for the University of North Carolina to win the national championship game. As a professional, he further enhanced his reputation for hitting clutch shots and winning championships. However, Jordan's place in the global culture depended on more than his basketball talents and success. He was made into a global icon by the golden triangle.

Michael Jordan's reputation and cultural significance grew exponentially as a result of his association with Phil Knight and Nike, which made him its lead athlete in its marketing. He also benefited from the growth of global media. According to LaFeber (2002:156–157), the linkages tying Michael Jordan to Nike and other major forces influencing the growth of the golden triangle at the time represented two major themes of the new information age and post-Soviet period. First was the "capitalist imperative" to expand markets, create new ones, and increase profits. Second was the accumulation of massive amounts of capital by transnational corporations and elite individuals and their development of markets that were receptive to American popular culture. The media combined with NBA and business interests in the golden triangle to promote Michael Jordan to a global audience. They associated his name with multiple versions of a top-selling Nike shoe, "the Air Jordan," used him in a major Nike advertising campaign that made the Nike swoosh known around the globe, and tied his name or brand to numerous other products he endorsed. Nike helped usher in the emergence of a new stage of consumer capitalism. In this stage, marketing was global, and economic growth was associated with creating powerful symbolic appeal across the global cultural economy.

In this cultural economy, Nike looked for athletes who could transform their sports with their attitude or style and bring to life its "Just Do It" tagline. At first, these were athletes such as antiestablishment working-class track star Steve Prefontaine (Walton 2004), then the irreverent John McEnroe in tennis, and after him, Michael Jordan in basketball (Smart 2005). Through clever advertising, Michael Jordan, Nike, and the swoosh became linked as a brand in the public mind, and this linkage made the athlete better known and his commercial sponsor richer. Television contributed to this relationship by increasing the global visibility of Jordan's athletic performances, the advertisements that featured him and the products he endorsed, and his image.

Success in the marketing of Michael Jordan could be viewed as an important factor in the emergence of a US-centric core in the global sports world in the second stage of the globalization of sport that began in the 1990s. Although football was king in the Big Four in the United States, Michael Jordan and the NBA were doing more to elevate the status of the US-centric golden triangle in the global cultural economy of sport. In this golden triangle, Michael Jordan became a member of "Team Nike" and demonstrated his brand loyalty on a number of occasions, for example, resisting efforts to wear official Olympic sponsor Reebok's team jacket as a member of the 1992 US Olympic "Dream Team" and avoiding criticism or comment when Nike was under fire for using sweatshops in poor countries to manufacture its goods. Michael Jordan became, in the words of writer David Halberstam (1991:76), "the first great athlete of the wired world." The new global media significantly contributed to the globalization of Michael Jordan—and Nike.

Since sport had not rid itself of racism in the United States or in many other countries, the promoters and marketers in the golden triangle developed a marketing strategy that downplayed or ignored Michael Jordan's color. He was marketed to white and black communities as a "crossover hero," and for many whites at least, he was without color (Smart 2005:123). According to Andrews (1996), the portrayal of Jordan's race was recast at different stages of his career to ensure the breadth of his appeal. At first, he was cast as a gifted athlete having "All-American" qualities and embodying the American Sports Dream. His image had to be reworked when his "All-American" (white) image was somewhat tarnished by stories about his alleged arrogance, selfishness, obsession with personal statistics, lack of respect for teammates, excessive competitiveness, preoccupation with his image, and gambling. Jordan himself was quoted as saying during this period that the media seemed to be increasingly portraying him as "Michael Jordan the black guy" (Andrews 1996:147). This kind of coverage seemed to recede after the tragic murder of his father, as his All-American image began to resurface and become more prominent once again.

After this period and at the end of his basketball playing career, the media coverage of Jordan's race focused on his return to the NBA after retiring and playing minor-league baseball. Without Jordan and with a new generation of young black stars who were portrayed as arrogant, irresponsible, and self-centered, the NBA's image had suffered. His return enabled the NBA and media to refocus on Jordan's All-American qualities that had appealed across racial lines and to defuse some of the negative conceptions of race that were associated with the younger black players. As a postscript, Michael Jordan found it much more difficult to be a star in management for the Washington Wizards or as an owner of the Charlotte Bobcats in the NBA. But with rare exceptions, this is true for even the most effective managers or owners. They do not generate the same excitement as a charismatic star player or coach.

The portrayal of Michael Jordan's race and his image in general demonstrates the power of the media to shape public perceptions of sports figures. Although Jordan the man may not have changed, media coverage of him did at various stages of his career. His enduring worldwide popularity clearly shows that media and corporate constructions of his image have typically been positive and effective across classes, racial and ethnic groups, and national borders. While white Americans may not have seen his color, young African Americans and black youths in other countries such as Great Britain may have identified with him and bought the products he endorsed *because* he was black (Andrews, Carrington, Jackson, and Mazur 1996). In fact, it may be that white youths bought Air Jordans and other Jordan-branded merchandise because he was a star basketball player, while black youths bought these things because he was a *black* basketball star. Ethnographic research in Canada by Wilson and Sparks (1996) that studied focus groups of black and nonblack adolescents provided support for this interpretation and also demonstrated the cultural power of commercial advertising using prominent sports figures.

Although athletes have been able to overcome racism to achieve global stardom and iconic status, the same cannot be said for female or gay athletes. Although Oscar Pistorius achieved international renown in disability and mainstream sports as the "blade runner," his run as a global sports hero was derailed by his conviction for culpable homicide in the killing of his girlfriend. He was the rare case of an athlete with a disability achieving global celebrity. Minority groups may have their own heroes. However, the golden triangle has generally found it easier to embrace sports stars who are white, male, and able-bodied and who reflect the racial and gender composition of the sports power structure. When they have been persons of color, their color has generally not been emphasized in the golden triangle, except when marketing to minorities.

There is a difference between sports heroes and celebrities. However, both are constructions of the media and golden triangle, which are able to make and unmake their heroes, as Oscar Pistorius and other fallen heroes have discovered. *Heroes* embody dominant and enduring social myths and cultural values of a society or a subcultural segment of society (Nixon 1984:172–175). They are idealizations of the qualities that people think are important or revered in a society, and in this sense, heroes are not real people. They are names and faces we associate with our values. Heroes are constructed by the mass media. It is difficult to sustain heroic conceptions of sports stars in the dynamic context of constant media scrutiny of public figures.

While the commercial media in the golden triangle try to keep sports stars in the public eye, this can mean that some are made celebrities, a few are lionized as heroes, and others are subjects of criticism or derision. It is the nature of contemporary popular culture to make people famous one day and then turn to someone else the next. This is why heroes seem to be harder to find today than in the past. In fact, there often seems to be a cynicism in the media. On the one hand, they need celebrities and heroes to sustain interest in sport, and so they create them. On the other hand, as they give more attention to the celebrities and heroes they have created, they inevitably find flaws. Celebrities rarely have much staying power, unless they have the qualities that can make them heroes. Few do. But even heroes fall short of our expectations when constant media scrutiny humanizes them.

Boorstin (1962, 1964) proposed that heroes are made by folklore and history books, while *celebrities* are images made by gossip, public opinion, and the fleeting tastes of the mass media. Rather than representing enduring cultural values, celebrities are public figures who are "known for being known." They are especially likely to achieve attention or notoriety in societies where the individual and a cult of personality predominate (Henderson 1999; Smart 2005:11).

With so many media outlets, it has become increasingly difficult for heroes to hide their human flaws from the public. Who can remain a hero for long with cameras and microphones following every move and recording every word and action on and off the field, and with probing or cynical reporters trying to find the hidden warts that heroes must be trying to cover up? Add to this the legion of amateur paparazzi and videographers who can publish their photos and videos on the Internet and quickly generate a worldwide audience. For these reasons, we are more likely to talk today about media celebrities of the moment rather than more traditional heroes. Heroes grow bigger in our imagination with the passage of time, but celebrities arise in the glare of constant media attention and then lose their hold on the public as they eventually become overexposed or are revealed as less heroic or inspiring than we thought they were.

Personal and sports-related scandals can turn sports celebrities and heroes into villains or scoundrels. Lance Armstrong is the classic story of the rise and fall of a sports hero. The Tour de France is one of the most grueling sports events, and he won seven consecutive races. He was widely admired in the United States by fans who generally lacked the knowledge and passion about bicycle racing and the Tour de France possessed by their European counterparts. In Europe and especially in France, his success caused some resentment and he had to fend off a barrage of criticisms and accusations of doping from the French press during his reign and afterward. However, in the United States, he was revered because he seemed to dominate his sport. Perhaps as important was that he had overcome cancer and then translated his sports fame into the establishment of an organization, which became the Livestrong Foundation, to support cancer victims and their families.

At first, the foundation was a joint venture with Nike, which had an endorsement contract with Lance Armstrong and produced a line of clothing and the yellow "livestrong" wristbands. All of this fell apart when the doping case against Armstrong gradually gained momentum with mounting evidence against him. After years of denials, Armstrong finally admitted his cheating in an interview with Oprah Winfrey in 2013 (Stanley 2013). While he seemed contrite about betraying his most ardent fans, including cancer survivors who were grateful for his charity, he seemed to imply that the cheating itself was necessary because the sport was so demanding and doping was so common (see Wieting 2000). He had waited too long for any kind of mea culpa or rationalization to be credible.

Probe 4.4: Images, Realities, and the Risks of Believing in Sports Heroes

It should be evident that the person is not the same as the image constructed, deconstructed, or destroyed by the media. On his Saturday *Weekend Edition* program on National Public Radio (NPR) on June 24, 2006, host Scott Simon hoped that the controversy about Armstrong the man would not tarnish the powerful and uplifting symbolic value of his livestrong wristbands for cancer victims. He added that these wristbands and the hope they symbolized had become bigger than Armstrong himself. His commentary followed a story on the NPR broadcast, which Armstrong denied, about his alleged hospital-room disclosure ten years earlier when he was recovering from cancer surgery that he had taken a number of performance-enhancing drugs such as EPO and steroids. After his public confession to Oprah Winfrey, the foundation that was identified with him and was an important part of his heroic image had to try to distance itself from the taint of his misdeeds to protect its own reputation and viability.

Armstrong's denials during his career were a demonstration of the hold of his heroic image over him as well as his fans. This was an image constructed mostly by US media about his stardom in a sport centered in a European golden triangle. His stardom and his rewards of fame and money from US media and corporations depended on his assertion of his innocence. We see in this story the complex ways different media in different golden triangles make, challenge, and unmake heroes. When Armstrong's resolve to sustain his cover-up was finally broken by relentless doping investigators and media probing, he had to admit he was not so heroic after all. He said he had a major "character flaw" that had driven him to protect his image. This flaw was having to get what he wanted, having to win, and having to be in total control. These qualities are probably not that unusual among the biggest sports stars, which may be part of the explanation for rampant doping in cycling and a number of other sports in the golden triangle. However, relatively few have lied so publicly and for so long to an adoring public that wanted to believe him. Other star athletes in the United States, such as MLB star Alex Rodriguez, have also struggled to maintain their innocence in the face of serious accusations and have ultimately been disgraced (Roberts and Epstein 2009; Sanchez 2014), but they may not have disappointed fans as much as Armstrong did.

Lance Armstrong's descent occurred over many years. Sometimes the fall from the pedestal is much more sudden for sports heroes. French soccer star Zinedine Zidane discovered how precarious the status of hero can be under the unblinking eyes of television cameras. Known affectionately as "Zizou" to his many fans around the world, he had led the French team to its only World Cup victory in 1998. He had come out of retirement to compete for the final time and to try to lead his national team in the 2006 Cup. As the games progressed, his play got stronger and stronger, until France became an unlikely finalist against the talented Italian team. Zidane had added to his legend by scoring the winning goal on a penalty kick in the semifinal game and then started the scoring in the final with another successful penalty kick. The Italians tied the game, and it went into overtime tied 1–1, with Zidane playing a key role in keeping pressure on the Italian defense. In the second overtime, he barely missed scoring a goal when his header was tipped by the goalie. Then it happened. In an instant of a pique of temper, he head-butted an Italian opponent, received a red card and was sent off the field, and ultimately had to deal with his team losing the game in a penalty kick shootout.

The announcers and commentators had extolled his virtues for several games, portrayed him as a national hero as well as a sports hero, and seemed to wish that he could end his career on a positive note with a victory. Then in an instant of infamy, they quickly shifted focus to references about how he had disgraced himself and let down his team and country. The sympathetic aging superstar seeking his last hurrah had become an object of scorn. Since his actions were shown on a screen in the stadium as well as across the world on television, they were not easily glossed over or ignored. This is unlike the case of Lance Armstrong, who was able to outsmart drug testing procedures for years and deny his culpability.

The television announcers and commentators expressed some sadness about this incident, but they did what they needed to do in this situation, that is, disavow their previous storyline and find another one. Zidane was quickly transformed from a hero into a villain with very human frailties, and the new story became his fall from grace and the difficulties his action had created for his team. The journalists similarly condemned Zidane and added to his remade image of human imperfections. Virtually within minutes of the end of the game, they posted stories on the Internet that focused on Zidane's red card. They also suggested that his action might not have been so out of character for this ostensible hero. The Internet news reports noted earlier notorious instances when the great star had lost his temper and received red cards for head-butting and stomping on opponents, and they reminded their audiences that he had been suspended for a game in the 2006 World Cup after receiving two yellow cards in the previous game (e.g., Pugmire 2006).

The status of superstar, hero, and cultural icon provided some degree of protection to Zidane's image after his less-than-heroic behavior. His outstanding performance up to the point of the incident could not be overlooked, and Zidane was voted the winner of the Golden Ball as the best player of the tournament by an international panel of journalists. However, what may have salvaged Zidane's reputation among his fans was his apology in an interview on a French television network (Moore 2006). He would not apologize to his opponent (Guardian 2010) but said he was especially concerned about the millions of children who saw his act. He admitted it was wrong and said he should have been punished, but he explained that he was provoked by repeated insults from Italian defender Marco Materazzi about his mother, who was ill at the time. "As a man," he said, he had no choice but to retaliate. Materazzi denied the accusations, but the press was more willing to believe the French superstar. His willingness to admit wrong distinguished him from Lance Armstrong, Alex Rodriguez, and other sports superstars who have denied wrongdoing, and allowed at least the French media to reconstruct him as a hero.

There are some heroes in a few sports, such as rodeo, who seem to be throw-backs to an earlier and simpler era. Pearson and Haney (1999) concluded from their ethnographic study of rodeo cowboys that these athletes seemed to embody qualities of the frontier and the American West, while also being risk takers as athletes in a dangerous sport and entrepreneurs relying entirely on their sports success for their economic livelihood. These athletes are generally outside the large-scale corporate culture of the golden triangle. The globalization of the golden triangle has made them anachronisms. For most, embracing the golden triangle with its intrusive media has been a path to success. We have seen that the intrusiveness and power of the media in the golden triangle can transform the celebrities and heroes they have made into something much less or much worse.

The Evolution of the Dominant Sports Culture in the United States

Whether or not the United States is exceptional in its sports tastes and cul-ture, its conception of the meaning and importance of sport has been closely intertwined with the evolution of cultural values, products, and practices in the larger American society. In American culture and society, a belief in indi-vidualism has long held a hallowed place. Americanization, modernization, and the globalization of capitalism have resulted in varying degrees of accep-tance of individualism and self-interest in other parts of the world, but in the United States there is little question about their central place in the culture and society.

Sociological theorists have recognized individualism as a central element of modern societies, and they have long debated its societal implications. Kivisto (2004:83) identified individualism as one of the "key ideas" in the history of sociological thought, and he pointed out that some theorists emphasized its positive implications related to freedom from social constraints and oppres-sion, while others focused on its more destructive tendencies to separate us from others and to undermine our commitment to reciprocity and the welfare of others in social relations. Frenchman Alexis de Tocqueville ([1853] 1969) observed a form of socially destructive individualism that he called "egoism" when he visited the United States over 150 years ago. This kind of individual-ism helps explain the decline of marriage, community, social capital, and civil society in contemporary US society. Individualism becomes destructive when individuals put themselves above or outside the group, have little commitment to the group, and only care about the group and other people to the extent that they can advance their individual interests. In these cases, individualism is out of balance with the societal need for strong group and community ties. Late twentieth-century and early twenty-first-century analyses of the decline of social commitment and community in the United States and the need for renewed civic engagement (e.g., Bellah, Madsen, Sullivan, Swidler, and Tipton 1985; Derber 2011; Putnam 2000) have reflected concerns about excessive and destructive individualism.

In sport, excessive individualism may take a number of forms. Individuals may realize that their own success is based on the success of their team, but they may not be willing to sacrifice their own chances to be the star or care enough about their team to give up the ball or the puck to a teammate in a better position to score. In addition, they may not be willing to give credit to teammates for their outstanding performance, to try their hardest in relay events or doubles matches when they could interfere with their preparations for their individual competition, to play a supportive rather than dominant role when the team needs it, to compete for their national team when it does not advance their personal career or pay them much money, or to stay with a team as a coach when a better offer comes along even though commitments have been made to new recruits and a contract will be violated by a move. As a result, individuals may score more points or goals, have a higher batting average, hit more home runs, throw more pass completions, win more individual races or matches, and go to more prestigious or better-paying positions, but they may leave their teams at a disadvantage and contribute to their losing. Thus, in the contemporary culture of individualism in sport, there may arise contradictions between individual motivations and team commitments.

Individualism and the individual entrepreneur are at the heart of traditional conceptions of capitalism. Individual rights are a central element of modern democracies, and the new economy of the neoliberal state focuses on the economic interests of individuals and corporations. At the interpersonal level, individualism involves the pursuit of self-interest, but it can develop into doing what is best for yourself at the expense of others and relationships with them. The contemporary culture of individualism is defined by these political, economic, and interpersonal elements. In contemporary sports, the golden triangle may emphasize the importance of individual stars to their team's success and create a cult of personality that turns these stars into celebrities and heroes. As a result, it may encourage these stars and their fans to think that their individual welfare and success are more important than their team's (Smart 2005:11).

In some sports cultures, such as Japanese baseball, the team traditionally has been valued more than the individual, and individuals have been expected to sacrifice for the team and suppress their individual interests and desires. In these cultures, it has been difficult for athletes from societies with more individualistic values, such as Americans, to adjust to the lack of attention to them as individuals (Smart 2005:41, footnote 6). For athletes and others in the United States, the importance of the individual is learned during socialization, which is why it is disorienting to be in a society where the culture places the interests and achievements of the group or team above the interests and achievements of the individual. In the United States, individualism occupies a central place in the dominant ideology of the American Dream. The American Dream and the American Sports Dream are primarily about the pursuit of self-interest and individual success.

The ideology of the American Dream is closely related to a set of popular cultural beliefs about US sport that sport sociologist Harry Edwards (1973) called the "Dominant American Sports Creed." Edwards (1973) formulated his conception of the most prominent beliefs about sport in the United States on the basis of his content analysis of statements about US sport and its effects found in newspapers, magazines, and a leading journal in athletics over several decades of the twentieth century up to the 1960s. He viewed the central or most common beliefs as ideological statements about the virtues of sport, which were meant to persuade people to participate in sport and support it. These dominant values and beliefs in the sport culture reflected the dominant cultural values and beliefs in the larger society, and this is because sport is part of the institutional structure of society. Just as belief in the American Dream has reinforced acceptance of the dominant structure of the larger society in the United States and the institutional structure of sport, belief in the Dominant American Sports Creed may have reinforced acceptance of the dominant institutional structure of modern US sport and society in the past.

According to Edwards (1973), the central themes of the Dominant American Sports Creed assert that (1) sport builds character by emphasizing such things as clean living, loyalty, and altruism; (2) sport teaches discipline by encouraging both self-control and obedience to authority; (3) sport encourages competitiveness, which results from courage, perseverance, and aggressiveness and which helps people meet the challenges of life and get ahead in society; (4) sport makes people more physically fit; (5) sport contributes to mental fitness by making people more mentally sharp and encouraging them to value education; (6) sport contributes to religiosity by encouraging acceptance of traditional Christian beliefs; and (7) sport makes people more patriotic (Nixon 1984:19–22). Like the American Dream, this set of beliefs was a persuasive argument—in this case, for the cultural legitimacy and significance of sport—despite lacking a basis in systematic research. People who were involved in sport believed the Dominant American Sports Creed because sport was important to them and the creed was an inspiring vision of sport. It implied that the virtuous qualities molded by sports participation would ultimately make athletes successful in sport and in life.

The Dominant American Sports Creed may have been part of the dominant culture of US sport through most of the twentieth century, but American society has changed, mediated images have become more pervasive and influential, consumption now may be more important than productivity or achievement, and the egoism described by Tocqueville—called "narcissism" by cultural critics such as Lasch (1979)—seems to have become a preoccupation in the United States and other contemporary Western capitalist societies. Indeed, to some extent, the American Dream now may be more about mediated images or the appearance of success than about actual achievement.

Derber (2011) has proposed a darker interpretation of the "New American Dream." This new version of the American Dream places an excessive emphasis on individualism, reflects a perverted view of morality, and encourages the pursuit of money, power, and fame at all costs. In sport, it can be seen as a distortion of legendary football coach Vince Lombardi's statement that "winning isn't everything, it is the only thing." He was talking about professional sports in which people are paid to win. The distortion was that it seemed to be interpreted too literally and to be applied in sports venues such as children's and youth sports, where it did not seem appropriate. The New American Dream encourages the belief that one cannot win enough or be successful enough, famous enough, rich enough, or powerful enough. The ego always has to be indulged. Derber proposed that this version of the American Dream could lead to an extreme form of deviance that he called "wilding." Wilding is individualistic behavior that serves the self by harming others and involves exploitation or manipulation of others. Wilding occurs when reasonable, moral, legal, and ethical behavior fail to produce the promised success of the American Dream—or American Sports Dream—and individuals turn instead to corrupt, immoral, unethical, illegal, and harmful actions to achieve their elusive success. Neoliberal economic policies promoting an unregulated capitalistic marketplace have contributed to wilding, especially when combined with an individualistic ethos rooted in a misplaced nostalgia for the frontier days in America. Some of the types of deviance and social problems that are the focus of the next chapter are examples of wilding and may be spawned by the New American Dream.

The contemporary sports culture in the United States has been shaped by the golden triangle and may bear some of the imprint of the New American Dream. Its core beliefs and practices have seemed to shift away from the idealized version in the Dominant American Sports Creed of sport's functions and benefits. The dominant belief system in US sport today may be more about what it takes to be a serious athlete than about the effects of participating in sport. Hughes and Coakley (1991; also see Coakley 2009:163–166) proposed that the dominant cultural standards that defined what it meant to be a serious athlete in big-time sport in the late part of the twentieth century were part of a belief system they called the "Sport Ethic." Its four major values and norms emphasized (1) dedication to "the game" above everything else; (2) striving for distinction by constantly striving to be the best, achieve perfection, and win; (3) accepting risks and playing with pain; and (4) believing that all things are possible and nothing can or will get in the way of success.

These values push athletes to their limits, make sports and athletic performances exciting and entertaining for spectators, and make sport profitable for its major corporate investors in the golden triangle. In specifying the path to success in sport, the Sport Ethic pushes athletes to do everything possible to win and achieve personal distinction. This can lead to a high quality of performance and competition, which serves the interests of the golden triangle. However, it can also lead to self-destructive behavior that damages the body and to forms of wilding when performances do not achieve the desired results. A perversion of the Sport Ethic and the American Sports Dream may explain the wilding that unmade Lance Armstrong, Alex Rodriguez, and many other disgraced sports stars and onetime heroes.

Sport and Religion

Whether in the United States or elsewhere, sports in the golden triangle can be interesting combinations of cultural contradictions. They can embody idealized conceptions of heroes and lofty purposes, while also being perverse manifestations of ego and exploitation. The paradoxical nature of sport requires explanation, which can take us into the realms of the secular and commercial as well as the spiritual and religious. On the one hand, sports are the business of the golden triangle. As such, they are highly organized, commercialized, and McDonaldized forms of entertainment. These sports become "mediasport" when the media of the golden triangle construct and globalize them to entertain their audiences around the world (Falcous and Maguire 2006). The popularity of mediasport helps the golden triangle to sell sports events and other products and make money from them.

Mediasport productions appeal to spectators and viewers in part because images and texts are skillfully created and manipulated to make them seem dramatic, exciting, and compelling. These qualities can transform sport into a kind of religious experience for those most passionate about it. Indeed, some have said that sport is appealing to fans as an escape from the pressures and problems of everyday life (Segrave 2000), while others have called sport a "secular religion" (Nixon and Frey 1996:63–66). That is, it has a special meaning, and for some, it provides a kind of sacred escape from the mundane problems of everyday life. It appears that televised sports are especially likely to be an escape for males and for fans of team sports (Raney 2006:320).

Of course, sport is not really a religion. It cannot solve the ultimate questions of human existence about life, death, and apparently needless suffering, and it has no supernatural deities. Yet for the most passionate sports "believers" or "followers," sport provides a sense of stability and authentic meaning that is not easily found in a world that often seems turbulent, chaotic, superficial, or contrived. It can be inspiring and absorbing, qualities often missing in people's highly organized or otherwise dull lives. Rojek (2001:53) suggested that sports celebrities can become objects of cult worship in a culture of celebrity, and like gods of ancient religion, they can serve as exemplars or role models in modern society. As Smart (2005:9) noted, however, they show us how important it is today to be consumers of material rather than sacred things. Nevertheless, their iconic status, similar to religious icons, gives them great power over those who idolize them.

The spiritual qualities associated with images of "magical" performances and "supernatural" talent enable the golden triangle to promote them more effectively as representatives of their worldly material interests. While these connections may seem quite abstract most of the time, sometimes they are made very concrete. Smart (2005:158) cites the example of a one-foot-high statue of David Beckham in his Manchester United uniform that was placed next to other statues at the foot of the image of Buddha in a Bangkok temple where minor deities normally were located. Local religious leaders commented that soccer could be viewed as a type of religion with millions of followers and that the statue reflected the high regard in which many held Beckham. There have been other similar types of images of Beckham, which reinforce the connection between sport and religion, even though his global image is a construction built from very secular interests.

We know that commercialism, image making, and sportainment characterize modern mediated sports and that sports heroes typically are much less heroic than they are portrayed. For devoted sports fans, however, these facts of sport tend to be minimized, denied, or ignored. Seen through the filters and mediascapes constructed by the golden triangle, sport is perceived as awesome, thrilling, compelling, real, and meaningful. This perceived version of sport can make it a "symbolic refuge" imbued with values, images, and meaning that transport serious fans into a world of fantasy, dreams, and pure enjoyment (Nixon and Frey 1996:55–56).

Even when their favorite teams and players do not live up to expectations, the sports faithful often remain faithful. They are buoyed by examples that fuel their hope that their faith will be rewarded—eventually. After all, the loyalty of the long-suffering Boston Red Sox baseball fans was finally rewarded with a World Series victory in 2004 after eighty-six years, and the Chicago White Sox baseball team overcame eighty-eight years of frustration for its loyal fans with a World Series victory in 2005, giving hope to Chicago Cubs fans, who have not seen a World Series championship since 1908. Similarly, in the birthplace of soccer, English soccer fans remain rabid, even though their national team has won only one World Cup, and that was in 1966. The appeal or love of sport is regularly stoked by beliefs that underdogs sometimes win, all things are possible, and loyalty will eventually be rewarded. When these things happen, even for rival teams or in other sports, these core beliefs and the attachment to sport are reinforced among the faithful. For the most dedicated sports fans, hope is more important than statistical tendencies, and fantasies are more compelling than studies and analyses of sport that probe beneath the sports veneer and reveal contrary or ugly facts.

Probe 4.5: Paradox of Sport as Sacred and Secular

From a sociological perspective, we can point to the paradox of sport as both a sacred escape and a manufactured commodity for sale. It is an object of love and devotion for many millions of fans around the world, and it is also a cultural product produced and sold by the golden triangle to make money. For both fans and investors, it has considerable cultural meaning and significance, and both derive something of value from this meaning and significance. This paradox is sustainable because golden triangles in various cultural settings create images and encourage beliefs that make sport and its stars seem special and different from the other celebrities of contemporary popular culture, perhaps even as sacred cultural icons. As we have already noted in regard to ideologies, reality may be less compelling than images or perceptions that capture our imagination or fulfill our desires or interests. Thus, the cultural values and practices of the contemporary global capitalistic cultural economy are reinforced and spread by the golden triangle as it builds and spreads sports and sports stars as culturally significant experiences *and* alluring commodities on a global scale.

For people in and out of sport who are religiously devout, treating sport literally as sacred or religious can be offensive. Furthermore, when the globalization of sport emphasizes secular and material aspects of modern culture, it can create social, cultural, and political disruptions. This has happened when modern global sport has clashed with established religious power or traditional religious values and practices, as in Islamic nations. In contrast, in the United States, the relationship between sport and religion has been complex. Along with those offended by the perceived exploitation or trivialization of religion in sport (Feezell 2013), other religious people have viewed the sports arena as a useful venue for expressing their religious convictions and proselytizing to get others to accept their faith.

In his series of *Sports Illustrated* articles about religion in sport in the 1970s, sportswriter Frank Deford (1976) coined the term "sportianity" to refer to the social movement of athletes and coaches who witnessed for Christ. This movement has involved an assortment of organizations, including the Fellowship of Christian Athletes, Athletes in Action, Jocks for Jesus, the Sports Ambassadors, and a number of others associated with specific sports. They have tended to be evangelical. That is, they have shared Christian fundamentalists' belief in scripture, but they have been more concerned about believers having a personal relationship with Jesus and about converting others to their faith (Hinch 2014; Steensland, Park, Regnerus, Robinson, Wilcox, and Woodberry 2000). They have sought religious converts by using religiously devout coaches and athletes to "sell" their religious message.

Evangelical athletes and coaches became important tools of sportianity as they engaged in what Higgs (1995) called the "religionizing of sport." This involved inserting their religion into sport and using their sports roles to proselytize. Coaches, sometimes controversially, brought their brand of Christianity to the locker room (see, e.g., Robinson 2014; Wolverton 2013b). Athletes became modern-day *muscular Christians*, whose lineage could be traced at least to the nineteenth century in Great Britain and the United States (Nixon and Frey 1996:68–69). Exemplars of this muscular Christianity were portrayed and saw themselves as role models who proclaimed their kind of Christianity as a path to a more righteous life. Former NFL player Tim Tebow is a recent illustration of this kind of muscular Christian. His period of celebrity in sport brought him a lot of attention. However, his unflinching public displays of religiosity also raised important issues about the ties between religion and sport in the United States (Feezell 2013).

During the 2011 NFL season, in particular, Tim Tebow captured the imagination of fans both because of his exploits on the football field and because of his many public expressions of his religious convictions. In fact, his tendency to celebrate on the field by prayerfully genuflecting on one knee came to be known as "Tebowing" and led to a flood of copycats, both serious and mocking. In an effort to ensure that his gesture was "used in the right way," his agents sought to trademark the move. He claimed that any money made from the trademarking would go to his charity (Associated Press 2012). His mixing of religion with commercialism seems apt for his religionizing in the golden triangle.

Trademarking Tebowing raises questions about the purity of his religious motives, despite his disclaimer about giving profits to charity. Krattenmaker (2010) has suggested that such instances of religion in sport may be more orchestrated than spontaneous. That is, they may be the result of well-organized and well-financed efforts by elements of the sportianity movement to encourage athletes and coaches to use sports settings to profess their faith and convert others to it. Krattenmaker proposed that pro athletes have been targeted by the evangelicals of sportianity precisely because they can command so much attention in the sports media spotlight.

Leaders of sportianity may be delighted to see Tim Tebow and other prominent athletes genuflecting before television cameras, reciting Bible verses as they walk the sidelines, or praising Jesus for giving them the determination and opportunity to be victorious. However, teammates, many fans, and the golden triangle may not share in this delight. As Feezell (2013) has pointed out, overt expressions of Tebow's "exclusivist" or narrowly defined brand of evangelical Christianity may be problematic in a number of ways. These kinds of displays may trivialize religion for those who think that God has much more important concerns than who wins in sport. They also may turn off teammates or fans who hold other religious convictions or who are not religious at all. The locker room can be very uncomfortable for minorities when it is filled with a narrow view of religion and the socially and politically conservative rhetoric that often accompanies evangelical or fundamentalist Christianity, such as opposition to abortion, homosexuality, and gay marriage (Hinch 2014).

The reality of twenty-first-century evangelical and fundamentalist Christianity in the United States is that this type of religion is losing its hold over Americans and especially young Americans (Dickerson 2012; Hinch 2014).

Religion in general seems to be less influential in American life (Newport 2010). For those in sportianity, this could be interpreted as a reason to intensify their religionizing efforts. However, they face a significant obstacle in the major demographic shifts happening in the United States and elsewhere in the world. Majority white populations may become minorities within a few decades, and with these changes will come an increasing diversity in religion. Along with the growing number of young people expressing no interest in formal religion, there will be more immigrant Catholics, Pentecostals, and Muslims (Hinch 2014). Thus, the relationship between religion and sport is likely to become more fluid and complex. For example, basketball may have already become the favorite sport of Muslims in the United States. Sacirbey (2012) suggested that the affinity in the United States between Muslims and basketball may be like the affinity between Jews and baseball portrayed in a documentary film with that name by sportswriter Ira Berkow. Each of these sports has provided members of these two religions with relatively more heroes than other big-time sports in the United States. Furthermore, in the case of basketball, the fact that the NBA is largely black and that 30 percent of Muslims in the United States are black strengthens the connection between basketball and Muslims as well as basketball and race.

Religious diversity in sports can lead to unspoken hostility or discomfort on sports teams when coaches and teammates zealously profess their particular faith and try to get others to join them (Wolverton 2013b). Thus, such sportianity-inspired religionizing can create divisions and tensions on teams, and possibly alienate some fans (Feezell 2013). In some cultures or cultural periods, being a devoutly religious athlete outside the religious mainstream can create hostility.

Muslims in sport have faced hostility, as Muslims, in a number of societies over the past several decades. For example, Muslim athletes in the United States and other Western countries have faced heightened antagonism for their religious affiliation during certain historical periods in recent history, including the 1960s in the United States and after September 11, 2001, in many Western countries. In the 1960s, prominent African American Muslim athletes experienced hatred and scorn in the United States for their conversion to Islam. The most prominent of these athletes were boxing champion Muhammad Ali and basketball star Kareem Abdul-Jabbar. They were viewed as anti-American for professing their "foreign" religious beliefs (Nixon and Frey 1996:72). Criticism of Ali was compounded by his opposition to the Vietnam War. Being black during a time of racial turmoil intensified racism for him, Abdul-Jabbar, and other Muslim athletes. After the terrorist attacks of 9/11, widespread prejudice and hatred toward Muslims as well as Arabs made it more difficult to be a Muslim in the US mainstream. Sport is embedded in that mainstream. Among Muslim women, their interest in sport has made them targets of hostility and discrimination under traditional and patriarchal Islamic regimes.

So, far from being uplifting, unifying, or inspiring, actual religion in sport can be a source of major rifts, tensions, and frustrations. It is no wonder that the golden triangle is much more comfortable with sport being a secular religion than with it being used or influenced by real religions. Religious speech and demonstrations such as Tebowing are not like patriotic displays that can make fans teary-eyed and feel a common bond. Religion can divide and breed animosity. The fear in the golden triangle is that religion could alien-ate fans and consumers of sport. The golden triangle produces a much less controversial kind of secular religion meant to excite, inspire, and get people to spend their money on sports and sports merchandise. Thus, its religion is about creating a passion for sport, building brand loyalty, and making money. The golden triangle is likely to tolerate and even exploit Tebowing and similar phenomena as long as people continue watching and spending. When interest wanes, its cameras, reporters, and sponsors will turn their attention in another direction. Open-water swimmer and sports commenta-tor Diana Nyad has referred to the "separation of church and sport" (Feezell 2013:140). It seems like an apt description of the philosophy embraced by the golden triangle as it goes about its work with the very secular business of sport.

Conclusion

The idea of sport as a secular religion could apply to a number of commercial-ized sports around the world that incite intense passion and devotion among fans. The modern sports cultures in which these sports are embedded have been shaped by the interplay of global forces of grobalization and glocalization. These globalization forces have added new sports and changed existing ones in many sports cultures. Some of these cultures have become very crowded, with older sports having to contend with competition from the increasing number of new sports that appeal to a younger population. Golf is an example of an ancient sport that has been trying to reinvent itself to make itself more appeal-ing to younger people and a wider audience.

Golf has been criticized for being too expensive, too elitist, and too tied to its traditions. It has been losing players and interest, especially among people under thirty-five, who have been turned off by the time it takes to play a round, the difficulty of mastering the game, and the number of rules. This has led to efforts to experiment with new forms for new players, such as a wider hole. This is akin to mounting a baseball on a tee in T-ball. Both innovations could draw novices into the sport by making them feel initially more adept at the sport. Not surprisingly, the wider hole has caused controversy among golf pur-ists (Pennington 2014). However, in the dynamic culture and marketplace of the golden triangle, a number of sports are being pressed to adapt to capture or retain the interest of players and viewers.

Technology entrepreneurs in the golden triangle are using new media and creating new sports to expand the sports market. For example, there are now fantasy sports leagues and video games that simulate the reality of major sports. A drawback of these virtual sports is that they may dilute interest in the real thing among their most ardent players. Entrepreneurs in the golden triangle have also been creating new live sports to attract the younger genera-tion. Initially, these activities attracted participants because they were part of an alternative youth subculture. They were an alternative to the bureaucra-tized or McDonaldized and commercial sports in the mainstream of the golden triangle. They were novel and added new levels of risk as "extreme sports." Extreme sports such as skateboarding and slopestyle skiing and snowboard-ing became more organized and commercialized as they became more popular and were incorporated into the golden triangle. The major competitions of a number of these sports have become part of popular televised events such as the ESPN X Games, and some have become part of mainstream mega-events such as the Olympics.

Extreme sports reveal the influence of forces of change in sport. They also show how the golden triangle "invents" new sports by co-opting emergent sports created for other purposes than building a brand or making a profit. Young people turned to alternative athletic pursuits because they were uninterested in or rejected the sports of their parents' generation. Along with being daring and fun, these activities gave their young participants chances for self-expression and control. Business entrepreneurs noticed these trends and began making new types of equipment and clothing for a variety of these activities, from snowboarding to skateboarding, dirt biking, hang gliding, rock climbing, and wind surfing. The golden triangle noticed, too, and created competitions to attract spectators and viewers and focused attention on the young stars of these countercultural sports to help them sell their events and products. Despite the reluctance of a number of participants, who feared losing their autonomy, their authenticity, and "selling out," core participants in a number of these new sports willingly competed and took advantage of the commercial opportunities their new celebrity status brought them.

Some of these alternative sports ultimately yielded to the influence of the dominant commercialized sports culture their originators had initially resisted or opposed (see, e.g., Heino 2000). As these sports and their stars changed to accommodate the expectations of the dominant sports culture, the golden triangle made its own accommodations to include them in the sports mainstream. These changes reflect the adaptability of the golden triangle and the flexibility of its culture. Sports are shaped and reshaped by the owners and officials who run sport, the corporate media, and transnational corporate sponsors in the golden triangle. But these people and organizations are responsive to changes in their environment and marketplace. They reshape their own cultural values and practices to retain their dominant position and profitability.

The dominant culture and cultural economy of sport are dynamic as well as complex. Those who shape this culture may influence the forces of change, but they themselves also change in response to dynamic socio-demographic, organizational, economic, political, and technological forces in their environment. Thus, downhill and slalom skiers share the slopes with snowboarders and slopestyle, big air, and other competitors on the snow. Along with race courses for cars and trucks, there are now race courses for motocross and BMX racing, and skateboarders perform tricks on courses with steps, ledges, walls, and ramps.

Slopestyle illustrates the appeal and risks of many of these new sports. It utilizes rails and jumps on a steep course navigated on a snowboard or skis. However, its injury rates have led some to propose significant modifications or even its elimination from the Olympics. Although some people may be thrilled by extreme risks, incorporating these dangers into organized sports in the golden triangle can pose unwanted risks of legal liability and a dubious reputation for these sports, the media covering them, and their sponsors. Thus, a *New York Times* article about slopestyle asked: "When is a risky sport too dangerous?" (Clarey 2014). The golden triangle may have wanted to sidestep this question with its newest sports, since it was already facing this kind of question with established "old" sports such as football. The challenge for the golden triangle is to figure out how to modify old sports and add new ones without crossing the line of excessive risk or danger from a physical, financial, or marketing standpoint. Its media and business sponsors and investors also must decide which sports warrant the most investment and promotion.

As new sports become part of the mainstream commercial culture of the golden triangle in the United States, they will be influenced by the values and practices of consumer capitalism and the Sport Ethic. This may seem ironic, since a number of the most popular extreme sports started as cultural alternatives to the dominant sports of the golden triangle. But the ability of the media and sponsors to sell sports and build fan bases can make sports and sports stars popular and rich. These are powerful inducements that can transform the most idealistic competitors and gradually make the Sport Ethic the guiding principles of their athletic careers. For fans of new and old sports, sports mega-events and other spectacles of mediasport may transport them from their everyday lives into a world of highly distracting entertainment.

Of course, the sports of the golden triangle are paradoxes of escape and commodification. The persistence of these paradoxes reflects the complex allure of the culture of big-time modern sports and its hold over the people who play the games and those who watch them. When sports wane in popularity, the golden triangle modifies old sports or finds new ones to cater to shifting interests and tastes. However, we must remember that the golden triangle is not all-powerful. Glocalization tempers its influence on a global scale, and domestically, the golden triangle must adapt its dominant cultural values, images, rhetoric, practices, and products to adapt to the changing demographics and tastes of sports consumers.

Thus, new sports share the stage with older established sports and even push some of them aside, and the golden triangle modifies its business plans to respond to the new cultural directions. In adapting globally, nationally, or locally, the golden triangle is acknowledging the forces of change in society and sport. These kinds of adaptation may ultimately be very disruptive of established cultural and social patterns in sport, even though they can be interpreted as forces that build and spread sport. Social deviance and social problems are unlikely to be mistaken for more constructive or benign social forces. Social deviance and problems are the subject of the next chapter.

Stop and Think Questions

1. What do we learn about consumer capitalism by watching sports on television?

2. What purposes are served when the US media portray Americans as exceptional in their lack of interest in soccer?

3. Explain why sports heroes may be more vulnerable than sports celebrities to a career-killing fall from stardom after reports of their deviant or unethical behavior surface in the media.

4. How has the US sports culture in the golden triangle changed in its evolution from the Dominant American Sports Creed to the Sport Ethic?

5. How does the golden triangle sustain the paradox of sport as sacred refuge and commercial commodity?

6. How does the golden triangle operate as a global network, and what is the difference between grobalization and glocalization when the core North American and Eurocentric golden triangles try to spread their influence overseas?

7. How do the media in the golden triangle create sports mediascapes, and how are these mediascapes related to the idea of sportainment?

5

Sport, Social Deviance, and Social Problems

People who subscribe to the Dominant American Sports Creed and accept the idea that sport builds character are likely to believe that athletes and coaches generally do what is expected, right, and good. Furthermore, those who make sports figures their heroes see these people as paragons of virtue to be honored and emulated. The fact is that real athletes and coaches frequently fail to meet these ideals of character, conformity, and virtue. The golden triangle creates temptations, pressures, conflicts, and perhaps even a sense of arrogance that may lead both stars and more ordinary athletes and coaches to break the rules of sport and sometimes the laws of society. This *social deviance* is a major focus of this chapter, and we will see that the perpetrators may be individuals or organizations.

Classical functionalist theorists such as Emile Durkheim ([1893] 1964, [1895] 1964) have argued that social deviance occurs in all societies and even has benefits for society such as making the meaning of cultural values and boundaries of normative behavior clearer, uniting people against a perceived threat, and spurring cultural and social change. Despite the possible functions of deviance, people in authority generally try to control it or give the impression of controlling it to maintain order. Furthermore, we tend to look down on people who engage in deviance. In looking at various forms of deviance in this chapter, we will see that perceptions of deviance and reactions to it can be varied and complicated, depending on the nature of the deviance and who is engaging in it.

This chapter is also about social problems created by the impact of recurrent and serious social deviance. *Social problems* are conditions in society that are widely viewed as sources of social disruption, tension, or difficulty for society (Nixon and Frey 1996:99). These conditions are defined by powerful people or organizations, the mass media, and many members of the public as highly undesirable because they are perceived as cases of deviance or disruption that challenge the social order *or* because they are conditions of society that cause difficulties or deprivations for broad or less advantaged segments of the population in a society. Thus, there are *social deviance–related social problems* such as rape, other forms of violence, and drug abuse, and there are *problems of social inequality* mainly affecting less advantaged people or minorities, such as poverty, illiteracy, prejudice, discrimination, and segregation.

We have considered a number of problems of inequality affecting women and minorities, and we will continue to examine these problems throughout this book. However, we are primarily interested in this chapter in social deviance–related social problems that are perceived as threats to the social order. Problems of social inequality may contribute to various types of deviance-related social problems in sport. Although sports officials and coaches have a vested interest in maintaining conformity to the rules and social order in their sports, they may implicitly or explicitly contribute to conditions that encourage deviant behavior among athletes and spectators. In some cases, officials and coaches may be deviants themselves.

Organized and organizational aspects of deviance and social problems are a major focus of this chapter. Thus, we are interested in deviance involving collusion in social networks such as teams, leagues, and even governing bodies. This kind of deviance generally involves extensive and serious rule breaking, but also may include unethical and immoral behavior. The unethical and immoral behavior violates basic values or principles of fairness or decency in sport and society. The rule breaking and unethical and immoral behavior contain elements of wilding when people engage in this behavior to serve their own interests without any concern about how it hurts other people or their organization. Wilding is also apparent in collective forms of deviance such as fan violence. Fan violence is another major topic in this chapter. The chapter will conclude with brief discussions of two other serious deviance-related social problems: hazing and interpersonal violence. Although they are not usually viewed as cases of corporate or institutionalized corruption, they have elements that reflect cultural and social elements of sports environments emphasizing physicality and aggression. They are also social problems that have become more serious as they have escalated into more wilding-like behavior.

Social Deviance and Sport

In the simplest sense, social deviance is breaking rules or violating social norms, and as I have noted, it may include violations of ethics or moral principles. When enough people break particular rules or when a particular type of rule breaking adversely affects a lot of people or people in power, deviance may be perceived as a social problem. Obviously, when viewed this way, deviance is something that needs to be eliminated or controlled to maintain social order. This is despite the possible social functions deviance might have. However, deviance is not always what we think it is. After all, norms may differ in different social and cultural contexts, which means that the same behavior could be deviant in some contexts and normative in others. Take the case of boxing. One would ordinarily be arrested for assault in most civilized societies for hitting another person. In boxing, though, the purpose of a match is to try to beat your opponent senseless. The more successful people are at this task, the more money they earn and more revered they are, at least among boxing fans.

Thus, whether a particular behavior is deviant depends on the applicable rules or norms. In addition, people of different status behaving the same way may be treated quite differently. A sports superstar might routinely break the rules of sports competition, such as elbowing an opponent in basketball or holding in football, and not be whistled for a foul or penalty. A player of lesser status might be a more frequent victim of the referee's whistle. Off the field, a sports superstar might be given a mild warning or be ignored for speeding, driving under the influence, or engaging in more serious offenses. A lesser player might not be allowed the same leeway. Coaches have been known to coddle their star athletes, while holding less talented players to stricter standards of conduct on and off the field.

It may seem odd, but people could be considered deviant if they conform too much rather than not enough. Coakley (2009:159–171) distinguished between *deviant overconformity*, which involves conforming too much, and *deviant underconformity*, which involves not conforming enough. Deviant underconformity is what we usually view as social deviance, and the social problems of primary interest in this chapter are related to deviant underconformity. Deviant overconformity is not usually viewed as deviance, because people are generally doing what they are expected to do, but this conformity becomes overconformity when it exceeds the boundary for normal or acceptable behavior and becomes risky or dangerous. For example, athletes who are expected by coaches to "train hard" in the off-season may overconform and hurt themselves by training too many hours a day and pushing their bodies too hard. Or, coaches may devote so many hours to their sport that they sacrifice personal relationships with family and friends, and high school or college athletes may devote so much time to sport that they hurt their performance in school.

In some cases, an intense desire to do what is expected or needed to succeed could lead initially to deviant overconformity such as overtraining and then to more conventionally defined forms of deviance. Intense coaches frequently implicitly or explicitly exhort their teams to "go the extra mile" and "do whatever it takes" to win. Less talented athletes may be frustrated that they are not doing enough when even their extreme physical sacrifices are not making them successful. As a result, "doing whatever it takes" may be interpreted as implying that they must be willing to cross the line into the realm of dubious or illegal practices, including cheating and doping, to help them succeed. Coaches who are highly committed to winning because they know it is necessary to keep their job may be similarly influenced to engage in deviant recruiting practices to bring in the athletes needed to win when legal recruiting is not successful enough.

The increasing influence of science, technology, and medicine in sports training and performance has pushed athletes and sport into new and uncharted territory. Hoberman (1992) criticized these developments as elements of the over-rationalization of sport, which has turned athletes into "mortal engines." The new "robots" of sport use new medications, new therapeutic strategies, and new equipment and other technologies to heal, rehabilitate, and strengthen their bodies and to improve their training and performance. Sports officials are constantly faced with the challenge of determining what makes competition "fair." In effect, this is an issue of identifying the line separating innovative and risky but legitimate overconformity from deviant underconformity or violations of the rules of the game that are meant to ensure fairness.

With a steady stream of experimentation and innovations, it can be difficult to know whether particular practices are acceptable or fair and should be permitted by the rules. For example, the question of whether it is fair to allow athletes with disabilities to compete in the mainstream with wheelchairs or prosthetic limbs is especially perplexing. These athletes have historically been excluded from the mainstream of sport, but the technology that allows them to compete in the mainstream may give them an advantage over able-bodied competitors. This was the controversy that swirled around Oscar Pistorius as he sought to compete in mainstream sports as the "blade runner." Thus, the effort to use technology to overcome the problem of exclusion of athletes with disabilities from sport may create new legal and practical issues and problems concerning access, the rules of competition, and fairness. As athletes and coaches continually push the norms or boundaries of what is acceptable, fair, or permitted in sport, they create new challenges for sports officials who must decide what is allowed and what is not in sport. For sport sociologists, this means that the study of social deviance and social problems is not always straightforward.

Theories of Social Deviance

Social deviance is not always clear-cut. The same behavior is not always deviant, different people technically breaking rules may or may not all be considered deviant, and going beyond what is expected could be seen as a type of deviant overconformity and provoke admiration or praise. This is true until the overconformity morphs into deviant underconformity or what we typically view as social deviance. Furthermore, the early adopters who experiment with innovations to raise their performance levels may initially be viewed with curiosity but not as rule breakers. They become deviants when sports authorities deem their innovative behavior to be dangerous or unfair and make rules against the behavior.

With the complexity of social deviance, it should not be surprising that different sociological theories define and explain it in different ways. To illustrate these differences in perspective, we will look at structural functionalist, social conflict, critical, and symbolic interactionist interpretations of social deviance. Although these theories make different assumptions about deviance, the combination of them gives us a range of possible insights about what deviance is, what causes it, and how it affects society and sport.

We have already considered in this chapter how structural functionalists can see social deviance as functional in some respects. In general, though, *structural functionalists* emphasize the importance of conformity to social norms for maintaining the established or institutionalized social order. Social deviance is a problem for societies because it disrupts the established or institutionalized social order that societies need to survive. *Social control* serves the purpose of maintaining or restoring order when deviance threatens it. Social control involves tactics, strategies, policies, and procedures that range from persuasion and inducements to punishment.

Robert Merton's (1938, 1957) *social strain theory* is an example of how structural functionalists explain social deviance. In his framework, conformity exists when beliefs are compatible with established cultural goals or values and actions are compatible with institutionalized norms and roles. Social deviance occurs when people fail to accept cultural goals or values or fail to act according to institutionalized norms and roles. For example, people engage in the form of deviance Merton called "innovation" when they embrace established cultural goals and values, such as winning in sport, but engage in behavior, such as cheating, that violates institutionalized norms and roles. Innovation is easy to understand in sport with the pervasiveness of the Sport Ethic at all levels of sport, from youth leagues and high school sports up to the Olympics and professional sports. If being successful in sport is very important and winning is the only thing that counts as success, we can understand the willingness to cross the line and break the rules when athletes or coaches lack the ability, opportunity, or resources to win the big game or win consistently. This is innovation in Merton's sense.

Probe 5.1: Social Control, Performance-Enhancing Drugs, and Inducements to Cheat

Whatever the specific causes of social deviance, structural functionalists assume that society is organized to root them out. Social control approaches in sport are illustrated by official responses to the use of performance-enhancing drugs (PEDs) by athletes. PEDs have been a problem in major sports venues since the 1960s (CNN 2014b). In sports venues such as the Olympics, the Tour de France, and Major League Baseball (MLB), the many well-publicized cases of illegal drug use have prompted social control efforts involving more extensive and more sophisticated drug testing, stricter enforcement policies, and more severe penalties. Social control can be difficult, though, when there are powerful inducements influencing people to try to win at all costs. This can lead to cheating. We are reminded of the discussion in the last chapter of wilding induced by the New American Dream. Thus, control efforts may have to overcome powerful cultural and social influences encouraging or abetting deviance. The increasing influence of cultural beliefs such as the New American Dream and the increasing prevalence of behavioral patterns such as wilding are difficult for structural functionalists to explain. They do not fit neatly into their perspective emphasizing conformity, stability, and order.

Structural functionalists generally assume that major cultural and social patterns contribute to social order and that disruptive elements in society tend to be held in check or controlled. *Social conflict and critical theories* seem more useful for helping us understand how disruptive elements and deviance become embedded in culture and social structure. For conflict and critical theorists, the maintenance of social order and operation of social control are tenuous and problematic in modern societies. This is because they see modern societies being driven by the capitalist pursuit of self-interest and reliant on rational forms of organization and technology that are often used to exploit or gain an advantage over others.

Marxist conflict theorists tend to look at social conformity and deviance in terms of their relationship to the interests of different social classes. They see the dominant normative structure of society, including the legal system, as a biased reflection of dominant class interests, and social deviance essentially as violating the rules, regulations, and laws of the dominant class. The dominant culture tends to reflect and reinforce the interests and pursuits of dominant classes. Thus, from a conflict perspective, social deviance is behavior that threatens or disrupts the dominant classes. More privileged and powerful people are likely to favor the tough prosecution of laws and other established norms to protect their own interests and to use the values of the dominant culture to justify their actions. At the same time, members of the upper class or elite in society have the power to disregard laws that interfere with the pursuit of their interests without being penalized. In fact, there is an area of sociology that focuses on white-collar and corporate crime and organizational deviance involving members of the elite (e.g., Simon 2012).

Consider the differences between structural functionalism and conflict theory as they apply to deviance and social control in sport. While structural functionalists tend to see social control as a means to maintain social order for the good of the sport in general and everyone involved in it, social conflict theorists see social control as a means to protect the narrower interests of the power structure of sport or golden triangle. Thus, from a conflict perspective, maintaining social conformity and social order in a sport keeps players and even coaches in their place and unruly fans under control. For example, players who speak out about the unfairness, oppressiveness, or incompetence of coaches or coaches who complain about lack of support from general managers or owners may be branded as "troublemakers" who are not "team players" and find themselves demoted, waived, traded, or fired. A sport under control preserves the prestige and profitability of the sport for the owners, investors, officials, and sponsors who constitute the golden triangle, and being "under control" means that control of the sport remains firmly in the hands of those at the top of the power structure.

From a social conflict perspective, the norms of sport reflect the interests of those with the most power, and some of those norms pose risks or dangers for athletes. For example, the Sport Ethic in the United States makes risk, pain, and injury seem normal or even heroic (Nixon 1993). In this kind of cultural context, players may be pushed toward deviant overconformity in their training and the intensity of their play, which ultimately leads to injuries for many of them. Most coaches and officials in pro football, for example, would acknowledge in principle that high injury rates are a problem in their sport and argue that they try to limit the number of injuries. Yet the popularity of their sport benefits from competition among athletes who train and play hard and disregard the resulting damage to their bodies. The National Football League (NFL) does not want to see its top players hurt and out of action or to be the focus of negative publicity about high injury rates. But it is not likely to curtail the stresses and risks for players as long as they have good enough replacement players to keep fans watching.

The golden triangle may perversely benefit from athletes taking risks and enduring pain and injuries. However, the athletes themselves may pay a high price for their overconformity. Injuries can end an athlete's career and cause serious and chronic disabilities. Putting aside the issue of how much athletes in the golden triangle of professional sports are rewarded for their physical sacrifices, what is relevant from a social conflict perspective is that players who want to play and succeed perceive that they have little choice about taking physical risks and making sacrifices. From this perspective, the system is skewed in favor of those who invest in and run sports and against those who play sports and have to accept the physical risks and damage.

Probe 5.2: Pushing Athletes to Be Mortal Engines

Neo-Marxist critical theorists help us see how sport can push athletes to risk their bodies as "mortal engines." They focus on how the application of organizational and scientific rationality in modern bureaucracies exploits and dehumanizes human beings. This happens in sport when organizational policies and practices and medical and scientific innovations are used unethically and illegally to improve athletic performance and make organizations more efficient, effective, and profitable. Athletes are pushed to experiment and take risks with their training and their bodies to do better, which serves the interests of their coaches, sports officials, and the media and sports investors in the golden triangle. Thus, athletes are pushed toward deviant overconformity by the culture of sport and by those who coach and run sports. When their overconformity becomes deviant underconformity, as in the use of PEDs, athletes tend to be held more accountable for their deviance than their bosses are. From a neo-Marxist critical perspective, the institutions of society such as sport are organized primarily to serve the interests of the bosses or those with the most power and privilege, at the expense of those whom they employ or who have less power.

Critical race theory provides important insights about how the power structure of sports treats the criminality of athletes. Athletes may be less involved in crime than their nonathlete counterparts from similar socioeconomic, racial, and ethnic backgrounds. However, criminal charges against big-time college and professional athletes generate a lot of media attention. In sports such as football and basketball in the United States, these media reports raise sensitive issues, since a disproportionate number of football and basketball players in the golden triangle are African American and a disproportionate number of the reported crimes in these sports involve black players.

A *USA Today* database of NFL player arrests was created in January 2000. By late November 2013, it had 687 entries, and 88 percent were black players (Schrotenboer 2013c). The most common reason for being arrested was driving under the influence (DUI). This accounted for nearly 30 percent of the arrests. The racial difference in these arrests may at least partially reflect racial profiling, since they involve traffic stops. After DUIs, the most common reasons for arrest were assault and battery, domestic violence, and illegal drug use, each representing about 12 to 13 percent of the arrests. Arrest rates of male college football and basketball players may have been even higher than those of players in the NFL and the National Basketball Association (NBA) (Wolverton 2010). The arrests of college athletes in these sports involved a relatively large number of black athletes because the racial composition of these sports is disproportionately black.

Many of the black football and basketball players recruited by colleges and signed by professional teams grew up in poor and gang-infested neighborhoods and had to fend off pressures to get involved in crime. A number had encounters with the criminal justice system. A structural functionalist might argue that providing opportunities to these young men gives them a chance to escape their backgrounds and become part of the mainstream. However, a critical race theorist would more likely point to racist exploitation of these young men and the self-serving way they are treated by those who coach and run the sports they play. Talented black athletes play a key role in football and basketball. However, playing these sports does not always lift poor minority athletes out of poverty and propel them toward the American Dream. Even when black athletes make it to the professional level, their careers are short

Newspaper headlines linking NFL name with domestic violence case involving Baltimore Raven star Ray Rice who assaulted his future wife in elevator at casino hotel; Rice was suspended indefinitely by the league and cut by his team after video of attack surfaced. (© Richard Levine/Demotix/Corbis)

and they may not gain the financial or economic security the American Sports Dream suggests. Thus, the people who run and coach commercialized sports benefit from having talented black athletes play for them. But a number of these athletes fail to escape the grip of their tough childhood or old neighborhoods, fail to fully assimilate into the culture of the dominant class, or fail to gain long-term financial and occupational security from playing sports. They may be the ones who show up in the crime statistics.

Racism makes minority athletes more vulnerable to deviant labeling by the criminal justice system and by the golden triangle. Black and other minority athletes must contend with the ways the media of the golden triangle label them. Racism filters the characterizations of these public figures. Even black superstars such as Michael Jordan are sometimes racially stereotyped when they seem to be drifting toward deviance. As we saw in the last chapter, when Jordan was reportedly involved in gambling, he commented that the media seemed to be increasingly portraying him as "Michael Jordan the black guy" (Andrews 1996:147). The implied link between race and crime is clear. Many minority athletes are not big enough celebrities or heroes to be shielded from the critical scrutiny or biases of the media and their negative insinuations and labels.

Probe 5.3: Race, Criminality, and the Golden Triangle

When black athletes get in trouble off the field, they may be shielded from criticism, arrest, and prosecution if they are big enough stars and their teams continue to need them (e.g., Bogdanich 2014). However, they may not escape the stereotypes linking race and criminality or the stigma of having been accused of a serious crime. A critical theorist might argue that the golden triangle keeps athletes in the spotlight as long as they continue to serve the interests of those who run and invest in their sports. When minority athletes carrying the baggage of tainted reputations are no longer deemed good enough to justify taking a chance on them, these athletes are likely to find themselves cut loose with an inadequate safety net or support system to cushion their fall.

The cases of Ray Rice of the Baltimore Ravens (involving his assault of his then-fiancée) and Adrian Peterson of the Minnesota Vikings (concerning his violent disciplining of his children) show that even big NFL stars cannot escape serious punishment from their sport when public criticism becomes too intense or widespread. Rice was dropped by his team and suspended indefinitely by the league, and Peterson was suspended, reinstated, and then suspended indefinitely after the Vikings received harsh criticism for his reinstatement. Critical race theorists raise the question of whether the league may be quicker to drop black stars than white stars of comparable status under these circumstances. Symbolic interactionists would point out that these stars became expendable when the image makers in the league could not successfully construct credible images of them as good men who made "mistakes" or had uncharacteristic lapses in behavior. Racial stereotypes might have made it more difficult to manipulate their images and gloss over their deviance. Image may be more important than substance in the golden triangle, since there are numerous cases of athletes charged with domestic abuse who kept on playing because their cases did not get the media attention the Rice and Peterson cases received (Crouse 2014).

The case of NBA Los Angeles Clippers owner Donald Sterling being banned from the league for his racist remarks would seem to be an example that contradicts the critical race theory analysis and its conception of the typical racial patterns in sport. However, a complicating factor in this analysis is that Sterling was long viewed as an uninterested and ineffective owner with a history of racism and sexual harassment complaints whom the league was happy to have a chance to remove (Golliver 2014a). From a critical perspective, this case was less about eradicating racism among owners and from the sport than about having better-run teams and a better image for the league. Image might have been the issue, too, when the Atlanta Hawks owner preemptively sold his interest in the team when news of his racist remarks became public.

From a critical perspective, negative or deviant labels are more commonly applied to athletes and perhaps especially minority athletes than to owners and other members of the power structure in the golden triangle. Labeling is a central concept in the symbolic interactionist perspective. *Symbolic interactionists* focus on how behavior is perceived and *labeled* as acceptable or deviant in particular social and cultural contexts and types of social interaction. From a symbolic interactionist *labeling theory* perspective, the key to understanding the nature and dynamics of social deviance is not the rule breaking itself but how people react to particular behavior and label it as rule breaking or deviance. These are matters with fuzzy boundaries that are negotiated in social interaction.

Labeling theory assumes that social deviance is socially constructed by people or organizations that label certain behavior or people as deviant because they are perceived as wrong, immoral, or breaking the rules. The social construction or labeling of deviance involves a process of identifying, defining, and responding to behavior as social deviance. The deviant labeling process is often affected by the status and power of the labelers over those who are labeled. For example, coaches have the status and power to make labels such as "troublemaker," "disruptive influence," or "disappointment" stick for athletes who play for them, but unless players are stars, it is difficult for them to make a label such as "incompetent," "unfair," or "abusive" stick for their coach.

When players are labeled as failures because they are cut or waived from a team, or if they are labeled as drug users by their league or domestic abusers by the media, the labels may *stigmatize* them or ruin their reputation. These labels also may change players' career opportunities and change their relationships with teammates, other players, the media, and other members of the golden triangle. Initial labels may "stick," too, after suspensions are served, jail terms are completed, and even after the athlete, coach, referee, or other alleged deviant is cleared of charges. We have seen that the mass media and golden triangle in general are powerful influences in labeling sports figures as deviants as well as heroes. Deviant labels can produce a "self-fulfilling prophecy" in which people believe the labels of them and change their behavior accordingly. For example, athletes falsely but repeatedly accused of taking PEDs may begin to think of themselves as deviants. Thinking they have nothing to lose, they may begin to do the things they were accused of doing, thereby becoming their label. Thus, labels are not merely descriptions of perceived behavior. They have the power to transform behavior.

Social Deviance and Contemporary Social Problems of Sport

Social deviance in sport can become a social problem when individuals or organizations engage in extensive or significantly disruptive rule breaking or unethical behavior. It is often easier to think of individuals rather than organizations as the "culprits" in cases of social deviance. *Organizational deviance* can be more difficult to see and understand than deviance by individuals because organizations often have more resources to rationalize, distract attention from, or cover up their deviant actions and because we may not be inclined to look for the sources of deviance and social problems in organizations and authority figures that are supposed to represent and uphold the normative order. We will begin our discussion of social deviance and contemporary social problems in sport with a general discussion of the social problem of organized and organizational corruption. Since structural functionalists tend to think of established organizations as playing a key role in maintaining the social order, social conflict, critical, and labeling perspectives may often provide better insights about social deviance at the organizational level in sports.

Organized and Organizational Corruption in Sport

Certain types of deviance, such as holding in football, pushing under the basket in basketball, flopping or diving to the ground in soccer to fake an injury or produce a foul call, and throwing at a batter as a form of retaliation in baseball, may be so common that they are considered by players to be "part of the game." Players learn these tactics when they learn to play the sport or to play in a particular context of the sport. The deviance they learn is *organized or institutionalized* because it is so widely expected. This is despite the fact that they are technically violations of the formal rules and can result in penalties or fouls.

Like individuals, organizations may stray from the formal norms and engage in rule violations on a regular basis. This is quite different from the organized deviance of individuals in a sport, because organizations are supposed to enforce the norms to ensure order and integrity in the sport. When the pursuit of individual or organizational success occurs in the context of the New American Dream, we can understand the drift toward deviance. When deviance by individuals or organizations gets out of control and turns into *organized or institutionalized wilding*, serious social problems can result. Organizations are supposed to control deviance. But when the organizations themselves are engaged in deviance, control itself is problematic. Organizational leaders are likely to try to manipulate public perceptions of their own or their organization's deviance to cover up or distract from the deviance in their sport. This is a dominant theme in the cases of the organizational deviance we will examine here.

Executives or high-level officials may engage in *white-collar crimes* such as embezzlement or fraud to make themselves richer (Friedrichs 2010). When these people pursue crimes or other types of deviance on behalf of their organization to improve or protect its competitive success, bottom line, power, or the status of its brand, they are engaging in *organizational or corporate deviance* (see Simon 2012). Organizational deviance generally involves some kind of *corruption* because it calls into question the integrity or reputation of the organization. The kinds of organizational deviance and corruption we will consider involve serious disregard for the rules of sport and the organization's own mission, policies, rules, or reputation. The cases involve doping in the Tour de France, match-fixing in soccer, a cover-up of a crime in college athletics, and the bounty culture in the NFL. What distinguishes these cases from the personal and collective deviance we will also consider is the embedding of the deviance in a social network or organization and the role of organizational officials in initiating or sustaining the deviance.

Doping and the Tour de France

According to Sokolove (2007), after the fall of the Berlin Wall and Communist East Germany at the end of the 1980s, government sponsorship of doping for nationalistic purposes gave way to doping practices increasingly driven by commercial influences and organized on the BALCO model of a loose network of athletes and coaches. BALCO refers to the Bay Area Laboratory Co-Operative, and it was at the center of a series of doping scandals involving US athletes. Among its prominent clients were US Olympian Marion Jones and San Francisco Giants star Barry Bonds, who publicly claimed only to have gotten "nutritional supplements" from BALCO. However, the US Anti-Doping Agency identified BALCO as the source of the banned steroid THG. More recently, MLB moved from the BALCO era to the Biogenesis era. Masking itself as an anti-aging clinic in Florida, Biogenesis supplied Alex Rodriguez with illegal drugs (Busfield 2014).

Although drug testing has become common throughout sports, the use of illegal PEDs continues. A small interview study of fifteen male and female European track and field athletes suggests some interesting insights into the use of PEDs. Thirteen of the fifteen admitted to PED use, while the other two said they were not users but had been offered banned substances. There were two main themes in their responses (Pappa and Kennedy 2013). First, the athletes viewed doping as a common aspect of highly competitive sports and often observed that their use of PEDs was abetted by members of the coaching staff. Second, despite the role of coaches, the athletes generally said they were responsible for deciding to use illegal drugs to help their performance. Thus, the drug use occurred in a social network, but athletes saw their use largely as a matter of individual choice.

The explanation for this apparent paradox is tied to the complex role of the golden triangle in influencing athletic performance and athletes' self-perceptions. On the one hand, the golden triangle makes winning in sport very rewarding, partly because success is so competitive. For this reason, athletes may believe they need to find ways, including cheating, to enhance their chances of success. The golden triangle benefits from athletes doing whatever they can to succeed, even though officials will not acknowledge that they contribute to the willingness to use illegal means of enhancing performance. On the other hand, athletes are exposed to a sports culture promoted by the golden triangle that emphasizes individual responsibility for success and failure. In the United States, this is a combination of the American Dream and the Sport Ethic. Thus, despite providing incentives to break rules to win, the golden triangle disavows any responsibility when athletes actually break the rules to try to win. Being well socialized by the culture of sport, athletes may often accept responsibility for their willingness to break the rules. Of course, this is what athletes say in a confidential research interview. It is evident from the persistent denials of highly prominent athletes such as Lance Armstrong, Barry Bonds, and Alex Rodriguez that athletes may not be willing to admit publicly to their deviance even though they do not blame their sport.

In bicycle racing, it has become difficult to believe that successful riders are "clean," since suspicions and denials of doping are so common. Wieting (2000) found evidence of cheating at various times in the history of the Tour de France, but the apparent difference now is that doping is institutionalized as part of the social and cultural fabric of the sport. It seemed to reach its nadir in the Tour de France during the Lance Armstrong era from the 1990s to the first decade of the twenty-first century. We have already considered Armstrong's deviant behavior and its consequences for him individually. However, the focus here is on the organizational context that seemed to breed, support, and sustain widespread patterns of doping in his sport.

Doping increased and became more entrenched in bicycle racing as teams became bigger, better organized, and better financed and developed more technically sophisticated means of enhancing performance. Similarly, as the sport grew in popularity, sponsors extracted more prestige from being associated with the winners and invested more in them and their teams. With so much at stake in such a physically and mentally taxing sport, the informal but influential "rules of the game" about winning increasingly condoned illegal or ethically questionable performance-enhancing measures, such as doping. Thus, despite the risk of adverse publicity for riders, their teams, and their sport when they got caught for doping, teams and the culture of the sport increasingly transgressed normative and ethical boundaries in order to win. For example, riders were provided with PEDs and injections of oxygenated blood before races, called blood doping, to give them an edge in their grueling sport.

Brewer (2002) saw the relationship between commercialization and the rise of doping as one of "unintended consequences." Rather than viewing doping as an inevitable and direct consequence of increasing commercialization, he thought that the rationale for increased doping was largely the performance pressures on riders who compete in an extremely demanding sport. Since there is more at stake in a more commercialized sport, commercialization can intensify the already-existing pressures to improve performance and to win that come from influences such as the Sport Ethic. A culture in which sports heroes are expected to do everything they can to win, find an edge, take risks, make sacrifices of their bodies, and even play hurt encourages the risky behavior of doping (Lipsyte 2005). Doping is what happens when deviant overconformity crosses over into deviant underconformity. It becomes institutionalized when team officials push for overconformity and routinely but covertly facilitate underconformity when overconformity is not enough. It may be a matter of "pluralistic ignorance" (Katz and Allport 1931) at first where teams cheat because they think everyone else is, but then it becomes a matter where many teams actually are cheating. When such cheating occurs in social networks involving teams and becomes systemic or part of the fabric of a sport, it is a serious social problem of corruption in the sport.

Teams and leagues that covertly play a role in facilitating deviance in their sport obviously do not want their role or the deviance itself to become a public matter. Reputations, media coverage, and endorsements are at stake. Thus, organizations aware of the deviance may try to control the labeling process. This is especially likely when team or league officials are actively involved in the deviance in some way. However, when word leaks out, sports officials who previously looked the other way may feel compelled to impose harsh penalties to protect their own and their sport's reputation. Damage control becomes more difficult when prominent stars and the officials themselves are indirectly or directly implicated. Repercussions of public revelations of corruption go beyond embarrassment and may ultimately lead in the worst case to the disbanding of teams or organizations. This is what happened in 2007 to the Discovery Channel team in the Tour de France.

Probe 5.4: Doping Revelations Scare Away Sponsors and Investors in the Golden Triangle

The Discovery Channel team had arguably been the most successful team in the Tour de France during the previous decade with eight winners in the previous nine races, but in 2007 its sponsors decided to stop supporting the team. Team officials made this decision despite the team's success and despite a "clean" doping report card. Some team members, including Lance Armstrong, had been accused of doping, but none had ever failed a test for banned substances. The owners of the team nevertheless decided to disband after winning the 2007 Tour. This is because the Discovery Channel had decided to end its involvement in cycling and because the sport's persisting drug scandals had made it difficult to find new sponsors. The team's general manager commented, "It's just not an environment conducive to a big investment" (Kennedy, Bechtel, and Cannella 2007). Thus, business interests were drawn to the golden triangle of this sport with the aim of enhancing their corporate brand by being linked with big winners in the sport. The sports investment lost its appeal when the sponsor's reputation was tainted by major scandals in the sport and by accusations specifically involving the team it sponsored. Sponsors can jump to another star in a sport when the deviance of a star is seen as unusual. But when the sport itself or teams in the sport seem to be infused with corruption, the only alternative to save the sponsor's reputation is to drop the entire team or withdraw entirely from the sport.

When athletes or coaches are caught cheating, the deviance can be dismissed as a case of wayward individuals. This is especially true when these individuals are not stars. However, when deviance ripples through an entire sport, is perceived as endemic or systemic, and involves people in prominent positions of authority, the entire sport may be tainted by a reputation for corruption. This is organizational deviance when teams, leagues, or governing bodies are involved. The irony in the Discovery Channel case is that the team died when it was at its peak of success and before its biggest star admitted his wrongdoing. It appears that the perceived pervasiveness of organized deviance creates suspicions that are sufficient to taint the reputation of sports organizations or an entire sport before actual proof surfaces. Images and reputations are what make sports popular and good investments in the golden triangle, and they are what can bring sports down for organizations as well as individuals.

Match-Fixing and Soccer

Similar elements of organized or institutionalized and organizational deviance can be found in the case of match-fixing in soccer. Match-fixing is not unique to soccer. *Fixing* is a form of bribery or extortion and refers to the manipulation of the outcome of sports contests for money from gamblers or those representing gambling interests, such as organized crime syndicates. Evidence of actual fixing scandals indicates that the sports establishment's concerns about adverse effects of gamblers and gambling interests on sport may be warranted. Fixing cases have characterized a number of sports, ranging from the notorious "Black Sox Scandal" in the 1919 World Series that involved eight members of the Chicago White Sox, including the great "Shoeless Joe" Jackson, who were banned from the league to "bagged" horse races, dubious knockouts in boxing, fixed outcomes of jai alai and cricket matches, point shaving in college basketball, and gambling-related missed calls by referees in the NBA (Munson 2008; Nixon and Frey 1996:115).

With the substantial salaries, prize money, and pensions earned by professional athletes in many major sports today, we would not expect athletes in these sports to be tempted by fixers. However, evidence (David 2006) revealed that just before the 2006 World Cup, teams were pressuring referees to fix matches in the top two Italian soccer leagues. In this scandal, four teams were penalized, with three teams, including the renowned Juventus, demoted to the second division. Thus, prominent and lucrative professional sports remain vulnerable to fixing, even when gamblers are not directly implicated. Prompted by this case, Italian prosecutors were investigating separate cases involving possible sports fraud, illegal betting, and false bookkeeping.

These prosecutions did not deter others from engaging in match-fixing. A *New York Times* investigative team found that a syndicate based in Singapore had fixed matches prior to the 2010 World Cup in South Africa and continued to raise concerns as the World Cup was set to begin in Brazil in June 2014 (Hill and Longman 2014). The syndicate used referees it had "bought" to fix exhibition matches among top-level teams to serve betting interests. FIFA, the global governing body of soccer, was apparently aware of this illegal behavior prior to the 2010 World Cup and had not been aggressive or effective enough in its policing to control this influence by the 2014 World Cup. The European Union's intelligence unit found 680 suspicious matches at the global level between 2008 and 2011. They included World Cup qualifiers and games in some of Europe's most prominent leagues and tournaments (Hill and Longman 2014).

The reach of match-fixing syndicates has been truly global, stretching from Europe and Africa to Asia (e.g., Amani 2013; Borden 2013; Forrest 2012; Hill and Longman 2014; Hughes and Pfanner 2009; Povoledo 2012). According to the *New York Times* report, Asia was especially fertile territory for the operation of these syndicates because underground or illegal gambling markets were largely unregulated there and these markets generated hundreds of billions of gambling dollars each year. Fixers were able to take advantage of financially stressed, lax, incompetent, or unscrupulous administration and vulnerable referees and players. They used incentives and threats to get referees to eject players and award penalty kicks, players to miss or allow shots, and teams to instruct their players to lose. FIFA officials realized the damage that revelations of match-fixing could do to the reputation of its sport, but it was understaffed for investigating and curtailing the influence of organized global gambling and fixing networks on its own. It needed the cooperation of its national federations, some of which were infused with corruption (Hill and Longman 2014).

Hill (2010) investigated why match-fixing occurs more in some leagues than in others and why some leagues collapse as a result of extensive match-fixing while others with equivalent levels of corruption are able to survive without losing support from the public or sponsors. He used newspaper articles, interviews, and court and police files to create a fixed-match database with over three hundred fixed matches in sixty different countries and fifty-five league or cup games. He concentrated his data collection in Asia and especially Malaysia and Singapore because this region and these countries were notorious for their long history of match-fixing. Leagues became "highly corrupt" when their normal operations were infused with bribery, illegal gambling, and match-fixing.

In general, Hill found that leagues with the most extensive match-fixing were characterized by poorly paid or exploited players, by perceptions among players that league and team officials were corrupt and involved in gambling and fixing themselves, and by large networks of illegal gambling. Hill noted, "In effect, players are paid badly to do their jobs well, but there is an alternative (illegal gambling and fixing) market that is willing to pay them very well, to do their jobs badly" (2010:222). The level of match-fixing was not by itself sufficient to explain which leagues collapsed. The collapse of local leagues was caused by a combination of factors: regular and extensive patterns of match-fixing, growing public awareness of this corruption, and the televising of a new alternative sports entertainment product, European soccer matches. Hill concluded that this combination of factors contributed to a 50 percent decline in attendance and private sponsorships of the corrupt local leagues.

League officials who can successfully control the labeling process and cover up the corruption in their league may be able to protect it from collapse. Corrupt leagues also may benefit from political support, even when their corruption has been made public. They are likely to find allies and apologists in the golden triangle and among fans if no better alternative is available for their investment and support. When public officials threaten tough prosecution of corruption, members of the golden triangle may become defensive. For example, the president of the Italian football federation, which governs Italian soccer, reacted to the suggestion from the prime minister to suspend soccer in Italy for two or three years by agreeing that the corruption scandal was "a very ugly page in our soccer." However, he added that suspending play was not the solution to the problem, since it would "(mortify) all soccer, penalizing those who work honestly, which are the majority in our system, and losing thousands of jobs" (quoted in Povoledo 2012).

Another member of the Italian soccer golden triangle, the editor of the highly respected Italian sports daily *Gazzetta dello Sport*, essentially agreed with this statement. He warned that shutting down the league would cost the country significant financial and job losses, since soccer was "a vital center of the national economy that lives off its image and sponsors" (quoted in Povoledo 2012). This is a powerful defense of soccer and its golden triangle. Although it may be overstated, it clearly reflects how much revelations of institutionalized corruption can disrupt established relationships in a society among popular sports, the golden triangle, and other important and powerful sectors of a society.

FIFA has been relatively ineffective in controlling illegal gambling and match-fixing due to its limited resources and lack of international cooperation. However, it has also faced its own allegations of corruption in decisions to name host countries for its World Cup (Gibson 2014; Wahl 2011), and it is not alone among global governing bodies in sport in being investigated for corruption. The IOC is another such body, which has a history of bribes and payoffs taken by its members (Jennings 2011). It is difficult to discourage corruption in a sport among athletes, coaches, referees, and team officials when officials at the highest level are tainted themselves by evidence or allegations of corrupt behavior, as Hill's research has suggested. The descent of a sport into patterns of deviance and corruption beyond match-fixing and gambling and involving bribes and payoffs of officials is further exacerbated by links to organized crime.

Chris Eaton is a leading expert on corruption in sports. He has worked with state and federal law enforcement agencies in his home country of Australia and with INTERPOL and FIFA and has been director of sports integrity at the International Centre for Sport Security in Qatar. He has argued that corruption is now a global problem in sport as a result of its global economic expansion and ties to the global economy. The problem, Eaton has said, is that the governance of sport has not kept pace with the surge in marketing and promotion, where a lot of the talent is now. With ineffective administration and insufficient monitoring, sport has become a highly visible and tempting target for greedy, unethical, corrupt, and criminal elements.

Eaton used the term "traditional match-fixing" to refer to cooperation between "friendly" teams to avoid relegation to a lower division or between "unfriendly" teams to force relegation. He observed that traditional match-fixing and opportunistic gambling conspiracies involving a few players and a referee had reached a point where they were "absolutely over-shadowed by criminals—including organised crime—infiltrating sport to serially corrupt results for betting fraud purposes." An example is the Singapore global match-rigging syndicate. Eaton also suggested that corruption in sport was a "'gold rush'—with the law left behind" (quoted in Williams 2013). This means that the success of the golden triangle has invited corruption, especially if it is not equipped to govern and regulate itself effectively. When this is true, corruption gradually and insidiously penetrates the fabric of a sport and becomes institutionalized and organizational deviance or corruption.

Eaton warned that the growing ties between organized crime and corruption in sport will ultimately erode trust in sport, which could erode the structure of the golden triangle itself. So far, though, powerful global and national golden triangles of sport have managed to survive these threats, even while leagues and teams at local levels sometimes collapse from corruption and top-level teams are relegated to lower divisions. Eaton proposed that stopping or reversing the penetration of sport in the golden triangle by organized crime and corruption will require intergovernmental cooperation. But international cooperation among national sports federations has been elusive. Intergovernmental cooperation seems even more difficult to achieve in a world where governments have so much trouble cooperating on issues much bigger than sports corruption.

A Cover-Up at Penn State

Big-time college athletics is another sports setting that has survived a long history of corruption, which has been characterized as systemic or institutionalized by critics (see Benedict and Keteyian 2013: chs. 14, 15; Branch 2011; Nixon 2014: ch. 5; Yost 2010). College sports fans have become accustomed to reading about prominent universities getting caught by the National Collegiate Athletic Association (NCAA) for one or more violations of its rules, such as academic cheating, recruitment infractions, and illegal payments. These are often cases of organizational deviance because they involve implicit or explicit complicity of athletic or university employees thinking they are acting in the interests of the athletic program or the university. Of course, there are also many cases of athletes or coaches acting badly as individuals (e.g., Benedict and Keteyian 2013: ch. 22). However, the cases of organizational deviance seem especially troubling precisely because they are institutional and not just individual matters. There is hypocrisy, too, when the deviance involves athletics because universities typically use athletics to market themselves and like to laud the character and accomplishments of star athletes and coaches.

Arguably the most egregious form of organizational deviance in the modern history of college sports occurred at Penn State (Nixon 2014:105–113). In November 2011, retired Penn State assistant football coach Jerry Sandusky was arrested for multiple counts of child sexual abuse. Although this case involved the deviant behavior of an individual, it became a case of organizational deviance when legendary coach Joe Paterno and Penn State officials conspired to cover up Sandusky's behavior. The details of the case are in a lengthy report prepared by an independent investigative team led by former FBI director Louis Freeh (2012). Sandusky's crimes caused widespread public revulsion and led to a conviction and virtual life sentence. However, it seems that the plight of the victims of his abuse received less media attention than the actions or inaction of Penn State officials, just as his abuse seemed less important to these officials than protecting the image of the football program and the university.

Coach Paterno escaped prosecution because he died a short time after the arrest of his former assistant coach. However, his perceived role in the cover-up had already cost him his job and tarnished his legacy. As part of its punishment, the NCAA vacated 111 of Paterno's record-setting number of victories during the period of Sandusky's abuse covered by the Freeh Report. The NCAA also imposed a $60 million fine and a number of other penalties on Penn State. The Penn State president Graham Spanier, senior vice president Gary Schultz, and athletic director Tim Curley were fired or resigned and also faced criminal charges of Grand Jury perjury, conspiracy, obstruction of justice, child endangerment, and failure to report suspected child abuse, a violation of federal law. The president got no support from the Penn State board of trustees because he failed to inform them of allegations against Sandusky.

The Freeh Report pointed to a "culture of reverence" as an underlying cause of the organizational deviance at Penn State. It is the virtual deification of a successful coach and his program by faithful fans, proud alumni, and a grateful local community. The media and sponsors of the golden triangle elevated the status of the coach and program and made support for Paterno and Penn State football a kind of secular religion similar to what was discussed in the last chapter. State College, Pennsylvania was "Happy Valley" and Paterno could do no wrong. When Paterno's teams faltered toward the end of his career, he had amassed enough social and political capital to ward off efforts by the president and athletic director to persuade him to retire. They understood his status among the Penn State faithful and also could not ignore the money, media attention, prestige, and public support he had brought to the university.

Probe 5.5: Big-Time College Sports Teams and Star Coaches Can Be a Mixed Blessing

Achieving institutional prominence through football obviously had its benefits for Penn State. However, ironically, tying a big part of Penn State's institutional brand to Joe Paterno and his successful football team was also why university officials failed to act responsibly when the Sandusky case came to their attention. The prospect of having their brand tarnished by reporting an ugly case of serial child sexual abuse by a long-time and respected former assistant under Paterno led to a fundamental dereliction of their duties. In the end, though, media exposure of the resulting cover-up led to far worse publicity and legal and financial consequences for the university than reporting the deviance would have caused. Thus, big-time teams and star coaches can be a mixed blessing for universities.

Organizational deviance in which the seriousness of a crime is exacerbated by an organizational cover-up has happened in other institutional settings in relatively recent US history. The Watergate break-in that cost Richard Nixon his presidency and the Catholic Church's own sex-abuse scandal are prominent examples. In these kinds of situations, people in power seem to get so caught up in preserving the power, reputation, and financial viability of their institutions or organizations as well as their own status that the law, ethics, rationality, and their responsibilities as leaders are forgotten or disregarded.

In my analysis of the corrupting influence of commercialization in college sports, I have used the idea of the "athletic trap" to help explain why presidents, trustees, and other university officials sometimes get caught up in athletics-related organizational deviance on their campus (Nixon 2014). The trap is defined as a complex array of social, economic, and political commitments that severely constrains athletic decisions by university leaders. It manifests itself in the apparent paralysis of presidents in the face of tough decisions about athletics. They seem either unwilling or unable to rein in their athletic director or their big-time programs or coaches. Having used athletics to market the university and build the support of alumni and boosters, they are not inclined to risk this exposure or support by punishing the most commercialized sports, even when they seem to be guilty of serious transgressions. Being in the golden triangle strengthens the grip of the trap, since presidents are also wary of losing the rewards it offers or promises. The problem with this uncritical and unrestrained support for athletics becomes obvious at the times of crisis when presidential leadership is most needed. Thus, the athletic trap makes presidents and their institutions vulnerable to organizational deviance, such as the cover-up at Penn State.

A footnote to the Penn State story is that Penn State was able to weather the storm of controversy. It took some serious hits to its reputation as a university and in football. However, it chose new leaders and a new football coach, and its most faithful supporters remained faithful. As an established big-time program, football had enough resources to continue to recruit top athletes and win a lot of games. In the 2013 season, Penn State was ranked fifth nationally in home attendance, averaging over 96,000 per game (Nelson 2013). As it often happens, institutions may be hurt by revelations of organizational corruption and incompetent or immoral leadership, but they survive, while their leaders are brought down by the corruption they could not or did not try to prevent. When popular sports and sports organizations are well entrenched in the golden triangle, their survival chances are enhanced. This was true for bicycle racing in Europe and soccer as well as for Penn State football, despite serious or persisting patterns of organizational deviance.

A Bounty Culture in the NFL

The culture of reverence at Penn State distorted the values and sense of morality of institutional leaders. Values and morality were also distorted in the last case of organizational deviance we will examine in this chapter. It concerns the bounty program of the NFL New Orleans Saints. It illustrates how normative behavior descends into deviance in a cultural setting where aggression and violence are valued. In March 2012, the NFL announced it had proof of an *illegal bounty program* set up by the New Orleans Saints defensive coordinator Greg Williams (Battista 2012; Holder 2013; King 2012; NFL 2012). Williams had just moved from New Orleans to a similar position with the St. Louis Rams. The program paid players for injuring opponents. The amount of the payoff was correlated with the amount of damage. "Knockout" hits that put players out of the game were worth $1,500, "cart-off" hits were worth $1,000, and payoffs doubled or tripled during the playoffs. A number of star quarterbacks were major targets, and Kurt Warner and Brett Favre were among those suffering knockout hits.

The bounty system helps us make a distinction between aggression and violence in sport. *Physical aggression* can be seen as physical contact and collisions within the rules of a sport. Aggression escalates into *violence* when contact is outside the rules and is intended to harm the opponent (see Nixon and Frey 1996:106–108). Aggression sports such as football can be brutal and lead to serious injuries, but the bounty system paid players to engage in violence.

Already sensitive to negative publicity about the escalation of violence, high injury rates, and the effects of concussions, the commissioner of the NFL responded quickly and imposed strong penalties on Williams and the other major wrongdoers. The commissioner had previously handed out stiff penalties in other cases threatening the image of the sport. For example, star players Alex Karras and Paul Hornung were suspended for the 1963 season for gambling on NFL games and for contacts with "undesirable" persons, and the New England Patriots and coach Bill Belichick were fined a total of $750,000 and lost a first-round draft selection as a result of the "spygate" scandal in which they illegally videotaped an opponent's defensive signals from the sideline during the 2007 season. Belichick's $500,000 fine was the maximum imposed by the league at the time, but he avoided a suspension.

New Orleans head coach Sean Payton was not so fortunate in the bounty case. Although he apparently was not involved in the administration of the program, the fact that he knew about it and did nothing to stop it led to his punishment. General Manager Mickey Loomis was suspended for half of the upcoming season because he failed to follow through on the team owner's orders to end the program once he had learned about it. Assistant Head Coach Joe Vitt's failure to inform Payton or Loomis about the program after he became aware of it cost him a six-game suspension without pay. Greg Williams was suspended indefinitely and was reinstated a year later. His journey had taken him from New Orleans and St. Louis to Tennessee, where he became senior assistant defensive coach for the Titans. The four suspended players had their suspensions vacated near the end of the 2012 season. An unusual twist in this case of organizational deviance is that the bosses received harsher penalties than the players. The greater power of the bosses often protects them from the harshest penalties.

The NFL wanted to sanitize its image in this case and demonstrate its commitment to two of its main principles: player safety and competitive integrity (NFL 2012). It was also upset with noncontract bonuses for interceptions and fumble recoveries, but the payments for hurting opposing players understandably received the most media and league attention. "Big hits" on opponents were not new, though. They were already a well-established practice in the league. The NFL Players Association cited a 1996 incentive program paid for by a defensive lineman on the Green Bay Packers that was allowed by the league (USA Today 2012), and some retired players talked about big hits and physical intimidation as a routine part of the game after the story of the Saints' program surfaced (Layden 2012). In addition, two of the teams for which Williams had previously coached reportedly had similar types of incentive programs (King 2012).

Probe 5.6: Attracting Corruption in the NFL and the Golden Triangle

One of the seamier aspects of this bounty program was the participation of well-known marketing agent and team consultant Mike Ornstein, who once had close ties to Sean Payton. He reportedly contributed bounty money on at least two occasions (NFL 2012). Ornstein had pleaded guilty in 2010 to federal fraud and money-laundering charges for scalping Super Bowl tickets and selling bogus jersey supposedly worn by NFL players. NFL officials talked about a "culture change" to control excessive violence in the league. In bringing about this kind of culture change, they also wanted to strengthen the league's reputation for rooting out corruption. The league's report of the bounty program expressed its concern about outside elements playing a role in organized corruption of this and other types. Alleged involvement by disreputable outside figures such as Mike Ornstein in the bounty program remind us that popular and lucrative enterprises in the golden triangle attract all kinds of unsavory and criminal elements from within as well as from the outside.

As sports corruption expert Chris Eaton suggested when talking about match-fixing in soccer, sports in the golden triangle depend on public trust, and weak governance opens the door to organized corruption that can undermine that trust (quoted in Williams 2013). NFL officials have seemed to be keenly aware of the need to protect the integrity of the league and its public image. The tough penalties meted out by the commissioner demonstrated the league's awareness and its capacity and willingness to act decisively and stringently. The bounty program may be a case where deviant overconformity turned into deviant underconformity when the league changed the rules. However, the NFL was not apologizing for changing the rules or trying the change the culture. It knew its reputation was at stake.

Collective Deviance: Fan Violence

The problem the NFL has in trying to control bounty programs and other types of hyperaggressive play in the league and bring about a culture change is that it can be difficult to know where to draw the line between legitimate and illegitimate aggression in a contact sport. Part of the problem is that the appeal of the sport may be tied to the hard hits. However, some sports and public safety officials have faced a bigger problem with aggression and violence beyond what happens on the field. On the one hand, they have had to prosecute cases of athletes and coaches who have gotten involved in violence in their personal lives. We have seen a repugnant example of this in the Sandusky sexual deviance case. The arrest statistics cited earlier in the chapter also indicated alleged and actual involvement of college and professional athletes in various types of violent crimes. Arrests, trials, and convictions of star athletes for rapes and murders have often made the front page of local, national, and international news publications. However, like some

English soccer fans back away from water cannons used by Belgian riot police after confrontation between German and English hooligans before EURO 2000 match between the two countries in Charleroi, Belgium in 2000. (Associated Press)

universities, leagues such as the NFL and MLB have seemed to take off-field deviance such as sexual assault and domestic violence a little less seriously than violence on the field (Webb 2012).

When deviant behavior involving individual sports figures on or off the field leads to a lot of media attention, the golden triangle tries to distance itself quickly from these kinds of sports figures and portray them as wayward exceptions. Even when arrests are on the decline, a seeming spate of high-profile arrests for violent crimes such as domestic abuse can make it difficult for a league to avoid public scrutiny and criticism (Irwin 2014). This is especially true when the league has a history of relatively light discipline for such wrongdoers (Pennington and Eder 2014). Negative publicity in these cases can make sponsors unhappy. The NFL, the Ravens, and the Vikings discovered this in the midst of the public relations debacle that was part of the fallout from their handling of the Ray Rice and Adrian Peterson cases (Armour 2014).

When violence is more organized and involves networks of athletes, coaches, referees, and others with authority, it is a little more difficult to dissociate these actions and people from the image and structure of a sport. When the people involved in the violence are not in the sport but are spectators or fans whose deviant behavior is not highly organized but is influenced by the sport, controlling the deviance is even more challenging for sports authorities. This kind of spectator or fan deviance is also a serious challenge for government and public safety officials when it develops into destructive mob-like violence.

Spectator and fan violence in soccer, called "soccer hooliganism," is the focus of this section.

Unlike players in contact sports, people who watch or follow these sports in their roles as spectators and fans are not permitted to engage in physical aggression. Sports-related spectator or fan aggression is almost always against the law and characterized as violence. Thus, *spectator and fan violence* involves any type of physical aggression related to a sports contest that is initiated by spectators or fans. It can occur in a variety of contexts, including the sports arena, a bar while watching a game, the street after a game, or at home as a reaction to the action or outcome of a game. Although the most serious cases of player violence on the field have led to condemnation inside and outside sport as well as civil lawsuits or criminal prosecution in the worst incidents, some types of spectator and fan violence have been viewed as a major social problem by authorities in society.

Passionate sports fans in a number of countries around the world have engaged in various types of violence, including riots, fighting, and assaults of referees, to express their dissatisfaction with the effort of their team, hostility toward opposing fans, or displeasure with decisions by referees (Young 2000:384, 390). In British soccer, this "hooliganism" has led to government investment in research to try to understand it and develop policy and security measures to try to control and curtail it. In recent years, fans of various sports have also engaged in *celebratory violence*, such as fighting, vandalism, and looting, following their team's *victory* in a big game.

British soccer hooliganism began before World War I and reached a peak in 1985 in Brussels, Belgium, prior to the final of the European Cup Championship between the British Liverpool club and the Italian Juventus club (BBC 2000; Haley and Johnston 1998). The match attracted approximately 60,000 spectators. A pack of belligerent British fans, many of whom had been drinking heavily, put pressure on a retaining wall of the aging Heysel Stadium, to get at opposing Italian fans, and this pressure caused the barrier to collapse. The collapse and ensuing panic crushed or trampled spectators, resulting in the deaths of thirty-nine people, most of whom were Italian, and injuries to hundreds of others. Following this tragedy, all British soccer clubs were banned from European Cup competition until 1991.

Despite its magnitude and the punishment it brought about, the Heysel tragedy was not the last occurrence of violence involving British soccer fans at home or abroad. In fact, there is evidence that a number of non-hooligan British fans who attended home and away matches had some practical reasons for supporting the behavior of hooligans. For example, they deflected the attention of violence-prone fans of other teams away from the non-hooligan and other nonviolent fans to the known hooligans supporting their team (Rookwood and Pearson 2012). Others of these nonviolent hooligan sympathizers, called "hoolifans," saw the hooliganism as justified under certain circumstances and appreciated the willingness of the hooligans to stand up aggressively for their team, even if the hoolifans were not willing to do so themselves. Although hooligans and hoolifans may still exist in British soccer, the police and soccer officials in Britain have substantially reduced this kind of violence among their fans (Mravic 2010). However, violence has occurred among fans from a number of other countries. In a few instances, British fans were involved as perpetrators or victims.

The venues and types of fan violence in soccer in recent years have varied. For example, Hughes (2012) reported several incidents that occurred during one month in the fall of 2012. They included an inebriated English fan who ran onto the field to hit the opposing goalkeeper in the face; Senegalese supporters who lit fires, stoned the players, and destroyed the seating because their team was losing in an African Cup of Nations game against the Ivory Coast; widespread fighting among fans before, during, and after a Ruhr derby soccer game in Germany, despite the presence of 1,200 police officers; the explosion of a firecracker near the faces of an injured Colombian player and the trainer who was treating him during a game in Cyprus; and Serbian hooligans who hurled racial abuse at black English players during an Under-21 match. Two years earlier, a Euro 2012 qualifier between Serbia and Italy in Italy was stopped after Serbian supporters threw flares onto the field and went over security fencing, causing injuries to sixteen people. It was not clear whether the rioters' motivation was related more to politics or soccer (Mravic 2010).

Probe 5.7: Politics and Soccer Passions Incite Soccer Riots in Egypt

In 2012 in Egypt, the soccer stadium again became a place for the mixing of politics and sport (BBC 2013; Tharoor 2012). Soccer riots at Port Said stadium killed seventy-four people and resulted in the suspension of league play. Fans of the local al-Masry team rushed the field shortly after the game and threw stones and firecrackers at the supporters of the visiting al-Ahly team from Cairo. The police were overwhelmed, the players ran for safety, and a number of those who died may have been trampled during the stampede precipitated by the violence. The notoriously fanatical supporters of the popular Cairo team were called "ultras," the same label applied to soccer fanatics in other countries (e.g., Duarte, Wilson, Walker, Bandini, and Doyle 2013; Hooper 2014; Scalia 2010). In Egypt, the al-Ahly ultras were implicated in the political protests against ousted president Hosni Mubarak in Tahrir Square in Cairo a year earlier. They were apparently targeted by al-Masry fans with opposing political views. A court sentenced twenty-one rioters to death, and all were supporters of the Port Said al-Masry club. The sentences led to even more violence, with eight more people killed, including two police officers. Strong opposing political views coupled with fervent support for competing teams in a sport that incites deep passions make the sports stadium a potentially dangerous place if security forces are perceived to be inadequate.

With the occurrence of soccer violence elsewhere, it is not surprising that organizers of the soccer World Cups in Brazil in 2014 and Russia in 2018 had concerns about the rising fan violence in their own countries (Gibson 2013). They also had to worry about the passions hooligan fans brought with them from other countries. In general, it appears that the combination of nationalism, team loyalty, right-wing extremist ideology, and alcohol often leads to violence among violence-prone hooligan fans. In Russia and Eastern Europe, there was the added element of ties linking right-wing fans to organized crime (Gibson 2013). The lethal combination of these factors was suggested as the source of racist fan behavior in Italy and Eastern Europe in the discussion of racism in soccer in Chapter 3.

Although North America has largely escaped the soccer hooliganism found in other parts of the world, it has not been without fan violence of its own in recent years. Major League Soccer (MLS) has had relatively few violent incidents involving fans, with some observers wondering if it was possible for the league to continue to escape the rampant hooliganism overseas (e.g., Parker 2013). The NFL and MLB were not as fortunate as MLS. A series of articles in the *Huffington Post* between 2012 and 2014 provided accounts of various types of fan violence in and around NFL and MLB stadiums (Huffington Post 2014). Fan violence has also occurred after National Hockey League (NHL) games in Canada (Assael 2011). Fan violence in North America has involved fights, brawls, stabbings, shootings, and the hurling of projectiles such as beer bottles at opposing fans. Sometimes the violence was precipitated by verbal taunts, other times simply by victims wearing a cap or jersey of the opposing team. Sometimes people were innocent victims in the wrong place at the wrong time, victimized by inebriated fans or ones frustrated with their team's loss (Huffington Post 2014). Whatever the cause, people were seriously injured or even killed in these incidents.

The challenge for the people responsible for preventing violent outbursts by fans is that fans also engage in celebratory violence, which means that violence could occur among "happy" as well as unhappy fans. Perhaps surprisingly, rioting after victories has been more common than rioting after losses in North American college and professional sports. Rivalry games, playoffs, and championships with close or unexpected outcomes have led to this kind of violence. Being a rabid fan and drinking excessive amounts of alcohol seem to be important factors affecting celebratory violence (Lanter 2011), and we can assume they influence "frustration violence," too. Both overreaction, such as the use of tear gas and other aggressive policing tactics, and underreaction, such as delayed, insufficient, or incompetent responses, may contribute to the escalation of fan violence (Assael 2011). When a past history of violence and alcohol, tension and aggression in the game, close or unexpected outcomes, and inadequate social control combine with violent propensities of fans, celebrations can escalate from revelry to rioting, and disappointment can turn into hostile and destructive outbursts.

Other Deviance-Related Social Problems in Sport: Hazing and Interpersonal Violence

We have focused in this chapter on types of organized and organizational deviance and corruption and collective deviance in sport that demonstrate how disruptive deviance can be when it becomes part of the culture or institutional structure. It may take a while for the deviance to be noticed or acknowledged and become recognized as a social problem. But when it is recognized and major figures in a sport are thought to be involved, it can be very damaging to the reputations of individuals, organizations, and the sport. This is especially true when authority figures are implicated in the deviance.

Hazing is an example of a social problem that is often institutionalized and may at least tacitly involve the cooperation or encouragement of sport authorities such as coaches. It is one of the two additional types of deviance-related social problems that we will consider in this last section of the chapter. The other problem is interpersonal violence or, specifically, sexual assault and relationship violence. We would not expect people in authority in sport or other institutions to condone this kind of behavior. But as we have seen in the case of Penn State, officials may fear tarnishing their institutional image by being associated with this kind of behavior and cover it up. They are not likely to admit that the culture that sport has spawned in their organization may contribute to the occurrence of this kind of behavior. We will see, however, that in both types of social problems considered in this section, the connection between sport and deviance is not necessarily unusual, random, or accidental.

Hazing has received a lot of publicity in recent years, but it is not a recent phenomenon. It is a form of initiation that has been a long-standing tradition in many types of groups and organizations (Trota and Johnson 2004). Hazing is important to mention here because it has often been viewed as relatively innocuous, if not humorous, and its damage has frequently been invisible or underestimated. But in the past decade it has become more apparent that it can involve intense experiences of alcohol use, degradation, humiliation, and physical and sexual abuse for new or probationary members at the hands of more established members of a group or organization (Wahl and Wertheim 2003). In some extreme cases, hazing has resulted in death.

Hazing is illegal in forty-four states, and it is difficult to estimate how pervasive it is. However, an insidehazing.com report cited in early 2014 estimated that more than 250,000 students experienced hazing when joining a college sports team, 40 percent said that the coach knew about it, and 22 percent said the coach was involved (cited in Mandelaro 2014). In addition, a 2009 study conducted by University of Maine researchers found that more than half of the 11,000 athletes involved in club, team, or some other organized sports they surveyed experienced hazing. The survey sampled fifty-three colleges and universities (cited in Mandelaro 2014). Ten years earlier, a survey by Alfred (NY) University found that 80 percent of NCAA athletes indicated that they had experienced some type of hazing in college, and 42 percent of the respondents said they also had experienced hazing in high school (Wahl and Wertheim 2003). Results from a 2005 NCAA survey provided a much more conservative estimate, indicating that less than 10 percent of student-athletes said they had been hazed as college athletes and about the same percentage said they had hazed their college teammates. The NCAA data also showed that over 50 percent of those involved in hazing said that alcohol was a factor and that alcohol was involved in relatively more of the women's than men's hazing cases (Hosick 2005). Estimates may have varied because hazing was defined in different ways, different questions were asked about hazing, and conditions for the administration of the questionnaires may have differed. In general, though, experts seem to agree that many hazing incidents are not reported because victims fear retaliation or isolation from teammates for revealing this behavior (Wahl and Wertheim 2003).

One of the common elements of hazing is the powerful group pressure to participate. There is a kind of "groupthink" in which powerful norms of group loyalty and cohesion create pressures to conform or go along with the group (Janis 1972). From the high school level to the professional level, strong expectations of displays of team loyalty and solidarity can discourage those being hazed from questioning dubious practices by teammates or coaches and encourage them to go along with the hazing. It is common for hazing in sports, especially at the high school and college levels, to involve secrecy to protect the hazing traditions of the team. This secrecy also protects the identities of aggressors whose actions may inflict pain and injury on initiates. Even when there are serious injuries, witnesses and victims usually honor the *code of silence.* Victims have apparently been too humiliated and fearful of their attackers to talk about what was done to them.

A notorious case of hazing involved a high school football team and the practice of sodomizing younger players during a preseason training camp. What happened afterward reveals a great deal about how deviance is perceived when a popular sport is involved (Wahl and Wertheim 2003). In this case, the status of coaches and the value of athletics in the school and in the community influenced how school authorities, members of the community, and students responded to hazing allegations. School officials and supporters of athletics in the school and community initially tried to minimize or bury the incident and rally behind the athletes accused of the attacks. It must be noted that the victims disclosed the hazing only when probed by their parents, who became aware of the serious injuries the hazing had inflicted on their children. When family friends of the victims called on the school board to fire the school principal and coaches, they received anonymous death threats. At a school board meeting following disclosure of the alleged incident, an estimated two-thirds of those in the audience, including parents, current and former athletes, graduates of the school, and faculty members, were there to support the coaches. Reporters trying to interview people in the community about the case generally received a very unfriendly reception.

Probe 5.8: Ignoring and Punishing the Victims in a Culture of Reverence

Perhaps most significant for the victims of the high school hazing was that when their identities became known to other students, they were made victims a second time, experiencing insults and derisive name calling from many of their classmates. Although the contexts and the specifics of the cases were very different, the effort to protect the reputations of the perpetrators of the deviance in this high school hazing case is not unlike what happened at Penn State University and what often happens when the reputations of popular sports, coaches, and athletes are threatened by allegations of deviance. In these cases, the real victims are ignored or even demeaned. The culture of reverence for sport can protect the deviants and deflect concern about the victims, and it can exist in high school athletics as well as at college and professional levels.

Hazing rituals in sport combine elements of team bonding, displays of power or dominance, and deeply entrenched patterns of aggression. A companion practice is *bullying*, and it has happened at all levels of sport. Bullying has been a concern in and out of sport in high schools, but it received considerable media attention when it involved members of the NFL Miami Dolphins in 2013. Richie Incognito's reputation for bullying teammates goes back to when he was a freshman at the University of Nebraska (Schrotenboer 2013b). He had a history of fights, suspensions, head-butts, taunting fans, spitting on opposing players, being dismissed from two college teams and his first NFL team, and an arrest for assault (Pelissero 2013). However, when Dolphin teammate

Jonathan Martin accused him of bullying, racism, and threatening e-mails, a number of teammates defended Incognito, and there was evidence that players throughout the NFL were divided in their opinions about the allegations (Mihoces 2013).

This kind of one-on-one hazing may be more common than the public and league officials realize because there seems to be the same code of silence about it in the locker room that characterizes other kinds of hazing. The problem in all these types of hazing in aggressive contact sports such as football is that players are supposed to be able to dish out and withstand taunts and aggression on the field and have the same kind of tolerance for it in the locker room. It can be difficult for players and coaches to determine the difference between what is acceptable aggression and violence and what is not.

There would seem to be little ambiguity about whether sexual assault and relationship violence such as domestic violence and date rape are socially acceptable or morally right. Much moral outrage has been expressed after cases of sexual violence involving prominent athletes have appeared in the media. We saw this in the case of Ray Rice, in which a video provided incontrovertible proof of his crime. However, the Penn State case showed how confused conceptions of right and wrong can become when reputations are at stake. When we looked at this case earlier in the chapter, our focus was more on the problem of the institutional cover-up than on the abuse itself. In this section, we will focus more directly on the problem of *sexual assault as a type of interpersonal violence*. Although sexual violence involves athletes and coaches at all levels of sport, we will consider here two cases of sexual violence in college settings. One involved alleged sexual violence that turned out to be much more complicated than first assumed. The other was a tragic case of *relationship violence* involving athletes.

Much has been written about the story known as "the Duke lacrosse sex scandal." In fact, one sports news source alone, ESPN.com, posted over seventy reports about this scandal between March 2006 and January 2007 (e.g., Price and Evans 2006; Wolverton 2006). The scandal turned out to be more complex than originally thought. The widely reported allegation of sexual assault by members of the Duke lacrosse team was actually untrue. However, the case is still worthy of attention here because it highlights important elements of college sports cultures that could lead to sexual assault or other types of interpersonal violence. Furthermore, it confounds popular stereotypes about athletes and interpersonal violence.

On the night of March 13, 2006, members of the second-ranked Duke lacrosse team attended a party at an off-campus house rented by team captains. Their entertainment involved alcohol and two African American exotic dancers who were hired from a local escort service to perform a striptease. One was a single mother of two who attended a local historically black college and earned money as a self-described "stripper." The other was an escort service worker who was wanted by the police for violating probation in a 2001 case involving embezzlement. The two women danced for a brief time and then abruptly left after one of the men made a vulgar sexual remark, another made a racial slur, and the women and men engaged in an argument. After leaving, one of the dancers alleged that she had been choked, sodomized, and raped. Acting in response to the public uproar about the initial media reports of the allegations and seeking to enhance his political prospects, the local district attorney zealously pursued prosecution. He charged three of the lacrosse players with forcible rape, a first-degree sexual offense, and kidnapping. Duke canceled the 2006 lacrosse season, the coach resigned, and a new coach was eventually hired. The district attorney was ultimately disbarred for his misguided and unethical actions when the facts became known and the players were exonerated (CNN 2007).

The Duke case was not the first involving allegations of gang rape against college athletes. But it drew national headlines and extensive coverage because, according to communications professor Robert Thompson of Syracuse University, it represented a "journalistic perfect storm" of the "national flash points of race, class, gender, (sexual) violence, money, and privilege" (quoted in Brady and Marklein 2006). The *sexual violence* charges raised the persisting concerns among feminist scholars, women's rights advocates, and critics of sport about close-knit men's sports teams, especially in contact sports, as breeding grounds for learning sexist ideas about gender relations and proving masculinity by dominating and using women.

The *racial* dimension of the case is that the strippers were black and the team was almost exclusively white. In addition, while 11 percent of the Duke University students were black, 44 percent of the residents of Durham, North Carolina, the town where it is located, were black. The additional fact that only one of the forty-seven lacrosse players was black suggests a racial divide between the town and the team and perhaps even the university. This might have encouraged the racist remarks known to have been made by players during and after the incident.

The elements of *class, money, and privilege* were reflected in the affluent backgrounds of the players, the much less advantaged status of the dancers they hired to entertain them, and the elite status of Duke University in a blue-collar town with a substantial minority population. Although there appeared to be some justification for questioning the validity of at least the rape charges against the athletes, it is evident that their privileged backgrounds and the substantial financial resources of their families made it easier for them to hire prestigious lawyers and to try to influence the media accounts of this event than it was for the accuser to manage her case in the public's eye.

The many media reports and analyses of this case presented a constantly evolving picture of a complex social problem that could be viewed from multiple, shifting, and sometimes contradictory perspectives. For example, Duke's prestigious national reputation was besmirched for a time by the allegations of rowdy behavior and rape, which raised broader questions about the nature of student culture at Duke and similar campuses. In addition, this case raised questions about the amount of money invested in athletics at Duke and the fragile relationship between athletics and academics and between athletes and the rest of the student body on this campus. Duke officials found themselves criticized both for acting precipitously before the facts were in to discipline the lacrosse players *and* for dragging their feet in responding to the situation.

The picture of privileged white athletes sexually exploiting and assaulting lower-status black women in the Duke case flips around the stereotype that rape is a crime of black athletes from lower-class backgrounds (Leonard 2007). But it also reinforces notions about the problematic implications of male bonding and hypermasculine socialization in certain men's team sports for all male athletes in these sports. At the same time, initial judgments of athletes "gone wild" were mitigated by facts that weakened the accuser's case and raised questions about preconceptions of guilt and innocence and about the meaning of justice for both accusers and accused.

One commentator (Johnson 2006) referred to a kind of *groupthink* that had occurred soon after news of the story became public, encouraging many faculty members and students to jump on a bandwagon of critics assailing the athletes for their alleged misdeeds before the facts of the case and guilt or innocence of the alleged attackers had been determined. This commentator also suggested that the allegations were consistent with the preconceptions of a number of critics of sports at Duke and elsewhere and that a type of *reverse prejudice* based on class and race and reflecting "political correctness" was at work early in this "non-rape" case, as he called it. The idea of a "rush to judgment" was reinforced when the North Carolina attorney general ultimately announced in April 2007 that all charges would be dropped (Lipka 2007).

In fact, initial opinions seemed to change when more became known about the case and when the rape charges were dropped. Sometimes overlooked by the media and other observers of this case was a pattern of crimes and misdemeanors involving Duke lacrosse players. For example, between 1996 and 2006, forty-one players were charged with misdemeanors in the local area, and in 2004–2005, fifteen of the forty-seven team members were charged with misdemeanor crimes that included disturbing the peace, public urination, and public drunkenness. Although they were less than 1 percent of Duke's undergraduates, lacrosse players were implicated in 33 percent of the arrests for open-container violations, with one-quarter involving disorderly conduct and almost a third involving alcohol-related unsafe behavior (Leonard 2007). Thus, their behavior was disproportionately deviant, which may have been why some critics quickly jumped to the erroneous conclusion that the accused players were guilty in the alleged sex scandal.

The complexity of this case should discourage premature conclusions about who is responsible for problematic behavior and whether the problem is what we think it is. It also shows how people in the golden triangle as well as people outside it, including critics of sport, use the mass media to try to construct their version of incidents of problematic behavior (see Leonard 2007). The Duke lacrosse "sex scandal" did not actually happen. Yet there were still troubling aspects of this case, with clear evidence of elitism, sexual exploitation of women, and racial tension and racism.

We see in this case what we saw in the Penn State case and in so many others involving deviance and sport. The resources of the golden triangle enable established sports programs to weather the storm of adverse publicity and rebound. Duke remained an elite university, and the lacrosse program became even more successful. Between 2007, the season after the scandal occurred, and 2014, it won three NCAA championships in men's lacrosse and was runner-up in another year. Thus, from competitive and marketing perspectives, cases of serious deviance or corruption may do less damage to institutional reputations and sports brands than institutional leaders fear, making both their cover-ups and their overreactions seem unnecessary or inappropriate.

It appears that sports programs are less successful in eradicating the sources of deviance-related social problems than they are at recovering athletically and commercially from the temporary stain to their brand that news of these problems causes. Certainly on college campuses and in college sports, wild parties with excessive drinking and risky and abusive behavior continue. Part of the challenge in controlling this behavior among college athletes is that rape and binge drinking are rampant on college campuses. A campus sexual assault study cited in a *Time* magazine cover story about the "rape crisis in higher education" in 2014 reported that 19 percent of under-graduate women in the United States were victims of sexual assault in college (Gray 2014:23). A major federally supported study of college drinking pub-lished in 2013 showed that 80 percent of college students drank alcohol and among them about half engaged in binge drinking, which generally means consuming five or more drinks in an evening (White and Hingson 2013). This study also found that in a year, over 690,000 students between the ages of 18 and 24 were assaulted by another student who had been drinking, and more than 97,000 students in this age group were victims of alcohol-related sexual assault or date rape.

The link between alcohol and interpersonal violence was tragically appar-ent in the killing of a University of Virginia women's lacrosse player by her ex-boyfriend, also a lacrosse player at Virginia (Wertheim 2010). Both teams were highly rated, and the men's team had won the NCAA championship in 2003 and 2006 and in the year following this tragedy, in 2011. By his own account, the aggressor had kicked in the locked bedroom door of the victim, who had recently ended their relationship, and shook her and repeatedly hit her head against a wall. He was nearly twice her weight, but perhaps more importantly, his actions occurred while he was in a drunken stupor. He had reportedly stalked his former girlfriend with threatening e-mails and texts after their breakup, before beating her to death.

Teammates of both athletes very likely were aware of their rocky relationship and perhaps even his stalking behavior, but may have been reluctant to say anything for fear of undermining the close relationships between members of both teams in the tight lacrosse community on campus (Wertheim 2010:31). Thus, the cohesion that coaches strive to achieve may have made the victim more vulnerable to the violence of a former intimate who could not handle rejection. His violence against her was a product of a history of violence, assaultive behavior, and, some said, a sense of entitlement as a lacrosse star from a rich family (Wertheim 2010:32).

The University of Virginia is one of many universities to experience cases of violence by athletes (Benedict and Keteyian 2013:chs. 5,22). As with hazing that turns into wilding, the interpersonal violence that occurs on these cam-puses reflects a potent combination of cultural encouragement of aggression on the athletic field with a lot of personal freedom, inadequate controls, and excessive amounts of alcohol that lower the inhibitions against using aggres-sion off the field. While not wanting to indict an entire sport, the cases at Duke and Virginia demonstrate how an athletic culture can tolerate, overlook, or even encourage highly intoxicated and aggressive expressions of emotion off the field that can produce damaging or deadly results. These two cases also suggest that serious deviance is not the exclusive province of minority or lower-class athletes and can happen at highly prestigious universities (Wert-heim 2010). Thus, the NFL arrest data reported earlier in the chapter, about black athletes and crime, do not tell the full story of athletes and social devi-ance. The deviant behavior of Lance Armstrong and Oscar Pistorius further illustrates the complexity of this story.

Conclusion

The golden triangle markets sports with ads and stories about the thrills and excitement of the games and the spectacular achievements of teams and individual stars. Those who run sports and represent the interests of coaches and athletes do not like these kinds of stories pushed aside by very different ones about acts of deviance and crime or corporate corruption. However, as in the rest of society, these latter stories are also part of the reality of sports in the golden triangle. In fact, there was enough crime in sport to fill twelve chapters of an edited volume, *Sport and Criminal Behavior*, a few years ago (Lee and Lee 2009). This chapter has examined major social problems related to a number of the types of criminal behavior covered in that book as well as some others reflecting serious and prevalent forms of deviance, crime, and corruption. Deviant behavior underlying these problems has made sports competitions unfair. Public exposure of deviance has tainted the brand identities of sports teams and programs, universities, leagues, sponsors, and even entire sports and their regulatory bodies. It has also stained the reputations of sports stars, changed the ways that some stars and their sports have been portrayed by the media, and caused sponsors to drop their support.

Yet major sports have been resilient in the face of adverse publicity. The most popular ones have typically been able to endure the negative publicity and bounce back, riding the support of loyal fans and the resources they have amassed from their past successes in the golden triangle. In addition, the celebrity status of high-profile athletes and coaches has been able to insulate many of them from negative publicity, and often from prosecution and conviction, when they have been accused of crimes.

The 732 arrests in the *USA Today* NFL arrest database in September 2014 would seem to convey a picture of substantial criminality in the league. However, in its defense, the NFL has pointed out that arrested is not the same as convicted (Schrotenboer 2013a). It has noted that its arrest rate is lower than the arrest rates for the general population and for adult males. In addition, an analysis of the arrest database in September 2013 showed that approximately one-third of the cases that were resolved in the legal system since 2000 resulted in acquittals or dismissed charges without penalty to the player. The remainder of these cases ended up in a conviction, plea deal, or a diversion program. Teams were much more likely than the league to punish players after arrests. My own analysis of the nearly 250 arrests in the database between January 2010 and September 2014 revealed that over 63 percent had no legal resolution. The league rarely fined or suspended arrested players. But approximately 8 percent of the arrests led to players being cut, released, or traded by their teams, and many of these decisions were made before their case was resolved.

Even though the crime rates among professional athletes in the NFL and other leagues and sports are lower than the rates in the general population, they are not necessarily lower than the crime rates in the more privileged sectors of society for a number of the crimes they commit. Athletes in the most commercialized professional sports can count themselves among the privileged during their playing careers. Officials are sensitive to accusations of widespread criminality in their sports because their financial status and success in the golden triangle depend on their public image. They recognize that actual patterns may be less important than the public perceptions that can influence the willingness of sponsors to invest in their sports.

Fans love sport and sports stars and are often willing to rationalize or forgive at least some of their failings. However, even the most passionate fans do not like their "sacred refuge" disturbed by too much reality, especially the ugly reality of serious corruption and deviance. Thus, sports are excused for corruption if well-publicized efforts are made to clean themselves up. Athletes and coaches are excused because loyal fans want to believe their claims of innocence—at least until the weight of evidence becomes too great to ignore. But even then, the most loyal fans may find ways to rationalize the deviance in terms of extenuating circumstances or as an aberration in an otherwise laudable life and career.

Although sports and sports stars may have some success in fending off negative publicity about deviance or corruption, the people who run sports in the golden triangle must project an image that they have control over their sports and are able to contain the "occasional" occurrences of wayward behavior. The public wants to believe in the integrity of their favorite sports because the impression of this integrity feeds the passion that keeps fans loyal. Fan loyalty is essential for a sport's success in the golden triangle because its media and corporate partners need audiences and markets to justify their sports investment. Thus, sports authorities often make public shows of their toughness in dealing with publicized problems and incidents of deviance and corruption. When they vacillate or seem slow to respond, they may find their job as well as the reputation of their league or sport at stake (Bell 2014; Rhoden 2014b).

League commissioners may be getting tougher in dealing with the criminal behavior of athletes outside the sports arena. Kim and Parlow (2009) examined league punishment of off-field criminal behavior of athletes. They noted that league officials recognize that bad publicity could translate into lost dollars and lost investment. When players get into trouble off the field, fans may buy fewer tickets and less merchandise and advertising revenue may decline as sponsors are scared away by the bad publicity. Kim and Parlow suggested that when the star power of popular players is dimmed by reports of their misbehavior, their commodity value to the league and the league's profitability may suffer. With the established sports media and social media paying more attention to the once-private behavior of sports figures, league officials are under pressure to respond firmly to reports of deviance to protect the league's image and profitability. When NFL commissioner Roger Goodell fumbled his handling of high-profile domestic abuse cases, he raised questions about his integrity and competence. On the other hand, new NBA commissioner Adam Silver in 2014 quickly established his reputation for toughness and decisiveness when he banned Clippers owner Donald Sterling for his racist remarks (Jenkins 2014).

From a structural-functional perspective, social control by league officials is essential for maintaining order for the good of the sport. From a conflict or critical perspective, social control is more about maintaining the appearance of order and integrity for the benefit of those who run and profit most from sport. Thus, in the latter regard, actions by league officials to discipline deviants focus more on damage control and keeping a sport popular and profitable through skillful public relations and marketing than on actually eliminating deviance and social problems or making athletes responsible for their misbehavior. This kind of social control as *image control* may impress the most loyal fans and serve the interests of the media and corporate sectors of the golden triangle. However, if it is not firm or convincing enough, it is likely to make knowledgeable but less passionate fans skeptical.

Despite the vested interest of the golden triangle to control deviance in the sports arena or at least to keep it out of the news, there are a number of factors that make it increasingly difficult to limit deviance at the individual and corporate levels of sport. For example, socio-demographic changes, such as the increasing social class, racial, and ethnic diversity of players and fans, have created divisions and tensions among fans, among players, and between fans and players that have sometimes erupted into violence. In addition, extremist political influences have intersected with sports passion, fanned the flames of racism or nationalism, and provoked fan violence. Among those in sport, the rewards of the golden triangle have been incentives to engage in various types of deviance to gain an individual or team advantage over opponents. They have also been an incentive for corporate deviance to cover up crimes in sport. With so much money bet on sports, they have attracted outside influences such as organized crime, which has resulted in illegal behaviors such as fixing outcomes of games. Finally, increasing access to new scientific applications and new technologies to enhance performance has pushed athletes, coaches, and teams to experiment more. In an increasing number of cases, it appears that this experimentation has gone beyond the boundaries of legitimate, acceptable, and fair competition.

Although the criminal justice system is supposed to be responsible for controlling the behavior of athletes in society and of spectators in and around the stadium, sports officials still must try to assure fans, consumers, and their partners in the golden triangle that their athletes, spectators, and sport are under control. This can be more challenging than enforcing the rules of their games. They need to figure out how to maintain at least the perception that they are in control and their players and fans are under control. They want to do this in a way that does not risk intervention from public authorities, since many sports have a delicate relationship to the laws of society about aggression and violence. They also would prefer to have primary responsibility for disciplining players when their sports-related *or* personal behavior is deviant. Being in charge of these matters enables sports to have more influence over the messages that get to the public about the meaning of these behaviors. Controlling the image is a big part of success in the golden triangle. In the next part of the book, about the social contexts of sport, we will see how commercialism and image-making play a role in sports from the levels of youth and high school programs to college, professional, and Olympic sports.

Stop and Think Questions

1. How does the aggressive behavior in many sports competitions help us see that conformity and deviance are matters of social context?

2. How are structural functionalists, social conflict or critical theorists, and labeling theorists likely to differ in their conceptions of social deviance and social control in sport?

3. Why is it difficult to arrive at general conclusions about the deviance or criminality of athletes in the golden triangle?

4. Why is organizational or corporate corruption so damaging to a sport, and which of the cases of organized and organizational corruption examined in this chapter has had the most damaging consequences?

5. Under what conditions are soccer hooliganism on the one hand and celebratory violence by fans on the other hand especially difficult for sports and law enforcement officials to control?

6. How did the Duke lacrosse "sex scandal" conflict with stereotypical ideas about race, social class, sexual violence, and athletes, and why were allegations of deviance somewhat justified despite the dropping of criminal charges in this case?

7. To what extent does the golden triangle complicate or facilitate sports officials' efforts to deal with criminal behavior by athletes?

Part IV

Social Contexts of Sport

6

Youth and High School Sports

The affluent suburban stay-at-home "soccer mom" has been part of the popular imagination in the United States since gaining currency in the media in the 1990s (Swanson 2009a, 2009b). She dutifully and selflessly spends hours carting her children to soccer and various other activities in her minivan or SUV. Like most stereotypes, this characterization is overgeneralized, but there is also some truth in it. Many real moms in both affluent and less advantaged families have encouraged and supported their kids' sports participation. However, the stereotype fails to capture the diversity of women's parental roles and the different ways they are involved in their children's sports. It also tells us little about how their kids experience sports.

This chapter is about how moms, dads, and other adults shape kids' experiences in sports. It is also about how the culture and organization of adult-run sports in the community and in high schools affect the young people who compete in them. "Socialization" is the term sociologists use to refer to this process of influence on participants and on their participation experiences in youth and high school sports. More generally, socialization involves social learning that affects how individuals form self-concepts, identities, and self-esteem. It also enables people to interpret how culture and the social structure relate to their roles and relationships. In these ways, socialization enables people to figure out how and where they fit in society. When we are well socialized, we know how we are supposed to act in our roles and relationships and how others are supposed to interact with us.

Just as socialization can give individuals a sense of order or predictability about their own lives, it also is a basis for social order in society. On a structural level, socialization contributes to social order by enabling people to develop relatively stable or reliable ideas about who they are, how they are supposed to relate to others in their various social networks, statuses, and roles, and how others are supposed to relate to them. In making society more predictable for individuals, socialization creates a basis for perceptions of order in society.

However, socialization can be complex because different social settings can have their own distinctive cultural influences, structural arrangements, and socialization processes. Thus, people may be exposed in different social settings to quite different ideas about who they are, how they should interact with others, and how they should play their roles. For example, learning to be part of a family is likely to be different in various important ways from learning to be part of a sports team, and learning to participate on a team in one sport may differ from learning to participate on a team in another sport.

Socialization is not only complex. It can also be messy. We can develop flawed self-concepts or be confused or annoyed by what others expect of us. But even when it is flawed, confusing, or annoying, we consciously or unconsciously rely on some sort of socialization to teach us about ourselves and the demands of society. Socialization in its various forms and settings continues throughout our lives.

Socialization and Sport

Although socialization is a lifelong process, this chapter will focus on socialization in youth sports, since youth is generally considered an especially formative period in our lives. I stretch the definition of "youth" here to include a focus on both childhood and adolescence, from elementary school ages through high school. Children and adolescents who participate in highly organized and competitive sports programs may have the common experience of being treated as "little adults." Much is expected of them as their parents and other adults invest a lot of time and money in their success. As a result, these young sports stars find that they have little time to enjoy being children or adolescents, as they spend much of their lives in serious training or competition. The rewards and stresses of competing in youth and high school sports programs in the golden triangle thrust these young people into the limelight, where winning and losing are much more consequential for them than they are for others in their age group who play sports less intensely or who do not play sports at all.

Sports participation can influence young people in all kinds of sports settings. However, participating in more competitive or elite sports programs is likely to leave deeper and more enduring impressions on young people. These impressions may not always be positive. This is at least partially because more elite youth sports programs are likely to be more influenced by the incentives, rewards, and stresses of the golden triangle. Looking around the globe, we see high-level training and competition in sports ranging from the major team sports of soccer, baseball, football, basketball, ice hockey, and rugby to the sports of tennis, golf, gymnastics, swimming, track and field, bicycling, skiing, and figure skating. That is, the influence of the golden triangles of popular professional and Olympic sports filters down to the level of children and adolescents. In some cases, we see children and teenagers competing on a world stage.

Consistent with the rest of the book, the primary focus of this chapter is on youth sports and interscholastic athletic programs that attract the interest of golden triangle media and sponsors and other businesses. The golden triangle is most interested in popular youth programs with commercial potential. Its media coverage tends to concentrate on the most talented young athletes at the most competitive levels of these popular sports.

The imprint of sport socialization on young people can be seen from two perspectives: socialization into sport and socialization through sport. Socialization *into* sport is the social learning process that teaches the rules, roles, skills, and relationships that are needed to participate in a sport. The intensity and seriousness of this socialization process can affect the proficiency and success of participants as well as the depth and seriousness of their sports commitment.

Socialization *through* sport involves the learning experiences that athletes take from sports participation into the rest of their lives. Whether or not sport is actually good preparation for life, extended and serious sports involvement is likely to leave an imprint beyond sport. We may see the imprint of socialization through sport in self-concepts, attitudes, aspirations, and social adjustment that athletes learned in sport. Socialization through sport is illustrated by sports programs that turn delinquent boys or girls into "good boys" or "good girls" who stay out of trouble and become model students and citizens. It also occurs when women rely on their competitive experiences in sport to prepare for competition and success in the corporate world. On the other hand, young athletes may have their aggressive impulses encouraged and reinforced in sport, but fail to learn how to restrain these impulses off the field. The result could be the abusive and violent criminal behavior that was discussed in the last chapter.

Participation Patterns

Sociologists have paid relatively little attention to the meaning of sports experiences for children and adolescents, especially before high school. This is part of an interesting paradox, since sport participation is at least a small part of the lives of large numbers of children and adolescents in countries such as the United States. Recognizing the paradox, Messner and Musto (2014) offered a number of possible reasons for the dearth of sport sociology research about kids. Among them are the greater convenience and perceived salience of studying college athletics and adult sports, problems of access to children as research subjects, a scarcity of research funding, the trivialization of youth sports as children's play, and a bias toward studying the sports that most interest them as adults, that is, the adult sports of the golden triangle.

Despite these reasons, it seems important here to pay attention to the participation of children and youth in sports, using the various sources of information we have in the news and sports media as well as in social science. Youth sports are important to examine because large numbers of kids are involved in them, because they involve so many adults, and because they are pursued seriously by many kids, often as a result of parental influences. The involvement of the golden triangle also implies that youth sports are a segment of the economy, which should elevate their perceived importance. Furthermore and perhaps most importantly from the perspective of young people, involvement in sports during the formative years of childhood and adolescence means that youth sports participation is likely to have some socializing influence on at least the more serious participants.

Socialization into sport can lead to socialization through sport when youth sports are pursued seriously over a number of years. In their survey of kids in sport for the Women's Sports Foundation, titled *Go Out and Play*, Sabo and Veliz (2008) found that 34 percent of girls and 61 percent of boys said that sports were "a big part" of who they were. Their research utilized a national random sample of nearly 2,200 third-through-twelfth-grade boys and girls in the United States. During high school, sport was still seen as an important component of the self-concept of 28 percent of the girls and 53 percent of the boys.

It is difficult to estimate exactly how many children and adolescents are involved in youth sports. However, one estimate based on Sports and Fitness

Industry Association (SFIA) surveys found that the number of children and adolescents in the United States between six and seventeen years of age who participated "regularly" or "frequently" in sports was approximately 21.5 million in 2011 (cited in Kelley and Carchia 2013). "Regularly" or "frequently" meant playing a sport such as ice hockey a minimum of thirteen times a year or a more accessible one such as soccer at least twenty-six times a year. Another estimate, which used data from the US Consumer Product Safety Commission's National Electronic Injury Surveillance System, indicated that over 46.5 million kids were involved in team sports in 2011 (Healy 2013). These data were based on a more liberal definition of participation than that of the SFIA survey. Sabo and Veliz (2008) found that 75 percent of boys and 69 percent of girls aged eight to seventeen reported that they had participated in organized sports the previous year. Their participation measure involved playing on at least one team or one club in a year. Sabo and Veliz also estimated that nearly 7.4 million high school students participated in interscholastic athletics during the 2006–2007 school year, representing 54 percent of all high school students.

Probe 6.1: Variations in Youth Sports Participation

Among those who did not participate in organized sports in the community or school in Sabo and Veliz's sample, 18 percent of girls and 13 percent of boys never participated and 13 percent of girls and 12 percent of boys had dropped out. Boys' participation was highest in the third to fifth grades (79 percent), dropped off somewhat in middle school (77 percent), and significantly declined again in high school (70 percent for ninth and tenth graders and 69 percent for juniors and seniors). Among girls, participation increased from the primary grades of three to five (70 percent) to middle school (72 percent), and then dropped off in high school (68 percent in grades nine and ten and 64 percent in grades eleven and twelve). About 27 percent of girls and 41 percent of boys were involved in three or more sports. Participation rates were higher in suburban than in urban and rural schools. This should not surprise us in view of our discussion in Chapter 3 of the financial struggles of schools in lower-income urban and rural areas (see Sabo and Veliz 2012). Sabo and Veliz concluded from their findings about youth sports participation patterns in *Go Out and Play* that girls who lived in urban areas and grew up in lower-income single-parent families were least likely to be involved in youth sports because they faced the greatest social obstacles to participation.

The *Go Out and Play* findings reinforce our previous conclusions about inequality, showing that access to sports is not equal across genders, social classes, communities, or families. This is also true for poor racial and ethnic minorities. The effects of inequality are initially seen in childhood but are likely to be repeated through adolescence. Being deprived of the chance to participate in sports in childhood can lead to a variety of lost opportunities. Children and adolescents who do not participate in sports lose the chance to gain a number of possible benefits that may result from youth sports participation. They include overall better health, positive body esteem, maintaining a healthy weight, popularity, more life satisfaction, and enhanced educational attainment (Sabo and Veliz 2008). These kinds of benefits first appear in elementary school and may continue on through high school.

While soccer moms are driving their kids to club and high school sports practices and games, less affluent moms and dads may be frustrated by the more limited sports opportunities available in their communities for their children, especially their daughters. They also are less able to afford the time and money required for participation in more elite youth sports programs in the community. Unless their children show unusual athletic ability or promise, they are unlikely to have the opportunities that are available to kids from more affluent families (Kelley and Carchia 2013; Sabo and Veliz 2008).

According to SFIA estimates or research by Sabo (cited in Kelley and Carchia 2013), 40 percent of adolescent boys play football and 40 percent play basketball, while 25 percent of adolescent girls play basketball and 23 percent play volleyball. Other popular sports among male teenagers in the United States are baseball (played by 24 percent), soccer (20 percent), and track (17 percent). Among teenage females, 17 percent play baseball or softball, 17 percent play soccer, 17 percent participate in track, and 12 percent swim. While these sports are generally offered by high schools, the most serious young athletes in these sports also tend to participate in elite club sports programs outside the school. The most talented or promising young athletes in certain sports such as tennis, gymnastics, swimming, and figure skating might attend academies in their sport or train with a private coach, which requires them to train and live away from home for extended periods of the year. This specialized training may begin at young ages for child athletic stars.

Along with the 7.4 million youths who participate in high school sports, there may be twice as many who participate regularly in sports outside the school (Kelley and Carchia 2013). Many of these nonschool sports programs are sponsored by or under the auspices of large youth sports organizations. For example, USA Hockey reported that 355,000 boys and girls participated in its youth programs in 2012, with 107,000 eight years old or younger. Numbers for Pop Warner, which is in forty-two states and a number of countries, were 250,000 football players and 180,000 participants in cheer and dance programs in 2010. The American Youth Soccer League indicated that in 2013, it had 50,000 teams and 600,000 players supported by 250,000 volunteers. Most are in the United States, but its programs are also in Moscow, Russia, the US Virgin Islands, and Trinidad and Tobago. Little League Baseball and Softball had 7,006 programs in seventy-nine countries in 2012. Little League reported 37,632 baseball teams with nearly 575,000 players as well as 9,041 softball teams with 135,765 players in 2013. Little League programs ranged from T-ball for the youngest participants to Junior Leagues for thirteen- and fourteen-year-olds. The US Tennis Association, US Kids Golf, USA Swimming, and USA Track also had programs for young players (figures cited by Messner and Musto 2014:106).

Although youth sports can be demanding, 41 percent of the boys and 27 percent of the girls who were involved in sports in Sabo and Veliz's study played three or more sports. This heavy involvement dropped off to 22 percent for boys and 14 percent for girls by high school, but these percentages still reflect the huge role of sports in the lives of large numbers of high school students. The involvement of kids in multiple sports makes it easy to see why the soccer mom is often seen as harried. However, involvement in multiple sports also raises questions about physical and emotional stresses on youth from trying to balance their assorted sports commitments with other after-school activities and school. These pressures are exacerbated by coaches in more elite sports programs who often expect extensive year-round commitment from their athletes. This conception of serious and demanding youth sports participation is at odds with idealizations of childhood and adolescence as times of exploration and fun without the commitments, responsibilities, and stresses of adulthood. The idea of the "little adult" again comes to mind.

We can think of several reasons why boys and girls get involved in sports, such as parental pressure, peer influence, media sports coverage, urging from teachers or coaches, curiosity, or genuine interest. The outcomes of their sports experiences and the kinds of lessons they learn from sport about such things as sportsmanship, fair play, and competition tend to reflect the influence of the attitudes and actions of their parents and other adults (Fullinwider 2006:7). These experiences are also likely to be significantly shaped by the contexts of cultural values and social organization of the sports they play. Children or teenagers who play the same sport, such as basketball, baseball, volleyball, or softball, can have very different sports and socialization experiences if the context of their involvement differs.

Cross-National Similarities and Differences in Youth Sports Participation

Research by Rees, Brettschneider, and Brandl-Bredenbeck (1998) is one of the rare cross-national studies of youth interest and involvement in sports and physical activities. Their study sampled suburban New York youths and German young people in Berlin. It suggested that globalization may create some similar sports interests and orientations for young people in different countries. However, it also showed that local and national cultural influences can lead to different kinds of sports interests and orientations among young people in different countries. We see from this study that the presence or absence of golden triangle influences in particular sports in different local, regional, or national settings is likely to affect how seriously young people view and play particular sports in these settings.

In this study, swimming, jogging, and basketball were named as popular sports or physical activities by the boys and girls in both New York and Berlin. However, bicycling was popular among the Germans but not the Americans. Only German girls mentioned dancing and gymnastics, only German boys mentioned table tennis, only American girls mentioned tennis and walking, and only American boys cited football and baseball among their top six choices. All except the German girls listed soccer.

The common interest in the "American" sport of basketball supports the Americanization theory. But there were also sports interests that were unique to each nationality. In the European golden triangle, bicycle racing is much more important than it is in the golden triangle of North America. This may explain why bicycling was very popular among German boys and girls but was not in the top six for either American girls or boys. The "European" sport of soccer was popular among American girls and boys and among German boys, but not among German girls, perhaps reflecting differences in organized sports opportunities for girls and boys in Germany. The American boys' top three choices of basketball, football, and baseball were distinctive in reflecting the kinds of sports promoted heavily by the golden triangle in their country.

Overall, it appears that the sports choices of the young people in the two cities in this survey were shaped by the global golden triangle of certain sports as well as by local or national factors affecting interests and opportunities. In addition, the imprint of the golden triangle could be inferred from male and female choices in both countries, although the boys in both countries seemed to be more influenced by popular golden triangle sports than the girls were. There was a significant cross-national difference in the role of schools in mediating sports choices. Nearly all students in US public schools were exposed to a heavy emphasis on organized and team sports, especially at the high school level. Whereas in Germany, students had relatively little experience with interscholastic sports, and physical education classes may have been their only exposure to organized physical activity.

There were significant gender effects that cut across cultures. Girls in Germany and in the United States rated the importance of fun higher than their male counterparts did, while the boys in these two countries rated the importance of competition higher than their female counterparts did. Competition was an especially important aspect of physical activity for the American boys. Regular practice was an important element of sport for both males and females in New York, but this part of sport was more important for males than females in Berlin. In general, it appears that while there are some overlapping conceptions of sport among teenagers in the United States and Germany, American boys may be most influenced by major sports in the golden triangle in their country and by the chance to play them in high school. For American boys, in particular, organized team sports in the school have been a primary source of identity and status for many years, and this kind of school-related socialization experience may be distinctive for American males in the global context.

Youth Sports outside the School and in the Golden Triangle

Although media coverage of youth sports is a tiny fraction of the coverage of their adult counterparts, we can still see much evidence of the involvement of the golden triangle in youth sports. For example, ESPN, *Sports Illustrated Kids*, and the adult version of the magazine cover a variety of popular youth sports events such as Little League and high school basketball and do an occasional story about a rising young sports star. Media attention contributes to the popularity of these sports. In addition, many major corporations invest in youth sports as partners or sponsors. A quick survey of the websites of youth sports organizations clearly shows these corporate connections.

We see that Pop Warner football includes athletic apparel and equipment manufacturers, a sports drink, a health and nutrition company, a retail health clinic, a motel chain, sporting goods retail chains, an insurance company, and the manufacturer of school yearbooks and class rings among its sponsors. The Amateur Athletic Union (AAU) offers over thirty youth sports programs and has a long list of Fortune 500 companies among its corporate partners. Its website states that its website network has over 100 million visitors each year and that its "youth sports marketplace" is a $1 billion per year industry. Similar networks and corporate relationships can be found in youth soccer, Little League Baseball, and the other popular youth sports programs. Furthermore, governing bodies of most sports in the golden triangle sponsor youth programs

Fan looks down on stadium in Williamsport, PA prior to start of 2000 Little League World Championship between US champ from Texas and international champ from Venezuela. (© Mike Segar/Reuters/Corbis)

to create a pipeline into their sports. The NFL-sponsored Punt, Pass, and Kick competitions illustrate the investment of professional sports leagues in creating their own pipelines. Nike's extensive network of sports camps shows the important place of children and adolescents in its business model. Its list of camps includes many different sports, such as tennis, golf, volleyball, basketball, soccer, field hockey, swimming, lacrosse, softball, running, baseball, football, rugby, water polo, gymnastics, and ultimate sports.

Nike and other major corporations are not involved in the more competitive youth sports for altruistic reasons. It is true that the sports media and corporate sponsors have directly supported community-based sports programs with civic purposes such as the Police Athletic League (PAL) and disability sports programs for young people and have also contributed to these kinds of programs through umbrella groups such as the National Alliance for Youth Sports. While the participants in these programs may derive a number of benefits from their participation, the media and corporations also benefit. This kind of support has great public relations value. It also has marketing value. The kids and parents involved in these and more competitive programs are an important market for the products manufactured, marketed, and sold by the corporate or business partners of youth sports organizations. In addition, big-time college, professional, and Olympic sports in the golden triangle need a steady stream of kids flowing into them, since they will one day become the next generation to fill their rosters. Youth sports, especially at more elite levels, serve this essential purpose for them.

More competitive or elite youth sports programs at the local level tend to be affiliated with larger and more organized or corporate sports organizations in the sport sector of the golden triangle. The biggest of these organizations are highly bureaucratic and complex, with numerous formal policies, rules, and regulations that are applied to various levels of competition. The central corporate body may provide resources as well as a regulatory framework for its sponsored programs, leagues, and competitions, and receives financial support from its members and outside corporate sponsors. Thus, for example, local soccer, basketball, football, baseball, tennis, or golf programs have ties to state, national, and sometimes international bodies that govern their sport. We have cited a number of the sports organizations that sponsor competitive youth sports programs. Junior Olympics is another example. It prepares promising young athletes with opportunities to develop their skills and move up the ranks in their sport on their way to the ultimate goal of Olympic participation.

Club sports involve locally organized teams or sports programs that often have the goal of providing high-level developmental and competitive opportunities for serious and talented young athletes. Clubs may be affiliated with state, regional, and national corporate sports organizations, including the national governing bodies of specific sports, such as swimming, figure skating, gymnastics, golf, basketball, and soccer. They are often subsidized by private sponsors, such as local businesses and wealthy individuals. Some clubs achieve elite status through their competitive success at progressively higher levels of competition. The larger corporate bodies with which clubs are affiliated may sponsor leagues, camps, competitions, and developmental and training programs for athletes and coaches. Nike's Elite Youth Basketball League (EYBL) has developed into one of the biggest and best-funded elite youth sports programs in the United States sponsored and run by a commercial enterprise (Wiedeman 2014).

Probe 6.2: The Golden Triangle and Chasing the American Sports Dream in Elite Youth Basketball

There may be no better example of the influence of the golden triangle on youth sports than elite youth basketball leagues in the United States. Elite youth basketball had been dominated for many years by the AAU, which is a nonprofit organization. However, in the 1980s, adidas and other athletic shoe manufacturers began to invest in youth basketball. They established all-star camps where aspiring basketball stars could display their talent and pursue their American Sports Dreams. Having concentrated on the professional level, Nike found itself behind its competitors in the youth market at the turn of the twenty-first century. In 2010, it made its big move into this market by spending millions of dollars on the creation of an elite league—the EYBL—modeled on the National Basketball Association (NBA). By 2014, this league was called "the sport's largest incubator of teenage talent" (Wiedeman 2014). The EYBL and other elite leagues and camps provide opportunities for coaches and referees as well as athletes to climb the sports ladder. It is also an opportunity for businesses and sponsors in the golden triangle to increase their brand visibility. Teams get cash from sponsors such as Nike, adidas, and Under Armour to outfit players in sneakers with their logos. Competitive venues are filled with company representatives handing out their products to players, who become billboards for the logos they wear. Thus, elite youth basketball is a junior golden triangle, with intense competition on the court, big-time recruiting, media exposure, substantial financial investments by sponsors and private donors, and athletes as commodities. There is even corruption such as under-the-table payments to get top players. The commercialization of this realm poses ethical and practical dilemmas for the truly altruistic. At least some of the individuals who have been involved with these elite teams have seen them as a means to lift talented players out of poverty and into a better life, but they have also recognized the seamier commercial aspects, the stress on young athletes' bodies, and the inevitable disappointment many were likely to experience (Wiedeman 2014). However, the reality is that making it into the golden triangle at the college and pro levels makes competing in this kind of commercial environment a near necessity for aspiring youths.

Although a majority of the boys and girls involved in youth sports may be involved in programs with a corporate structure, relatively few ascend to the elite level of big-time corporate sports. In addition, many other youths participate in *recreational sports programs* sponsored by city and county recreational departments or nonprofit organizations that are primarily intended to help children learn a sport, promote fun, or, in the case of PAL, keep kids out of trouble. There tend to be major *structural differences* between these kinds of youth sports programs and the more serious nonschool programs we will call "corporate youth sports programs." For example, the organization of corporate youth sports tends to place more emphasis than recreational sports on (1) paid professional coaches; (2) selectivity mechanisms such as competitive tryouts; (3) fees for membership and access to facilities; (4) expensive clothing, equipment, coaching, training, and travel; (5) competitive intensity and the significance and rewards of winning; (6) sport specialization with mandatory year-round participation in practice, training, and competition; (7) spectators; and (8) commercial sponsorship. In addition, the organization of corporate youth sports is more likely to involve larger, more complex, and more bureaucratic structures and more external or nonlocal regulation and control. It should be easy to see the influence of the golden triangle in these kinds of youth sports programs because they can be expensive to run.

Some young people opt out of traditional forms of sport to pursue *alternative or extreme sports*. In Chapter 4, we considered how some extreme sports were transformed from alternative recreational subcultures into highly organized and commercialized sports with professional athletes. An ethnographic study of youth participation in a BMX bikers subculture showed that participation in this activity is quite different for those who pursue it in different contexts or "spaces" (Rinehart and Grenfell 2002). The researchers studied a group of young people who participated in BMX riding in two different types of settings: (1) a grassroots context where the more experienced riders set up the ramps, courses, and jumps themselves and (2) a BMX indoor/outdoor riding circuit at a skate park that was organized as a corporate commercial venture by adults to make money by providing a safe place to practice BMX riding skills. In contrast to the commercial site, the grassroots site did not cost money to participate and was free from adult supervision, organization, and interference. In addition, the riders could take risks and ride as they wished at the grassroots site. Because they were freer from external adult intervention, their own site was more play-like and relaxed, and the riders were more spontaneous and more cooperative and helpful toward each other.

The more recreational youth-driven site coexisted with the corporate commercial site, and the BMX riders moved in and out of both types of venues.

It might seem surprising that young BMXers who had a chance to ride at their own site would be attracted to the commercial site. It was expensive for many of them, it had formal rules, and riding there was more intense as riders tried to "get their money's worth." However, commercially organized sports and facilities construct powerful marketing messages to attract customers. The skate park studied by Rinehart and Grenfell advertised itself as "cutting edge" and "rider friendly" and promoted the kinds of clothing, equipment, and other products that appealed to many young people. Thus, we can see that trying to understand how alternative or extreme sports socialize young people is complicated by their participation in both countercultural and mainstream contexts that are organized in very different ways. When young people participate in sports venues influenced by the business model of the golden triangle, they find themselves pushed increasingly toward the marketplace where sports entrepreneurs can sell them their products and services.

High School Sports and the Golden Triangle

The use of "pay-to-play" fees to fund public school athletic programs, the struggles of public high schools in poor neighborhoods to retain their athletic programs, and the more limited access of less advantaged kids to athletics were discussed in previous chapters. It should be evident from these discussions that many high school athletic programs are not as well funded as programs at well-endowed private secondary schools, programs at schools in wealthy communities, or youth sports programs with major corporate support. The willingness and ability of a school to support athletics depend on factors such as the wealth of the community, the value of athletic programs to the community, the willingness of taxpayers to support public education and athletics in the school, and the willingness of parents to pay the fees needed to cover the costs of the children's interscholastic sports participation. Furthermore, most students in the poorest schools in the United States do not play school sports (Kelley and Carchia 2013). While some school districts are not able to afford athletic programs and most poor children lack access, there are more affluent schools that support a large array of sports and have lavish facilities for their athletic teams. Some even stand behind their athletic programs when money spent in athletics seems to be wasted.

Probe 6.3: Being "Big-Time" in High School Sports

Allen, Texas, built a football stadium that some in the community touted as the premier high school facility in the country (Prisbell 2014). It was built in 2012, cost $60 million, seated 17,000, and included a three-tiered press box. Its football team was the pride of the community, having won state championships the two previous years. The stadium generated criticism outside the community for its excess and for adding fuel to an "arms race" of escalating spending in school sports among those communities that could afford it and some that could not. Allen was clearly one of those communities that could afford such spending. With the backing of 64 percent of the voters, the city of 89,000 passed a bond proposal in 2009 for $119 million, which included funding for the stadium, $23.2 million for a performing arts center, and $36.5 million for a service center. The stadium area also included a practice area for men's and women's golf, a 5,800 square-foot practice area for wrestling, and a huge new weight room. The stadium was built with a high-definition video screen. Although cracks were found in the stadium's structure, causing it to be shut down until repairs could be made, most local residents continued to support the decision to build the stadium. They believed it "put Allen on the map" and saw it as the "jewel of the community."

There are school districts willing and able to spend huge amounts of money on athletics to feed their sports passion, to try to distance themselves from their competitors, and to gain prestige for their community. As in college sports, the "haves" in high school sports operate in a very different world of resources and competitive success than the "have-nots," who struggle to keep up. At the high school level, poorer communities with more meager tax bases may decide that athletics is a luxury or that those who want their children to participate in sports will have to "pay to play." Public and corporate support for high school athletics has a limited reach, and the golden triangle does not distribute its largesse evenly across the terrain of high school sports.

In the more privileged stratum of high school sports, there is clear evidence of the golden triangle. Along with the construction of lavish new stadiums, high schools sign deals for naming rights, attract Internet broadcasting revenue, and significantly raise coaches' salaries (CNBC 2012). In many small towns in the South and Midwest, sports are popular, and high school sports are the major source of local entertainment. In these communities, the market for high school sports has grown and made them more attractive investments for the golden triangle. Local networks and ESPN began covering high school events in the 1980s. When some school districts had to deal with reduced public funding, they sought commercial deals to keep their programs competitive. Taxpayers paid for a new football stadium in Allen, Texas, but the shoe company New Balance invested $500,000 in the renovation of the high school football stadium in Gloucester, Massachusetts. Local businesses have made similar types of investments in other communities across the country. In addition, school districts have been negotiating increasingly lucrative broadcasting rights contracts. For example, the New York City public schools signed a two-year $500,000 deal with MSG Varsity Network. It is part of Cablevision, presents high school content, and concentrates much of its 24/7 programming on high school sports.

Part of the attraction of high school sports to the golden triangle is that three times as many students attend high school as attend college and a large number of high school students are involved in interscholastic athletics, making high school sports a potentially huge market (CNBC 2012). The media and corporate sponsors do not negotiate with a central governance body equivalent to the NCAA at the college level. They instead deal with state-level interscholastic athletic associations in many cases to obtain broadcasting rights and then license them to cable companies, which generate advertising fees to cover their costs. This is the standard formula for generating revenue through the media in the commercialized sports of the golden triangle.

With some television coverage at the national level, we can see why winning and high national rankings have become very important in big-time high school sports. National exposure has also intensified recruiting pressure on top high school athletes (Halley 2013). High school sports stars in boys' basketball and football may receive hundreds of text messages along with stacks of letters, and colleges may spend hundreds of thousands of dollars on high school recruiting in each of these sports in a single recruiting season (Newman 2014; Wolverton 2014a). In addition, commercially sponsored sports leagues such as the Nike EYBL try to recruit the most talented high school prospects to wear their branded products when they compete in their leagues. Recruiting high school sports stars has itself become a big business in the golden triangle. Recruiting services that find and rank top high school age prospects for big-time college and football programs are valuable commodities. For example, Yahoo bought Rivals.com for $100 million in 2007 (Rovell 2007). While some questioned whether the investment was worth it, it nevertheless reflected the perceived value of information about star high school athletes in the golden triangle.

College athletic recruiters give a lot of attention to top high school athletes in big-time sports, which can add a lot of pressure to the lives of these young people. They also may find themselves caught in a competition among club teams, private and public high schools, and sports academies and elite leagues to get them to play for them. A number of these athletes are dropping out of high school sports to play exclusively for travel teams affiliated with youth sports clubs or academies, seeing them as a better route to a scholarship from big-time college programs (Sondheimer 2012; Wiedeman 2014). This kind of competition for star athletes is an inevitable by-product of the increasing commercialization of youth sports and the increasing involvement of the golden triangle in them.

A study of high school athletics commissioned by the National Association of State Boards of Education (NASBE) pointed to concerns about the exploitation of high school athletes and a distortion of academic and moral values. This was a decade earlier than the latest wave of spending and commercial investment in big-time high school sports (NASBE 2004). Among the issues identified in this study were the influence of shoe manufacturers, ambitious and self-serving coaches, questionable recruiting practices, steroids and other performance-enhancing drugs, lavish gifts to athletes, and increasing specialization encouraged by club sports. Commission members urged state boards to play an active role in making sure that academics remained the top priority in public education, that the integrity of competition was protected, that access was available to all students who wished to participate in high school sports, and that schools were acting responsibly in raising and spending money for athletics. The report suggested an underlying concern among commission members that high school athletics was straying from the ideals that originally justified sports in the school. Commission members called for research to clarify how high school athletic participation actually affects students. This is an important research question, especially since what happens during the high school years can have a lasting effect on the lives of young people.

Justifications and Benefits of High School and Youth Sports

With new immigrants entering the United States in large waves at the end of the nineteenth century and early twentieth century, assimilating these new Americans into American culture and society was thought to be an important purpose of the high school and a useful function of high school sports (Nixon and Frey 1996:125). The New York Public School Athletic League took the lead in 1903 among US public school districts in establishing interscholastic athletic programs. Advocates of these early programs saw them as having valuable socialization or character-building functions. In effect, their assumption was that socialization into school sports would lead to productive socialization through sports, making former athletes better adjusted and more successful as adults.

Research reviews and reports from a more recent period (e.g., Carlson, Scott, Planty, and Thompson 2005; Fullinwider 2006; NASBE 2004) have suggested a number of positive academic outcomes of interscholastic athletic participation, including higher grades, a better academic self-concept, fewer disciplinary problems in school, fewer missed days of school, lower dropout rates, higher tenth-grade standardized test scores, better preparation for college, higher high school graduation rates, higher college attendance and graduation rates, and higher educational aspirations two years after high school for athletes than for their nonathlete counterparts. These outcomes may be related to the level of athletic commitment in an interesting way. For example, athletes who identify themselves as "jocks" and see themselves as *more committed* to sports *may not do as well academically* as other athletes who do not identify themselves as jocks (Miller, Melnick, Barnes, Farrell, and Sabo 2005).

As noted earlier, Sabo and Veliz's (2008) study *Go Out and Play* showed that high school sports participation tended to improve health, enhance body esteem, help maintain a healthy weight, increase popularity, and increase life satisfaction, as well as enhance educational achievement. They concluded that sports participation overall was "an educational asset" for many girls and boys in the United States. While it was not the only factor affecting academic performance and the other kinds of positive outcomes just cited, it was among the factors with significant effects on these outcomes. As suggested earlier, how much sports affects these outcomes seems to depend on grade level, family income, and school location. When he revisited research about the educational benefits of school-sponsored sports participation for a national educational summit in 2012, Sabo (2012) reached conclusions similar to those of his and Veliz's *Go Out and Play* study.

In his overview, Sabo provided valuable insights for interpreting the role of interscholastic athletic participation in the education and social adjustment of young people. First, he asserted that participation in school sports was a real and potential educational resource, since it could be related to the academic development of many boys and girls. For this reason, he argued that athletic programs in the school were more than "fun and games" for participants, but instead should be viewed as an *institutional resource* and form of *social capital* for students, their families, and the community. He used "social capital" in the sense that Putnam (2000) had proposed, meaning that school sports programs had elements of trust, social norms, and social networks that increased integration and cohesion in groups, the community, and society. Fullinwider (2006:16) suggested in this same vein that being on a high school team was a form of socialization that increased students' respect for their school and its academic values. Furthermore, the team linked students to important social networks, enhanced their status, and encouraged the kind of character traits that are associated with academic commitment and success. High school athletes also may be able to draw from the social capital of their contacts in sport to help them in their pursuit of a college education and to find jobs. In addition, organizations, communities, and societies benefit from having individuals who are able to work with others from different backgrounds as a result of their experiences with diversity in school sports networks.

Sabo concluded from his collaborative research on adolescents in tennis (Sabo, Veliz, and Rafalson 2013) that youth sports could be seen as a "catalyst" or mediator of positive educational outcomes. This meant that participation in sports was not by itself a direct cause or effect of positive educational and psychosocial outcomes. However, it was associated with these benefits when it was interwoven with an assortment of other factors that shaped the socialization of young sports participants. These other factors included the influences of family, school, community, peer group, coaches, teachers, and cultural beliefs. In combination, these factors could tie young people to the institutional order and encourage a healthy sense of self, positive behaviors and friendship choices, and a commitment to school and education that was likely to lead to good social adjustment during the teenage years and afterward. It would also seem that positive outcomes that occurred when young people participated in sports might reinforce the desire to keep playing sports. The general implications of this argument are that school sports participation may be associated with a number of factors that lead to better educational outcomes and better social adjustment and that society benefits when young people grow up well educated and well adjusted.

The better grades, school attendance, graduation rates, and postsecondary educational aspirations found for high school athletes in comparison with their nonathlete counterparts may be at least partially explained by the need for athletes to meet academic standards to remain athletically eligible. The concern raised by some critics that black high school athletes from the inner city were forsaking academics to pursue athletics is somewhat allayed by the facts that athletes must have passing grades in all or most of their academic courses to be able to play high school sports in many public school districts and that they must meet increasingly tougher initial academic eligibility standards to qualify for college athletics. Athletics may be especially important for students from less socially and economically advantaged backgrounds who lack academic motivation from other sources, such as the family and peers in their community. We are reminded of Edwards's (1998) appeal to young black athletes in poor communities and their families to continue to nurture their athletic dreams, but to do so with their eyes open about what it takes academically to play college sports or succeed in life in general.

The benefits of participation in corporate youth sports programs outside the school are not as well documented as the effects of participation in school sports. While low-keyed community recreation programs may be fun and have social benefits, it is not clear exactly what benefits are gained from participating in more competitive and intense corporate youth sports programs outside the school. It seems obvious that the young athletes who are successful in these programs get opportunities to move up the sports hierarchy to college, Olympic, and even professional sports. However, this intense participation may be at a cost. The same may be said for big-time high school sports participation. These costs are among the reasons for criticisms of more competitive, and demanding, youth and high school sports. When we consider these criticisms, we need to keep in mind that they tend to be focused on high school athletic programs and corporate youth sports programs that look like junior versions of big-time sports in the golden triangle. Before considering the criticisms, though, we will address one more common justification of youth sports. For some, it is and has been the ultimate justification. It is the idea that sports keep kids out of trouble, and it is both a practical and a moral argument. It assumes that sport is good for kids and also good for the community.

The Ultimate Justification: Keeping Kids out of Trouble

If we frame the justification that sports keep kids out of trouble as a question, we might ask: Can sports save kids from gangs and keep them out of trouble? This is the kind of question that economist Steven Levitt and journalist Stephen Dubner relished. In their work on "freakonomics," they applied data to questions that often were unasked because the answers seemed so intuitively obvious (Levitt and Dubner 2005). Their answers to many of these questions were interesting because they were counterintuitive or went against prevailing popular opinion. Dubner took on the popular idea that sports is a good outlet for young people and keeps them out of trouble. The article he posted on the *Freakonomics* website in 2006 was provocatively titled "Put Down That Basketball! Sport Causes Crime!" (Dubner 2006). He presented a portion of an article in *L'Equipe*, the French sports newspaper, which included comments by French criminologist Sébastien Roché, who was the director of the state-funded National Centre for Scientific Research. The article also included comments by Jean-Philippe Acensi, the founder of the Education through Sport agency, and Jean-Francois Lamour, the government minister in charge of Youth, Sports, and Associations. Roché was interested in the factors associated with teenagers' involvement in delinquent activities. His interest was heightened by the street riots in the suburbs of Paris in 2005. Some characterized the rioters as young terrorists. Roché saw them as outside the mainstream, but more likely they were young and poorly educated street delinquents than terrorists (Sakurai 2005).

The French government had invested in sports programs for youths in tough neighborhoods to try to keep them constructively occupied and out of trouble and keep the streets quiet. Roché challenged the value of these investments. He cited prior research conducted in France, including his own, and in the United States that supported the argument that sports participation among teenagers did *not* reduce their involvement in delinquency. He believed that the riots confirmed his argument, since there was a range of sports and cultural activities available for young people in the neighborhoods where the riots occurred. He was not in favor of cutting public subsidies for sports programs, since they could be a healthy source of recreational fun. However, he opposed the idea of using youth sports programs as a "political tool" to maintain social order or socialize young people (cited in Dubner 2006). He argued that despite conventional wisdom in France (and elsewhere), there was no evidence that these programs kept deviance-prone males, in particular, out of trouble. In fact, he concluded on the basis of his own research that playing sports did not reduce the number of crimes.

He went a step further, in making the controversial assertion that sports may increase the likelihood of delinquency among some young men by giving them a chance to enhance physical abilities that could be useful for street crime. These abilities could include running, channeling impulsive behavior, and using force. He added that sports often provided young men with their first opportunity to fight. Roché's research on which he based his conclusions was not persuasive for critics who noted that he relied on interviews of young men and did not use more compelling statistical data. Dubner did not fully embrace Roché's arguments, either, but recognized that the link between sports and violence was compelling. We have seen this link in both the violence involving hooligan fans and the interpersonal violence that athletes have inflicted off the field.

Roché's research may not offer definitive evidence that sports participation *causes* violence, but it is suggestive enough of the link between sport and delinquency for at least some teenage males that it deserves a closer look. He surveyed French teenage boys from Saint Etienne in 1999 and from Grenoble in 2003. In general, he found that the more time young men devoted to sports, the more likely they were to have committed a serious crime. This was especially true for working-class boys. Participation on a club or association team compared with less organized involvement in sports seemed to have a positive effect on delinquency rates only among thirteen- to fourteen-year-olds and white-collar boys. In general, though, in a population of one hundred boys and young men between thirteen and nineteen years old who participated in sports seven to eight hours a week, 24.5 percent, on average, said they had committed at least one serious crime. "Serious crimes" included car theft, burglary, racketeering, drug or other criminal traffic, stone throwing, or violence resulting in medical intervention.

Acensi, founder of the Education through Sport agency, agreed that claims about sport reducing delinquency were overblown, but attributed the disappointing outcomes to poor management rather than to the capacity of sport to have more positive consequences. Lamour, the youth sports minister, was more outspoken in his criticism of Roché's research and conclusions. He pointed to the deficiencies of Roché's interview studies and their lack of statistical corroboration. He countered with the familiar justifications of youth sports that focus on its claimed social and educational value. This was the conventional wisdom—that young men otherwise inclined to reject mainstream culture and disobey the rules or law benefited from playing sports because they were socialized into the mainstream. They learned what society expected of them and how to interact effectively with others in team settings. This is called a "social control" argument in the deviance literature and is part of Sabo's argument of athletics as an institutional resource.

Roché conducted other research that raised doubts about the conventional wisdom regarding youth sports involvement and deviance and the applicability of the social control argument. For example, he coauthored a statistical study showing that 33 percent of males and females aged fourteen to nineteen who played in extracurricular sports reported that they were drunk in the past twelve months, while 22 percent of those who did not participate in these kinds of sports activities reported being drunk in the previous year (Bègue and Roché 2009). They did not distinguish between more and less formal types of sports involvement in this study. It is noteworthy that selling alcohol to minors (age sixteen before 2009 and age eighteen afterward) is illegal, although consumption by a minor is not. Drinking among young people is generally not as associated with drunkenness in France as it is in the United States. The finding that girls and boys involved in sports are more likely to get drunk is contrary to the notion in social control theory that being involved in more institutionalized activities, even more informally organized ones, tends to increase acceptance of established norms and behaviors. Excessive drinking among the females in sport is especially noteworthy, because males generally were substantially more likely to get drunk than were the females.

Along with his earlier research, Roché's research with Bègue cast serious doubt on the social control argument in relation to sport and deviance or delinquency. Travis Hirschi's (1969) classic social control theory of delinquency emphasizes the importance of social bonds for staying out of trouble. Having attachments to others such as parents and friends, being involved in activities that embody established social norms, being committed to conventional behavior, and embracing societal codes of morality are assumed to be elements of the social bonds that make people more likely to do what society expects of them than to engage in deviant behavior such as delinquency. Since sports can be seen as creating these elements of social bonds, we would predict that participating in sports will keep adolescents out of trouble. However, the studies of teenagers in France clearly contradict this theory. Research findings in the United States also raised questions about a straightforward application of this theory to the relationship between youth sports participation and delinquency.

Kelley and Sokol-Katz (2011) did a sophisticated statistical analysis of data from the National Longitudinal Study of Adolescent Health to examine the relationship between sports participation and delinquency among adolescents. They tested three hypotheses derived from assumptions in social bond theory about attachment and involvement. Theoretically, being more involved in sports should leave less time for other activities, such as delinquency. Thus, their first hypothesis was that those involved in sports would be less delinquent than those not involved. Their second hypothesis incorporated the idea of degree of involvement and predicted that those with the most involvement in sports will exhibit higher levels of delinquency than those less involved. This seemingly contradictory hypothesis was based on the idea that more involvement in sports could give athletes more exposure to social influences supportive of behaviors such as risk taking and troublemaking or delinquency and less time to be involved in conventional activities that could challenge these social influences. These influences may arise precisely because highly involved athletes are more cut off from the social bonds that encourage conformity as they spend more time in sports. This suggests the problematic consequences of too much involvement in a peer culture that values testing the normative boundaries. The third hypothesis predicted that athletes more attached to their parents in more cohesive families and more attached to or accepted by their friends would be less delinquent. Delinquency was measured in terms of behaviors such as being drunk or high at school, smoking regularly, experimenting with various types of drugs, doing graffiti, lying to parents, running away from home, vandalism, stealing, burglary, interpersonal violence, use of a weapon, and involvement in group violence. Less serious delinquency was distinguished from more serious delinquency. More serious delinquency included acts such as damaging property, stealing a car, committing burglary of a building, getting into a fight, and using or threatening use of a weapon.

In their broader analysis of the data, Kelley and Sokol-Katz found a number of positive factors that were generally associated with playing high school sports, including a greater sense of mastery, higher self-esteem, more perceived peer acceptance, more attachment to school, better attendance, and a higher expectation of attending college. These are the kinds of benefits Sabo observed in relation to interscholastic athletic participation. They are the types of benefits that would seem to result from social bonds formed in athletics that keep adolescents from losing their way and getting into trouble. However, Kelley and Sokol-Katz found that among the various measures of delinquent behavior, only regularly smoking cigarettes was curtailed by playing sports. On the other hand, athletes were significantly more likely than nonathletes to do graffiti, run away from home, steal more than $50, steal a car, damage property, engage in fighting, physically hurt someone, and participate in group violence.

These results contradicted the first hypothesis that sports participants would be less delinquent than nonparticipants. The relationship between sports participation and delinquency did not seem to be affected by whether athletes participated in contact or noncontact sports. The particular sport may matter, but its effect on delinquency may depend on how much the team culture within the sport encourages antisocial or delinquent behavior. We have seen, for example, how hazing on some high school sports teams has been embraced by the athletes and also at least tacitly encouraged or tolerated by the coaches. This type of culture could encourage deviance off the field.

The second hypothesis was supported. Even though playing one sport was not a significant predictor of delinquency, playing two or more sports was a strong predictor. It appears that those more heavily involved in sports and more drawn to risk taking tended to commit more serious delinquent acts. Data also supported the third hypothesis. Those with stronger attachments to their families and those who felt more accepted by friends were generally less delinquent. Furthermore, parental involvement in all of their children's decisions predicted lower rates of less serious delinquency but did not significantly affect rates of more serious delinquency. Additional analysis showed that males had higher levels of more serious delinquency and whites tended to be less involved in more serious delinquency. It was also found that those from more affluent families had lower levels of general delinquency. Risk taking was also broadly linked with delinquency.

The researchers did not dismiss the potential value of participating in high school sports, but they pointed out that the relationship between athletic participation and delinquency was complex. Focusing on the attachment and involvement aspects of social bond theory, they found that the theory failed to provide an adequate explanation of delinquent behavior. The theory generally predicts that delinquency is more likely when bonds to society and self-control are weak. However, they found that students who were highly involved in activities thought to be conventional and in the mainstream of society also got involved in delinquency. The effects of sports on involvement in delinquency may depend on the degree of involvement, the kinds of relationships that athletes develop in sport, and the nature of the culture within the sport or team. Kelley and Sokol-Katz suggested that we may need to reexamine our conception of sports as a source of mainstream conformity and as a builder of character among young people.

Sports would seem to be a positive antidote to the negative effects of gang involvement among teenagers in tough inner-city neighborhoods. There are over 20,000 active street gangs in the United States, with some affiliated with larger criminal enterprises (Dohrmann 2008). However, even playing sports does not insulate young athletes in these neighborhoods from being severely wounded or killed by gang violence. It can be difficult to escape the gangs, and the choice often faced by teenage boys and even some girls in gang-infested neighborhoods is to join a gang or try to leave the neighborhood. Their families often do not have the means for them to escape. Anderson (1999) found that although most parents in these neighborhoods wanted to protect their kids from gangs, gang influence was difficult to avoid.

Faced with the dangers of crime and violence, police hostility, and parental neglect, some young men in these neighborhoods adopted a "street code," which involved "nerve" or the ability to stand up to threats, which put them at risk of being hurt, killed, or sent to jail. This was their subcultural adaptation to social disadvantage and discrimination. Being poor and disadvantaged and having relatively few perceived mainstream or conventional opportunities made the chance to rise up the ranks of the gang attractive. The fact that gangs controlled their neighborhood also made it difficult to escape being pulled in or influenced by them. This was a life-and-death decision for young men trying to survive in these neighborhoods. Cities such as Compton, California, with a population of 96,000, reportedly had thirty-four active street gangs with over one thousand members in 2011. Some blocks had several. Athletes sometimes found themselves in the middle of gang competition to recruit them, since they could add visibility and prestige to a gang's reputation (Benedict and Keteyian 2011:84). Thus, some star athletes might experience pressure from both gang recruiters and college recruiters at the same time. However, being known on the streets as a member of a particular gang could make these athletes targets of rival gangs.

Probe 6.4: Sports Participation Does Not Insulate Young Athletes from Gang Influence

The president of a Pop Warner football program in a tough neighborhood in Oakland, California, commented, "It used to be that if you play sports, everyone protected you" (quoted in Dohrmann 2008:56). He added that this was no longer true. In the neighborhoods destroyed by poverty, unemployment, crime, and gang violence, everyone was a potential victim. Coaches got used to attending the funerals of their players caught up in the violence. There are prominent examples of young men from these neighborhoods getting out through their sports prowess and reaching the college and even professional sports levels. However, in relative terms, they are the exceptions. Even among those who have seemed to escape, their old neighborhood ties may continue to exert an influence. It is not unusual to see the names of college and professional athletes from these tough neighborhoods on police blotters as criminals or victims.

Sabo's catalyst hypothesis assumes that youth sports participation is associated with a number of positive educational and psychosocial outcomes. This happens when playing sports is intertwined with a number of other factors that facilitate these outcomes by intensifying social bonds. It appears that youth sports can also be a negative catalyst when sports participation is linked to a different set of factors associated with severed social bonds and problematic social adjustment. Some young men might want to escape the gangs, crimes, and violence of their neighborhoods, but these factors may be much stronger than those that draw them into sports. If they play sports, they face a powerful array of influences that make it difficult to stay away from people and situations that could get them in trouble. Those who grow up in poor and unstable families and neighborhoods are likely to have more difficulty becoming part of the mainstream and forming the social bonds that insulate them from delinquency and other trouble. Sports may be an institutional resource promoting social bonds and social control primarily for the middle-class kids who already have the attachments, involvements, commitments, and beliefs that insulate them from deviance and make them more receptive to the positive behaviors we associate with sports involvement.

Issues and Problems of Youth and High School Sports

The delinquency research and stories of gangs and sport show that sports do not protect teenagers from getting into trouble or experiencing serious problems in their lives. While minorities, males, and kids from less affluent backgrounds and unstable or dysfunctional families and neighborhoods seem most vulnerable, all sports participants may be at some risk, especially when they are heavily involved in highly competitive sports programs in their school or community. Youth sports may generally be an institutional resource and catalyst for various positive outcomes for participants, their schools, and their communities. However, when youths get excessively caught up in the cultural incentives and pressures of sports in the golden triangle, the positive aspects and effects of sports participation may be diminished or reversed. The effects of sports participation also may be affected by negative social influences outside sport.

We have seen that the positive rhetoric about the benefits of youth sports may be exaggerated, misleading, or mistaken. The NASBE (2004) commission study cited earlier proposed that state boards of education need to consider policies and programs that make students, especially those from minority backgrounds, aware of the limitations of concentrating exclusively on sports and neglecting their studies. This recommendation is consistent with the results from research by Eitle and Eitle (2002). The Eitles' research suggested that to be able to benefit from their high school experience, high school students from less advantaged backgrounds need to keep their eyes focused on activities that give them an opportunity to develop *cultural capital*. Athletics may not be one of these activities. The Eitles defined "cultural capital" in the high school context as elements of the middle-class lifestyle that are distinct from elements of the lifestyles of the lower and working classes. Cultural capital such as trips to museums and art galleries and classes such as art, dance, and music enabled a student to do better in middle-class institutions such as the school, which place special value on these kinds of practices. Middle-class students have more cultural capital of other types as well, such as more educational resources at home.

The Eitles found that relatively higher rates of male participation in football and basketball were associated with being more culturally disadvantaged and being less involved in courses and activities that increased cultural capital. Male students from economically disadvantaged backgrounds were more interested in the status gains and opportunities they could get from playing football and basketball than in chances in school to enhance their cultural capital. Unlike their generally more affluent classmates who played sports and were involved in activities that built their cultural and social capital, the more disadvantaged football and basketball players gained very little academically or educationally from their concentration on sports. To the extent that students from less advantaged backgrounds trade opportunities to accumulate cultural capital for their concentration on certain sports, they may pay the price of not building the kind of educational motivation and background needed for better academic achievement.

The Eitles' research suggests that being too committed to sports may be costly for high school athletes from low-income and minority backgrounds. Other young people from disadvantaged backgrounds may not have any chance to benefit from athletic participation. Their socioeconomic background may make sports in the school and in the community inaccessible, either because they cannot afford to participate or because their school or community cannot field teams. In addition, despite Title IX, there continues to be a *gender gap* in school sports. This is especially true outside the suburbs and also applies to youth sports programs in the community. Sabo and Veliz (2008) suggested that variations in the gender gap in sports participation reflected economic differences, race and ethnicity, and characteristics of families, which influenced opportunities and access.

Some critics of high school sports in the United States believe that with America falling behind other nations in various academic rankings, investing in sports in schools represents misplaced priorities. For example, US public schools typically spend more tax dollars on average per athlete than they spend per student in math. When high schools are under financial duress and must consider drastic budget cuts, they often seem reluctant to trim their budget for popular athletic programs (Ripley 2013). These critics often see athletics in the school as an expensive distraction from what schools need to be doing, which is improving the quality of their students' education.

School principals and advocates for athletics often justify their schools' investment in athletics by citing the kinds of benefits Sabo's research found and by arguing that athletic programs keep kids out of trouble. In fact, having more students involved in sports may have positive effects for schools as well as for the participants. For example, Veliz and Shakib's (2014) national study of 4,644 US public high schools in 2009–2010 showed that schools with higher rates of athletic participation for both sexes and across racial and ethnic groups had lower rates of student suspensions, less violence and assault, and higher scores on math, foreign language, and science Advanced Placement (AP) exams. Their argument was that schools that provide more athletic opportunities for their students are also giving them a boost academically through these opportunities. This illustrates Sabo's idea of athletics as an institutional resource. These findings also seem to demonstrate socialization through sport. The researchers also found that girls who participated in interscholastic athletics were more likely to enroll in AP classes than were male athletes.

On the other hand, we have seen that there are a number of factors that affect whether kids get involved in sports and how much they benefit from them. We have also seen that being highly involved in sports could increase the likelihood of kids getting into trouble. Sabo's idea of athletics as a catalyst implies that it is not participation in athletics by itself that leads to positive educational and psychosocial outcomes. A combination of factors including family, school, community, peer groups, coaches and teachers, and cultural beliefs affects whether athletic participation has positive outcomes. Among those from less advantaged backgrounds who have the most to gain, committing too much time to sports could deprive them of opportunities to build cultural and social capital from other kinds of activities and also could distract them from their studies. It is ironic, too, that girls seem to benefit from athletic participation because they are less likely than boys to participate, they are more likely to combine sports with other extracurricular activities, and they are not as likely to see sports as an important part of their identity. In fact, girls, minorities, and low-income students tend to have fewer chances to play high school sports and take advantage of the possible benefits. Furthermore, schools in poorer districts do not have the resources to offer enough sports opportunities to accommodate all the students who may be interested. Sports programs in these schools also have to contend with the formidable and intimidating influence of gangs in their neighborhoods. Thus, the chance to take advantage of the possible benefits of athletic participation depends a lot on socioeconomic factors at the individual, institutional, and community levels.

Even when kids have a chance to participate in sports, they may decide not to try out or to drop out. Especially at the varsity level in high school and in highly competitive corporate youth sports programs in the community, those with ordinary athletic skills often find or decide that they are not good enough to make the team. They also may not be motivated enough to meet the serious demands of these programs. Other reasons they drop out are because they are not having fun, they become more interested in other activities, they do not get along with the coach or teammates, or they want or need to spend more time on studying and boosting their grades.

While many parents encourage their kids' sports participation and are disappointed when they quit, they also may have some ambivalence about their kids playing sports. A major source of this ambivalence is a fear of injuries, especially concussions. Research has shown that this is the greatest fear among parents about their kids' involvement in sports (Kelley and Carchia 2013). This fear seems to be justified. According to a survey of emergency room (ER) visits by the nonprofit advocacy group Safe Kids Worldwide, 1.35 million youths per year are injured seriously enough in sports to go to a hospital ER (cited in Healy 2013). This means that youths visit hospital ERs for sports-related injuries approximately once every twenty-five seconds. They represent one in five kids who go to ERs for treatment of an injury. The data were from the US Consumer Product Safety Commission's National Electronic Injury Surveillance System and focused on injuries in fourteen popular sports activities, including football, cheerleading, soccer, and basketball. Other data from this source indicated that the most common sports injuries for children and youths in the six to nineteen age group were sprains and strains, fractures, contusions, abrasions, and concussions. The most frequent injuries involved the ankle (15 percent), the head (14 percent), finger (10 percent), knee (9 percent), and face (7 percent). The cost of treating these injuries each year was more than $935 million.

The concussion rate in high school football is especially alarming because it is the highest among high school sports and because we are learning more about its serious short-term and long-term effects (Gregory 2014). Concussions are traumatic brain injuries (TBIs), and kids take longer to heal from them than do adults. Although the symptoms of concussions generally disappear within two weeks, in 10–20 percent of cases, symptoms may still be experienced from weeks to months to years later. Compounding the concern among parents of high school football players is research showing a link between concussions and debilitating neurological conditions such as dementia and Alzheimer's disease among retired NFL players. Statistics derived from the US Centers for Disease Control and Prevention (CDC), the National Institutes of Health (NIH), and the National High School Sports-Related Injury Surveillance Study showed that the concussion rate per 10,000 high school players in games was 33 in football in 2013–2014. This was 78 percent higher than the rate at the college level (Gregory 2014). It was also much higher than the rate of 18 for girls soccer and 12 for wrestling, boys soccer, and girls basketball (Gregory 2014). Male and female athletes in other high school sports were also at risk of concussions (e.g., Farrey 2013), but the consistent hard hits in football made it especially worrisome. The statistics also show that we should be concerned about the risk to girls as well.

Probe 6.5: Sports Can Be a Greater TBI Risk for Girls than Boys

The data about gender differences in concussion rates may be surprising in light of common gender stereotypes about physical aggression and risk. Research has suggested that in sports with similar rules and comparable physical demands, such as soccer, basketball, and baseball/softball, females seem to have a greater risk of concussions and may experience more severe concussions (e.g., see Healy 2013; Kerasidis 2014). Furthermore, after suffering a concussion, recovery time may be longer for boys than girls, but girls are likely to experience more symptoms, more loss of memory, and slower reaction times. Adolescent symptoms can include headaches and worsened attention deficit disorders, depression, and anxiety (Farnan-Kennedy 2011). Girls may be more vulnerable to TBIs for anatomical reasons, such as less developed neck muscles and smaller head-size-to-body ratios than boys. There also may be cultural reasons (de Lench 2014). For example, parents may have more protective attitudes toward girls and be more sensitive to possible injuries to them, resulting in more medical attention and thus more reported injuries. Boys also may be more likely to underreport their injuries because hypermasculine sports cultures may discourage their acknowledgment of pain and injury. Whatever the rates and reasons for concussions in youth sports, it seems important for the people who run these programs to recognize the risk to both sexes and to structure their sports to try to minimize the risk. This is not so easy, though, when sports almost inevitably involve impacts to the head.

Being more serious about a sport means putting in more hours of training and competition, which makes young athletes more vulnerable to overuse injuries to the tendons, bones, and joints of their growing bodies. Medical researchers have estimated that children and adolescents who play a sport more hours per week than their age are 70 percent more likely to have serious overuse injuries (cited in Healy 2013). With so much concern about high obesity rates of children and adolescents who are not active enough, the increasing incidence of overuse injuries in youth sports is ironic and troubling since these injuries may result from a Sport Ethic in youth sports nurtured by parents, other adults, and the golden triangle (Hyman 2009).

It appears that the more competitive and demanding youth sports become in school or corporate programs, the more they put kids at risk—of emotional distress, burnout, and serious injury. However, "big-time" youth sports in these settings are organized to promote the highest level of competition among the most talented athletes. The benefits associated with playing sports may diminish when the levels of commitment and physical demands reach a threshold where the benefits start decreasing. In Kelley and Sokol-Katz's research, this was playing two or more sports. Those who are serious about a particular sport may be involved in at least two sports programs, one in school and the other at an elite club level outside the school.

When high school and corporate youth sports become junior versions of college, professional, and Olympic sports in the golden triangle, the welfare of the young athletes can get lost in the pursuit of winning, status, and financial gains. We can marvel at the prodigious talent of eleven-year-old Lucy Li when she became the youngest qualifier for the US Women's Open in golf in 2014 (DiMeglio 2014). She said she planned to have fun, but we might wonder whether it makes sense physically or developmentally to allow young children to compete against adults in a highly publicized event. Participating in this commercialized environment immediately transforms this young girl into a commodity in the marketplace and subjects her to a wide range of influences that people her age rarely experience.

On the institutional level, when high schools get involved in an "arms race" competition of escalating expenses to catch up with or surpass their rivals and achieve state, regional, or national recognition, they may divert resources that could be spent for academic purposes. The problem is that once schools take sports seriously, it may be difficult to scale down their ambitions and put athletics in a proper perspective in relation to academics in the school. In the community, sports programs that are organized solely for the purpose of achieving athletic success for athletes or the team will have even fewer constraints on their athletic ambitions. They usually need outside investment, which makes them more vulnerable to the influence of sponsors and the media in the golden triangle.

The answer for the biggest critics of high school sports would seem to be to eliminate sports from the schools and provide community recreation and club alternatives outside the school for those interested in organized participation. Community recreation programs generally require public funding or major contributions from private donors, but they could provide healthy and fun-oriented activities for kids with less motivation or more modest skills. However, those wanting more competitive and serious opportunities for their kids are likely to turn to club and other elite programs. This pushes kids in the direction of the golden triangle, as they aspire to sports careers at higher levels.

Although the competitive pressures, commercialization, and media exposure are not nearly as much, big-time sports at the high school and elite corporate youth sports levels still bear striking similarities to sports at the highest level. For example, top high school sports programs in boys basketball participate in nationally televised games; receive fees plus expense money to play in these games; and generate equipment contracts for themselves, broadcast rights fees for ESPN and regional sports networks, and investment from corporate sponsors (Wertheim and Dohrmann 2006). In addition, print publications such as *High School Basketball Illustrated (HSBI)* have annual subscription rates of $400, and online recruiting services such as Hoop Scout.com can cost $500 per year or more (Zengerle 2010). It appears that youth football is trying to emulate big-time youth basketball in its physical and time demands on the athletes, commercialization, and pursuit of ties to college recruiting services and the media (Staples 2011).

In big-time high school and youth sports, it is not enough to win locally. There are bigger ambitions, such as playing in nationally televised games, being ranked nationally by publications such as *Sports Illustrated* and *USA Today*, or competing in national championship games. The success of the Nike EYBL is a reflection of these ambitions. In addition, young athletes have been drawn into "sneaker wars" (Boston Globe 2006; Hohler 2006a, 2006b, 2006c). They have been courted by coaches of elite teams and representatives of manufacturers of sneakers and sports gear. For example, we have seen that in elite youth basketball, representatives of sneaker manufacturers such as Nike, adidas, and Under Armour have competed for talented young athletes to participate in their leagues and camps and to wear their logo-imprinted products. This commercial competition has exposed increasingly younger athletes to significant pressures and dubious practices, and has distracted a number of them from serious attention to their studies. Some of the coaches and promoters involved with elite teams have acknowledged paying young basketball players for expenses that were not related to their sport, which could later jeopardize their NCAA eligibility.

**Probe 6.6: Becoming a Sports Prospect and Commodity
at a Young Age**

One of the socialization lessons for talented young athletes and their families is that boys and girls with athletic talent in certain sports, such as Lucy Li in golf, are valuable commodities for corporate sponsors, appealing subjects for the mass media, a source of revenue for sports academies and camps, and a vehicle for professional coaches and trainers and elite sports programs to enhance their status and careers. Even talented athletes in elementary school may draw the interest of the golden triangle, as the case of a ten-year-old basketball prospect in the Baltimore area showed (Saslow 2006a). Such players could look forward to being ranked by college recruiting websites as fifth graders. Thus, the social world of this boy involved the possibility of national attention in elementary school, special coaches to hone his skills, and overtures from a number of AAU coaches and local private school recruiters. The young prospect's father wanted him to be "comfortable and carefree" and "a little kid at home," but he also told his son he had to be serious, "an impact player" on the court, and not waste his big chance at sports success. His mother was acutely aware that her son was only ten years old and that many people wanted to "buy" him. She wanted people to know that her son was "not for sale," but the world of youth sports constructed by the golden triangle transforms talented athletes of any age into commodities.

When an athlete from a low-income family has exceptional talent and plays a highly commercialized sport, a family's limited resources may not pose an obstacle to participation in elite youth sports when the young athlete can attract sponsors. For example, Five-Star Basketball Camp was started in New York in 1966 and has grown into a network of camps across the country. Its website (fivestarbasketball.com) boasts that over five hundred of its alumni have played in the NBA and that over five hundred of its staff have coached at the college Division I or professional level. Grants from its foundation enable talented but financially disadvantaged prospects to attend. This enables Five-Star to provide a camp experience that attracts top prospects, who in turn attract top coaches and big-time college recruiters. Playing in these camps and leagues such as the EYBL along with interscholastic athletics constitutes a serious nearly year-round commitment for young athletes. However, moving up the sports ladder seems to require such commitments and their associated sacrifices of the normal social and family life of a child and teenager. Only the most disciplined are able to manage their priorities and also be serious students.

Affluent families are able to subsidize the big-time sports aspirations of less talented young athletes or their parents. For example, Alsever (2006) wrote about a young baseball player whose parents spent $30,000 between the time he was ten and sixteen for coaches, private trainers, performance tests, baseball camps, tournaments, and travel with elite teams to advance his career prospects. He was the starting catcher on his high school team, but he had no guarantee that his parents' investment would pay off. Children and adolescents from less affluent families with equivalent but not exceptional talent do not have the same opportunities for access to elite sports development as their peers. Without expensive sports training and experience with a competitive club team, they may even be at a disadvantage in trying to gain a place on their high school team. Thus, social class is likely to be a significant filter in access to participation in certain high school sports as well as elite youth sports in general.

The sports network in which the golden triangle draws talented young prospects from various backgrounds into a big-time realm of youth sports is global, which we can see from a series of articles about young Nigerian boys with dreams of playing in the NBA. Saslow (2006b, 2006c, 2006d) showed how the path from a one-bedroom apartment in Enugu, Nigeria, to the United States could include stops in Lagos, Nigeria, Senegal, France, and Belgium, as young basketball hopefuls try to join the nearly fifty countrymen on NCAA men's basketball teams. As Saslow (2006b) observed, young Nigerian prospects were treated as commodities by the various coaches, scouts, and middlemen who hoped to profit from these prospects if they became college and NBA stars. Even though it was a violation of NCAA rules, US colleges paid Nigerian coaches about $5,000 for each talented player they identified and delivered. One coach alleged that approximately half of the colleges paid for this service because the international market for players had become so competitive. Some players tried to market themselves, even though they often needed help to deal with visa problems. A number of these players first play for US high schools as a stepping-stone to playing in college, and they hope at least to be able to return home with a college degree if their professional basketball dream does not become a reality.

When promising young athletes, from Nigeria or the United States, learn that their commodity value no longer attracts interest, as many will ultimately learn, their adjustment to being more ordinary athletes or even nonathletes will depend on how much of themselves they have invested in their American Sports Dream. For all but a relatively few athletes, serious sports involvement ends in adolescence. Those who have thought of themselves only as athletes and have dreamed only of a future in sport are likely to have difficulty dealing with the transition from seeing themselves as star athletes with a promising future to also-rans and, ultimately, former athletes (Adler and Adler 1991). They are not likely to be as prepared for the future as their non-jock peers are, especially if they have sacrificed their studies and other opportunities to accumulate educational and cultural capital outside sport. In addition, they may have to deal with the lingering effects of having sacrificed their bodies to pursue their big-time sports dream.

Possible inequities in sports access and opportunities raise a number of public policy questions about youth sports investment. For example, we may ask whether the often indirect educational and socialization benefits from high school athletic participation are extensive and important enough to justify public investment in school sports and whether the public interest might be more broadly and better served by investing tax money in public recreation programs outside the school. These kinds of questions are made more salient where high school athletic programs are becoming highly commercialized and increasingly influenced by private interests.

Conclusion

An important aspect of most kids' involvement in high school and youth sports programs in the community is that they are organized and controlled by adults. Edward Devereux (1976) used the term "Little Leaguism" to refer to this aspect of youth sports. While the obvious reference is to Little League Baseball, the term was meant to have a broader application. This feature makes these sports experiences less like play, which may explain why not having fun was cited by nearly 40 percent of girls and boys as the reason they quit a team sport. It was at the top of their list of reasons for quitting (Kelley and Carchia 2013). A big part of not having fun may be not having a chance to make decisions about their participation or feeling too much stress in trying to meet adult expectations. Pushing kids more intensely and frequently into organized sports programs and other adult-organized activities for their enrichment, development, or distraction deprives these kids of opportunities to do things they enjoy and can control.

Parents and youth sports organizers may worry about dropout rates in youth sports, but Devereux was more concerned about the costs of the spread of Little Leaguism. He was worried that these kinds of programs threatened to destroy the spontaneous culture of play, recreation, and games among children (cited in Nixon 1984:31, 32). He was writing nearly four decades ago, and his concerns were not likely to be allayed by the expansion of Little Leaguism since then. Instead of encouraging kids to go out and play on their own, soccer moms drive them to practices and games for their school and youth sports teams. Suburbs groom fields for organized sports programs, leaving less open space for spontaneous play. Inner-city neighborhoods may want to provide more recreational programs and spaces to try to keep kids out of trouble, but they typically lack the resources to support these programs or keep recreational spaces usable and safe. In rural areas, it can be expensive and logistically challenging for kids to get together to play games on their own when they live some distance away from each other. The result is that parents who can afford it get their kids involved in organized sports, and if they show promise, the parents might hire personal trainers or coaches or send their kids to camps or academies to hone their skills. Otherwise, the kids stay home, play video games, or otherwise remain sedentary in the affluent suburbs. Or, they fend for themselves on the street in tough urban neighborhoods or in small rural communities, where parents might wish there were organized sports programs to keep their kids occupied and out of trouble.

But what do they lose by having less time or fewer chances to play on their own with peers? Devereux argued that the decline of spontaneous play on the sandlots, streets, or playgrounds deprived kids of a number of valuable social-ization opportunities as well as the joy of engaging in activities of their own making. When they decide on their own what games to play, what the rules will be, who gets to play, how to mediate disputes, and how long they will play, they can develop a sense of autonomy or independence, initiative, creativity, and skills of making and enforcing rules and resolving conflicts. These qualities are needed to form independent and mature moral judgment and a secure and socially adjusted sense of self. In addition, in spending more time at their own play, they can avoid more of the hypocrisy, inflated expectations, and intense pressures that adults bring to the world of Little Leaguism. In this world, there may be too much exposure to adult responsibilities and adult flaws too soon. Little Leaguism exposes children and adolescents to coaches and parents who talk about sportsmanship but push their players to do whatever it takes to win, who get upset with "losers," and who constantly remind kids they need to try harder (Fine 1987).

All of this can lead to what Devereux called "a premature loss of childhood innocence," which could make young athletes more cynical, more insecure, or more confused about values, rules, and their identities. Devereux's concerns about the absence of play are validated by extensive research by experts on play such as Stuart Brown (Tippett 2014). He has argued that play is essential for normal human development, character formation, and social adjustment and may be a means of lessening the chances of children growing up as violent adults. The play research has found the specific outcomes that Devereux sug-gested, including learning empathy, trust, and problem solving, while being a source of fun. The pleasure undoubtedly comes from not having any particular purpose, which removes the adult expectations and pressures associated with the formal adult organized and regulated activities of Little Leaguism.

Parents do not seem to be too concerned about the pervasiveness of Little Leaguism or what their kids are losing when Little Leaguism steals time from more spontaneous child's play. In fact, adult control may be part of the reason that Little Leaguism is appealing to them. They may worry that their kids will get into trouble if they have too little adult supervision and too much freedom. Mistakenly or not, they may think of organized sports as a safe haven because adults are, or are supposed to be, firmly in charge. Coaches rarely depart from this pattern of largely autocratic control in the more serious realms of high school and club sports. However, the closely supervised and tightly regulated nature of Little Leaguism means that kids lose chances to learn how to be responsible and exercise authority. There is an interesting documented case that deviates from this general pattern. It involved a California high school football coach who tried to make sport a lesson in democracy for his players. It is distinctive because this type of experiment has been so rare in youth sports and because the parental reaction was quite hostile, despite the team's success on the field.

George Davis led his team to a then California state record of forty-five consecutive wins between 1960 and 1964 (Amdur 1971; Nixon and Frey 1996:131–133). Davis liked winning, but unlike other high school coaches, he was also committed to using sport to teach his players lessons about being citizens in a democracy. Believing that an important part of his role as a high school coach was to be an educator, he wanted his players to understand that citizenship involved active participation in decision making and both individual and shared responsibility for getting things done. His lessons about democracy involved having his players vote for the starting line-up, allowing them to decide what positions they should play, and giving them a chance to provide input about their roles during competition.

Like most "serious" athletes then and today, George Davis's players had little or no prior experience with this kind of responsibility beyond their informal games on the playground, and not surprisingly, they initially reacted with some reluctance and uncertainty. Yet, opposition from parents and fans to this experiment in democracy might seem surprising. After all, a school sport was being used for educational purposes, providing a strong justification for having sports in the school. However, the parents who opposed this experiment seemed to perceive it more as a coach abandoning his responsibility than as an educator teaching about democracy. Even winning was not enough to offset expectations that sport teach boys about accepting adult authority rather than about learning how to exercise authority responsibly themselves. Although parents, fans, and high school coaches generally have not embraced George Davis–like experiments in democracy, his players ultimately learned how important it was for them to trust in each other, accept peer leadership, and share responsibility for the team's success. George Davis believed that his players would become better citizens if they learned about the importance of these aspects of shared decision making on the football field.

Parents sometimes seem unaware of their own inconsistencies and ambivalence about child rearing and their kids' involvement in sports. However, empirical studies have provided clear evidence of the contradictory messages parents often express to their kids about their sports participation and the pressure parents and coaches are putting on kids in youth sports. For example, the Liberty Mutual Insurance Responsible Sports program (Liberty Mutual 2013) conducted a national survey of 1,000 parents of seven- to seventeen-year-olds in organized youth sports and 501 youth sports coaches. The survey found that 77 percent of the parents placed high importance on their child's coach being a caring person, and that relatively fewer (59 percent) thought it was as important that the coach be skilled in that sport. On the other hand, 36 percent of the coaches cited problems with parents' unreasonable expectations about winning. This was contrary to the fact that 75 percent of parents said a major reason they got their children into youth sports was for them to have fun.

The survey looked at sports involving kids in the elementary school, middle school, and high school age groups. It showed that coaches of kids in all these age groups valued competitiveness more than did the parents of the kids they coached. Among both coaches and parents, though, competitiveness was widely valued for all these age groups, and it became important for more of them as the kids got older. Among parents, 58 percent with elementary school–age children in youth sports said competitiveness was somewhat or very important, while 78 percent with middle school–age children and 88 percent with high school–age children felt the same way. Among coaches, 76 percent of those coaching the youngest kids, 85 percent of those coaching middle school–age kids, and 91 percent of those coaching kids of high school age said competitiveness was somewhat or very important. These findings are not surprising, since parents often enroll their kids in youth sports programs because these programs are organized to be competitive. However, parental views of competitiveness seem to be at odds with parents' expressed interest in their kids having fun, unless, of course, winning and fun are equated.

The interest in competitiveness might explain why 55 percent of coaches reported parents yelling negative things at their own children from the sidelines. In addition, 44 percent of the coaches reported that parents yelled negative things at referees, 40 percent said parents yelled negative things at other children, and 39 percent said they yelled negative things at coaches. Nearly all parents (90 percent) said they were involved in attending their kids' practices and games, but nearly half of coaches (46 percent) said they had a problem with a lack of parental involvement. Finally, in regard to the serious issue of concussions, most parents said they discussed the risks of concussions with their children, and they were more likely to do so as their children got older. However, while 82 percent of parents said they were concerned about the concussion risk in youth sports, a much smaller percentage (47 percent) said this concern influenced their decision about which sport their children would play. Their kids were more likely to express concern about concussions with their coach (35 percent) than with their parents (12 percent), perhaps feeling that talking to their parents might result in a decision to prohibit their participation in a sport the children wanted to play.

While parents may push their kids into youth sports, they apparently try less hard to keep them involved as they get older. A number quit or get cut, but many continue playing through high school. As noted earlier, 53 percent of boys and 28 percent of girls in high school say that sports are a big part of who they are (Sabo and Veliz 2008). Recall, too, that approximately 7.4 million kids were involved in high school sports, according to the *Go Out and Play* study. Many others were also involved in youth sports clubs or other sports programs outside the school. The vast majority of the parents of these kids thought competitiveness in these programs was somewhat or very important, and a significant percentage got upset enough with their kids' efforts to yell at them from the sidelines. These findings highlight the significance of Devereux's arguments about lost opportunities when kids are involved in Little Leaguism instead of more informal or spontaneous play on their own initiative.

So, on the one hand, there are so-called helicopter parents, who hover over their kids and make all their decisions, and soccer moms, who overorganize their kids' lives in an effort to put them on the path to later success or at least to keep them out of trouble. These types of parents are likely to feel quite comfortable with Little Leaguism, even though their kids' involvement in sports could affect their lives and the lives of other family members and strain the family's resources. On the other hand, there are parents who exercise little or no parental responsibility, who let their kids go wherever or do whatever they want, or who keep little track of their kids. Somewhere in between are the parents who embrace Devereux's ideas and try to provide the combination of nurturing, protection, and safe opportunities for trial and error that kids and adolescents seem to need for healthy development. These are the parents who allow their kids the freedom to play on their own, while also supporting them in the organized activities they want to pursue. They teach responsibility and an understanding of limits, but also allow them to succeed and fail and encourage them whatever the outcome. At least in regard to sport, it seems increasingly difficult to be this kind of parent, because Little Leaguism is so pervasive. Parents also seem to be suspicious or hostile when coaches fail to be assertive enough in exercising their authority over the kids, as George Davis learned.

The increasing influence of the golden triangle over youth sports and interscholastic athletics means that more of the most talented young athletes will be turned into commodities whose interests and welfare are secondary to the sports, media, and sponsors who invest in them. It also means that the parents who can afford it will spend more of their time and money on sports for their kids and that communities that can afford it will spend more of their tax money and raise more money to build more extravagant sports facilities for their most popular sports. Parents and communities that cannot afford these commitments and investments will find themselves strained or drained.

We should not forget that sports participation may be an important catalyst and institutional resource that can lead to a number of beneficial outcomes for young people, their schools, and their communities. There might even be circumstances where sports participation keeps kids out of trouble or minimizes the trouble they get into. However, the value of participation in sports for children and adolescents and how much they enjoy it are likely to be influenced by their socioeconomic status and whether the adults who run their programs are more concerned about their own interests or the interests and welfare of the kids for whom their programs are supposed to exist. The issue of the welfare of athletes arises again in the context of college athletics, especially where the golden triangle is most influential. College athletics is the focus of the next chapter.

Stop and Think Questions

1. How do socialization into sport and socialization through sport differ, and what are examples that show the difference?

2. What do the sports interests of US and German teenagers reveal about the globalization of sport, and how do their interests and participation reveal both Americanization and the influence of local culture?

3. What is "Little Leaguism," and how may soccer moms and helicopter parents reinforce Little Leaguism and deprive their children of chances to play?

4. How does high school sports participation act as a catalyst for positive educational outcomes, and to what extent do sports keep kids out of trouble?

5. How does the golden triangle turn talented young athletes into commodities, and what is an example of this process?

6. Why is football the most dangerous sport for adolescents in the United States, and in what sense are certain sports more dangerous for the adolescent girls than for the boys who play them?

7. How do social class and race shape the sports experiences of young people in the United States?

7

College Athletics

The Penn State cover-up in Chapter 5 introduced us to college athletics with a look at the seamy side. In this chapter, we will take a broader and more detailed look at college athletics as a form of commercial entertainment (see Clotfelter 2011). It is the world of big-time college sports, and the intercollegiate golden triangle plays a prominent role in this world (see Nixon 2014). The people who run college sports on the campuses and in organizations such as the NCAA paint an idealized picture of intercollegiate athletics with genuine student-athletes who pursue their education while also playing sports. The inconsistency or tension between the commercial realities of big-time college sports and the rhetoric of the amateur student-athlete and educational justifications is an important part of understanding this big-time sports world and how it affects those involved in it.

Athletics was the first significantly commercialized aspect of US higher education. This commercialism and intercollegiate athletics itself had rather humble origins. According to sports historians (e.g., Betts 1974), college athletics began with an eight-oared barge or crew race between Harvard and Yale on Lake Winnipesaukee in New Hampshire in 1852. While there were no paying spectators and no mass media coverage, this event could be characterized as professional as well as commercial. It was the idea of a railroad owner and real estate developer. His railroad went from Boston to Lake Winnipesaukee. His idea was to market vacation lots he wanted to sell in the southern New Hampshire lake area through a sports event. Crew was a popular sport at that time, and he hoped to get wealthy friends and families of the Harvard and Yale rowers to ride his railroad to the race and invest in his vacation lots (Deford 2005). The athletes were induced to compete with offers to pay all their expenses and provide "lavish prizes" and "unlimited alcohol" (Bok 2003:35).

Although we generally do not think of Ivy League institutions as athletic powerhouses today, their role was pivotal in the growth, popularization, and commercialization of college athletics in the United States. By 1850, Harvard had organized intramural and interclass competitions and a sports day for its students. The sports day was called "Bloody Monday." It was quickly copied by other institutions and became a model for sports competition between colleges and universities (Nixon 1984:106–110; Nixon and Frey 1996:142–144). Intercollegiate sports in the United States did not begin with the organizational trappings that we typically associate with college athletics today. For example, in their earliest days, students controlled their sports, faculty members were involved if students wanted them to be, and colleges and universities did not officially sanction or authorize them (Nixon 1984:106–107). These sports were more similar to the student-run "club" model on many campuses today than to university-run sports programs, and this model had its roots in the student governance of athletics in private secondary schools of England in the nineteenth century. The model persists today in secondary schools and universities in Great Britain (Sage 1998:229).

During the second half of the nineteenth century, college sports—including both intramural and intercollegiate programs—grew slowly and steadily and eventually evolved into activities that were bureaucratically organized and controlled by higher-education institutions and alumni. Students lost control of their sports as administrators, faculty members, and alumni sought increasingly bigger roles in athletics. Many faculty members and administrators were dubious about the purposes of athletics in academic institutions, they saw athletics growing beyond the capacity of students to run them responsibly or effectively, and they had concerns about issues such as professionalism, financial mismanagement, and poor sportsmanship. At the same time, alumni wanted to see better-run athletic programs to generate both greater success on the field and more revenue. These concerns and desires led to the formation of faculty athletic committees, which either gave institutions regulatory control over student athletics or delegated authority over athletics to faculty, students, and alumni.

By the early 1900s, students had completely lost control over athletics, and, as athletics became more bureaucratized and commercialized, the faculty role in college sports diminished and the role of administrators and alumni grew. As college athletics expanded throughout the late nineteenth century and into the twentieth century, colleges and universities hired professional coaches, marketed to paying spectators, and recruited athletes to compete for their teams. Athletics came to be seen as a vehicle to serve institutional ends. The basic structure of college athletics as we know it today was largely in place by the 1920s, with smaller colleges broadly emphasizing physical recreation and intercollegiate athletics as part of student life and many bigger institutions organizing intercollegiate athletics as a form of entertainment with elite athletes.

The Popular and Peculiar Institution of Big-Time College Sports in the United States

As intercollegiate athletics became more popular in the late nineteenth century, colleges and universities tried to create more uniform standards for competition, academic eligibility, and other matters. This standardization usually occurred within newly formed conferences of similar types of institutions. Football, which began with a game between Princeton and Rutgers in 1869 and developed into a uniquely US form (see Riesman and Denney 1951), became a very popular college sport. In 1876, the popularity of football resulted in the formation of the Intercollegiate Football Association by Harvard, Yale, and Princeton. Despite regulatory efforts, a number of problems arose in college football concerning issues such as academic integrity, professionalism, institutional control, and injuries and even deaths of players (Betts 1974; Nixon and Frey 1996:145).

By 1905, concerns among faculty members, college administrators, and prominent officials had risen to a level where there were calls for abolishing the sport. The Intercollegiate Athletic Association of the United States (IAAUS) was formed in 1905 to address these concerns and establish regulatory control that emphasized responsible and effective institutional control, academic integrity, ethical behavior, and the welfare of student-athletes. The IAAUS became the National Collegiate Athletic Association (NCAA) in 1910, and it remains the dominant organizational and regulatory body in college athletics in the United States. The NCAA has been able to preserve college football and has overseen the organizational, popular, and commercial growth of college athletics in general. It remains formally committed to its organizing principles, but it has had to contend throughout its existence with many of the same issues and problems that faced the IAAUS at its inception.

The commercialized entertainment-oriented form of college sport was justified by college officials as a means to market the institution to prospective students, increase student morale and institutional loyalty, build alumni support, enhance the institution's visibility and reputation, and make money. I have called this the "institutional enhancement rationale" (Nixon 2014:8–9).

Although promotion of the university's "brand" or identity in the marketplace from athletic success may boost student enrollment on some campuses (Moody's 2013), on most campuses the claims in the institutional enhancement rationale have generally been overstated or untrue. But this has not seemed to diminish support for big-time athletics (Nixon 2014:ch. 1).

The National Football Foundation (2014) reported that NCAA football drew more than 50 million spectators during the 2013 season, its highest attendance ever. The University of Michigan led in attendance, with an average of over 111,500 spectators per game. Michigan broke its single-game attendance record in 2013 when 115,109 attended its game with Notre Dame. According to a survey of ticket prices on the online ticket seller TiqIQ, tickets for this game were expensive, with prices ranging from $372 to $727 per seat (Stankevitz 2014). It was not even the most expensive college football game to attend in 2013. The Texas-UCLA game earned that distinction in the TiqIQ survey. Its tickets cost from $144 to $770.

Other major revenue generators in college football are conference and bowl game payouts. For example, the Big Ten conference projected bowl game distributions of $4.7 million for each member institution in 2014–2015 and $7.1 million per school in 2016–2017 (Carmin 2014). Department of Education data showed that the football programs at perennial powers Texas ($104 million), Michigan ($85 million), and Alabama ($82 million) produced the most revenue in 2011–2012 (Jessop 2013). ESPN paid more than $150 million per year for broadcast rights to all five Bowl Championship Series (BCS) bowls, which were the most prestigious. The BCS championship game paid $30 million to the two contenders in 2013 (Smith 2013a).

In men's basketball, the NCAA reported that Syracuse University had an average attendance of over 26,000 during its 2013–2014 men's basketball season. Two other men's college basketball teams drew over 20,000 per game that year. The signature event in men's college basketball, so-called March Madness, reached a nineteen-year high in viewership in 2013, with the combination CBS, TBS, TNT, and TruTV attracting an average of 10.7 million viewers per game. The championship game between winner Louisville and Michigan had an audience of 23.4 million. Only the Alabama–Notre Dame BCS Championship game attracted more college sports viewers that year (26.4 million). The tournament also generated $1.15 billion in ad revenue (Van Riper 2014).

The popular and lucrative world of big-time college sports is an interesting mixture of contradictions. Benedict and Keteyian's (2013) book *The System* captures these contradictions in its subtitle, *The Glory and Scandal of Big-Time College Football*. They observed that college football was never more popular—or more chaotic. Yet the public and fans seem to be paying less and less attention to the chaos and problems. A poll conducted for the Knight Commission in 1990 showed that 75 percent of respondents thought college sports were out of control, and another poll in 1993 showed that 52 percent of respondents held this belief. In 2005, the percentage holding this belief had declined to 44 percent (Knight Commission 2006). Thus, there was a trend of *declining* concern about the state of college sports. This is despite the fact that most poll respondents in 2005 expressed concerns about professionalism, commercialism, the high salaries of coaches, the influence of companies and media in the golden triangle, and competitive pressures on athletes. Although they recognized these problems, 83 percent of survey respondents said their overall view of college sports was positive. The success of universities and the intercollegiate golden triangle in selling the institutional enhancement rationale is an important reason why big-time college sports remain popular. This is despite the dubious validity of the institutional enhancement rationale on most campuses and widespread public questions and concerns. Another significant reason for the continuing popularity of big-time college sports is the effectiveness of the intercollegiate golden triangle in creating entertaining and compelling spectacles that fans love.

Over the past century, big-time college sports have been able to withstand a series of attacks from reform-minded journalists, faculty, and investigative bodies. In 1926, a prestigious commission funded by the Carnegie Foundation conducted a series of investigations of college sports that resulted in well-publicized reports in 1929 and 1931 (see Savage 1929). These reports were critical of the increasing use of professional coaches and trainers and the special treatment of athletes. Other commissions and reports followed. They raised concerns about issues such as professionalism and commercialism, governance and the lack of university oversight, the influence of gambling, academic corruption, runaway expenses, and the status and welfare of student-athletes. Although the Knight Commission has had some impact on academic standards for athletes over the past two decades, none of the commissions or reports has done much to derail the big-time college sports juggernaut of the intercollegiate golden triangle or reduce the influence of the commercialism that is the root of many of the problems in big-time college sports (Nixon 2014; Nixon and Frey 1996:160–162). The golden triangle has pumped too much revenue into big-time college sports and provided too much exposure for universities to turn their backs on their media and business partners.

Even more than at the high school level, the golden triangle influence in college sports has made the interests of student-athletes secondary to the interests of the people who run their sports and make money from their efforts. As Clotfelter (2011:52) suggested, big-time college sports have never really been about or for students. For over a century, it has been commercialized mass entertainment organized primarily to serve the interests of the major institutional players in the golden triangle. The main beneficiaries are the universities, their top-tier athletic programs, the major conferences, the NCAA, and the media and the other businesses that represent the major sectors of the golden triangle. Their underlying interest in building brand recognition and making money have had little to do with education or students.

Prominent sports writer Frank Deford (2005) referred to the mix of higher education and big-time athletics as "America's Modern Peculiar Institution." With its extensive and lucrative ties to the golden triangle, big-time intercollegiate athletics has been a uniquely US phenomenon. The highly commercialized sports of the intercollegiate golden triangle are characterized by extensive recruitment, offers of athletic scholarships, and implied promises of professional or Olympic opportunities for the most talented. The scholarships and dreams they evoke are incentives for serious young athletes from the United States and abroad to play big-time college sports in the United States. They are not dissuaded by the realities of limited opportunity, just as fans are not turned off by the seamy side of college sports they see or hear about or by facts that cast doubt on the institutional enhancement rationale (Nixon 2014:ch. 1).

Probe 7.1: Big-Time College Sports as Social Capital

According to Frederick Rudolph (1962), in his book *The American College and University*, "By 1900 the relationship between [college] football and public relations had been firmly established and almost everywhere acknowledged as one of the sport's major justifications" (385). A more recent variation of this justification of big-time football and commercialized college sports in general was offered by the then chancellor of the University of Kansas, Robert Hemenway, who was also the chair of the NCAA's Division I board of directors (quoted in Suggs 2004). He asserted that successful football and basketball teams produced a sense of community and a kind of "social capital" that justified their expense. He said, "Social networks have value," adding, "that's what we create with 50,000 or 60,000 in the football stadium. . . . When I go to meet our alumni, the first thing they ask about is how we're doing on the field." In a related comment, former University of Maryland president Dan Mote said, "A very visible, very successful athletic program gives you lots of entrées. It changes the understanding of state government, the state legislature, and of the business community and alumni" (quoted in Bok 2003:50).

Stratification and Organizational Conflicts in College Sports Today

College presidents and trustees at "big-time universities"—that is, ones with big-time sports programs on their campus—often talk glowingly about their most visible athletic programs, coaches, and athletes. It is obvious that the athletic programs that they value most are the ones that give their institutions the most visibility, prestige, and clout in their states and across the nation. Their bias toward these big-time programs is a reflection of the *athletic trap*, which was created and is reinforced by the golden triangle. Recall from Chapter 5 that this trap is defined as a complex array of social, economic, and political commitments that severely constrains athletic decisions by university leaders. These decisions favor the interests of the most popular sports programs on their campus, which are generally football and men's basketball at the highest level of college sports.

Popular sports are the most valued and supported on campus because they attract the most investment from boosters and the media and businesses in the golden triangle and are believed to do the most to enhance the institution's brand. College presidents may find themselves in the athletic trap either because their school already plays at the big-time level or because they want or are feeling pressure to move up to the big time. The trap is difficult to escape because financial obligations, relationships, and expectations regarding big-time sports are firmly in place. Alumni, boosters, fans, and some trustees do not readily give up their desire or passion for these sports programs. Part of the resiliency of established big-time programs can be attributed to their association with the brand of the university. University leaders do not easily give up these historic commitments to big-time sports on campus.

The outcome of the skewed investments of the golden triangle and the resulting sports biases among university leaders is a high degree of stratification in college sports on campus and beyond. There are "haves" and "have-nots" and there are big gaps between them. This stratification has various dimensions. First, there are top-tiered revenue-generating sports that have the best facilities, the best coaches, and the most scholarships. They are usually football and men's basketball, but some campuses may make relatively big investments in other sports such as ice hockey, lacrosse, or women's basketball. Title IX is a complicating factor, but it has not prevented institutions from investing much more in football and men's basketball than in women's sports. The hierarchy in many big-time athletic departments is football and men's basketball at the top tier, women's basketball at the next level, followed by an assortment of other sports that offer athletic scholarships and generate some revenue. The men's and women's programs that generate little or no revenue and offer few, if any, scholarships share a common low status. However, when Title IX is made an issue or more money is needed for struggling top-tier programs, lower-tier men's programs are most likely to go on the chopping block and be cut.

Beyond individual universities, we see stratification in the NCAA and among the conferences. The NCAA reported that it had 460,000 student-athletes playing 23 sports at 1,084 institutions in 2014 (Emmert 2014). The competing National Association of Intercollegiate Athletics (NAIA) is far behind in size and visibility. The NAIA had approximately 300 members and 60,000 student-athletes in 2014. The members were mostly small colleges and universities along with conferences. Since NAIA members are outside the intercollegiate golden triangle, we will not be paying attention to them. The big-time athletic programs at the top level of the NCAA that rely on their ties to the golden triangle are the primary focus of this chapter.

The NCAA is internally stratified, with a hierarchy of three major divisions, from the highest or "big-time" Division I to the lower-level Divisions II and III (NCAA 2014). Division I member schools have to compete in at least seven sports for men and seven for women, or six for men and eight for women. At least two of the men's sports and two of the women's sports must be team sports. Division I schools with football are classified as either Football Bowl

Subdivision (FBS) (formerly Division I-A) or Football Championship Subdivision (FCS) (formerly Division I-AA). All Division I members must meet minimum financial aid award standards and cannot exceed a stipulated maximum award level. However, football programs in the FBS must meet a minimum attendance requirement (15,000 average). They also tend to spend much more on their football programs than do schools at the FCS and lower NCAA levels, and they generate much more revenue. This is because FBS football teams draw many more spectators and benefit much more on average from media exposure and sponsorships in the golden triangle. In 2013–2014, there were 120 FBS schools and 125 FCS schools. The remaining one hundred member schools in Division I have big-time basketball but not football programs.

For a number of years, football teams from eleven conferences and a few independents such as Notre Dame, Army, and Navy in the FBS competed in the BCS for the right to participate in one of five major bowl games, including one each year that was designated as the national championship bowl game. FBS teams that did not qualify for one of the five BCS bowl games could qualify to play in another bowl game. The "College Football Playoff" replaced the BCS in 2014. It uses a new format, with a rotation among six semifinal bowl sites leading up to the championship game. In the first College Football Playoff championship game, played January 12, 2015, Ohio State defeated the University of Oregon 42–20.

The BCS bowl games were the most prestigious, most widely publicized, and most lucrative bowls, and they generated the most television revenue. However, there has been a proliferation of less-elite postseason football bowl games, reflecting their perceived potential to generate revenue for the sports entrepreneurs, advertisers, and media that constitute "local golden triangles" associated with these games. They are also perceived as important sources of revenue and publicity for football programs, their institutions, and their conferences once the regular season has ended. Returns can fall short of expectations in even the most lucrative bowl games, though, as schools pay travel expenses and are saddled with the cost of unsold game tickets they must purchase (CBS Miami 2014; Harris 2011). Schools competing in less prestigious bowls at the FBS level and in FCS playoff games rarely make money and also get relatively little media exposure for their investment.

In general, within Division I, there is a stratification of conferences. With a lot of television money at stake, conferences have been competing over the past decade for members in the biggest or most attractive television markets. This has led to a lot of movement or *churning* among schools seeking to affiliate with the most prestigious conferences offering the biggest payouts to their members (Nixon 2014:37–40). The churning has generally involved the movement of top and bottom teams out of conferences and into new ones. This dance of conference realignment has attracted the most attention at the FBS level, since the most media and sponsorship revenue is at stake at this level. This dance has been propelled largely by the quest for more lucrative television contracts in football, with conferences and some major individual football powers such as the University of Texas establishing their own networks in partnership with media corporations such as ESPN. The NCAA has retained its hold over basketball with its lucrative long-term television contract for March Madness. But with control over football television contracts mainly under the auspices of the conferences and major football programs, the NCAA has had to sit on the sidelines and watch schools and conferences battle with each other in the realignment dance.

Big-time college sports had achieved some stability at the highest level in the early years of the BCS with six elite conferences: the Atlantic Coast Conference (ACC), Big East, Big Ten, Big 12, Pac-12, and Southeastern Conference (SEC). However, the Big East was essentially a basketball conference, experiencing much less success in football. As a result, the more prominent football schools in the conference gravitated to other conferences that were more successful in football and offered the promise of bigger payouts from television. The turbulence or conflict involving conference realignment that began around 2010 reshaped the landscape of college sports. During the ensuing three years, about 25 percent of major football programs had changed conferences, and relatively few unaffiliated major schools remained (Bostock, Carter, and Quealy 2013). By 2013, the Big East was so decimated by departures that the Elite Six became the Big Five. The stature of the Big Five was defined by its TV revenue, with average distributions of TV revenue to individual conference teams estimated to range from $17 million to $23 million in FY2013 (Moody's 2013).

Moves by the University of Maryland from the ACC and Rutgers from the Big East to the Big Ten illustrate the underlying dynamics of churning and conference realignment (Mandel 2014). Neither school was a football power, and Maryland had slipped in men's basketball since winning a national championship in 2002. The attraction of the Big Ten, with its much bigger financial payouts to member schools, is fairly obvious, but the reason for the Big Ten's interest in these schools may not be so obvious. It becomes clearer in the context of the conference's shrinking population base in the Midwest. Maryland and Rutgers enabled the conference to increase its presence in the populous Northeast and reach the lucrative Washington, DC, and New York media markets. As usual in the golden triangle, money was the major driver of change.

Probe 7.2: Tensions and a Power Grab in the NCAA

In 2014, a number of prominent college sports experts wrote about a possible "power grab" by the Big Five that could result in a new NCAA division (Porto, Gurney, Lopiano, Ridpath, Sack, Willingham, and Zimbalist 2014). If unsuccessful in gaining the autonomy within the NCAA they desired, conference members threatened to establish their own organization outside the NCAA. They would bring with them the formidable resources from their golden triangle media and business partners, especially from football and the new College Football Playoff. This effort was motivated by a desire for more power to control their own destinies, including the power to keep more of the golden triangle revenue for themselves. The big revenue and wealth gap between the Big Five and the other conferences would grow much bigger. The NCAA was already facing serious threats from antitrust lawsuits and from a push toward unionization by football players at Northwestern University (Strauss 2014). By the late summer of 2014, the NCAA had bowed to pressure from its most powerful conferences and granted them more autonomy (Tracy 2014). They got the right to make their own rules on various issues concerning athletes and competition. This was another blow to NCAA control over college sports and the status and power of have-nots in the organization. It also raised questions about whether the changes would create even more distance between the NCAA and its stated educational mission. In addition, within the Big Five conferences, there were concerns among the less wealthy athletic departments that they would not be able to afford the costs, such as new athlete stipends, that greater autonomy could bring (New 2014b).

One sports commentator used the term "class warfare" to refer to relations between the haves and the have-nots in the NCAA in 2014 (Dodd 2014). He discussed the nature and implications of the gap between the 65 schools in the Big Five (the haves) and the other 286 schools in the NCAA Division I (the have-nots). He discussed the worry among the have-nots that the haves' moves toward autonomy would deprive them of the resources they needed to compete at a high level. The have-nots have riled the haves by standing in the way of changes the haves wanted so that they could provide more support for athletes. They wanted this authority in part to stave off the push toward more market-based compensation (i.e., "pay for play") and employee rights for athletes.

An example of tensions between the haves and the have-nots concerns cost-of-attendance stipends. The haves wanted a cost-of-attendance stipend for athletes to supplement their athletic scholarships. The Presidents Council in the NCAA approved the stipend, but it was voted down by the have-nots, who feared it would add another cost to budgets they were having difficulty balancing. A president of a Big Five school expressed a view shared by a number of his peers in commenting that "a lot of people want to be in Division I but do not want to do Division I" (quoted in Staples 2012). What he meant was that only some schools could afford to compete at the highest level, while others wanted to be at this level without the resources to be there. Presidents of schools in the big-time elite seemed to resent the influence of schools that they thought did not belong in the big time and should not have a vote on big-time issues. What seemed like class warfare to some actually was the desire by the elite or Big Five schools to separate their big-time programs from the have-nots and the rest of the NCAA (Nixon 2014:59).

Although inequalities spawn tensions and conflict in college sports, there is an even more fundamental source of conflict within big-time college sports. It is the amateur status of college athletes, which involves the legal treatment of them as students and which prohibits them from being paid as employees. In 1956, the NCAA created the athletic grant-in-aid or athletic scholarship to provide financial aid for athletes on the basis of their athletic ability rather than academic qualifications. This treatment of college athletes involves basic contradictions that represent a clash between two very different models of college sports, which I have called the "collegiate model" and the "commercial model" (Nixon 2014:6–8). Simply described, the collegiate model is an idealized conception of college sports organized around the interests of athletes as students. It has some credibility at the least commercialized level in the NCAA, Division III. However, this conception has little relevance to the big-time college sports world oriented to the commercial model, which focuses on the uses of college sports for commercial purposes. This is the world of the intercollegiate golden triangle.

We often hear lofty rhetoric about college sports from college presidents and NCAA officials that projects an image embodied in the collegiate model, but the realities of big-time college sports are more closely aligned with the commercial model. So when highly commercialized big-time college sports programs are extolled for their commitment to amateurism and the welfare of student-athletes, the rhetoric seems out of sync with reality or even disingenuous. Although athletic scholarships are construed by university and college sports officials as grants to support the education of big-time athletes, the fact that college athletes are paid on the basis of their ability to play a sport is in itself a contradiction of the collegiate model. Critics have long taken issue with the hypocrisy in big-time college sports in invoking the collegiate model when the commercial model is more appropriate. More recently, a number have focused on the inadequate or unfair compensation of star athletes in big-time college sports and have advocated a "pay for play" model that drops the pretense of amateurism and allows athletes to be paid in the same marketplace as their coaches. The conflict between collegiate model rhetoric and commercial model realities is a central theme of this chapter. We will examine in upcoming sections the increasing turbulence in big-time college sports coming from direct challenges to the collegiate model rhetoric.

From the AIAW to NCAA Women's Sports

Another important source of conflict in college sports has revolved around women's sports and gender equity. In Chapter 3, we briefly considered the meteoric rise and fall of the Association for Intercollegiate Athletics for Women (AIAW) from the early 1970s to the early 1980s during the period of the passage and initial implementation of Title IX. We looked at the AIAW then in the context of gender inequality. We examine it here in relation to its conflict with the NCAA.

The NCAA faced a serious challenge to its power and financial status in the 1970s following the passage of Title IX. As women's college sports exploded during this period, a new organization arose to foster this growth and provide major competitive opportunities for women in college athletics. The AIAW was established by an organization of women physical educators in 1971 as the first major governing body for women's intercollegiate athletics (Morrison 1993; Nixon and Frey 1996:147–148). It grew out of an earlier organization, the Commission on Intercollegiate Athletics for Women (CIAW), which was formed in 1966 to sponsor national championships for women. However, it soon became clear that a much larger institutional membership organization with wider institutional representation was needed for this purpose, and thus the AIAW replaced the CIAW.

Like the men's IAAUS, the AIAW began with a principled approach and high-minded goals. Its organizers embraced an amateur model of athletics akin to the collegiate model and tried to establish policies that respected the rights of student-athletes. Its founding principles emphasized striving for and rewarding excellence in sport. But they also focused on using sport as a chance for education and development for those who do not win; women governing and leading women; women serving as role models to empower other women; providing numerous, inclusive, and diverse sports opportunities for women and opportunities for women with different skill levels; and accommodating athletes who wished to transfer, return to school after dropping out, or try out for the Olympics (Morrison 1993:61–62). Many AIAW members wanted to create an organization that differed from the NCAA and men's athletics in being less bureaucratic and less commercialized and more responsive to the needs of student-athletes. At first, there were no athletic scholarships, no transfer limitations, and no limits on the number of sports a college or university could offer. The AIAW also depended on self-policing and the integrity of individual institutions rather than a formal enforcement unit to maintain control over possible excesses or deviance in athletic programs.

As an indication of the lack of "big-time" or large-school dominance in the early years of the AIAW, a tiny eight-hundred-woman college in Pennsylvania, Immaculata College, was able to win the first three AIAW national basketball championships between 1972 and 1974 (Byrne 2005). However, even during these early years, conflicts arose about the direction of the organization. The AIAW began to drift toward a more competitive, professionalized, and commercialized sports model that favored bigger institutions. For example, in 1973, AIAW institutions began offering athletic grants-in-aid or scholarships rather than strictly need-based scholarships to athletes, and in 1975, television covered a regular-season women's college basketball game for the first time (Jenkins 2007). Immaculata defeated the University of Maryland in that game and then went on to play in front of 12,000 spectators in the first women's college game at Madison Square Garden in New York City later that season. Immaculata was AIAW runner-up in 1975 and 1976, but it lacked the money and desire to continue competing at the top level of the evolving women's basketball game.

The first nationally televised broadcast of the AIAW basketball championship, which was tape delayed, was in 1978, and by then, the larger universities had begun to take over the sport, with UCLA defeating Maryland (Jenkins 2007). Title IX, which had created the interest in women's sports that was needed to justify the investment of television and the golden triangle, ironically may have created an environment in which it was increasingly difficult for smaller institutions to compete successfully against much bigger ones, as Immaculata once did (Byrne 2005). Pushed by Title IX to create more opportunities and better funding for women's sports, the bigger universities became increasingly difficult competitors for much smaller institutions with much smaller athletic budgets and recruiting capabilities.

The AIAW was able to grow during the 1970s despite some organizational problems related to administrative inexperience and internal disagreements among member institutions. Its growth was made easier by the absence of organizational competition or interference from the NCAA, which had no interest at the time in sponsoring championships in women's sports. The AIAW grew from 278 charter member institutions in 1971 to 950 members in 1981, and in 1980–1981, it sponsored thirty-nine championships. Thus, the AIAW was able to take advantage of the surge in popularity of sports among girls and women that was made possible by Title IX. The AIAW estimated that at the beginning of the 1980s, 120,000 women—in comparison with 180,000 men—were competing in college sports (Eitzen and Sage 1997:293; Nixon 1984:122). Along with providing regular and high-level competitive opportunities for female athletes in college, it gave women the chance for leadership roles as coaches and athletic administrators. However, the growing success of the AIAW ultimately led to its demise, as it tempted the NCAA to get involved in women's sports.

In the context of the growing popularity of women's college sports and the uncertainties associated with the future influence of Title IX on NCAA men's sports, NCAA member institutions voted at the association's 1981 convention to sponsor women's championships and govern women's sports without any additional cost to member institutions (Nixon and Frey 1996:148). In addition, the NCAA offered a television package for both men's and women's championships that guaranteed a national audience for the women, and it scheduled its national championships for women at the same time the AIAW scheduled its championships. Although the women received less support than the men to travel to championships and less championship revenue, the assorted inducements offered by the NCAA to the women led to a rapid decline in AIAW membership as institutions switched from the AIAW to the NCAA. Within months of the NCAA vote, there was a 20 percent drop in AIAW membership and a 48 percent decline in Division I AIAW championship participation. Perhaps the final blow was notification by the NBC television network that it would not televise future AIAW championships and that it would not pay the approximately $500,000 it had agreed to pay the AIAW between 1981 and 1983. The intercollegiate golden triangle chose sides and the AIAW had to face the consequences. With these new realities, the AIAW executive board concluded that it could no longer operate effectively on behalf of female college athletes and decided to dissolve the association in 1982 (Morrison 1993:64).

Although joining the NCAA has resulted in benefits for women's sports programs in participation opportunities, funding, media attention, and commercial support, it also has had costs. Under the AIAW, women's college sports were administered and coached by women. But as we saw in Chapter 3, under the NCAA, many female directors of women's athletics became associate directors of athletics for women's sports, and many women coaches lost their jobs to male coaches, who saw new opportunities in a more professionalized and commercialized world of women's college athletics.

The Business of College Sports in the Intercollegiate Golden Triangle

The battle between the NCAA and the AIAW clearly showed that in the business of college sports, the golden triangle goes where the best branding and revenue opportunities are. The idea of college sports as a business may seem at odds with the status of universities as not-for-profit educational enterprises. Clotfelter (2011:33) observed that universities have a number of organizational peculiarities. For example, they lack the clearly defined objective of making money; they have shared governance in their academic domain; and they allow a lot of autonomy to the faculty members, who are the employees who conduct the main "business" of the university, which is education, research, and service. These organizational characteristics make universities unlike most business corporations. Commercialized athletics makes universities look much more like businesses. This is because big-time athletic departments and teams are organized with more centralized and autocratic control structures. In addition, athletic directors have no reservations about engaging in commercial activities or trying to increase revenue. They embrace being in the commercial entertainment business, without necessarily acknowledging it. Accountability is another element that makes athletics more businesslike than the academic side of the university. It is much easier to measure accountability and hold people accountable in athletics than in the academic realm, where educational quality and other goals are somewhat vaguely defined and hard to measure. The primary indicators of success in big-time athletics (i.e., attendance, revenue, winning, and rankings) are much easier to measure than academic goals and objectives.

Clotfelter (2011:35) pointed out that the university's vague institutional goals and decentralized structure of power have made it possible for activities not directly related to higher education to become part of the university structure. Thus, it was possible in the early years of commercialized college sports for college presidents to make vague claims about the relationship of athletics to education or the mission of the university. Their primary purpose was actually to use athletics to gain publicity and attract external financial support to increase enrollment and institutional viability. This became a "bargain with the devil" as presidents found themselves in an athletic trap that increased its grip as athletics became more entrenched on campus and more popular with the public and eventually with the golden triangle. They found themselves struggling to maintain control over this part of the university (Nixon 2014:ch. 6).

Thus, commercialized athletic programs tie universities to the world of commerce and the economic marketplace. They have the capacity to enhance recognition of the university name or brand and produce revenue to an extent academic programs cannot. The network of relationships in the intercollegiate golden triangle is the vehicle that makes these outcomes possible and makes big-time college sports look like a business. There are a variety of business relationships involving big-time universities in the golden triangle. They include selling radio and television broadcast rights, getting advertisers to invest in these broadcasts, allowing sponsors to display their brands on campus, and generating income from the sale of licensed clothing, mugs, and other products using university and athletic logos and other images. These commercial activities have enabled the big-time college sports business to grow over the past few decades.

With all this commercial activity and all the money that has flowed through the intercollegiate golden triangle, it is not surprising that 78 percent of the respondents in the 2005 Knight Commission public survey believed that athletic departments at colleges supporting big-time sports programs generated profits. An even bigger majority believed that, generally, successful teams produced more alumni donations for their university. In addition, 57 percent of self-identified college sports fans in the survey thought that spending more on salaries and operating expenses usually enabled teams to win more. There is no reason to assume public perceptions have changed since then, with the escalation in coaches' salaries and the inflation in the media contracts. The researchers noted, however, that at the time existing evidence failed to support these beliefs (Knight Commission 2006). The hold of big-time college sports may be so strong that it can sustain some of its biggest myths despite compelling contradictory evidence.

There are a number of oddities and paradoxes associated with the economics of big-time college sports. First, in the years following the economic downturn that began in 2008, public universities had to deal with reduced state subsidies, budget and program cuts, faculty salary freezes and less hiring, and rising tuition in higher education. Yet several years after the economic downturn, athletic department budgets and revenues at big-time universities continued their pattern of growth. Using data gathered by ESPN from the NCAA and the US Department of Education, Lavigne reported in 2014 that athletic

University of Texas football game at Longhorn Stadium. (© Noamfein/Dreamstime.com)

revenues were at their highest levels and that payrolls had surged an average of 40 percent since 2008. Total revenue for schools in the FBS increased by about one-third, or $8 billion, since the downturn, with substantial increases in ticket sales, donations, and television contracts. Despite this financial surge, big-time college sports continued to be a losing proposition over this period for all but a relatively few big-time universities.

The NCAA president reported in 2014 that member schools collectively spent about $13.8 billion per year on athletics, including $2.7 billion on financial aid. Although athletic spending was only 3.8 percent of institutional budgets on average, this spending was problematic in most cases because it produced a deficit of operating expenses over athletics-generated income. This deficit collectively was $6 billion per year (Emmert 2014). Some very big deficits of tens of millions of dollars were at the FBS level. Data over the past several years have consistently shown that between twenty and twenty-three big-time universities in the FBS generated enough revenue without institutional subsidies to cover their costs in athletics (Lavigne 2014). This represented about 10 percent of Division I schools playing football, and all were in three of the Big Five conferences in 2013—the Big 12, SEC, and Big Ten (Moody's 2013). Everyone else in commercialized college sports runs a deficit without subsidies.

The financial boom in college sports has obviously not produced the same returns or benefits for everyone. On the one hand, the wealthiest athletic department, the University of Texas, generated $166 million in revenue and a surplus of $18.9 million in 2012–2013. Ohio State University had the biggest athletic surplus, $24 million, that year from revenues of $140 million (Bennett 2014). Ohio State's surplus is a little misleading, though, because it had to pay $16.6 million in debt service on bonds issued to fund athletics new construction and renovations. At the other end of the financial scale was Rutgers, which reported the biggest deficit among FBS schools of $47 million without subsidies (Lavigne 2014). We can understand why it was so eager to move to the Big Ten, with its generous conference payouts.

Division I schools use subsidies, such as student fees, to try to balance their athletic budget (Berkowitz, Upton, and Brady 2013). Athletic subsidies increased by a median 25 percent between FY2008 and FY2012 (Moody's 2013). Athletics is a part of the institutional budget for schools at the Division III level because it is not expected to pay for itself. Division III budgets are much less than at higher NCAA levels. Deficits can be quite large in the FBS because the costs are highest at this level. We can understand why most institutions rely on subsidies, especially at the FCS level and in the lower ranks of the FBS. At some schools with little visibility and few connections in the golden triangle, subsidies can account for 85 percent or more of the athletic budget (Nixon 2014:34). However, it is striking that at the level of the richest haves, schools still use subsidies to support athletics. In 2012, 23 of the 228 athletic departments in public institutions in Division I of the NCAA made enough money from athletics to cover their expenses without subsidies. However, of the 23, 16 received subsidies, and 10 of the 16 received a bigger subsidy in 2012 than in 2011 (Berkowitz, Upton, and Brady 2013). This may seem odd, or greedy, but it more likely reflects the *arms race* in big-time college sports.

The arms race is a well-documented pattern of escalating spending in big-time college sports (Nixon 2014:ch. 4). According to a report by the well-known investment research and risk analysis firm Moody's Investor Service, athletics expenses at NCAA Division I schools almost doubled on average between 2004 and 2013, while other institutional expenses rose 58 percent during this period (Moody's 2013). It subtitled its report *Big-Time Sports Pose Growing Risks for Universities.* The risk taking is driven by the imperative of winning to create more publicity, enhance the university brand, and attract more investment from the intercollegiate golden triangle. Winning also attracts better athletic recruits. As in the nuclear arms race, competitors believe that if they do not outspend their opponents, they will fall behind them. Unilateral disarmament is not perceived to be an option for those who want to remain competitive and successful in the big-time sports world. The athletic trap makes rational decisions about spending in athletics much more difficult for college presidents. As a result, they pay the coaches of their big-time teams in football, men's basketball, and, in some cases, women's basketball more and more money, and they build bigger and more extravagant stadiums, arenas, and training facilities to attract the best coaches and best athletic recruits.

Probe 7.3: Spending and the Need to Win in Big-Time College Sports

Clotfelter (2011:116) observed that the main objective of athletic departments, unlike for-profit businesses, is not to make money for its own sake. It is to win, and money is needed to be able to be a big winner. It pays for coaches and facilities that bring in the best athletes. The problem is that athletics is structured to have winners and losers, and it can be difficult and very expensive to be a consistent winner. The arms race is a consequence of this competitive reality. Clotfelter (2011:121) cited "Bowen's axiom" to explain the relentless upward pressure on spending in higher education in general, but it applies especially well to the athletics arms race: you raise all you can and spend all you have. Saving money does little to help you keep up with your extravagant foes. It may not be possible to win at the top level of college sports or move up the hierarchy without spending a lot of money, but spending does not guarantee success (e.g., Tsitsos and Nixon 2012). However, the lure of success in the golden triangle, the uncertainty of winning, and the compelling logic of the arms race push institutions to spend more to succeed or stay competitive.

Coaches, athletic directors, other top athletic administrators, and building contractors have been major beneficiaries of the arms race in big-time college athletics. For example, Alabama football coach Nick Saban signed a contract in 2014 that promised him at least $6.9 million per year for eight years. This contract was unanimously approved by the compensation committee of the University of Alabama System board of trustees (Berkowitz 2014). Two days later, Kentucky basketball coach John Calipari signed a seven-year contract extension worth $52.5 million. In the two previous years, Duke basketball coach Mike Krzyzewski earned $7.2 million and $9.7 million (Uthman 2014).

The arms race in coaches' salaries, which my colleague Bill Tsitsos and I (2012) have called "the star wars arms race," is illustrated by what happened to coaches' salaries in football between 2006 and 2012 (Nixon 2014:73). During this period, the number of football coaches in the FBS with salaries of at least $5 million increased from zero to two, the number earning at least $4 million went from zero to four, the number earning at least $3 million increased from one to thirteen, the number making at least $2 million rose from nine to forty-two, and the number receiving salaries of at least $1 million increased from forty-two to sixty-six. Overall, the salaries of FBS head football coaches rose 70 percent to an average of $1.64 million. In 2013, the average cost per win of football coaches in Big Five conferences was $259,409 in the Pac-12, $311,452 in the ACC, $357,278 in the Big Ten, $399,982 in the SEC, and $506,289 in the Big 12 (Trahan 2014).

The escalation of top-level coaches' salaries has also driven up the salaries of some "mid-major" basketball coaches, some athletic directors, and some women's basketball coaches to above $1 million per year (Nixon 2014:74–76). Striking contrasts can be drawn between these salaries and the more modest salaries of faculty and college presidents (Newman 2014). The irony of the big salaries in big-time college sports is that they are disproportionately paid by public universities, which dominate the highest levels of the commercialized college sports world.

The arms race may seem necessary and even rational, albeit worrisome, to athletic decision makers. But the fact is that spending more and more without the assurance of rising income to cover the rising costs does not really make logical sense from an accounting standpoint. However, the perceived need to compete and win, tradition, hope, and the athletic trap twist the logic of investment in big-time college sports. How do institutions afford the arms race? They struggle financially, rely on subsidies, and cut low-revenue or nonrevenue men's sports to have more money for their top-tier sports. Women's sports are usually protected from cuts because of fear of Title IX lawsuits. Having trustees, regents, and legislators who are caught up in the hoopla of big-time college sports, believe the hype or myths about it, or trust in the promise of next season enables big-time universities to stay in the arms race and big-time college sports despite defeats on the field and deficits in the budget.

The stratification of college sports means that competition in the golden triangle as well as on the field is not fair. The haves enjoy an advantage over the have-nots, and they are able to build on that advantage from year to year. We have already looked at the revenue and surpluses produced by the most successful FBS athletic departments. Although slightly dated, statistics from 2009–2010 more precisely show the gap between the haves and the have-nots. The median net athletics-generated revenue minus subsidies for FBS schools that year was $35.3 million, for FCS schools it was $3.3 million, and for all Division I institutions without football it was approximately $2 million. Net losses averaged $9.4 million at the FBS level, $9.2 million at the FCS level, and $8.6 million for institutions without football in 2009–2010. Deficits were obviously bigger in relation to revenues for schools not in the FBS. Their smaller stadiums, arenas, and fan bases and their more limited exposure in the golden triangle restricted their revenue-generating potential (Moltz 2011).

While having a lot of resources does not guarantee big-time success, lacking them makes consistent success from year to year much more difficult or even unobtainable. Competition in the marketplace of big-time college sports is biased toward the richer and more powerful conferences and schools with established big-time credentials. This marketplace is also biased against the economic interests of college athletes. In the next two sections, we will consider how the NCAA and big-time sports programs exploit athletes in the pursuit of their own economic interests.

The NCAA Cartel

According to some critics of the NCAA as a business, one of its most significant peculiarities is that it has been allowed to ignore antitrust laws and operate as a cartel. A *cartel* is a cooperative economic network of firms in a market that is organized to exert restrictive or monopolistic influence on the production and/or sale of a commodity or on the wages of workers in that market (Nixon and Frey 1996:146). With the intention of promoting economic competition, Congress passed the Sherman Antitrust Act of 1890 to prohibit trusts and other monopolies that restricted competition in the marketplace. However, the Supreme Court decided in 1922 that Major League Baseball (MLB) was not engaged in interstate commerce or trade and hence was not a commercial activity subject to the antitrust laws. In effect, this decision made it possible for MLB, other professional sports leagues, and the NCAA to claim their sports were not really businesses. In fact, they were businesses that benefited from their special or peculiar status, and they took advantage of it by organizing as cartels.

The NCAA made the argument that antitrust legislation did not apply to it because it was a voluntary organization involved with amateur sports whose procedures were determined by the consensus of members. When faced with threats such as the AIAW, it used its superior resources to eliminate this threat and expand the scope of its monopoly over college sports. The NCAA formed a football television committee in 1953 to restrict television broadcasts of members' games. This move enhanced the NCAA's dominant position in college sports and gave it significant leverage in its negotiations of broadcast rights fees with television networks. For a sixteen-year period until 1981, the ABC network was given the exclusive right to broadcast regular-season NCAA football games. After a while, though, major football programs wanted more power over media negotiations and the flow of media revenue. Many of the top football schools and conferences formed the College Football Association (CFA) in 1979 to represent their interests. Their efforts to negotiate their own television rights contracts led to battles with the NCAA, which culminated in a Supreme Court case in 1984 involving the University of Oklahoma and the University of Georgia. They had sued the NCAA over its monopolistic control of television broadcast rights. The court sided with the plaintiffs, resulting in the loss of the NCAA monopoly over football broadcasts and the rise of the rival CFA. The CFA eventually had its own internal problems and disbanded in the late 1990s. The void was filled by the BCS, which controlled postseason play in football. The latest iteration of big-time schools' control over football is the College Football Playoff. While the NCAA was forced to cede control over football, it retained control over basketball and media broadcast rights for its premier event, the men's basketball tournament. This has been a source of the continuing dominance by the NCAA in big-time college sports (see Nixon 2014:35–37).

The NCAA has also benefited from its control over college athletes. According to many economic experts, the NCAA's relationship to its "student-athletes" has constituted a labor cartel. For example, Zimbalist (1999) argued that the NCAA organized itself to restrict the economic freedom and legal rights of labor (i.e., athletes) in college sports in many ways. The *capitalist marketplace* is generally supposed to permit workers to try to maximize their economic opportunities and sell their services to the highest bidder. Other workers in big-time college sports, such as coaches, have taken full advantage of their opportunities in the athletic marketplace. The star wars arms race is clear evidence of this. Coaches have even broken contracts at times to move on to more lucrative opportunities. But the core "workers" in the business of college sports have not enjoyed the same economic rights as their coaches.

You might point out, as the NCAA does, that college athletes are students and are not really "workers" in a conventional sense and that many big-time athletes are compensated with scholarships, which allow them to attend and graduate from higher-education institutions that may be very prestigious and may cost as much as $60,000 or more per year. Yet, star athletes do not have a chance to earn the rewards of the highly commercialized world of college sports that are available to star coaches, and their economic rights as athletes are far more restricted than are the economic rights of coaches. They have not even been able to control the commercial use of their names, images, and likenesses (NILs) in video games, clothing, and other commodities sold by the intercollegiate golden triangle. In fact, the economic structure of the NCAA as a cartel has not been set up to benefit workers, per se, whether athletes or coaches. Its purpose has been to generate exposure, build brands, and make money for the organizations in the sports, media, and private business sectors of the intercollegiate golden triangle. Unlike athletes, coaches have been able to take advantage of the commercialism in big-time college sports because they have not faced the same economic and legal restrictions.

Being able to standardize and cap the major form of athletic compensation, the athletic grant-in-aid, is a fundamental element of the NCAA business model and allows it to keep this potentially much more expensive cost factor under control. Zimbalist (1999) noted a number of examples of structural factors that have restricted athletes but also have contributed to the success of the NCAA cartel: (1) athletes are treated as amateurs—or student-athletes—and are not allowed to receive direct compensation for their play; (2) until the rule was modified in the 1998–1999 academic year, athletes could not have a job during the school year; (3) the number of athletic scholarships in each sport and the maximum financial value of individual scholarships are limited; (4) athletes are not allowed to employ an agent to represent or counsel them; (5) athletes who sign a letter of intent to attend a college must attend that institution or they will have to wait a year before competing for another institution; and (6) athletes who transfer from one college to another must sit out a year.

Some rules, such as the requirement of the National Basketball Association (NBA) that basketball players wait a year after high school graduation and until age nineteen to enter the professional draft, show the cooperative relationship between the NCAA and other golden triangles to serve their mutual economic interests. The minimum-age rule assures the NCAA of access to outstanding athletes for at least one year. Although the best of these athletes may play for one year and then try to play professionally—the "one and done" pattern—it gives colleges access to outstanding athletes who otherwise might have skipped college and gone directly to the professional level. It also provides another year of seasoning for top prospects and gives the NBA a clearer sense of their readiness for the professional game.

There are also rules that reflect the stated educational purposes of the NCAA, such as the rule that athletes must meet NCAA-prescribed initial and continuing academic eligibility standards to be permitted to compete. However, the kinds of NCAA rules cited by Zimbalist help institutions limit their costs, give them some assurance that the athletes in whom they have invested a great deal in recruiting will play for them, and enable coaches to maximize their control over athletes as they try to maximize their own chances of success. Notwithstanding efforts to improve the academic readiness and performance of its student-athletes, the NCAA and big-time member institutions have benefited a great deal from the operation of the NCAA as a labor cartel. In recent years, however, this arrangement has been under increasing attack.

Threats, Attacks, and Changes in the NCAA

In 2014, the NCAA seemed to be under siege. It faced a seemingly endless series of threats and attacks from multiple sources. In addition to the move by Big Five conferences and schools to achieve autonomy, the NCAA had to deal with a number of lawsuits concerning the rights of athletes to engage in negotiations for use of their NIL rights in commercial products without being punished by the NCAA (McCann 2014a). The NCAA and eleven Division I conferences also faced a lawsuit filed by four current and former college athletes charging they illegally put a limit on football and basketball scholarships that was "substantially below" both the value of the players in the marketplace and the cost of attending college (Solomon 2014b).

Another major challenge to the NCAA in 2014 was a decision by a regional office of the National Labor Relations Board (NLRB) to support an effort by Northwestern football players to form a union (Grasgreen and Lederman 2014). The director of the NLRB Chicago office stated that all grant-in-aid scholarship players for the "Employer's" (i.e., Northwestern University) football team who were eligible to play were "employees" under the NLRB Act. As such, they were permitted to form a union and engage in collective bargaining as their counterparts in professional sports leagues did. The ruling cited a number of factors as justifications, including the idea that the football players performed services for the benefit of their employer and received compensation in the form of the scholarship and the idea that scholarship players were "subject to the employer's control in the performance of their duties as football players" (quoted in Grasgreen and Lederman 2014). The definition of the student-athlete as an amateur was the centerpiece of the NCAA commercial model, which meant that this ruling directly challenged this model. The ruling did not apply to walk-on players without scholarships because they did not qualify as employees.

None of the challenges faced by the NCAA and big-time college sports received as much publicity in 2014 as the suit brought by former UCLA basketball star Ed O'Bannon, who played on the 1995 NCAA national championship team. Unhappy as a college player that he could not get a share of the revenue made from using his image in video games, he later filed suit against the NCAA and the Collegiate Licensing Company claiming violations of the Sherman Antitrust Act. O'Bannon said the point of his lawsuit was not the money. It was getting the NCAA to change its rules about how it governed college sports and treated college athletes. He wanted more due-process protections for athletes, and he wanted them to be able to be compensated beyond the value of their athletic scholarship. O'Bannon was not naive. He realized how powerful the NCAA was and how entrenched its governance structure and business model were. He thought that a legal ruling and even a players association such as the one sought by Northwestern football players might not be enough to bring about the desired changes. He believed that more extreme action such as a player-led boycott might be needed (Wolverton 2013a).

Federal judge Claudia Wilkens ruled in the O'Bannon case that the NCAA could not prohibit compensation to college athletes for use of their NILs. But she capped the compensation at $5,000 per year for each year the student-athlete was academically eligible. This left open the possibility of both the NCAA and the plaintiffs appealing the decision (McCann 2014b). Thus, the idea of amateurism was seriously challenged, but the extent of the challenge was unclear and was subject to additional legal action.

Just prior to the O'Bannon trial, the NCAA reached a settlement in a lawsuit brought by former Arizona State quarterback Sam Keller and other plaintiffs. It awarded $20 million to "certain Division I men's basketball and Division I Bowl Subdivision football student-athletes who attended certain institutions during the years the (video) games were sold" (Rickman 2014). Electronic Arts (EA) and the Collegiate Licensing Company, which had been codefendants in the O'Bannon suit, previously agreed to a $40 million settlement, pending court approval. The combined amounts of the two agreements could pay individual athlete claimants more than $1,000 for each year their image appeared in EA video games (Solomon 2014a).

On top of all these serious threats was a US Senate Commerce Committee hearing, "Promoting the Well-Being and Academic Success of College Athletes."

Ed O'Bannon in his office in 2010 surrounded by memorabilia from his years as a UCLA basketball star; in 2009, a lawsuit bearing his name was filed against the NCAA seeking compensation for college athletes whose names, images, and likenesses were used for commercial purposes. (© Isaac Brekken/AP/Corbis)

NCAA president Mark Emmert faced questions about the rights of college athletes from legislators dubious about the claims of amateurism in a highly commercialized environment (New 2014a). The president's 8,000-word written testimony was a sweeping defense of college sports, including the big-time programs (Emmert 2014). He asserted that college sports provided more financial aid to more student-athletes than ever before, giving many of these young people a path to a college education and degree they otherwise might not have enjoyed. He also asserted that student-athletes had higher graduation rates than ever and that they entered college with better academic preparation than in the past and left better prepared for leadership roles in society. He acknowledged that his organization and its members had "witnessed some issues and challenges in every sport in every division." He noted that big-time football and men's basketball programs got the most attention and criticism. But he pointed out that the athletes in these programs were only 3.5 percent of all NCAA student-athletes. He realized, though, that the welfare of these athletes in big-time programs was the main reason he was called to testify before the Senate committee.

Arguing that his organization and its members were doing the best they could to take care of all NCAA student-athletes, he made a strong defense of what he called "the American collegiate model of athletics as compared to other models." He declared that NCAA student-athletes generally did not play sports to gain "tangible benefits" but instead were students and were treated as students. He made the broad statement that participation in NCAA sports was "a meaningful extension of the educational process" that gave student-athletes a chance to participate in a fair competition against other students in an educational environment. Emmert rejected the idea that athletic scholarships were compensation, calling them "educational support." He also rejected the idea that NCAA student-athletes were employees. These comments directly contradicted the NLRB ruling for scholarship athletes.

The NCAA president's rhetoric about his organization's commitment to a collegiate model rings hollow when applied to big-time college sports. A commercial model seems to provide a much more apt description of the NCAA's guiding principles in its dealings with the intercollegiate golden triangle. The NCAA and its member institutions may genuinely have concerns about the education and welfare of student-athletes at every level of the organization. However, the reality is that big-time college athletes have been treated as commodities in the golden triangle. This was the point of the NIL suits. They have also had few economic or legal rights. This was the point of the Northwestern athletes' effort to unionize.

Beyond the rhetoric, the NCAA's actions betrayed the realities of big-time college sports as business. The Keller case revealed the difficult balancing act for the NCAA, as it asserted a collegiate model but engaged in actions more closely aligned with a commercial approach. For example, although some current as well as former FBS football players and Division I men's basketball players could receive a monetary payment from a settlement fund in the Keller case, the NCAA was not willing to acknowledge that this was payment for athletic performance (Rickman 2014). It clearly was not in the interests of the NCAA to concede that it was actually operating with a commercial rather than collegiate model. In particular, it did not want to open the door to "pay for play."

The implications of the various rulings and court decisions involving the NCAA were likely to play out over a number of years. However, whatever the details of specific outcomes, the NCAA appeared to be on the defensive. In response, it seemed to engage in some preemptive actions to protect itself and as much of its underlying commercial model as possible. Downplaying his power in the Senate hearings, Emmert suggested a number of reforms he wanted to see, including guaranteed four-year athletic scholarships, scholarships that paid for the full cost of attendance, and better health care, safety, and insurance provisions for athletes. In the latter regard, he was sensitive to criticisms of the handling of concussions and other serious athletic injuries. He noted that these changes would have to be approved by NCAA member organizations. He also had to answer questions about member institutions' handling of sexual assault cases involving athletes, especially since over 20 percent of colleges and universities allowed athletic departments to have oversight of these cases (New 2014a).

Probe 7.4: Denying the Basic Necessities to Star College Athletes

Senator Cory Booker of New Jersey, who played football at Stanford University, commented that the issues raised in the hearing were problems when he was a college athlete twenty years earlier. He was particularly troubled by the exploitation of athletes expected to devote sixty to seventy hours per week to their sport, but could not afford the basic necessities (New 2014a). For example, the NCAA had been embarrassed when

University of Connecticut basketball star Shabazz Napier said after his team won the NCAA men's championship in 2014 that he sometimes went to bed "starving." Despite the provision for a meal plan in the UConn student-athlete guidelines, he did not have enough food and could not afford to buy any. Napier was happy to see the NLRB ruling on unionization at Northwestern. He appreciated his athletic scholarship but found it did not cover all his expenses.

Napier's case drew sympathy from Connecticut state legislators who saw in it the reasons Northwestern athletes wanted to unionize. The legislators wanted to put pressure on the NCAA to pay more attention to the welfare of student-athletes (Ganim 2014b). In fact, shortly after Napier's comments and with evidence from its own research that Napier was not the only NCAA athlete who received inadequate nutrition, the NCAA Division I Legislative Council approved a rule that permitted Division I programs to grant unlimited meals and snacks to all their athletes (Jessop 2014). Inattention to this matter left the NCAA open to criticism that it did not care about meeting the most basic needs of athletes. It appears that the NCAA is willing to listen to athletes if they are able to be compelling in front of a national audience. Of course, the NCAA has not been so responsive to calls for more fundamental changes.

The public has generally taken the side of the NCAA in matters of compensation of athletes. In the context of suits claiming the NCAA was "an unlawful cartel" and the efforts of student-athletes to unionize, the *Washington Post* and ABC News sponsored a scientific national poll of US adults about underlying issues in these actions (Prewitt 2014). Overall, 56 percent of respondents said they were fans of college sports, but there was a large gender discrepancy, with 66 percent of males and 47 percent of females saying they were fans. Among income groups, the most affluent earning $100,000 or more per year were most likely to say they were fans (64 percent). Similarly, Republicans (61 percent), the most educated with postgraduate education (64 percent), nonwhites (60 percent), ideological conservatives (60 percent), people aged sixty-five and older (58 percent), and Southerners (65 percent) were more likely than their demographic counterparts to say they were college sports fans.

The poll found that only 33 percent of respondents were in favor of paying salaries to athletes beyond their current scholarships. Forty-seven percent were strongly against this idea. The only demographic or political group favoring the idea was nonwhites, whose support was 51 percent. Seventy-three percent of whites were against paying athletes as salaried employees. The racial difference is not hard to explain if we recognize that it is easier for minority group members to identify with poor minority athletes such as Shabazz Napier who were experiencing financial hardships under the existing NCAA rules.

The NCAA should not have been too comforted by the results. Forty percent of men versus 27 percent of women and 37 percent of self-professed fans of college sports versus 27 percent of nonfans said they were in favor of paying college athletes. Furthermore, 47 percent of the public was in favor of permitting athletes to form a union to negotiate their rights and working conditions, which was the same percentage that opposed this idea. A striking 66 percent of nonwhites supported unionization, while 56 percent of whites opposed it. About two-thirds of respondents under forty supported unionization, while 57 percent of those over fifty were opposed to it.

It appears that the same kind of paradox in public attitudes about college sports that existed in 2005 continued to exist in 2014. The public had widespread concerns but still generally expressed support for college sports. If we exclude those who rarely or never followed college sports and we view as "fans" those who said they closely or occasionally followed college sports or only followed their favorite college teams, then 59 percent of the respondents in the 2005 Knight Commission survey were self-identified college sports fans. This is only a few points higher than the percentage of self-identified college sports fans in the 2014 *Washington Post*–ABC News poll. The 2014 results seemed to show some sympathy for efforts to change the NCAA's commercial model and the status of big-time student-athletes, with a large majority still not willing to accept the idea of paying colleges athletes a salary.

In 2005, the fans were much more likely than respondents in general (51 vs. 31 percent) to say that college sports were more like amateur sports than professional sports. The fans were also less likely than the average respondent (51 vs. 73 percent) to strongly or somewhat agree that college sports as big business conflicted with the values of higher education. At the same time, a nearly equal majority of fans and other respondents (58 and 59 percent) strongly or somewhat agreed that college athletes were exploited by corporate advertisers. This response by fans might seem surprising, but even more surprising are the findings that 63 percent of fans (vs. 68 percent of others) strongly or somewhat agreed that colleges should reduce their expenditures on big-time sports such as football and basketball and that 73 percent of fans (vs. 82 percent of others) strongly or somewhat agreed with a hypothetical initiative to require colleges to show that sports-related commercial contracts did not conflict with academic values.

It appears that fans still followed sports despite the apparent desire among a large number of them to see some commercial aspects kept under better control. Misgivings did not undermine their passion, with 68 percent of the fans saying they had a very positive overall opinion of college sports and another 30 percent saying they had a somewhat positive opinion. These are the kinds of fans who in 2014 recognized the need for better representation of athletes' rights but nevertheless bought the NCAA argument that being paid was not something that should occur in the amateur pursuit of college sports. Like it or not, though, the NCAA and big-time sports were changing as the myth of amateurism and the collegiate model in big-time college sports became more exposed.

The Myth of Amateurism and the Collegiate Model in Big-Time College Sports

For the vast majority of the 96.5 percent of NCAA student-athletes not at the top level, many or most of the NCAA's president's claims based on the collegiate model may be true. The NCAA president cited research showing that whether or not they receive athletic scholarships, student-athletes are generally more likely to complete their college degree, get a good job, and have a higher income than their nonathlete counterparts (Emmert 2014). These patterns even applied to Division I football and men's basketball players and to low-income and minority athletes. Using its own measure of graduation rates, the Graduation Success Rate (GSR), the president also cited data showing that the six-year graduation rate for student-athletes in 2013 was 82 percent, eight points higher than in 1995. Furthermore, he said, the GSR in 2014 was 71 percent for FBS football players and 73 percent for men's basketball players. He noted that since 1995, the graduation rate had risen 17 percent for men's basketball and 22 percent for African Americans in the sport. The GSR increased 8 percent in football since 1995, with an 11 percent increase for African American football players. He attributed these impressive increases to tougher NCAA academic standards. The NCAA president also pointed out that five members of the Commerce Committee, to whom he was testifying, and six of the previous eleven US presidents had participated in NCAA sports.

All of these observations seem to make a compelling case for the validity of the collegiate model and relevance of the amateur student-athlete idea in all of college sports. However, we have already seen that President Emmert's argument is not the whole story of the college athlete in big-time college sports. He ignores the constraints from the NCAA's operation as a labor cartel and the NCAA's exploitation of big-time college athletes. He also ignores cases of academic corruption and the lack of seriousness that a number of big-time college athletes display toward academics. This may be due to their lack of preparation or the overwhelming demands of balancing academic with athletic role responsibilities, which the Adlers (1991) found in their case study of a big-time men's college basketball team. Realizing that they cannot or do not want to meet the rigorous academic demands of a college education, these athletes turn to an "eligibility education."

It appears that Division I football players at the highest FBS level have had a harder time graduating than have football players at the FCS level. A measure called the "adjusted graduation gap" (AGG) compared the six-year graduation rates of football players with those of full-time male students on their campus. The four-year average FBS conference AGGs from 2010 through 2013 ranged from –13 in one conference (i.e., thirteen percentage points below the all-male student average for schools in the conference) to –28 in another conference at the other end of the continuum. Five of the six lowest-performing conferences were in the Big Five. For football players at FCS schools, the four-year average AGGs ranged from +7 and +1 (i.e., seven points and one point *above* the all-male student average for schools in their respective conferences) to –18 (reported in DeSantis 2013). Additional data comparing five-year average AGGs (between 2010 and 2014) for football players showed a six percentage point difference between the Big Five (–20) and other FBS conferences (–14). The gaps were greatest for black players in both sets of conferences (Southall, Sexton, and Waring 2014). Among tournament teams in big-time college basketball in 2014, women graduated at much higher rates than did their male counterparts (87 vs. 72 percent) (Pelts and Haldane 2014). These various results suggest more academic distractions or conflicts for athletes in more commercialized programs. The race results suggest the academic challenges of minority athletes having to balance sports and books and perhaps also their willingness to drop out of school to pursue their American Sports Dreams.

It appears that at the highest level, big-time (male) athletes focus disproportionately on sport and only enough on academics to remain eligible to play sports. In this regard, Ed O'Bannon testified in his antitrust trial that he was "an athlete masquerading as a student." He went on to say that he did "basically the minimum to make sure I kept my eligibility academically so that I could continue to play" (Wolverton 2014b). O'Bannon said that the demands of basketball—which could be forty-five hours per week—did not allow him to take certain classes and pursue his preferred major. He estimated missing thirty-five classes each season due to team travel, and usually worked only about twelve hours per week on his studies. He left school needing seven more classes to graduate.

In the Adlers' study, this kind of orientation was encouraged by the subculture of players' basketball teammates, which inflated the importance of basketball in their lives as well as their perceptions of their own importance. This was because their team was so highly ranked, they received so much attention from the media and boosters, and they had deluded themselves into thinking they would play pro basketball. They chose less demanding majors, chose courses on the basis of when they were scheduled, and tried to find shortcuts in their classes so that they could meet the demands of their coach on the basketball court. As a result, players developed unrealistic expectations of their postcollege opportunities in sport and were not well prepared for lives outside basketball after their careers ended.

Some of these ostensible student-athletes in big-time college sports are quite open about their priorities. One Ohio State football player who was sitting out his freshman year as a redshirt in 2012 used his Twitter account to express his lack of interest in being a genuine student. He was quoted as asking, "Why should we have to go to class if we came here to play FOOTBALL, we ain't come to play SCHOOL, classes are POINTLESS." The article was revealingly called "Ohio State Freshman Takes the 'Student' out of Student-Athlete" (Myerberg 2012). The young man was probably a bit chastened to see his tweet get so much attention, but it was nevertheless revealing. I argue that this kind of attitude is more common in big-time college sports than coaches, athletic directors, and presidents admit. It reflects the predominant influence of a commercial rather than a collegiate model in the big-time realm.

So-called student-athletes are usually less candid about their feelings concerning their education. More typically, this kind of honesty is expressed after athletes have completed their eligibility, as in the case of Ed O'Bannon. Two other former college athletes talked about the challenges of being a student in testimony before the Senate Commerce Committee. Both were football players in big-time programs. Myron Rolle was a star at Florida State and went on to a Rhodes Scholarship. Devon Ramsay played for the University of North Carolina (UNC) and was declared ineligible by the NCAA, a decision that was later reversed. Rolle saw himself as an exception and recounted the academic difficulties experienced by many of his teammates. He said they "go through this academic machinery and get spit out, left torn, worn, and asking questions." He also said that "student-athlete" was a misnomer, since the demands of big-time college sports left little time for studying (see New 2014a; Wolverton 2014c). Ramsay commented to the Senate Committee that the NCAA was more concerned with "signage and profit margins" than with the welfare of athletes.

Like other big-time universities in the intercollegiate golden triangle, Ramsay's institution, UNC, seems to have had its institutional priorities distorted by its commitments to big-time sports. It became embroiled in a series of scandals, including a very serious academic fraud case. The football program was accused of having players accept improper benefits of $27,000 from sports agents and their representatives, of having a tutor complete work for players and also provide improper benefits, and of having a former assistant coach receive money from an agent for steering UNC players to the agent (George 2012). The NCAA penalized the university for failing to monitor its athletic program, one of its most serious charges. It imposed sanctions including a postseason bowl ban for the 2012 football season, fifteen lost scholarships, and probation for three years. The football coach was fired, and the athletic director resigned after forty years at the school.

As serious as the corruption in the football program was, it paled in comparison with the bigger case of academic fraud, which involved many athletes. The NCAA did not sanction it at the time because the case involved regular students as well as athletes. It leaves such cases to institutions to handle. Yet the case revealed serious fraud in the education of many student-athletes. Classes offered by the African and African-American Studies Department involved little or no instruction or class time and little or no work, but resulted in a disproportionate number of "A" grades. This was known as the "paper classes scandal" (Ganim 2014c). Many athletes enrolled in these classes. The initial findings from a university investigation revealed that there were fifty-four "aberrant classes" that largely enrolled UNC athletes, who were mainly football and men's basketball players. The investigation also seemed to show that the advisors in the academic support program for student-athletes had directed them to no-show or fake classes to help keep them eligible (George 2012). The inquiry first covered the years from 2007 to 2011 but was later expanded in scope. The university and the NCAA were criticized for saying the scandal was not just about athletes, but the NCAA decided three years after the 2011 UNC investigation that it would reopen its own investigation (Ganim 2014c; Norlander 2014). This is because of reports that a number of athletes were admitting they were pushed into the bogus classes by athletic advisors, and charges by a whistle-blower that many star athletes were able to use the classes to remain eligible to play. What made this case an athletic scandal as well as an academic one is that 45 percent of the enrolled students in the suspect classes were athletes, who were only 5 percent of the undergraduates on campus (Stripling 2014). More than four years after the scandal was acknowledged by campus officials, the university was still trying to get beyond the story and restore its reputation. In 2014, another investigation, this one headed by a former US Justice Department official, was under way to try to provide a definitive report of what happened and why (Stripling 2014).

Probe 7.5: The Myth of the Student-Athlete at Great US Universities

The fake classes may have been the tip of the academic corruption iceberg at UNC. According to research at the university conducted by Mary Willingham, a reading specialist there between 2003 and 2010, many of the big-time athletes were not prepared to do college-level work (Ganim 2014a). She looked at the reading levels of 183 football and basketball players who had played at UNC over a span of about eight years and found that 60 percent read between the levels of fourth and eighth graders. From 8 to 10 percent read below the third-grade level. The university disputed her findings and tried to discredit her (Stripling 2014). She resigned after being publicly criticized for her research. However, what may have been more damaging were her conversations with a local reporter as a whistle-blower about the academic fraud and phony classes. She filed suit against the university claiming she had to deal with a hostile work environment for three years after telling her boss she was talking to the reporter (Blythe 2014).

Her allegations, along with public statements about academic misconduct by former UNC athletes, caught the notice of the NCAA and led to its reopening its investigation. The charges and countercharges prompted by the Willingham findings should not distract from a deeper problem, which was not confined to UNC. Prestigious academic institutions were admitting academically unprepared "student"-athletes to play sports (Stripling 2014). This kind of scandal should not be surprising when we consider the pressures on these athletes found in the Adlers' research. These pressures drove them to pursue an eligibility education by whatever means were available.

In its own study of twenty-one public universities across the country in states with open records laws, CNN found that most of the schools had between 7 and 18 percent of revenue-sport athletes who were reading at an elementary-school level. Many of these athletes scored in the 200s and 300s on the SAT critical reading test. In most cases, the team average on the ACT reading test was below the national average of 20, with some athletes scoring in single digits (Ganim 2014a). The CNN report also cited research by a University of Oklahoma professor showing that around 10 percent of revenue-sport athletes were reading below a fourth-grade level.

What seems most shocking is that UNC is recognized as one of the great public research universities in the United States. However, it is a little less shocking when we recognize that other top universities have had similar issues. These kinds of scandals, especially when they involve academics, nevertheless sear the reputation of the institution, at least in academic circles (George 2012; Stancill 2013). They force loyalists on the university faculty to become defensive, even though students keep applying and athletic boosters keep giving (George 2012). However, the stress and embarrassment from these scandals are not so easily ignored by the people who run the university and athletics. At UNC, the athletic corruption cost a coach and an athletic director their jobs, and the academic corruption pushed the university's president to resign. It became, in the words of a reporter for the *Chronicle of Higher Education*, "a scandal that won't die" (Stripling 2014). These scandals do not seem to go away until universities decide to focus more on the truth and how to fix things than on trying to manage public perceptions, minimize the damage to their university brand, and protect athletics.

The grip of the athletic trap becomes palpable to college presidents when they become embroiled in athletic scandals and see no way out. They may get so frustrated by their inability to control athletic excesses and scandals that they resign. This is what happened at UNC (Associated Press 2013). Holden Thorp had a long tenure as a professor and chair at North Carolina before assuming the presidency there in 2008. He began with great expectations and had some notable accomplishments, but he was ultimately derailed by the series of athletic scandals just described. Less than five years after assuming the presidency of the institution he loved, he decided to resign. He commented that presiding over a big-time athletic program can be overwhelming and distract presidents from more important institutional commitments. Although he recognized the importance of presidents taking control of athletics, he seemed skeptical about their ability to escape the athletic trap and exercise real control over big-time programs. He understood the nature of this trap and how it could constrain presidents and skew institutional priorities. This may be part of the reason he moved on to become provost at Washington University in St. Louis, which has modest athletic ambitions. As he departed, he commented that universities needed to put athletic directors in charge of athletics and make them accountable if "things don't work." He added: "Let's be honest and tell everyone when we select (presidents) to run institutions that run big-time sports that athletics is the most important part of their job" (quoted in Associated Press 2013).

When presidents feel the grip of the athletic trap and lose control of athletics, it becomes more difficult to ensure the academic integrity of big-time athletics and the welfare of student-athletes as students. This is why the highly respected author and historian Taylor Branch referred to the NCAA's collegiate model and conception of the amateur student-athlete as a myth. This was a major point of his piercing criticism of the NCAA in his much-cited 2011 article in the *Atlantic* magazine (Branch 2011). When he made this point in his testimony to the Senate Commerce Committee investigating college sports, he clearly contradicted the arguments made by the NCAA president at those hearings.

Student-athletes are exploited when universities do not ensure that they are getting a genuine college education and concentrate instead on using them to help them be successful in big-time sports and in the golden triangle. This exploitation is antithetical to the noble conception of the amateur student-athlete in the collegiate model. As the author of *Moneyball* and *The Blind Side* Michael Lewis (2007) once suggested, everyone associated with big-time college sports was getting rich "except for the people whose labor creates the value." Clotfelter (2011:209–210) observed that this exploitation had a racial aspect, since a disproportionate number of the athletes in the most commercialized and biggest revenue sports, football and men's basketball, were African American.

Probe 7.6: Getting "Rent" for Big-Time College Athletes

The economic concept of "rent" helps us see more precisely how exploitation of big-time student-athletes works. Clotfelter (2011:118–119) explained how rent applies in this context. First, coaches must recruit talented athletes to win. But with a limited supply of talented athletes in the labor market of big-time college sports, their "price" could rise substantially under free market conditions governed by supply and demand. These would be conditions where the NCAA did not operate as a labor cartel. If the NCAA were not able to set the upper limit of compensation for athletes or cap the value of athletic scholarships, the price athletes could command would rise to levels dictated by the marketplace and supply and demand. But this marketplace would have much more unpredictable and inflated prices than the current economic system dictated by the NCAA. Those who recruit top athletes receive a kind of rent. It is the difference between the revenue and publicity for their university that the athletes generate and the amount the university invests in them. Revenue and publicity can be substantial in big-time programs, while the cost of scholarships is relatively much less, especially at public universities. Thus, the more revenue and publicity talented athletes help produce, the more rent their university or athletic program generates from them. In the cartel-like environment of the NCAA recruiting process, the rent that schools may get from signing top prospects gives coaches incentives to humble themselves in the face of these prospects and also gives the best athletes significant bargaining capital to use with the schools courting them. This process could lead to illegal inducements from coaches or boosters. That is, rent creates the temptation to cheat. This is an unintended consequence of this exploitative system. But the bottom line is that no matter how good athletes are, their compensation—or "educational support" in the NCAA's terms—is capped at a level less than they could command in a free market. This is part of the reason for the antitrust suits against the NCAA and efforts by athletes to unionize.

Cheating and other types of corruption prompted by the desire to get and retain the best athletes make platitudes about the virtues of college sports and the collegiate model seem empty and false. When institutions engage in academic fraud, violate NCAA rules, and exploit supposed student-athletes, they demonstrate that the idealized conception of the amateur student-athlete in the collegiate model is a myth. They show that big-time college sports is about building brands and making money from commercial entertainment in the intercollegiate golden triangle rather than about education and the welfare of student-athletes. *Sports Illustrated* magazine published a five-part series in 2013 alleging multidimensional corruption in the Oklahoma State University football program from 2000 to 2011 (Dohrmann and Evans 2013). The alleged corruption was even more extensive than the case at UNC that we just considered. The magazine's investigation focused on academic misconduct, financial misdeeds, illicit drug use and drug dealing, sexual favors in the recruiting process, and a general failure to live up to the promises that playing a college sport and getting a college education are supposed to offer.

The reaction to the *Sports Illustrated* series reveals a great deal about the current state of big-time college sports and public attitudes toward it. Rather than provoking outrage against Oklahoma State and the big-time college sports system (see Benedict and Keteyian 2013), the series seemed to spawn more criticism of the report itself. Former players refuted the allegations against them, and even other journalists pointed out some apparent inaccuracies in the reporting. Of course, many people in the intercollegiate golden triangle make their living from the commercial success of big-time college football at places such as Oklahoma State. This is why a media outlet in the golden triangle with the stature of *Sports Illustrated* takes a risk when it criticizes its bread and butter and attempts to do real journalism about corruption in big-time college sports. This is similar to ESPN's production of investigations by its *Outside the Lines* program, which brought to light allegations of academic corruption at UNC (e.g., Delsohn 2014).

The most interesting part of the reaction to the *Sports Illustrated* series may be that very few people seemed too surprised. Even in Stillwater, the home of Oklahoma State, people may have felt more unlucky than surprised or shocked. A sportswriter for the *Tulsa World*, Jimmie Tramel, commented that "Oklahoma State feels like they won the anti-lottery" (quoted in Sports Illustrated 2013). The implication is that there is a widespread perception that everyone in big-time college sports was engaging in some kind of corrupt behavior and Oklahoma State had the misfortune of being singled out. This cynicism clashed with the testimony of the NCAA president and his rhetoric about the collegiate model, but the continued support of fans of Oklahoma State and other big-time sports programs reflects the capacity of sports passion to suppress any desire to act on the cynicism. On the other hand, the Oklahoma State University Regents took the *Sports Illustrated* allegations seriously enough to spend more than $100,000 in the months following the publication of the series for an investigation to determine the validity of the report (Tramel 2014). Boards are undoubtedly more aware now of their need to act after the Sandusky scandal and cover-up at Penn State.

Conclusion

In the world of big-time college sports, coaches are paid more and admired more than college presidents and professors, college athletes are often exploited commodities, and educational values are distorted by the influence of the intercollegiate golden triangle and the promised glamor of succeeding in the world of big-time sports entertainment. The irony is that despite the actual importance of athletics at big-time universities, the universities rarely include any language in their public mission statements about the role of commercial sports entertainment. Economist Charles Clotfelter (2011) emphasized this point in his carefully researched book *Big-Time Sports in American Universities.* He argued for more openness about the place of big-time sports entertainment on campus.

Instead of making this admission and acknowledging that amateurism and the collegiate model were a myth in big-time college sports, big-time universities and the NCAA were more focused in 2014 on defending their version of the collegiate model. This model was actually a commercial model at the highly commercialized big-time level. The economic realities of big-time college sports are the reason for the myth of amateurism and the collegiate model at this level. However, the NCAA's continued commitment to its standard business practices and operation as a labor cartel are why it came under intense fire in 2014. In fact, 2014 was simply a perfect storm of assorted attacks all reaching their peak that year in lawsuits and unionization efforts. As noted earlier, criticisms of the NCAA were not new, and it previously had to yield to challenges from big-time football schools, conferences, and the courts that robbed it of its monopolistic control over big-time football. It still controlled basketball and the massive television revenue from March Madness, but the fight over autonomy with the Big Five conferences and schools seemed to be further undermining its control over big-time college sports. Athletic and financial competition in big-time college sports was not fair, and the Big Five wanted to be sure it stayed that way.

College sports participation may approximate the collegiate model for the vast majority of NCAA athletes. But it is participation in the big-time realm by a small percentage of these athletes that captures the most attention, generates the most revenue, and is relied on most by big-time universities to build their brand and make their mark on the college sports scene and beyond. At the same time, this small sector of the college sports world is also where the financial deficits are biggest and grow most in the arms race, where universities are most susceptible to embarrassing corruption in athletics, where academic priorities and the collegiate model are most compromised, and where student-athletes are actually "athlete-students" (Nixon 2014:154) and are exploited.

Although the power of the NCAA may be eroding, big-time college sports in general has withstood serious challenges and reform efforts in the past. Past history tells us that calls for reform, even from prestigious organizations such as the Knight Commission, do not necessarily result in any significant change. Significant change could still happen in college sports, though, but not because the NCAA or college sports leaders want it to happen or have much influence over it. It could result from an "asteroid," an idea suggested by scholar Charles Clotfelter and former Ivy League executive Jeff Orleans (see Nixon 2014:144–145). Asteroids are external events or powerful outside influences that the people who run big-time college sports—the NCAA, the conferences, the athletic directors, and the presidents—cannot control. The NLRB ruling and the Ed O'Bannon case are potential asteroids.

Even with its efforts to raise academic standards in college sports, the NCAA has been notoriously reluctant to do anything to alter its commercial model of highly commercialized big-time college sports. The rhetoric about the "amateur student-athlete" resonates with lofty ideas about the college athletic scholarship as an opportunity for a college education that many athletes might not be able to pursue without it. In fact, it is difficult for ostensible student-athletes in big-time programs to devote enough time to be as serious as students as they could be. Athletes often bypass normal admissions standards and enter their institution underprepared for the academic demands they will face. They also must live with the consequences of the academic and physical sacrifices made while fulfilling their athletic commitments as scholarship athletes. Whatever the ultimate outcome of the NLRB ruling, lawsuits, and other challenges in 2014 and beyond, they have shone a bright light on the actual status of scholarship athletes in big-time athletic programs as "athlete-students" and challenged the NCAA and college presidents to reconsider how they currently treat athletes in their big-time programs.

The NCAA and its leadership councils of presidents have long fended off or dismissed challenges to their treatment of big-time college athletes as students rather than athletes. They will have difficulty ignoring the perfect storm of forces mounted against them in 2014 and its aftermath. These forces may ultimately create enough pressure on the NCAA and big-time university presidents to get them to acknowledge the "shamateurism" or pseudo amateurism (see Nixon 1984:184) in big-time college athletics, treat scholarship athletes in big-money programs as the professional athletes they actually are, and acknowledge their commitment to the welfare of athlete-students beyond their playing days.

A central principle of reform advanced by the Knight Commission in its earliest policy statements in the 1990s was that college presidents needed to take the lead in bringing about serious academic, organizational, financial, and ethical reform in big-time college sports. While on its face this idea seems to make logical sense, achieving it has been difficult. Caught up in the athletic trap of social, economic, and political commitments that severely constrain their ability or willingness to act, they have largely maintained the status quo in big-time athletics. The question is whether university presidents with big-time sports programs will see newly surfacing turbulence and challenges in big-time college sports as threats or opportunities.

Presidents have been caught in the athletic trap. As a result, they have often seemed to perceive too much risk and too many powerful people to offend if they pressed for meaningful change that might award athletes with the support, compensation, and rights their academic and physical sacrifices warranted. They had another opportunity to take charge and assert bold institutional control over big-time athletics amid the turbulence coming to a head in

2014. Failing that, they faced a bigger risk than backlash from bold decisions. They risked being buried by old and new asteroids, including the momentum from the most powerful conferences' efforts to take over big-time college sports.

The golden triangle will invest in college sports as long as people continue to watch, attend, and buy college sports products, from clothing to video games. The exposure and money they pump into college sports make significant reform of the commercial model very difficult, even with the prospect of various real and potential asteroids. The public may see warts on the face of big-time college sports, but these issues and problems have not done much to temper its enthusiasm. The golden triangle gives the public highly entertaining sports, and this entertainment fuels passions and mutes concerns. The same can be said for professional sports, which have also weathered many past and recent storms of controversy. Professional sports is the focus of the next chapter.

Stop and Think Questions

1. What happened to college sports when universities and colleges began to organize or sponsor intercollegiate athletics, and how did the universities and colleges justify their involvement in athletics?

2. What are the various ways that athletic departments, the NCAA, and athletic conferences are stratified, and how does stratification affect the experiences of college athletes?

3. Why was the AIAW established when it was, and what caused its demise?

4. What are paradoxes that have been found in surveys of public attitudes about college sports, and how can these apparently contradictory findings be explained?

5. How is "rent" related to the ties of big-time college sports to the golden triangle, how does rent reflect the fact that big-time college athletes are really "shamateurs," and how does the operation of big-time college sports as a cartel create the possibility of rent?

6. How does the case of academic corruption at the University of North Carolina demonstrate the myth of the student-athlete, and why are cases of academic corruption such as the "paper classes scandal" predictable at big-time universities?

7. Why is the NCAA president's defense of the collegiate model both valid and not valid, how has this model been challenged by lawsuits, political oversight, and actions by student-athletes, and how does the athletic trap make it more difficult to implement a genuine collegiate model in big-time college sports?

8

Professional Sports

Unlike at the youth and college sports levels, there is little question about the role of the golden triangle in professional sports. The emphases on commercialism and money are key elements of the definition of professional sport. There may be disagreements about how much professional athletes should be paid. But unlike college sports, pay for play is an accepted part of pro sports. As in these other sports realms, the amount of money invested in professional sports by the media and sponsors has increased, and the amount paid to athletes and coaches has also increased over the past few decades. Clashes have occurred between players and management over money and working conditions on a number of occasions in different professional sports during this period. Until the 1970s, professional athletes in the most popular North American sports leagues were largely restricted in the amount they could earn and the team for which they could play. It took legal battles and the kind of labor activism the Northwestern football players were seeking for pro athletes to achieve the economic freedom and legal rights they have today. With so much more money pumped into professional sports by the golden triangle, there is much more at stake today when athletes negotiate their individual contracts and when player unions negotiate their collective bargaining agreements. Conflicts over money, collective bargaining, strikes, and lockouts are not what fans want to see in professional sports, but they have become part of the game in these sports.

The things we learned about professional sports and athletes in Chapter 5 are things that fans try to ignore. Corporate corruption and individual deviance do not cast these sports or athletes in a positive light. They include cases of doping in cycling and Major League Baseball, match-fixing in soccer and some other sports, a bounty culture of violence in the National Football League, and various kinds of off-field interpersonal violence and other crimes. Fans might become disillusioned, frustrated, or angry at times, but as at the college level they tend to keep coming back to the sports they love.

There are cases, though, where the corruption and cheating are so disappointing that the reputation of a sport is seriously tarnished and the careers of athletes are ruined. Cycling and Lance Armstrong are two prominent examples. Like most professional sports in North America, cycling has generally been on the periphery of its golden triangle. However, during the reigns of Americans Greg LeMond (1986, 1989, 1990) and Lance Armstrong (1999–2005) as Tour de France overall champions, the sport had a surge in popularity. It was not established enough, though, to withstand the bad publicity accompanying the allegations and admission of doping by Armstrong. With no other US champion

233

to cheer for or invest in, the sport's popularity with the American public and in the golden triangle of North American pro sports took a nose dive.

Thus, while the US public seems to love its pro sports, it does not love all of them equally. This is true for golden triangle investors as well. In the United States and North America, the National Football League (NFL), the National Basketball Association (NBA), Major League Baseball (MLB), and the National Hockey League (NHL) are the most popular pro sports among fans and in the golden triangle. In the rest of the world, there are countries where pro sports such as cricket, rugby, auto racing, cycling, tennis, and golf appeal to large numbers of fans and golden triangle investors, but soccer rises above all of them. The dominance of the North American Big Four and soccer in their respective golden triangles is the reason they will receive the most attention in this chapter.

The Golden Triangle and the Pro Sports Industry

A major theme of this book is the significant and growing influence of the golden triangle on a global scale. "The" golden triangle actually includes many golden triangles at every level of commercialized sport. They are loosely connected by sports, the media, and businesses with overlapping interests in different sports domains. These golden triangles have made commercialization and the capitalistic pursuit of profit through sport a pervasive aspect of big-time sports at every level. I have tried to show how processes such as organizational rationalization, commercial partnerships, the pursuit of profits, and capitalist expansion in the global cultural economy have linked the major actors in the golden triangle in general. Big-time sports have relied on ties in the golden triangle for exposure and revenue. This is certainly true in the professional sports industry.

Different golden triangles in pro sports have their own spheres of primary influence in particular sports or geographical regions. Within the North American golden triangle of pro sports dominated by the Big Four, each sport and sports league has its own sphere of influence, just as soccer and other professional sports outside North America have their own spheres of influence. Even with overlapping ties to the media, commercial sponsors, and other businesses, there is economic, as well as athletic, competition within and between these spheres of influence. However, all of these professional sports and their golden triangle partners share a common goal of making money. They are capitalistic in this sense, but as we saw in the case of big-time college sports, the pro sports industry in the United States has been characterized by a peculiar kind of capitalism that has allowed antitrust behavior. Being permitted to operate as cartels has allowed particular sports such as MLB and the pro sport industry in general to grow relatively unimpeded by concerns about exploiting its labor. This privilege granted by the courts and perpetuated by legislative inaction has been an important growth factor for the major professional sports leagues in North America. The next section will have more to say about the pro sports industry and cartels.

The pro sports industry in North America and in other parts of the world has grown for a number of reasons. A key factor contributing to this growth has been the burgeoning of market economies in the global economy. They have been fertile environments for investment in pro sports. Pro sports investment has been especially attractive in demographic areas with a large or affluent potential fan base that can make leagues and teams popular and franchise values soar. Pro sports are successful when they are able to produce entertaining sports products in collaboration with their media and business partners in their golden triangle. However, these partnerships are not equal. Over time, pro sports have become increasingly dependent on media exposure and money, which has tilted the balance of power in the golden triangle toward the media for the most popular sports. This has been true for the intercollegiate golden triangle as well.

The influence of the media in the core golden triangles of professional sports in Europe and North America can be seen in the amount of money the media pay for broadcast rights. This influence may be increasing as the amount paid for TV rights deals has continued to increase. Consider, for example, the top five European soccer leagues. The amount of revenue generated by these leagues in the 2012–2013 season was $4.19 billion for the English Premier League, $2.85 billion for the German Bundesliga, $2.68 billion for the Spanish La Liga, $2.34 billion for the Italian Serie A, and $1.84 billion for La Lige 1 in France (Masters 2014). The Bundesliga was the only one of these leagues for which media broadcast rights contracts were not the largest source of revenue. Germany relied relatively more heavily on revenue from match-day sales of tickets and concessions and commercial sales of licensed product. According to a report by TV Sports Markets in 2013, television rights contracts in England and Germany had increased the broadcast revenues of the top five soccer leagues in Europe by 25 percent, amounting to $6.7 billion per season (cited in Panja 2013).

Even though the Premier League reportedly made over $4 billion in revenue in 2012–2013, it lagged behind three of the four top professional leagues in North America. The estimated revenue during that period was $9 billion to $10 billion for the NFL, $8 billion to $8.5 billion for MLB, and $4.6 billion for the NBA. The NHL had a lockout in 2012–2013, but it had generated $3.3 billion the previous year (Gaines 2014). A major reason for the difference in revenue was television money. In 2014, the annual revenue from television rights fees contracts was estimated to be $4.9 billion in the NFL, $1.5 billion in MLB, $930 million in the NBA, and $635 million in the NHL (Brown 2014a; Turner 2014). A new media rights contract signed by the NBA in 2014 and covering nine years beginning in 2016–2017 was for $24 billion or $2.67 billion per year. This near tripling of the previous NBA contract showed the continuing importance of media money to Big Four sports (Golliver 2014c). There were a number of power players in the media sector of the golden triangle of the North American pro sports industry in 2014, including Fox, NBC, CBS, ESPN/ABC, TBS, TNT, NBC/Versus, and the Canadian Roger Communications.

Sitting just outside the Big Four was National Association of Stock Car Auto Racing (NASCAR), which governed the most popular stock car racing series in North America. The popularity of NASCAR soared until 2007, when attendance and TV ratings took a big dip. However, it has grown again in recent years, and by 2014 it was benefiting from new television deals with Fox and NBC that paid an estimated $820 million per year, which was 46 percent more than its previous television contracts (Badenhausen 2014).

With the worldwide popularity of soccer and the popularity of youth soccer in the United States, it is interesting to consider briefly how well professional soccer does in the United States and Canada. There were nineteen teams in Major League Soccer (MLS) in 2014, sixteen in the United States and three in Canada. The league's television deal clearly indicates its relative standing in the North American golden triangle. It paid the league $70 million per year, a fraction of the contracts negotiated by the Big Four and NASCAR. It was $10 million less than the English Premier League's deal with NBC for North America (Turner 2014). This could be seen as a positive sign in view of the global prestige and popularity of the Premier League, but of course, it also means that the North American sports media have more confidence in European soccer on their continent than they have in their homegrown product. MLS was aware of the importance of increasing its television revenue to fuel future growth and be able to attract big stars in the sport. However, while attendance seemed solid, surpassing average attendance in the NBA and NHL in some recent years, it struggled with falling viewership. Only ten of the nineteen teams made a profit, and an estimated 90 percent of the average team's revenue came from sources other than television (Smith 2013b).

As important as television money is in keeping teams and leagues afloat financially, it obviously is not the only major revenue source in commercialized sports or the pro sports industry. Teams must sell tickets and get spectators into the stadium or arena so that they can buy food, drinks, and souvenirs. In addition, as MLS demonstrates, pro sports leagues and teams must also have a variety of relationships in the business sector of the golden triangle to be successful or even financially viable. In MLS, teams depend heavily on revenue from sponsorships as well as from ticket sales. Some are able to profit from the sale of luxury seats and stadium rental for non-MLS events (Smith 2013b). NASCAR generates substantial revenue from ticket and licensed merchandise sales, but commercial sponsors have an especially important place in their financial formula, paying for the right to emblazon race cars with their names and for other branding opportunities in the sport and at individual events. Along with television, sponsors are a major source of prize money for which drivers compete. Of course, television contributes far more revenue to NASCAR than it does to MLS, which is why NASCAR is near the top of the hierarchy of North American professional sports, while MLS is much farther down the ladder.

In European soccer, increasing transfer fees are putting more stress on club budgets. The fees are paid to obtain star players, and they go to the selling clubs and not to the players. The ten most expensive transfers at the time of the 2014 World Cup ranged from $12.2 million to $128 million (Johnson 2014). Rising transfer fees and salaries of athletes in European soccer and rising salaries of athletes in other professional sports across the Atlantic are made possible by increasing major revenue streams for leagues, teams, and sports in the core golden triangles on these two continents. However, at the same time, these rising cost factors are making it more difficult for many teams to make a profit in their sport. In the Premier League in 2012–2013, thirteen of the twenty clubs made an operating profit. The previous year, only half of the clubs made a profit. The financial stress felt by many clubs can be explained by the fact that over 75 percent of the revenue increase from media contracts and other sources went to player salaries (Masters 2014).

A similar arms race in player salaries was happening in North America, too, and some sports were more able than others to absorb the cost. Recall that barely half of the teams in MLS made a profit in 2012. Even for the wealthiest leagues with a lot of television revenue to share among teams, profitability was not guaranteed. The *Forbes* magazine annual list of the most valuable franchises in major professional sports showed that in 2012 only one of the thirty-two NFL teams failed to make a profit. But its reports for the other three leagues in the Big Four showed that in 2013, four of the thirty NBA teams, eleven of the thirty MLB teams, and eleven of the thirty NHL teams lost money.

Probe 8.1: Blackout Policies Are a Political Football

Media revenue may be a cash cow for many pro sports teams, even if they do not spend these riches wisely. However, there may be a point where sports can depend too much on the media. This has historically been a concern, especially in the NFL. It established blackout policies over four decades ago to try to ensure that television broadcasts of local games did not hurt live attendance. These policies have become a political football, as politicians are highly sensitive to complaints from local fans (and voters) that they are being unfairly prevented from watching television broadcasts of their favorite team playing at home. US senators have put pressure on the Federal Communications Commission (FCC) to eliminate these rules, saying they are obsolete and arguing instead that blackouts should be decided by broadcast rights holders and distributors of the broadcast games (Eggerton 2014). The irony is that these kinds of policies only become an issue when a sport has become popular enough to warrant big television contracts and extensive television exposure. It has become a political football because fans have come to believe that watching their favorite team on television is their right.

Despite concerns about giving away its product for free and possible oversaturation, the professional sports industry has generally aggressively pursued increasing revenue and exposure from the media. This has given the media sector substantial power in the golden triangle. The presence of the media can also be seen in the sports sector, with a significant number of owners having a background in the media industry. We already discussed in Chapter 2 the prominent place of media executives in the power elite in the golden triangle. The entertainment business also is closely tied to the media and sports worlds, and Harvey, Law, and Cantelon (2001) found that media and entertainment businesses in the Big Four pro sports leagues in North America were highly represented among franchise owners. They found that almost one-third (31 percent) of the owners of these franchises had these kinds of business backgrounds. Media conglomerates have tried to expand their businesses by investing in sport. The one exception to this pattern among the major North American professional sports leagues is the NFL, which has prohibited corporate ownership since 1970.

Business fluctuations can affect sports team ownership and the composition of the golden triangle media and business sectors. However, the basic contours of these sectors and their relationship to the sports sector remain the same. It is difficult to imagine professional and other commercial sports being as popular or financially successful as they are today without the ties and transactions linking them to media and business investors in the golden triangle.

Although specific motivations and interests may vary across different sectors of the golden triangle, shared incentives and interests are the money, status, and power that can be made from their partnerships. These partnerships enable golden triangles in the pro sports industry to impose their interests on the sports public, employees of sports businesses, and competing firms outside the boundaries of these networks of power.

Monopoly Capitalism and the Operation of Pro Sports in North America and Europe

In the last chapter, we considered how the National Collegiate Athletic Association (NCAA) has operated as a labor cartel to restrict the rights and economic opportunities of athletes. This arrangement has existed to keep the cost of financial support of athletes under control. Even though they pay their players more directly as professionals, professional sports leagues have also operated as cartels and restricted the rights and economic opportunities of their athletes. As *monopolies*, these pro sports cartels have been the only major suppliers of goods and services in their sport at the professional level in the core golden triangle on their continent. This has given them tremendous power in negotiations with the media, unions and players, their own owners, and the public in their golden triangle (Quirk and Fort 1999). This structure of monopoly capitalism and its restriction of economic competition have made these leagues and many of their franchises wealthy and contributed to their stability. They have been able to manipulate prices and wages in pursuit of profits. These league cartels have also operated as *monopsonies*, as the only buyer of certain goods or services in their market. This arrangement has meant that athletes wanting to play a professional sport at a major league level have typically been limited to one league and have only been able to negotiate a contract with the team drafting them. We will take some liberties in the use of these economic terms and focus broadly on *monopolistic practices* under *monopoly capitalism* in professional sports league cartels.

The courts and Congress have shielded pro sports in the United States from prosecution for violating antitrust laws. For example, according to the US Department of Justice website, under the Sherman Antitrust Act, monopolies are illegal when they "monopolize any part of interstate commerce" or "when one firm controls the market for a product or service . . . and it has obtained that market power, not because its product or service is superior to others, but by suppressing competition with anticompetitive conduct." In 1922, the US Supreme Court ruled that MLB was not a commercial activity and exempted it from the antitrust laws (Nixon and Frey 1996:175–177). In effect, it exempted the others in the Big Four as well.

The failure of Congress to intervene further protected this special legal and economic status. However, the implicit antitrust exemption enjoyed by the other pro sports leagues has not been so secure. For example, the courts ruled over a half century ago that the NFL's practice of selling television rights for the entire league violated the antitrust laws. But Congress responded by passing the Sports Broadcasting Act in 1961, stipulating that the NFL could not televise games on Friday nights or Saturdays during high school and college football seasons. In return for protecting the high schools and colleges, the NFL was permitted to bundle the league's television rights, which gave it substantial leverage in negotiations with the media. It also prevented popular big-market teams from making their own deals, which could freeze out less popular small-market teams from a big share of television revenue. The media were required to include games involving both more and less popular teams in their packages (Florio 2014). Along with this help from Congress, the league has faced congressional pressure regarding its blackout policy, as noted earlier.

The Big Four have generally been successful in retaining monopoly control over league territory, making it difficult or impossible for other leagues to compete effectively in the same territory and controlling who gets to be a member of the league and where they can be located. Quirk and Fort (1999:118) made the economic argument that a foundational element of the business structure of professional sports leagues as monopolies was the "exclusive territorial franchise" that was assigned to each team owner in the league. The franchise gave owners a local monopoly over their territory within the league. Teams have still had to compete with other professional sports and college sports for attendance and television viewers as well as with the wide range of other entertainment options available to the public. However, the powerful brands of the Big Four have given their member teams significant advantages over many of their competitors in the marketplace.

Probe 8.2: Public Financing of Stadiums and the Abuse of Monopoly Power in Pro Sports

Quirk and Fort suggested that one of the major abuses of the monopoly power of the major professional sports leagues in North America has concerned public financing of stadiums and arenas for current or prospective league members. Leagues and teams have exercised this power repeatedly in recent decades by threatening not to locate a new team in a city as promised or to relocate an existing one if the city or state government did not agree to fund a new stadium or arena. There has been much debate about the public costs and benefits of these kinds of investments, which we will discuss later in the chapter. However, pro sports franchises clearly have been big beneficiaries of this public largesse. The subsidies often written into long-term rental contracts for these new facilities have reinforced the monopoly position of leagues by creating significant obstacles to potential rival leagues in their sport. Rival leagues would be hard-pressed to find affordable facilities of comparable size and quality in the same locations for their teams. They also would be unlikely to negotiate media contracts that would give them the exposure and a fraction of the revenue of the established league. The big contracts signed with the Big Four leave little for other leagues.

Although the Big Four have been relatively stable leagues, all have had to merge with rival leagues or absorb teams from other leagues at some time during their history. But these moves only made the resulting leagues more dominant. The area where league dominance has been especially consequential has involved the labor market and control of players. The player reservation system or reserve clause in MLB gave teams complete control over how players entered the sport in the draft, where they played, and how much they were paid. Players had no recourse other than holding out or quitting if they were unhappy with the terms of their contract. Their owner had the right to trade, sell, or release them as if they were property. The other leagues in the Big Four had their own versions of the reserve clause.

Bolstered by court decisions, a Congress reluctant to intervene, and players uninterested in organizing, these practices endured in these leagues for a long time. But by the 1970s they were facing serious challenges. Players went to court and arbitration hearings and ultimately unionized and engaged in collective bargaining. Their advantage over the Northwestern football players was that these unions were league-wide. They also had some very effective labor negotiators at their helm (Nixon and Frey 1996:175–177, 192–194). Furthermore, they turned to strikes when they perceived owners as unwilling to meet their demands. Owners have retaliated with lockouts. Fans have generally been unhappy about the labor battles in their favorite professional sports and have often seemed to resent the greed of the players as well as that of the owners (Schwarz 2002). But this environment of professional sports reflects the existence of a freer marketplace than existed in earlier decades of these professional sports leagues, when owners kept a disproportionate amount of the revenue.

The major professional sports leagues in North America have seen a significant amount of their monopolistic control erode as a result of court rulings, interleague competition, collective bargaining, strikes, and agents more aggressively representing the interests of their player clients. Despite this erosion of power, they have continued to wield enough power to remain popular and become even wealthier. They have negotiated bigger media contracts and better commercial deals with their business partners in the golden triangle. However, franchise owners in these leagues have seemed to lose sight of the value of being in a cartel and being allowed certain monopolistic practices and instead have gotten into an arms race in hiring free agent stars, which has drained their resources. As we have seen, escalating player costs have made it difficult for many pro sports teams to balance their books. The much more open labor marketplace in contemporary professional sports is a stark contrast to the labor environment in these sports just a few decades ago.

Although professional sports leagues in North America have lost or given up monopolistic control in recent decades and have engaged in costly arms races, they nevertheless still operate in ways that other industries in the United States cannot. Within leagues, teams agree to the sharing of pooled league revenue to achieve competitive balance and maximize the chances of profitability for owners. They also collude in other ways to give the league as much control as possible in negotiations in the golden triangle and in its economic environment. This collusion best serves the collective interests of the owners when individual owners agree to cooperate and cede their individual competitive rights to the centralized controlling body of the league. However, as we saw in the case of big-time college sports, when individual firms—such as schools or franchises— try to break away and make their own deals, the cartel is weakened. The NCAA lost its battle over television rights to big-time football schools and, as a result, lost its control over the football postseason to competing organizations.

In pro sports, it has been difficult at times for leagues to throttle the aggressive and entrepreneurial inclinations of team owners. There have been a number of powerful renegade owners in a number of the Big Four leagues. For example, leagues have imposed salary caps to try to maintain competitive

balance among the richer and poorer teams and to control spending on salaries. Called a luxury tax in MLB, this cap has been violated by wealthy owners
of rich teams such as the Yankees and Dodgers. They have accepted the financial penalties of exceeding the cap to sign talented and expensive free agents
or retain their own stars. In the NFL, Oakland Raiders owner Al Davis had legendary battles with the league commissioner over a number of issues, including his right to move his team from Oakland to Los Angeles (Weber 2011). He
went to court and overcame league opposition and eventually moved his team.
After unhappiness in his efforts to get a new stadium in Los Angeles, which he
claimed were sabotaged by the league, he got league approval to move back to
Oakland.

Owners have also battled with other owners when they thought their team
interests were at stake. For example, the MLB Baltimore Orioles opposed the
proposed move of the Montreal Expos to Washington, DC, in 2005. They feared
that the relocation of the team into "their" territory would cut into the team's
fan base, attendance, and media revenue. As compensation, the league allowed
the Orioles to have majority ownership of the cable network MASN, which aired
Baltimore Orioles and Washington Nationals games, and they got a substantially bigger portion of the MASN rights fees. When this distribution arrangement ended in 2012 and the Nationals were supposed to begin receiving a "fair
market share," the teams could not agree on what constituted a fair market
share (Barker 2014; Calcaterra 2014).

Despite these internal rifts, monopolistic practices have continued to give
professional sports leagues considerable control in their marketplace. This control is achieved through practices such as the rookie draft, regulation of team
entry, exclusive territorial franchise assignments, rules for free agency, salary
caps, pooling of television rights fees, and revenue sharing in the distribution
of media money to league members. These practices have been important elements in the economic model used by the Big Four leagues in North America.
This model has created what economists call a "closed" market system, and it
can be contrasted with the "open" systems characterizing the elite professional
soccer leagues in Europe (Andreff 2011). In the closed system, leagues are
independent entities with restricted entry. Joining the league requires league
approval of an expansion franchise in a location dictated by the league. This
approval generally must be by a majority of existing franchise owners. Competing leagues are allowed to form, but the legal and economic rights enjoyed
by the dominant professional league in the sport make it difficult to succeed.
Competing leagues usually operate according to the same closed model used
by their dominant rivals.

NASCAR is an interesting variation of the North American model of ownership and monopolistic control (Newman and Beissel 2009). NASCAR differs
from other major sports in North America in large part because it has been
dominated by a single family. At the inception of NASCAR in 1947, Bill France
Sr. was made the principal leader of the loosely aligned group of regional race
organizers. He quickly consolidated his control over the sport by establishing
an autocratic family-dominated governance structure meant to keep races
competitive and retain control in the family's hands (Newman and Beissel
2009:520–521). The France Family Group was able to use its monopoly control
over NASCAR to forge a complex network of companies, subsidiaries, and affili-
ates to run the sport. An important piece of the family's empire was controlling

interest in the International Speedway Corporation, a publicly traded company that owned or had investments in a majority of the tracks used on the NASCAR circuit. The France Family Group dictated sanctioning fees, the scheduling of races, and the distribution of television revenue (Newberry 2002/2005).

NASCAR became one of the most popular and wealthy sports in the North American golden triangle. However, in 2014, the France Family Group's monopoly was in jeopardy. This was ironic because NASCAR had become so lucrative, with its new television rights deal paying $820 million per year. A potentially powerful new organization, Race Team Alliance (RTA), was formed by nine prestigious Sprint Cup racing teams (Ryan 2014). It ostensibly was interested in cutting costs, but it very likely was more interested in changing the existing formula for splitting revenue in the sport, which was 65 percent to tracks, 25 percent to teams in prize money, and 10 percent directly to NASCAR and the Frances (Pockrass 2014b). The Frances shared a significant portion of track revenue with Speedway Motorsports Inc. (SMI). Long a rival of the France Family Group, SMI sided this time with the Frances, not wanting to give up its share of the revenue pie.

Although NASCAR was organized and is operated differently than the Big Four leagues, it is similar in the closed model it employs to run its sport. This model contrasts with the open model in European soccer. The soccer leagues are in hierarchies governed by national federations in their sport, and these national federations are subject to regulation by their international federation, which is FIFA in soccer. FIFA has six continental confederations under its auspices. The one coordinating soccer clubs in Europe and part of Asia is the Union of European Football Associations (UEFA). An important element of European professional soccer leagues in UEFA that makes them open is the promotion/relegation system. The basic principle of promotion and relegation is that teams move or are moved between divisions in the sport's hierarchy in a country on the basis of how well they perform. In general, top teams in a division move up to a higher division, and bottom teams move down to a lower division at the end of the season. This is supposed to reflect a commitment to meritocracy and motivate teams to do as much as possible to try to win. It is also supposed to assure fans of a competitive product on the field. These sports systems are not open, however, in terms of opportunities for rival leagues to form in a country, since a second high-level professional league in the sport in a specific country is not permitted by the international governing body.

The closed model in North America is supposed to reflect a relatively greater concern about profit maximization than on-field success, and the open model in European soccer is supposed to emphasize the importance of winning over profits. Economic research suggests that this contrast between the profit-maximizing North American model and the more win-oriented European model is oversimplified or incorrect (e.g., Dietl, Grossman, and Lang 2011; Késenne and Pauwels 2006; Szymanski 2003). Teams or clubs may actually be interested in both profits and winning, but struggle to achieve a balance between the two. As we have seen, owners of pro sports franchises in the Big Four leagues are sometimes reluctant to adhere to monopolistic practices meant to ensure competitive parity and profitability for their league because they have sought a competitive advantage for their team. Thus, they have seemed to place winning above profits in the quest to achieve the prestige of owning a championship team. The pursuit of championships can be expensive, and free spending on players can deplete team profits and also threaten league parity. Buying a championship team can have a long-term payoff, though, since more successful teams are likely to have more value in the marketplace when owners want to sell their team. This shows that winning can be expensive in the short term but have a big financial payoff in the long term. The relationship between profits and winning is obviously more complex in North America than sweeping generalizations about objectives of profits *versus* winning imply.

In Europe, the soccer marketplace is more open in some countries than in others, and opportunities for clubs to win *and* make a profit also vary across nations and leagues. The promotion/relegation system has had different financial and performance effects on leagues with different economic models. The globally prestigious brand of the Premier League has led to big media contracts in recent years and has attracted investors from around the world. In 2013, half of its twenty teams were entirely foreign owned, with six of the teams having owners from the United States (IBNLive 2013). However, investing in a Premier League club did not guarantee immediate returns. Until the most recent television contracts, as many as half or more of the teams in the league did not make a profit, which was noted earlier.

The top teams in the Premier League found it relatively more difficult to generate big profits than top teams in the other elite European soccer leagues. This is because the Premier League used a revenue sharing model similar to the model used in North America, and the other leagues did not. The Premier League has benefited from lucrative revenue streams from television, commercial activities, and ticket sales. But profits for top teams in the league have been limited by escalating investments in players and by revenue-sharing formulas that distribute television revenue more evenly among teams than in other elite leagues. In these other leagues, teams often are allowed to negotiate rights contracts on an individual basis, which enables top teams to take a relatively bigger portion of television revenue than in the Premier League (Yueh 2014). This may be why five Premier League teams were among the ten most valued soccer franchises on *Forbes* magazine's list for 2012–2013, but four teams in other elite leagues were among the top five in earnings that year.

The promotion/relegation system can encourage less talented and less successful teams in elite leagues to take big risks with expensive player transfers and hiring new managers in order to be more competitive on the field and to avoid relegation. These actions seriously damage the financial well-being of a league. This is why UEFA (2014) introduced a plan called "Financial Fair Play" (FFP) to "improve the health of European football clubs." Its FFP rules are meant to have the same effect as the monopolistic measures used by North American pro sports leagues such as salary caps. That is, they are meant to control runaway spending and ensure the sustained financial viability of leagues.

Players have benefited from cracks in league cartels and the erosion of league power over them. In North America, players in the Big Four have fought restrictive practices with aggressive agents and unions, in the courts, and in salary arbitration and achieved free agency. With weakened control over the labor market and much more television money to spend, owners in the Big Four leagues in North America have gotten involved in arms races to sign the most talented free agents. NASCAR faced a potential threat to its monopoly control after the formation of RTA. In Europe, players have taken advantage of the promotion/relegation system. The cost of star players has soared as teams have paid bigger salaries and higher transfer fees in efforts to be promoted and win championships or to avoid relegation. But arms races that inflate the salaries of star players on both continents can also disrupt team finances in ways that ultimately diminish the overall quality of the team and its performance. This is especially true when there are salary caps and FFP rules in place. North American leagues have used salary caps to try to get costs under control, and these caps are often a contentious issue in collective bargaining between management and players in these leagues. UEFA has imposed the FFP rules to deal with its own arms race. Star players are not likely to object as long as salaries continue to escalate, but under the FFP rules, teams may decide to cut other players' salaries to be able to afford stars and stay within their budgets. Thus, measures that benefit leagues may be resisted by players when they see their own financial interests threatened. Monopolistic practices by leagues and teams in an increasingly free market environment for players can lead to complicated and contentious economic relationships in professional sports.

Professional Sports below the Top of the Golden Triangle

Despite a variety of financial and legal challenges and some fluctuations in support over their histories, the most popular sports leagues in North America and in European soccer have grown and prospered in recent decades. Some sports such as NASCAR are knocking on the door of the elite in the golden triangle. Sports such as golf and tennis are less popular than the Big Four but are seen on television around the world because they attract affluent spectators and viewers, a valued demographic for the media and commercial sponsors. Golden triangles around the world are filled with professional sports of all kinds that have less recognized global brands and generate much less revenue than the sports that are very popular and very visible in the core golden triangles in North America, in Europe, and on other continents. There are professional sports with appeal in many countries outside the United States that get little attention in the United States. They range from badminton and cricket to rugby and table tennis. In North America, other sports such as lacrosse and indoor soccer are trying to establish themselves at the professional level. There are also professional sports outside the mainstream, such as surfing, that have existed for decades, and others such as snowboarding and skateboarding that are newer. Sports such as horse racing and jai-alai have derived part of their popularity in the United States from the betting opportunities they provide. However, off-track betting hurt attendance at the race track, and the proliferation of lotteries, casinos, and other gambling venues has hurt both of these sports in the United States.

Road racing is an example of a low-profile professional sport struggling for financial support and publicity. It is also a kind of hybrid in that it allows recreational runners and professionals to compete against each other. It has relied on appearance fees to attract the best runners. In the past, professional runners made their living in this sport from these fees and sponsors. Appearance fees were a major portion of the incomes of many runners. The sport can be expensive for them, with training, travel, and competition costs. Appearance money enabled them to afford to compete, even when their race results did not earn much prize money. However, aggressive new investors in the sport have changed the economic model by discontinuing appearance fees. Competitor Group, which organized more than eighty prestigious events around the world, announced in 2013 that it would stop paying appearance fees to star runners (Pilon 2013). Competitor Group was owned by a private investment firm, whose business is to raise, manage, and invest financial capital. It was one of a number of these kinds of firms to invest in the sport. Equity firms now own the Ironman Triathlon, have majority ownership of the shoe and apparel company Brooks Sports, and have made a substantial investment in the shoe company Newton Running.

These kinds of firms were buying into road racing as a "niche industry," since there was a burst of interest in distance events among affluent recreational runners who were willing to pay large fees to participate in events and buy running-related products. The elite runners were often not so affluent and were finding it difficult to make a living in their sport. These runners complained of the greed of Competitor Group, but the new investors were less concerned about them than the large number of affluent recreational runners who were willing to pay increasingly expensive entrance fees. Race organizers would continue to pay for the travel and lodging of top runners and offer cash prizes to the top finishers. But this would leave a lot more professional runners with less money in their pocket at the end of the race. Organizations such as Competitor Group are using the latest online marketing strategies to attract participants, but they are targeting their efforts at recreational runners using attractions such as musical performances at the race sites. They are paying for these attractions with money once used for appearance fees.

This brief case study of one struggling professional sport shows what the bottom of the hierarchy in the golden triangle looks like. When investors see an opportunity to make money from a sport, they seize it. But these kinds of sports lack the established infrastructure, revenue, and media visibility to move up the hierarchy. Their organizational and financial instability also make them vulnerable to the aims or whims of new investors who are interested in the sport as an investment and not as a sport. Like others in the golden triangle, when they think they can make more money elsewhere, they will move on. Unlike the more popular and established professional sports, these sports do not have a line of other investors waiting their turn.

Women's professional sports such as tennis and golf have been popular for decades, but they lack the amount of resources of their male counterparts. Top female stars can make millions of dollars in prize money and endorsements, but the average earnings of women on these "tour sports" is far less than that of their counterparts on the men's tours. Women's professional sports leagues have struggled to gain a foothold in the golden triangle and popular culture. The women's professional basketball league, the Women's National Basketball Association (WNBA), is the most established of these leagues in North America. It was founded in 1997 with the strong support of the NBA (Voepel 2014). All of its original eight teams were owned by NBA franchises. This changed after 2002, when the league allowed independent owners and the possibility of teams being located in non-NBA cities. The league expanded to sixteen teams, but had to retrench in face of financial difficulties. It started the 2014 season with twelve teams, with only the New York, Phoenix, and Los Angeles franchises remaining from the original eight. The fate of the Los Angeles Sparks was in doubt prior to the season, until a new ownership group stepped in to buy the team.

The WNBA's instability is a reflection of the more limited resources and visibility of the league. It was buoyed in 2013 by a six-year extension of its ESPN television contract until 2022, which paid the league $12 million, or $1 million per team (Lefton and Ourand 2013). Although it was a big boost for the league, it was dwarfed by the nearly $1 billion per year the NBA got from its television rights deals. These drastically different comparative revenue pictures explain why there were fifty-two players in the NBA in 2014 who *each* earned more than all of the WNBA players combined (Adler 2014). The fifty-second player on the NBA salary list earned $10.75 million, while the WNBA's total payroll for players was $10.37 million. However, even with its instability, its limited revenue, and its relatively brief thirty-four-game schedule played in the summer, the WNBA has had the distinction of surviving as a women's professional league and becoming a recognizable brand in North American professional sports.

Other women's professional sports leagues have had much more difficulty surviving. The National Women's Soccer League (NWSL) was the third attempt at a women's professional league in the sport since 1999 (McCann 2014). The two prior leagues lasted only three years each. The NWSL had nine teams that played a twenty-four-game schedule between mid-April and mid-August. It began its pivotal second season with limited revenue streams but had the support of the governing bodies of soccer in the United States, Canada, and Mexico. They agreed to subsidize the salaries of the national team players from their respective nations. However, salaries typically ranged from $6,000 to $30,000, and to control costs the league had a salary cap in the first year of $200,000 per team. This amounted to an average of less than $15,000 per player. It is difficult to attract top players and sustain their commitment with such low pay. The NWSL signed one-year agreements to televise league games. But the contract was for fewer than ten games. Although the league gained some exposure, it did not get money from rights fees.

The struggles and relatively limited success of women's professional sports leagues in North America might seem surprising in view of the popularity of elite women's college basketball in the United States and the US women's soccer team during World Cup competition. However, the golden triangle has not seen enough interest in women's professional leagues in these or other sports to make significant investments in these leagues. Growth and financial stability of these leagues are tied to popularity and golden triangle support. Without these things, women's sports leagues have generally sat on the same low rung of the golden triangle hierarchy as struggling low-profile men's sports leagues. Efforts to establish women's professional sports leagues outside North America generally have been less successful than in North America.

With rare exceptions, professional leagues and sports at the top of the pecking order in the golden triangle have been played, coached, and run by men. The men in charge have protected the dominant status of their leagues and sports with a variety of monopolistic practices. They have also relied on the golden triangle to keep fans interested and entertained and to provide reliably abundant and growing revenue streams that have enabled these sports to attract outstanding talent. In addition, the most successful professional sports leagues have been able to use their popularity and monopoly position in their sport to convince public officials that they need a league franchise in their city to be a "big league city." Public officials and the public are persuaded that big-name professional sports teams have great value in branding the cities where they are located (e.g., see Bois 2011). They assume that the media and business partners of these leagues and teams will bring publicity, investment, jobs, and commerce to their city. Of course, cities prefer to be associated with a champion in a big league sport, so that they can bask in the reflected glory of the sport's success and claim that it is a reflection of the place where the team plays.

Being truly big league as a team in a league that operates as a monopoly has advantages and opportunities would-be competitors lack. These things also mean that fans and the public are vulnerable to exploitation because, at least in North America, they rarely have a voice in team and league decisions. In the next section, we will see that the governance structure of professional sports may have a lot to do with how these sports interact with fans and the public.

Sports Monopolies, Fans, and the Public

Implicit in the business model of the golden triangle is the loyalty of the public as fans and consumers. All of the enterprises in the golden triangle depend on fans and consumers to watch and spend money on commercialized sports. Without fan interest, stadiums would be relatively empty, and television, sponsors, and merchandisers would take their business elsewhere. Yet the welfare

2014 World Cup Final pitting Argentina against champion Germany in Rio de Janeiro, Brazil; soccer is the world's most popular sport and is the dominant player in the Euro-centric outside the US. (© Celso Pupo Rodrigues/Dreamstime.com)

of ordinary fans or the public does not seem to be a priority of major professional sports. These sports know they need public support, but they often seem to act in ways that exploit or ignore fan interests.

The importance of fan involvement is not universally ignored by professional sports teams. In European soccer, fans play a major role in the ownership and governance of top teams in two of the elite leagues. Spain won the men's soccer World Cup in 2010 and Germany won in 2014. In Spain, La Liga clubs, including elite first division Real Madrid, FC Barcelona, and Athletic Bilbao as well as CA Osasuna, have had "socio" ownership structures. Real Madrid was ranked number one, and FC Barcelona was ranked number two on the 2014 *Forbes* list of the most valuable soccer franchises. The value of Real Madrid was estimated at $3.4 billion and of FC Barcelona at $3.2 billion. The estimates were based on a number of financial indicators such as income, revenue, and debt and reflected their popularity and the value of their global brands in the golden triangle. However, rather than exploiting their supporters or ignoring their interests to boost their profits, these clubs gave their supporters a chance to be owners and play a role in their governance.

Real Madrid had a reported 93,000 member owners in 2013 who paid approximately $195 each for full-year annual adult memberships (Badenhausen 2013). FC Barcelona had a reported 222,000 members in 2014 who paid approximately $240 each for their memberships (DeMause 2014). Membership bought adult members a share of club ownership, the opportunity to get ticket discounts and the right to buy season tickets in the supporters' sections, and the right to vote on important team decisions such as the hiring of team management and sponsorship deals (DeMause 2014). A case study of FC Barcelona between 2003 and 2008 showed how the club was able to balance a not-for-profit economic model and democratic governance with an effective commercial strategy and a corporate social responsibility policy and remain one of the most successful and valued franchises in its sport (Hamil, Walters, and Watson 2010).

Probe 8.3: The Success of the German Bundesliga 50+1 Socio Ownership Model

Germany's Bundesliga has its own distinctive form of member ownership and democratic governance, and it is even more pervasive among its clubs than socio ownership is in La Liga. Elite clubs such as Bayern Munich are run as private companies. But like most other clubs in their league, with the exception of company teams Wolfsburg (automaker Volkswagen) and Bayer Leverkusen (chemical company Bayer), teams in the Bundesliga are required to be majority owned by local members (Evans 2013). This "50+1" rule is less stringent than the prior 100 percent rule, which existed in the early 1990s, but it still gives individual team supporters a significant role in the governance structure of teams (Kapadia 2014). Even with smaller budgets than clubs in other leagues in Europe, Bundesliga teams have been very successful in European Champions League competitions. In addition, their philosophy of building talent within the country has resulted in a higher percentage of domestic players in the league than in other elite European leagues such as the Premier League. Since teams have not been as vigorously involved in bidding wars for players, this saved money. In addition, having more homegrown rosters has made it easier for fans to identify with players.

Fan control has had a direct financial payoff for supporters of member-owned teams. These teams have lower season-ticket prices. For example, according to the BBC Sports Price of Football study, the average season-ticket price in the German Bundesliga was about 27 percent of the average price in the English Premier League—$220 versus $808—in the fall of 2014 (AP 2014). The Premier League prices were the highest in Europe. Arsenal, winner of the elite English FA Cup in 2014, had the most expensive season tickets, ranging from $1,614 to $3,204. The 2014 Premier League champion Manchester City had the cheapest season-ticket price in the top English division—$476—but this was over two times more than the price of the average season ticket in the Bundesliga. It was also almost three times more than what FC Barcelona fans paid for a season ticket, i.e., $476 versus $164. The Bundesliga and FC Barcelona had socio ownership models not found in the Premier League.

Even though Bayern Munich relied on the 50+1 socio model common in the Bundesliga and its fans could pay as little as $174 for a season ticket, it was still a very financially successful enterprise. It relied heavily on ties in its golden triangle to local companies, which tended to be big, global corporations. Its commercial strategy and financial success were important reasons why Bayern Munich was number four on the *Forbes* list of most valuable soccer franchises in 2014. The only team in the top four not controlled by fans, Manchester United, was ranked number three.

Socio systems in soccer are like other types of democratic organizations. They give a voice to the rank and file but are not managed on a day-to-day basis by the rank and file. However, giving the fans a voice in these clubs means that they have a chance to play a role in hiring, budgeting, commercial deals, and other key decisions that affect the operation of their club. Fans can push for quality on the field, wider access to the stadium through cheaper ticket prices, and sensible and thrifty budget management. FC Barcelona's community involvement extends beyond the sport in its commitment to corporate social responsibility through its charitable foundation. By giving fans a chance to invest in the team *and* a voice in its decisions, clubs are able to nurture more of a sense of belonging or connection to the team as it also generates revenue for its operations (Herranz 2014).

The economic and governance models of La Liga and Bundesliga clubs are a striking contrast to those characterizing privately owned clubs such as Arsenal and Manchester United. Their high ticket prices and extravagant expenditures suggest some indifference to the welfare of ordinary fans and their bottom line. There have been efforts to establish "supporter trusts" in English soccer. These arrangements involve fans of particular clubs forming associations that are represented on the boards of these clubs. This kind of fan influence has generally been restricted to the lower levels of British professional soccer (Madden 2012). The powerful owners of top Premier League teams such as Arsenal, Manchester City, Manchester United, Chelsea, and Liverpool are not likely to step aside to allow fans to control their teams.

Member-owned teams are less common in elite European soccer leagues than are the private for-profit corporate models of ownership that exclude supporters from roles in governance. This is despite a report commissioned by the European Union (EU) in 2005 to study issues in European soccer that recommended more involvement of fans in team governance (Garcia 2007). Member ownership does not completely insulate teams or leagues from problems in their sport such as bad or corrupt management or prevent league domination by a few elite teams (DeMause 2014). In addition, the Spanish socio system has been under fire in recent years, ironically in the EU, for violating EU trade policies by prohibiting the sale of clubs to outsiders such as foreign investors (Corrigan 2013). In addition, badly managed socio-owned lower-division clubs were pressured by the Spanish government to change to a private investment model in the hopes of making them more able to pay off their rising tax debt.

Despite its imperfections and failings, the Spanish socio system was deemed an ideal by UEFA president Michael Platini (Corrigan 2013). Platini argued that others should emulate the socio model because it encouraged enduring attachments of fans to their team and investment in local youth development programs, kept ticket prices within the reach of ordinary fans, and compelled teams to keep their financial house in order. All these things contributed to the long-term stability of teams, leagues, and the sport and were in line with the UEFA FFP rules.

There are few examples of teams in major professional sports in North America that have had fan ownership. The NFL Green Bay Packers is the only franchise in the Big Four leagues with an ownership model that seems similar to the European socio model (DeMause 2014). The franchise was established in 1923 as a publicly owned not-for-profit enterprise. The team has raised capital from five stock sales between 1923 and 2011, and in 2014 it had 352,427 stockholders who owned a total of over 4.7 million shares of the franchise. To prevent an individual from taking control of the team, the articles of incorporation do not allow any individual to own more than 200,000 shares. The club is governed by a board of directors and seven-member executive committee (Green Bay Packers 2014).

At a cost of $250 per share, Green Bay Packer ownership seems comparable to being a member owner of an elite European soccer club. However, membership benefits for Packer shareholders are hard to identify. They receive no dividends, their shares cannot be traded, and they have no securities-law protection. Investors are informed when they buy the stock that they should not expect to profit from their investment. Their purchase did not even move them up the list of 96,000 people waiting to buy tickets in 2012 or give them a discount on licensed clothing or souvenirs. They are allowed to attend the annual meeting and buy special shareholder merchandise, but they get no clout in team decision making for their investment. All this prompted a *Wall Street Journal* blogger to ask, Are the Green Bay Packers the worst stock in America? (Saunders 2012). Yet when shares were offered for sale in 2011, more than 250,000 were sold. Fans may appreciate the symbolic value of being shareholders, but their role in governance is more similar to the powerlessness common among fans of Big Four teams than to the more consequential role of member owners in Europe. Interestingly, the NFL prohibits other franchises from using the Green Bay model. The small size of Green Bay is why it is permitted for the Packers, but there seems to be little danger that this kind of model would be embraced by the current owners of any of the other teams in the Big Four, even with its negligible impact on their control of their teams and the revenue it generates.

Fans of North American sports, like their counterparts in European soccer who support teams with profit-oriented private ownership, pay a high price for their support. Ticket prices have been steadily rising beyond the reach of fans with average incomes. Some have even proposed that attending professional sports events in North America has become the province of the elite, suggesting the basic contradiction between high ticket prices and publicly funded facilities (Lamberti 2013). It is an especially expensive excursion for families. The *Fan Cost Index* (FCI) is a measure of the cost of attending a sports event for a family of four and includes the cost of four average-priced tickets, two small draft beers, four small soft drinks, four regular-size hot dogs, parking for one car, two game programs, and two least-expensive, adult-size sports caps. It is calculated each year for the Big Four leagues by Team Marketing Report, a publisher of sports marketing and sponsorship information. In 2013–2014, the average FCI for MLB teams was $212.46, for NBA teams was $326.60, for NHL teams was $359.17, and for NFL teams was $459.65. All of these FCIs were higher, by at least 2.3 percent and by as much as 3.7 percent, than the previous year. In NASCAR, races can cost from $60 per ticket to over $2,000 for special package deals, with tickets for its premier event (the Daytona 500) costing an average of $253 (Nilsson 2014).

With the cost of attending professional sports events steadily rising, television would seem to provide a free or cheap alternative for watching favorite teams or sports. However, watching sports on television is often not free. Fans who like to watch sports such as Mixed Martial Arts (MMA) and boxing often find that the biggest bouts are available only on a pay-per-view (PPV) basis. This can be expensive. For example, championship Ultimate Fighting Championship (UFC) MMA bouts cost nearly $60 for high definition and $50 for standard definition transmissions in 2014. In addition, rabid fans of other sports can also pay extra on their monthly cable bills to add specialized or premium sports packages in different sports, ranging from the Big Four to college football and basketball, MLS, golf, and the Premier League. These premium packages usually add about $10 per month to cable bills. Blackout policies mean that ordinary fans with basic cable access to NFL broadcasts may find that they cannot watch their home team play at home if the stadium is not sold out three days in advance of kickoff. Thus, fans get to watch games at home only when there are enough other people willing to pay the increasing price of admission and attendance or if they are willing to pay extra for a special NFL package.

Perhaps it seems reasonable that fans should have to pay for the sports they watch on television. After all, it costs money to produce televised sports events, and the cost of watching at home is usually only a small fraction of the cost of being in the stadium or arena. However, fans are not the only ones paying for these sports broadcasts. People who do not watch sports on television are also paying. Hruby (2013) explained the implications of this arrangement with his concept of the "sports cable bubble." He described it as an "unseen economic engine" that pours money into sports and television and as a "value balloon" that was being pushed ever higher by rising cable and satellite bills. The money has inflated professional sports franchise values and fueled arms races in professional athletes' and college coaches' salaries. He proposed that the expectation that this balloon would keep rising indefinitely was why the sports cable bubble was a bubble.

NFL Baltimore Ravens vs. Cincinnati Bengals in Monday Night Football (MNF) game in Baltimore in 2012; MNF has brought NFL football to a prime-time audience since 1970. In the 21st century the Sunday-night counterpart of MNF was the TV ratings leader and was joined by many other NFL broadcasts among the top-rated shows in the US. (© Lawrence Weslowski Jr/Dreamstime.com)

Television is the major conduit of money flowing through the golden triangle to professional and other commercial sports, which inflates the balloon and keeps it ascending. Hruby singled out ESPN as a "cash cow," paying out hundreds of millions of dollars to college and pro sports and more than one billion dollars a year to NFL Monday Night Football. It could do this because it was earning about $10 billion each year from television and digital and magazine ads, and cable and satellite affiliate fees. About two-thirds, or approximately $6.5 billion, came from cable and satellite affiliate fees, which are charged on a per-subscriber basis each month. They pass that cost on to their subscribers. This cost has been referred to as a "sports tax" paid by cable and satellite subscribers (Hruby 2013).

This sports tax is particularly noteworthy because subscribers pay it whether or not they watch sports or ESPN, since ESPN and other sports channels are bundled with their other basic channels. Of course, they can pay more if they want any of the premium sports channels or PPV options. Unbundling ESPN and other sports channels from the basic monthly package would cost their subscribers more money for these premium services, but would lower the cable and satellite bills for the subscribers who did not choose them. This unbundling could be the pin that bursts the sports cable balloon and seriously disrupts the fundamental business model of professional sports and other commercial sports in the golden triangle.

Probe 8.4: Sustaining the Sports Cable Bubble at Public Expense

Legislative unbundling measures seem unlikely to pass precisely because they would threaten to burst the sports cable bubble and disrupt the financing of major professional sports. But some viewers uninterested in sports or in continuing to pay the cost of sports on pay television are making their own decisions to unbundle. They are dropping their cable or satellite service and turning to on-the-air programming or using online services such as Netflix and Hulu. There are new companies emerging to provide new technologies to access broadcast television on the Internet. Until they grow big enough, they are unlikely to make a dent in the sports cable bubble or the exploitation of viewers with no interest in the sports for which they are paying. However vulnerable the sports cable bubble is, we can understand why the major players in the golden triangle do not want to see it burst. It is a cash cow for sports as well as the cable and satellite companies. However, the business model of North American professional sports is not fan-friendly and may be costly to the general public as well in North America. Blackout policies, ticket prices, pay-television agreements, and patterns of team ownership and governance demonstrate that the golden triangle generally does its business in North America in ways that cost, exploit, or exclude fans or the public.

North American professional sports leagues generally have a different relationship to the public than elite European soccer leagues have. This distinction is especially evident in the case of public subsidies for stadium and arena construction. They exist in North America but are much less prevalent in Europe. These subsidies are an important consequence of the monopolistic power of North American pro sport leagues to dictate who gets to play in their league and where they play.

The European teams may occasionally use publicly financed stadiums built for other purposes, such as the Commonwealth Games or the Olympics. In general, though, they are much less likely than the Big Four to ask taxpayers to fund all or most of the construction costs for a major renovation or a new building (Waldron 2014). FC Barcelona provides a good example of the contrast in funding models. It wanted a new stadium to replace its aging facility so that it could increase revenue and keep up with its rivals in the elite European soccer leagues. It decided a new stadium would be too costly and instead proposed a major renovation that updated the old stadium and added several thousand new seats. At this point, a Big Four owner would typically make an appeal to government officials to finance the construction project. For FC Barcelona, like the rest of European soccer, this was not an option. It planned to cover the entire $813 million cost with private financing. The financing package included a combination of cash reserves, club revenue, the sale of naming rights, and private debt. The project was financially risky, but whatever cost overruns occurred would be the responsibility of the club and not the taxpayers. By contrast, in the United States, taxpayers were paying billions of dollars to finance the construction and maintenance of stadiums for privately owned professional sports teams (Waldron 2014).

Wealthy elite European soccer clubs such as FC Barcelona and Real Madrid get tax breaks, which prompted an investigation by the EU. But the investigation of the impropriety of these tax breaks had to do with giving these teams an unfair competitive advantage and had nothing to do with stadium subsidies. European clubs typically do not turn to taxpayers for this kind of help. This is not a matter of altruism, but may have more to do with the promotion/relegation system. This structure includes a wide array of teams spread across the cities and towns in a country, including more than one team in some communities. As a result, many teams have close and deep ties to their community and are not likely to be "the only game in town" if they move, making it more difficult to pose a credible or compelling threat of moving to another location if their local government refuses to fund stadium construction (Waldron 2014).

In the United States, these kinds of threats are more credible and compelling because there is a long history of franchise relocation, as owners have looked for greener (in a dollar sense) pastures. Wunderli (1994) observed a kind of game in pro sports that happened when stadium leases expired. It involved owners getting the permission of the league to relocate and then using the opportunity to offer their franchise to the city offering the best financial package. The game usually included the expectation of a new or substantially renovated stadium or arena that would enable the owners to make more money from expanded or luxury seating and lucrative deals for parking and concessions. Owners eventually came up with the idea of personal seat licenses (PSLs), which are paid licenses to purchase season tickets for particular seats. They usually lasted for the life of the stadium or until the license was forfeited by the owner. This arrangement gave owners the motivation to build a new stadium after the flow of revenue from the sale of PSLs largely or entirely stopped. Congress was also a possible player in this game, since the league's monopolistic control over franchise location and relocation was illegal.

The franchise relocation game could develop into an intense competition between current and aspiring home cities, and it often involves a lot of threats (to leave) and promises (to retain or attract teams). Wunderli concluded that "at the end of the game, one city *may* win, the league may or may not win, one or more cities will lose, and the owner will almost certainly win" (1994:83). He could have added that the devoted fans in the home city rarely get to take an active role in this game. But the public certainly plays a big financial role because elected officials agree to invest public funds in the stadiums and other facilities that they think will keep or attract a team, and they seldom consult their constituents. When owners move their franchise or build a new stadium in their existing location, they often leave behind a stadium and many years of unpaid debt service (e.g., see Belson 2010).

Wunderli compiled a list of the cities vying for a Big Four franchise between the 1971 and 1982 seasons and their win/loss records in the "franchise creation, movement, and demise game." There were fifty-seven cities on the list, and a number benefited from league expansion during this period. This was a high-stakes game. It was estimated in 1984 that in the previous years, approximately $6 billion had been spent on stadium construction or renovation in baseball and football (Wunderli 1994:86). This was before the steep inflation in building costs that happened over the past thirty years since then and did not include the arenas for basketball and hockey. This game left a lot of unhappy losers, especially in cities where existing franchises were relocated.

In an article in the *Atlantic*, Easterbrook (2013) argued that professional sports leagues turn public subsidies into private profits. This was because team owners received publicly known *and* hidden subsidies. The public was usually aware of the construction costs but were less aware of the breaks on property taxes owners received or the low or negligible rental rates they paid. There were also hidden subsidies of regular facility maintenance, infrastructure operating costs such as power and plumbing, and improvements that were often substantially paid by city, county, or state governments. Long's (2012) research on public/private partnerships for major league sports facilities in North America revealed that when all of the known and hidden subsidies were taken into account for NFL stadiums, twelve of the thirty-two teams made a profit from subsidies alone. They got more public funding than they needed to build their facilities. Only three NFL teams—the New England Patriots, New York Giants, and New York Jets—paid three-quarters or more of their stadium's capital costs.

Long estimated that when known and hidden subsidies of all the 121 major league professional sports stadiums in use in 2010 were considered, the public paid $10 billion more than typically reported in the press (Kuriloff 2012). The property, infrastructure, and operational costs and lost property taxes increased public spending on the 121 facilities by 25 percent. Overall, in the average public/private partnership for these stadiums and arenas, cities assumed 78 percent of the full cost, including known and hidden costs, and teams assumed 22 percent. Football and baseball stadiums, averaging approximately $480 million each, were more costly than basketball and hockey arenas, which cost $170 million on average. Long noted that because leagues had a monopoly on the supply of franchises and could control where teams were located, teams had considerable leverage in negotiating deals for facilities. This explains the imbalance in the public and private contributions. Smaller cities tended to be at an especially big disadvantage in these negotiations because it usually cost them more to retain franchises interested in moving to a bigger market or because they had to pay more to compensate a team moving from a bigger market.

Professional sports leagues have built different types of facilities as their sports and ideas about the purposes of sports facilities have evolved. While stadium and arena planning has sometimes accommodated the tastes of fans to make them more appealing, this planning has generally been driven more by the profit motives of owners. Ritzer and Stillman (2001) argued that as sports facilities grew in size, they became increasingly rationalized or McDonaldized, risking their appeal to fans. Based on rational economic logic that more seats equals more money, arenas and stadiums got bigger and bigger. In addition, they staged increasingly spectacular displays to attract spectators, with an assortment of types of entertainment along with the sports event itself, including music; fireworks; exploding scoreboards; concession stands selling food, beer, and ice cream; distinctive architecture; and flags to commemorate past successes and to honor the nation. This has long been part of the history of professional sports.

Ritzer and Stillman observed that Major League ballparks evolved from the cozy, small, and distinctive Fenway Park in Boston, Ebbetts Field in Brooklyn, and Forbes Field in Pittsburgh to the cold and nondescript county stadiums built in the 1960s through the 1980s. They argued that these second-generation ballparks contributed to the significant drop in MLB attendance in the late 1980s and early 1990s. Fans had become disenchanted with the big salaries of players who left their local fans to take advantage of free agency and get a bigger salary. They were also unhappy with owners who demanded that taxpayers fund new stadiums, and they found little appeal in the sterile environment of the *late modern ballpark*. Orioles Park at Camden Yards in 1992 began a new era of stadium construction.

The construction of a new Baltimore Orioles stadium at Camden Yards in 1992 began the postmodern period for ballparks. The ballparks of this period were called "postmodern" because they were meant to capture the nostalgia of the past through architecture that called to mind the charm of the earlier ballparks, while also making a day or night at the ballpark thoroughly entertaining. However, these new ballparks only simulated the charming environment of the early modern ballparks. Beneath the appearance of a return to the past, there was clear evidence of postmodern rationalization and McDonaldization. Owners charged more for tickets and offered special seating, such as luxury boxes, for very high prices. They also developed new ways for spectators and other consumers to spend money in and around the ballpark, such as food courts, video arcades, merchandise stores, and amusement park play areas, turning the ballpark into a virtual shopping mall. Furthermore, merchandise giveaways, scoreboard displays, fireworks, sideline antics by mascots, and cascades of water marking various parts of the game as well as entertainment between innings distract from the game and seem to be intended to make attending a ball game entertaining for those not really interested in baseball.

Probe 8.5: Building Cathedrals of Consumption in the Postmodern Era

Ritzer and Stillman were concerned that the new ballparks ultimately replaced a leisure escape experience for fans with a "mass-produced, manipulated, rationalized, simulated, and commodified" consumption experience (2001:111). They were "cathedrals of consumption" (Ritzer 2011:5), encouraging spectators who have already spent a lot of money for admission to the game to spend even more. Thus, the ballpark experience has become an important commodity in the contemporary cultural economy of sport constructed by the sports club owners and promoters and their media and corporate partners. Nostalgic ideas of authenticity are part of the construction of this experience, but Ritzer and Stillman contend that this is actually very calculated. The golden triangle has blended an appearance of nostalgic authenticity with rationally calculated commercial strategies to expand sports markets and make them more profitable. This kind of commercial and capitalistic motivation seems ultimately more important to the golden triangle than preserving or restoring authenticity in sport.

Global Expansion and Migration in Pro Sports Marketplaces

The Big Four professional sports leagues and other major professional sports in North America and elsewhere in the world have prospered in their golden triangles. As the postmodern ballparks have shown, they have also gotten richer through expanding their markets to reach consumers as well as fans. Efforts to expand have gone in other directions, too. Economic competition and the

capitalist growth imperative to increase profits have spurred economic globalization in professional sports. This globalization has involved the movement of
professional leagues and sports into new countries and on to new continents
and the migration of athletes around the world in pursuit of more and better
opportunities. Some athletes have embodied the global aspirations of emerging powers in the capitalist global economy. Chinese NBA star Yao Ming is an
example of these types of athletes.

As a Chinese sports celebrity, he was a vehicle for moving capital through
global economic networks. At 7'6", he was the tallest player in the NBA when
he played for the Houston Rockets between 2002 and 2011. Wang (2004)
argued that Yao represented a new phenomenon of Chinese transnationality
in the modern cultural economy and global sports culture, which he called
"the China Global." He represented a complex cultural icon with an identity
that could be associated with Asian, Chinese, and Asian American cultures.
He represented China and the Chinese market in the global cultural economy,
and he also increased ticket sales among a growing number of Asian American
NBA and Houston Rockets fans in the United States.

Just as Michael Jordan represented the realization of the American Dream
for African Americans and blacks elsewhere in the world, Yao Ming represented the realization of the American Dream for those with Asian, Chinese,
or Asian American backgrounds. Wang proposed that in Jordan's case, his
global appeal was based on an all-American image that transcended race, but
that in Yao's case, his appeal was based on his transnational ethnic identity
as the China Global, which crossed national and cultural borders. Just after
Yao retired, Jeremy Lin had a sudden and brief burst of NBA superstardom,
known as "Linsanity." He appealed to the general sports public because he was
a Harvard graduate excelling in the NBA, which was unusual. He captured the
attention of Asian Americans because he was the son of Chinese immigrants,
which was also rare in the NBA. Thus, his appeal stemmed in part from his
contradiction of stereotypes, particularly ethnic ones.

Professional sports leagues have been trying to internationalize their operations for decades. The NBA has been the most aggressive in global marketing
and the most adept at using social media among the North American Big Four
in the pursuit of globalization over the past few decades (Groves 2013; Larmer
2005). In 1989, the NBA commissioner made his first trip to China to try to
arrange a television deal with China's state-run television monopoly for free programming that would expose the Chinese people to the NBA. Although he met
some initial official resistance, he learned that the Chinese people were already
watching pirated videotapes of Michael Jordan and the Chicago Bulls. The commissioner was more successful in his forays in other countries. Before going
to China, he had already extended the reach of the NBA into Europe, played
regular-season games in Japan, and signed the first NBA player from the former
Soviet Union (Larmer 2005). More recently, the NBA was eyeing the huge and
largely untapped basketball market of India, focusing its attention on a 7'1½"
Punjabi teenager. Satnam Singh Bhamara was being groomed in a US sports
academy to become the first Indian player to reach the NBA (Thamel 2013).

These NBA globalization initiatives and parallel efforts and plans by other
North American sports have made the global sports marketplace quite crowded
and competitive. Klein (2006) studied efforts by MLB to "grow its game" internationally. These efforts have included searching for new talent in the global

marketplace, creating development programs to nurture foreign talent in foreign countries, and then bringing the best of that talent to MLB in North America. The presence of so many foreign players on MLB rosters may be the most obvious manifestation of this globalization process. As noted in Chapter 3, TIDES data showed that nearly 30 percent of MLB players in 2013 had Latino or Asian backgrounds. MLB reported on its website that on opening day 2014, there were 224 players on MLB rosters who were born outside the United States. This represented 26.3 percent of the active, disabled, and restricted-status players in the league. This was down slightly from the 27.7 percent (243) two years earlier. The Dominican Republic supplied the highest percentage of foreign players in 2014, 37 percent (83).

As we might expect from its globalization efforts, the NBA also has a significant number of international players born outside the United States. It reported on its website that it started its 2013–2014 season with ninety-two international players from thirty-nine countries and territories, which were records. Assuming each team began the season with a maximum roster size of fifteen, this meant that over 20 percent of the 450 players were internationals. Ninety percent (27) of the thirty NBA teams that season had at least one international player. The Spurs had the most international diversity, with players from seven countries. France supplied the most international players, with nine, followed by Canada's eight.

In the NHL, internationalization refers to the representation of players born outside Canada, since ice hockey is Canada's national sport and its players have long dominated NHL rosters. The internationalization of the NHL is indicated by the increasing number of US-born players in the league. According to the NHL website, when the league grew from six to twelve teams in the 1967–1968 season, 2 percent of the players were from the United States. During the 1979–1980 season, when the US hockey team defeated the heavily favored Soviets in the Olympics for the gold medal in the "Miracle on Ice," the percentage rose to 12 percent. It climbed to 17 percent in 1996–1997, the season when the US team won the World Cup of hockey. The number of US-born players in the league continued to climb in the new century, and by 2012 there were a record 214, or 23.1 percent. They were from twenty-eight states and the District of Columbia, and Minnesota supplied the most players, with forty-six. New York's twenty-nine was greater than all of the countries, except for Canada, the Czech Republic, and Sweden.

The NFL is striving for a more global image, but it still draws relatively few players from outside the United States. According to the calculations of a senior analyst for Bleacher Report (Kacsmar 2013), 97.1 percent of the NFL players in 2012 were born in the United States. The total of 1,947 players included everyone who played at least one game in the 2012 season. Fifty-six were born outside the United States. The country supplying the most foreign-born players was Germany (11), followed by Canada (8). There were other players from Africa, the Caribbean, the British Isles, Europe, the South Pacific, Australia and New Zealand, and Asia, but most of these places supplied small numbers of players. Although the best Canadian players may have aspired to play in the NFL, they had a homegrown alternative, the Canadian Football League. Since the CFL was trying to avoid US domination of the league, it limited the number of international players on each forty-four-man roster to twenty.

In many of the elite European soccer leagues, rosters are highly diverse. In 2013, foreign players were at record-high levels. The CIES Football Observatory in Switzerland examined the composition of 478 clubs in the top divisions of Europe's thirty-one most successful soccer nations, including those in England, Germany, Spain, Italy, and France, and found that overall 36.1 percent of their players were foreign (cited in Harris 2013). In six countries—Belgium, Cyprus, England, Italy, Portugal, and Turkey—more than 50 percent of their top league's players were born outside the league's territory. Brazil supplied the most foreign players to these leagues, 515 in 2013 and 524 a year earlier. Brazil was followed by France, Serbia, Argentina, Portugal, Spain, Germany, and Nigeria as suppliers of foreign talent. The league with the most foreign players making at least one first-team international appearance in 2012 was the English Premier League (42.5 percent), followed by the Bundesliga (35.6 percent).

The extensive amount of migration of players into the European soccer leagues reflects the global popularity of soccer. We also see evidence of significant amounts of globalization of MLB, the NBA, and the NHL and even some representation of foreign players in the NFL, as the league tries to increase its global presence by playing some games overseas. In some cases, players develop in the sports systems of their native countries and then become good enough to play for elite teams in other countries. MLB is an example of how top professional sports leagues operate overseas to increase the popularity of the league brand. They also develop foreign talent that can eventually be imported to improve the quality of the league and its international image. MLB has an international arm, MLBI, which is expected by owners in the league to increase foreign revenue by the sale of television rights overseas, getting corporate sponsorships and selling licensed products outside the United States, and organizing overseas events. Another crucial function is to build interest and talent in foreign countries. This is what Klein (2006) called "growing the game."

When players migrate from their native countries, they deplete the supply of homegrown stars in their home country's professional leagues. The migration process reflects the relative prestige of different leagues in a sport around the world and in some cases with more than one professional league, the prestige of leagues within a nation. Money surely attracts players to the best leagues, but prestige can be an important factor as well among the best players in a sport. They want to play and win at the highest level of their sport (see Sage 2010:89–93). The elite leagues have both the financial resources and prestige that attract elite players. As in the world economy in general, leagues in poorer countries often lack the resources and prestige to compete with the elite leagues in richer countries for their own star players. As a result, the movement of elite athletes through migratory networks in sport is out of poorer countries into richer countries with more elite sports academies and leagues (see Campbell 2011; Poli 2010).

In a sport such as soccer, which has less prestige in the United States than in Europe, the dilemma for MLS has been that the US national team has seemed to benefit more from having its players develop in elite European leagues than in MLS (Borden 2014). Elite European soccer teams are accustomed to having rising US stars come to them. However, a number of these teams have begun to grow their game in the United States and Asia by extending their reach to these foreign marketplaces. For example, Bayern Munich hired a director of internationalization and strategy to implement a globalization strategy (Sandomir 2014). His job was to increase revenue in new international markets by marketing sponsorship and partnership opportunities to companies outside Europe, to make new fans in these countries, and to sell them licensed merchandise. Audi, Allianz, and adidas—partial owners of Bayern Munich—pushed for these new international business ventures. There were interlocking links across golden triangles to exploit. For example, adidas was a sponsor of MLS, and its CEO was the supervisory board chair of Bayern Munich. Bayern's internationalization strategy was facilitated even more by a five-year Fox television deal with the Bundesliga to begin televising games in the United States in 2015.

The Bundesliga deal paralleled a similar one the Premier League had in place with NBCSN. A Premier League team, Liverpool FC, had an office in Boston because its owner lived there and also owned the Boston Red Sox. This cross-ownership linked powerful golden triangles on two continents, which was another globalization strategy. However, the efforts by the Premier League and Bundesliga to penetrate more of the US market posed serious potential problems for the much less established MLS. MLS could gain valuable exposure and credibility from its association with these elite European leagues and from having success on the field in exhibition games against teams from these leagues. On the other hand, MLS is trying to build its own reputation and fan base and wanted someday to emerge from the shadow of the elite foreign leagues.

In general, it appears that globalization is following a variety of paths in professional sports as popular leagues and sports try to increase their popularity and expand their commercial reach across the global marketplace. The tendency has been for elite leagues and sports to develop and expand globally in ways that primarily serve their own interests. In the less common cases where they join forces with less established leagues and even with teams in different sports, the cooperation seems to foster mutual growth. This occurred in 2014 when the MLB New York Yankees partnered with the Premier League Manchester City to create New York City FC, an expansion team in MLS (Sandomir 2014). This kind of cooperation and mutual growth seem to be facilitated by interlocking commercial interests across golden triangles of different leagues and sports. However, to the extent that the global expansion of professional sports follows the patterns of growth in the global economy, we can expect that the benefits of growth will accrue more to the established rich and powerful elite leagues in more affluent countries than to lesser ones in less affluent countries.

The Stresses and Problems of Professional Sports Careers

Although athletes at the highest level of professional sports earn considerable fame and fortune, this is not the whole story of careers in professional sports. There are serious stresses and problems faced by professional athletes that are not part of romanticized images of the life of a professional athlete. Success can be fleeting, as rivals vie for spots on rosters or in the rankings or as bodies fail. There are many professional athletes who languish in the minor leagues or in lower divisions and never make a comfortable living. In addition, there are many men who earn the same modest salaries or prizes as most female professional athletes because they play sports below the highly commercialized tiers of the golden triangle. Former NBA star and US senator Bill Bradley

(1976) referred to his professional sports career as a "life on the run." He wrote about the stresses and sense of impermanence from constant travel and the loneliness from being on the road so much. In addition, as public figures, professional athletes often have to deal with invasions of their privacy, and, as famous public figures, they need to try to hold in check a "gloried self" (Adler and Adler 1991) that exaggerates their sense of self-importance and may lead to irresponsible personal behavior. Some are more successful than others at staying out of trouble.

Another stressful aspect of life on the run for professional athletes with families is the challenge of trying to balance the demands of family and career. Both can be "greedy institutions" for professional athletes, in the sense that both demand the exclusive and undivided commitment of those involved in them (Coser 1974). As a result, professional athletes can feel torn by the competing demands of family and career. In addition, spouses and families can feel that they have been relegated to a lower status than the sports career of their husband, wife, or parent (Roderick 2012). Their perceptions are often correct.

Brandmeyer and Alexander (1983) used the concept of the "vicarious two-person single career" to describe the lives of many wives of professional baseball players. The concept refers to the situation where the employer of the husband and the husband expect his spouse to conform dutifully and even happily to the stereotypical supportive role of a "husband-oriented wife." For athletes, this is because his sports success would presumably be the means for achieving "their" American Dream. However, this vicarious two-person single career means that women and their children must endure long periods of separation from their athlete husbands and fathers and relocations that uproot them from their homes, schools, and friends. This concept also implies that women must be willing to sacrifice their own career aspirations to support their husbands' careers. The vicarious two-person single career may be less appealing to contemporary wives and partners of professional athletes because they are less willing than women in the past to conform to stereotypical roles of sports wives. They may be less interested in making the personal or career sacrifices of "trailing wives," following whatever path their husbands' peripatetic careers take them (Roderick 2012).

There are other factors that may contribute to stress for sports wives and their marriages. For example, the loneliness of life on the run for male professional athletes may also result in succumbing to the temptations of infidelity. In addition, when they are home, these men may take out their frustrations by abusing their wives (see Nixon and Frey 1996:201). These and other issues can make it difficult for sports marriages and relationships to survive. They explain why professional athletes have higher-than-average divorce rates (see Roderick 2012:318).

While men can marry their sports careers and expect their wives to take care of their home and children, women in professional sports are more likely to face the conflicting role demands of athlete, wife, and mother when they have families. It is a very difficult balancing act with these greedy institutions, which is why we sometimes see female professional athletes involved in relationships with male professional athletes or entertainers. Their balancing act may be made a little easier by their mutual understanding of the stresses of their respective careers.

Women have had their best professional opportunities in winnings-based sports such as tennis and golf. However, both women and men in these kinds of sports have had to deal with the "structured uncertainty" of these sports (Spencer 1997; Theberge 1981). These sports typically lack the contractual guarantees of salary-based sports. Athletes in these sports have to pay their expenses of travel, equipment, coaches and training, and fees. Although they may have their own sponsors, athletes in winnings-based sports depend on the paycheck they get from each competition, and the amount they earn in competition depends on how well they do. In this sense, these sports are structured to be *meritocratic*. That is, the most successful competitors generally make the most money as athletes. Salaried athletes in team sports get paid whether they play or not, and their pay is related to their contract and generally not to how well they do in a particular competition. Thus, another part of the gender-based stresses faced by women in professional sports is that they have relatively few opportunities in the kinds of sports that provide men with both more security and better financial opportunities. In their winnings-based sports, the pool of prize money reaches far fewer of them and puts less money in their pockets on average than in the pockets of their male counterparts.

The Toll of Professional Sports Careers

Even for the stars, a professional sports career can take a toll that lasts a lifetime. For those who were not as successful as they expected to be or who squandered the wealth earned from their sports careers, the toll can be especially hard to accept. Debilitating pain and injuries are part of the life of professional athletes, and they make young men feel old. The intense physical demands of their sports careers contribute to the aging and disablement of professional athletes. These effects leave an enduring imprint on the lives of many athletes long after their playing days are over.

Physical risk taking and injuries are part of the job of a professional athlete. Data from the US Bureau of Labor Statistics have indicated that professional athletes were in one of the five occupations that had more than 1,000 injuries per 10,000 workers, with their rate being higher than 2,000 injuries per 10,000 workers. During the 2000s, injury rates increased in three of the Big Four sports leagues: the NFL, MLB, and the NHL (Fitzgerald 2014). In the other league, the NBA, there are many players who "play hurt" and are taped up like mummies so that they can continue playing (see Drakos, Domb, Starkey, Callahan, and Allen 2010). The most common injuries differ across sports, but many are debilitating enough to cause athletes to lose playing time and sometimes an entire season. Some may end careers. An ongoing UEFA injury study found that between 2001 and 2012, there were 8,000 injuries causing loss of playing time. Injury rates did not change during this period. The twenty-five-man rosters averaged fifty injuries per season, or two per player (Ekland 2013). As we might expect, long seasons stretching into the postseason tended to have adverse effects on player performance and make players more vulnerable to injury. Debilitating injuries can hurt players' career trajectories and be costly if the players do not have guaranteed contracts. Disabled players also are costly to teams in lost productivity and in salaries that teams must pay for players unable to play (MacGregor 2014; Nightengale 2012). When stars go on the disabled list, their injuries can affect the chances of teams winning championships or even making the playoffs.

Evidence suggests that despite having their bodies damaged by their careers in sports, athletes in the Big Four leagues and elite European soccer seem to live longer than the actuarial tables predict for men in their age cohort (e.g., Bell 2012; Engber 2012; Morris 2014). This finding seems to hold up overall for each of these sports, even though there have been disagreements about the relative longevity rates of different sports. There are variations within these sports. For example, the huge size that is an advantage for NFL defensive linemen during their careers may be the reason they have a 42 percent *higher* risk of dying from heart disease than average men in their society (Bell 2012). In addition, some sports or pseudo sports such as WWF wrestling seem to have *higher* than average mortality rates (Morris 2014).

Even if professional athletes are able to prolong their lives as a result of benefits derived from playing their sport, those extra years may not be pleasant ones when they have to deal with chronic pain and disabilities from their sports careers. The NFL illustrates the highs and lows of playing the most popular sport in the United States. It is a sport that makes players celebrities and even heroes among adoring fans. They are revered in part because they make or can take hard hits. They are admired for their ability to play in pain. Playing hurt or in pain seems to be a necessity in a sport where serious injuries can happen on any play, and where players sustain bumps and bruises on every play. Players acknowledge the need to play hurt. An excerpt from a book about Washington quarterback Robert Griffin III (RG3) that appeared in *Sports Illustrated* was called "You Gotta Play Hurt" (Sheinin 2013). RG3 had put himself back on the field when he obviously was suffering from a serious knee injury, which ultimately led to surgery. As a budding star, he was the team's "franchise quarterback" on whom it had pinned its hopes for success.

RG3's return to action raised a lot of questions about the wisdom of playing hurt and the responsibility of the league, coaches, teams, and the medical staff to protect injured players. These kinds of questions have also been at the center of the concussion controversy in the NFL. In 2013, the league was facing lawsuits from 4,500 players who claimed that team physicians did not tell them of the risks of playing with concussions (Jenkins and Maese 2013). They were a little more than 22 percent of former NFL players who are still alive. The flip side of this relationship is that players were not very open about their aches, pains, or physical problems. They knew they could not complain to coaches or doctors, or they could risk their chance of playing. They would rather accept the risk of injuries and even disability than take the risk of complaining, being placed on the disabled list, and being considered not tough enough. *Washington Post* interviews with NFL players and agents revealed that hiding or downplaying injuries was part of a "code" adhered to by players (Jenkins and Maese 2013).

When they are young or in the midst of their careers, NFL players and other professional athletes may not think much about what their bodies will be like when they are older. This was true of former NFL quarterback Brad Johnson. However, at age forty-four and a few years removed from his seventeen-year career in the NFL, he had to deal with chronic aches and pains (Klemko 2013). His pain began during the latter stage of his career and was severe enough for him to use painkillers to lessen the pain from tendonitis in his throwing elbow and shoulder and from three serious injuries. He qualified for disability payments from the league because he had "substantial disablement arising out of NFL football activities" (cited in Klemko 2013). He also received health insurance payments from the NFL for five years after his career ended and would be eligible for extended benefits if he developed a neuro-cognitive disease or other condition that prevented him from being employed. He was fortunate because his benefits were better than those received by earlier generations of retirees in his sport, and much better than those received by players with abbreviated careers or careers in most other professional sports.

Despite the damage done to them by football, the majority of retired NFL players who have been surveyed in recent years have reported that they view their careers in the NFL very positively. A 2009 University of Michigan Institute for Social Research (ISR) study of 1,063 retired NFL players found that 78 percent of older retirees (age 50 and older) and 69 percent of younger retirees (30–49) responded this way (Weir, Jackson, and Sonnega 2009). The results of an online *Washington Post* survey of five hundred retired NFL players conducted four years later were similar, with 69 percent saying they were very happy and 21 percent saying they were somewhat happy (Jenkins, Maese, and Clement 2013; Washington Post 2013b).

According to the ISR study, 30 percent of the older retirees and 16 percent of the younger retirees responded that injuries were *not* an important factor in their decision to retire from their sport, implying that injuries influenced most retirement decisions in the sport. Younger retirees were much more likely than were men in their age group in the US population in general (29 percent vs. 9.1 percent) to rate their health as fair or poor. Older retirees were somewhat more likely (26.2 percent vs. 23.6 percent) to rate their health as fair or poor. Arthritis rates were five times higher than the general male population of their age for younger retirees and twice as high for the older retirees. When the NFL retirees were compared with their age cohorts on eight items concerning functional limitations, the retirees reported more difficulty performing all eight tasks, including climbing stairs, standing for extended periods of time, stooping, bending, kneeling, and lifting and carrying ten pounds. Although rare, the reported rates of dementia, Alzheimer's disease, and other memory-related diseases were much higher for both groups of retirees than for the general male population—1.9 percent (vs. 0.1 percent) for the younger retirees and 6.1 percent (vs. 1.2 percent) for the older group.

The incidence of on-the-job injuries, disabilities, and memory-related diseases among NFL retirees was higher than average for men of their age, and their self-ratings of health were lower. However, the players earned more than average men of their age during their careers and the league paid better retirement pensions than many occupations in the United States, which suggests that the players should have had the means to take care of their career-related ailments. Yet the ISR research showed that significant numbers of the retirees under the Medicare eligibility age of sixty-five had unmet health care needs. For example, among the retirees in the younger (30–49) group, 7.3 percent could not afford prescriptions, 10.1 percent could not afford surgery, 5.3 percent could not afford mental health care, and 15.9 percent could not afford dental care. The percentages were fairly similar for the older (50–64) group of NFL retirees. In Chapter 2, the financial struggles of a number of former professional athletes in the NFL and other sports were noted. This may be part of the explanation for the difficulty some NFL retirees in the ISR survey said they had in meeting their health care needs, with 10.3 percent of the younger retirees and 9.7 percent of those in the older group reporting incomes below twice the poverty level.

The *Washington Post* (2013a, 2013b) survey results paint a similar picture of the experiences of NFL retirees. Almost 90 percent said they had aches and pains every day, and 92 percent said most or nearly all of their aches and pains were due to their football careers. Ninety-three percent reported they had one or more major injuries that caused them to miss at least one game, and 52 percent said they had three or more of these injuries. Fifty-two percent reported three or more orthopedic surgeries, and 44 percent had joint replacements. Ninety percent said they had at least one concussion during their careers, 60 percent said they had three or more, and 67 percent of those who had concussions indicated they had ongoing symptoms from those head injuries. Many of these retirees seemed to have limited trust that team doctors were primarily committed to their welfare. Nearly half of the respondents (47 percent) answered that the team doctors made the interests of the team their main priority. Only 13 percent thought their health was the doctors' main concern.

The NFL engaged in a lengthy dispute with former players about compensation for the claimed effects of concussions from their football careers. In 2013, the NFL reached a $765 million agreement with the 4,500 retirees who had sued over work-related brain injuries (Smith 2013). Players who were diagnosed with a qualifying condition (usually dementia) received lump-sum payments that were correlated with age and career length. The players would not have to prove that playing football caused their condition. However, as generous as the settlement might appear, the amount might not be adequate to cover all future claims as more cases are diagnosed (Schwarz 2014).

Probe 8.6: The NFL as a "League of Denial" about Concussions and Memory-Related Diseases

The inferred connection between rates of concussions and memory-related diseases in the NFL has been a focus of much debate and criticism. Concerns have been heightened by the perceived priorities of team doctors. In a widely cited book called *League of Denial*, ESPN investigative reporters Mark Fainaru-Wada and Steve Fainaru (2013a, 2013b) argued that the NFL had sponsored its own research to refute more objective and scientifically sound evidence showing this link, out of fear of bad publicity and legal and financial liability. The NFL-sponsored research essentially claimed that players were not at risk of serious damage. But it was flawed by various research biases and conflicting interests. The authors likened the NFL's response to the concussion threat to the way the tobacco industry responded to research about the deadly effects of its product, by trying to discredit and silence those who threatened its business. According to the ESPN investigation, the NFL had been trying for over two decades to suppress damaging evidence and discredit the scientists who did the research. The league benefited from publications by NFL-friendly researchers downplaying the effects of hits to the head area on brains. Finally the weight of scientific evidence produced by independent researchers became too compelling. League efforts to get medical journals to retract articles by those researchers also failed. By the 2000s, top neuroscientists were finding that football caused higher rates of depression, memory loss, and brain damage (Van Natta 2013).

The University of Michigan research cited earlier showed that the NFL would be dealing with far higher rates of memory-related illnesses among its former players than in the general population. The league acknowledged in a federal court document in 2014 that it expected almost one-third of retired players to experience long-term cognitive problems and to have them at "notably younger ages" than in the general population (Belson 2014b). Furthermore, government research in 2013 showed that NFL players were four times more likely than men in the general population to die of Lou Gehrig's Disease or Alzheimer's (Schwarz 2014). The NFL has been cushioned by its popularity and wealth, and will be as long as the fans remain faithful, the golden triangle continues to invest in it, and the government does not intervene. However, other levels of football or other sports with serious concussion risks may be nervous about the precedent set by the NFL because they may lack the resources needed to compensate victims.

The *Washington Post* survey found that 56 percent of the retirees said they frequently played hurt and another 32 percent said they sometimes played hurt. Most (57 percent) said they did so because they wanted to play *and* the coaches wanted them to play. However, when they retired, many seemed to view differently the code that had abetted their playing hurt. Forty-nine percent said they wished they had played through pain less often. However, 68 percent said they did not think they had a choice (Washington Post 2013a). The number of concussions they reported affected their thoughts about playing through pain. Twenty-six percent of those with two or fewer concussions said they wished they had played through pain less often, but 59 percent of those who had three or more concussions felt this way.

Officials at all levels of football and other collision sports are now voicing concern about the culture that encourages or pushes players to hide injuries and try to play hurt. The NFL commissioner began talking about moving toward a "safety culture" but acknowledged it would be difficult to get players to become more open about their injuries (Jenkins, Maese, and Clement 2013). Players may not change as long as they think coaches want them to play hurt and perceive financial and competitive disincentives to sit on the sideline. In addition, all their prior experience in sport taught them that pain is part of the game.

Probe 8.7: The Culture of Risk, Pain, and Injury in Sport

In my own research, I documented the culture of risk, pain, and injury in sport (e.g., Nixon 1993, 2004; also see Young 2004). It overlaps with the Sport Ethic, which was described in Chapter 4. One of its basic tenets in its conception of what it means to be a serious athlete is to accept risks and play with pain. In this context, injuries become "normal." The sports media, sports executives, coaches, and players reinforce physical risk taking by emphasizing the Sport Ethic and glorifying as "heroic" those who endure pain and injuries to continue playing. Sports officials may introduce rules, tighten enforcement, or impose suspensions and fines as means to control injury rates and the aggression and violence affecting them. However, it is not necessarily in the financial interests of sports officials and executives to transform the structure or culture of their sports to ensure safety, despite the public urging of the NFL commissioner and others running similarly risky sports. Furthermore, sport as physical competition is inherently risky whether or not contact is involved, and risk is part of its attraction for athletes. Athletes pushing themselves to peak and sometimes violent performances also make sports more exciting and more appealing to fans. However, adhering to the Sport Ethic and the code takes a toll. Especially for those in the most physically damaging sports, the aftermath of their usually relatively brief professional sports careers is likely to involve adjusting to the lingering or chronic effects of injuries. They have to find ways to cope financially, emotionally, and physically, and it will be outside the media glow that seemed to glorify their physical sacrifices when they were playing. Coping is more difficult when the damage is more serious and enduring and the financial compensation from their sport is less.

Conclusion

Professional sports are an unusual business. Teams and athletes engage in athletic competition, and leagues and sports pursue profits in what is supposed to be a competitive capitalistic global economy. But leagues, associations, and confederations typically restrict economic competition, with their cartel-like arrangements and monopolistic practices. Even with these economic advantages, a number of team owners still manage to lose money. The prestige of winning championships drives them to pay higher and higher salaries in arms races to get top talent in their sport to play for them. In going on these spending sprees, they undermine the cooperation that keeps costs under control in their league and act more like the entrepreneurs many of them were before they bought a professional sports franchise.

At the highest levels of the golden triangle of professional sports, organizational and economic models have evolved over time and sustained these sports in the face of a variety of challenges. Some teams in the North American Big Four have struggled competitively and financially, but the popularity and overall financial health of these leagues have carried them through tough times. When the waning of popularity and financial losses have been too much for teams to continue, leagues have relocated franchises to cities with more enthusiastic fans awaiting them. In the elite soccer leagues of Europe, relocation has not happened between cities, but instead between divisions in league hierarchies, and it happens routinely in soccer. With their more hierarchical structures and promotion/relegation systems, they have regularly shifted teams up or down divisions to maintain competitiveness and fan appeal. Facing escalating spending that threatened the financial health of many of its top leagues, UEFA established FFP rules.

Despite their dependence on fan support, most major professional sports leagues have tended to overlook the interests and welfare of their fans. The publicly owned teams in European soccer are an exception, giving supporters who modestly invest in them both a piece of team ownership and a voice in team decisions. The more typical case is the exploitation of fan loyalty. For the general public much less interested in professional sports than passionate fans, there is also a price to pay for local professional sports. They help pay the tax bills for publicly subsidized professional sports facilities from which private owners derive substantial revenue. Thus, unlike those in the public who are fans, the general public sees little payoff for their indirect sports investment. They also see public funds diverted from public projects, such as schools, recreation centers, and community infrastructure, that serve the general public interest more than a professional sports stadium or arena does. The public also may continue paying for stadium construction bonds and maintenance costs after a team leaves for greener pastures in another city, where the game of building a new sports facility to attract a big league team and make the city big league is replayed.

Talented and exciting sports stars are a big reason why fans flock to the stadiums or arenas of NFL, NBA, MLB, NHL, and UEFA teams and to the variety of venues of other popular professional sports. The athletes and their teams and sports are valued branded commodities in the global golden triangle. The biggest stars become rich and famous, at least for a while, but relatively few professional athletes leave their sport without paying a price with their bodies. Many keep paying this price for the rest of their lives.

The NFL has seemed secure in its perch at the top of the sports hierarchy in North America. But the actions by the league and its commissioner seemed to reflect a somewhat more tenuous reality. Its popularity and wealth made it a target of critics of its blackout policies, antitrust exemption, and public subsidies of its huge stadiums. Publicity about the bounty system, sexual assaults, domestic violence, and other crimes by players led to additional criticisms. Unlike the widely respected new NBA commissioner (Jenkins 2014), the NFL commissioner, Roger Goodell, seemed defensive (Gregory 2012). The publication of *League of Denial* sharpened one of the most serious lines of attack against the sport itself. Goodell had to convince the public and legislators that his sport was not too dangerous and that the league was doing as much as it could to deal with concussions. But he had to deal with revelations about the league's longtime cover-up of research showing the adverse effects of the repeated head injuries suffered by most players. Even its settlement of its lawsuit with players wanting compensation for their brain injuries was under fire for being inadequate (Schrotenboer 2014). Thus, while the NBA was enjoying good press, the NFL was being attacked on a number of fronts. Meanwhile, the NFL was much less successful in its efforts to internationalize its players and appeal than its main competitors in the North American and European golden triangles of professional sports.

Thus, even popular and wealthy leagues have vulnerabilities. They may be taking their biggest risks when they ignore the welfare of their players and do not pay enough attention to their fans. Fans seem to have unswerving loyalty despite being exploited or having their interests ignored. But there may be a limit to their tolerance of rising ticket prices, public subsidies, franchise relocation threats, and breakdowns in labor-management negotiations that lead to stoppages of play. Professional sports owners, commissioners, and athletes need to be careful not to appear too business-like or greedy and risk diminishing the passion and excitement that keep fans loyal to their teams and sport. Findings from an unscientific online reader survey for the *SportsBusiness Daily* conducted in 2006 seem to convey an important warning to the people who run professional sports (SportsBusiness Journal 2006). Asked what they thought was the biggest threat to sports, 28.3 percent of respondents said "disconnect with fan base" and 21.6 percent said "use of drugs/integrity of the game." Other responses were "rising ticket prices" (15.4 percent), "inflated salaries"

(14 percent), "overcommercialization" (12.1 percent), and "losing competitive balance" (5.3 percent).

These results imply that the people who run and play professional sports must strike a balance between their economic interests and the desire of sports fans to see games and stars that interest them and appear exciting *and* authentic. How well these people maintain this kind of balance in the context of the forces of change in society and the global cultural economy may be the key to understanding the future popularity and commercial success of specific professional sports and professional sports in general. The future of sport is an explicit focus of the next chapter, which is about the politics of sport and the social, economic, and political influences likely to shape the future of sport.

Stop and Think Questions

1. Why are professional sports leagues "peculiar businesses" in the United States, and how does the golden triangle make them successful?

2. How does NASCAR differ organizationally and as a business from the Big Four North American pro sports leagues, and why hasn't NASCAR reached the status of the Big Four in the United States?

3. Why does the distinction between open and closed market systems over-simplify the difference between the economic structures of the Big Four leagues in North America and those of elite European soccer leagues, and how is the ownership model of the NFL Green Bay Packers similar to and different from the socio ownership model in some segments of European soccer?

4. In what sense are contemporary sports stadiums in the United States postmodern and "cathedrals of consumption," and why is the funding of pro sports stadium construction in the United States often an abuse of the power of pro sports leagues and franchises?

5. Why have the NBA and MLB been more successful in globalization than the NFL has been, and in what ways has elite European soccer been more successful in the United States than MLS has been?

6. What are the biggest sacrifices that professional athletes must make in pursuing their athletic careers, and what is the most important message from *League of Denial* for NFL players, and possibly athletes in other major professional sports in the North American golden triangle?

7. Why are fans so important to success in the golden triangle, and why is their status in the most commercialized sports in North America generally inconsistent with their importance to these sports?

Part V

Power, Political Economy, and Global Sports

9

Politics, Economics, and Sport in a Changing World

Throughout this book, we have been considering the effects of powerful and pervasive socio-demographic, organizational, economic, political, and technological processes that have expanded the reach and influence of corporate and commercialized sports around the world. We have seen how the power of the golden triangle has combined with these social processes to influence what sports we see, how they are organized and run, who the stars of sport are, and how sports are played, seen, and consumed. In this chapter, we will emphasize politics and power, and consider how people have used power in the political arena to make and shape decisions that have influenced sport in the past and will influence its future.

Politics refers to the political realms of society where power is exercised by governments or governing bodies. These political realms also include the actions of citizens and others outside government who try to influence how they are governed, the rules and policies of governments or governing bodies, and the enforcement or effects of these rules and policies. Power is used when the officials of a sport try to protect their sport's integrity and its established rules. For example, it does this by imposing stiff fines and suspensions for violent plays on the field and for violations of a league's drug policy. Power is also used when fans write letters or complain to reporters about the competence of a coach, the commitment of a team owner to getting the best players, or the price of tickets. The US Congress exercised power when it investigated doping in professional sports and clearly conveyed the message that if the leagues did not develop stronger drug policies and enforcement procedures, it would intervene. It conveyed the same intervention threat when a Senate committee investigated the status of student-athletes in big-time college sports. When officials create new rules to make their sport more exciting or to increase the pace of games, they are exercising their rule-making power, and they usually do these kinds of things to increase the appeal of their sports to the sports public. These are all cases of *political power*, which involves the exercise of power by governmental and nongovernmental actors in the political arena. Political power is the primary focus of this chapter.

Power has been a pervasive theme of this book, and we have considered various forms of power exercised by governments, regulatory bodies in sport, individuals, and of course the golden triangle, which I have characterized as the dominant network of power in the corporate and commercialized sports world. Following the lead of Max Weber, sociologists generally use the term "power" to refer to the capacity of people acting individually or collectively to get what they want from others in the face of their perceived or actual resistance. Power is a kind of social interaction in which people try to get what they want from others by effectively using resources, ranging from persuasion to material inducements and threats to coercion. This book has devoted a lot of attention to the *economic power* of golden triangles, which involves the power wielded by organizations and individuals in the economic arena, where goods and services are manufactured, distributed, and consumed. We have seen that golden triangles also exercise *cultural power*, which is about the power of organizations or individuals to create or disseminate influential cultural ideas and products such as the Sport Ethic, sports events, and images of sports stars. In a cultural economy, economic and cultural power overlap as economic enterprises try to beat their competitors at the production, marketing, and sales of cultural goods and services. Golden triangles compete and sometimes cooperate with each other in this global cultural economy, and sport itself is a major cultural product of these golden triangles.

Sociologists usually refer to the legitimate political power wielded by formal organizations or agencies of government as *authority*. In modern societies, authority is usually legitimized as the rule of law. Max Weber conceptualized this rational-legal kind of authority as a characteristic of modern bureaucracies, and it is linked to a position in an organization. Holding a position of authority means that you have a right to expect people to accept your decisions and policies as binding, as long as they are within formally defined boundaries. The authority of a professional sports league commissioner is illustrated when players pay fines or serve suspensions without question or turn to a formal appeals process to try to modify a league decision. The players recognize that the league commissioner has the authority to make these kinds of decisions and that questioning them requires following formal procedures. Authority systems are hierarchical, which means that when policies or rules conflict, the relevant policies and rules of the superior authority have precedence. For example, when the US Congress passed Title IX, it meant that public schools and colleges were compelled to create gender-related opportunities and practices consistent with the principle of gender equity embedded in the new federal law.

When people in positions of authority want others to do things they have no right to expect them to do or when their authority is weak, they may turn to *interpersonal, group,* or *organizational power*, which involves mobilizing individual or collective resources to get their way. For example, owners of sports franchises have no right to expect taxpayers to fund a new stadium, so they may believe they have to threaten to move their team to another city to get local politicians and voters to approve new stadium construction. The National Collegiate Athletic Association (NCAA) has authority to govern its member institutions, but it has no authority over the US government. Thus, the NCAA has used its organizational power to try to influence the US Congress not to regulate its commercial activities and not to remove the tax-exempt status of its members. Similarly, Major League Baseball (MLB) and other professional sports leagues have implemented drug policies to try to avoid congressional intervention in their sport. One of the resources that the NCAA and professional sports can use to try to sway legislators, government officials, and the public is the prominent place of their sports in the popular culture. Sports officials, coaches, and athletes can use the popularity of their sport as a political resource when the people they want to influence are passionate about sports, admire sports stars, or recognize the value of sport in society or the sports business in the economy. People may be deferential and more easily influenced under these conditions. Thus, sports officials try to boost or protect the image of sports for political purposes as well as for economic reasons.

When people have no formal authority but want to influence the public, governing officials, or governing bodies to change beliefs, attitudes, behavior, rules, or policies, they rely on interpersonal, group, or organizational power. For example, high school athletes with physical disabilities have gone to court to get school athletic officials to allow them to compete in mainstream inter- scholastic athletics events; women have used Title IX to try to reduce gender discrimination in high school and college athletics; college athletes who have been disgruntled about their lack of compensation for the use of their names, images, and likenesses for commercial purposes have sued the NCAA; other college athletes have sued for the right to unionize as employees; and profes- sional athletes have used agents or organized as unions to negotiate with own- ers and management in their sport.

We will pay special attention later in this chapter to other cases of indi- viduals and organized social movements that have indirectly and directly challenged sports officials and the power structure of sport from within and outside sport. These cases of *oppositional power* have focused on issues rang- ing from the revival of a sports franchise to globalization, the environment, and human rights. These cases of oppositional power suggest that the use of power is often prompted by inequalities and involves struggles to make sport and society fairer for people with lower status and fewer resources. However, we have also seen cases of oppositional power where fans have acted collec- tively and violently against political and sports authorities as an expression of their racist politics. This happened when Jackie Robinson integrated MLB in the United States and has happened more recently when foreign and domestic players of color have become more prominent in European soccer. We have also seen recent examples of oppositional politics in sport where soccer venues have become arenas of protest in Egypt and elsewhere in the Middle East.

Power, Politics, and Political Economy in Sport

The relationship between politics and sport can be understood from various sociological perspectives. For example, a *structural functionalist* might focus on how sport contributes to political stability, national integration, or support for a political regime. These things could occur when the sports accomplishments of national sports teams overcome divisions, fuel nationalistic pride, and unify nations. This was the theme of a number of news stories when the Iraqi soccer team upset the Saudi Arabian team 1–0 to win its first Asian Cup Champion- ship (e.g., Farrell and Gelling 2007; Wahl 2007). Across Iraq, this victory pro- duced celebrations, flag waving and other expressions of national pride, and a chance to forget the ravages of war, sectarian violence, and suicide bombings. The fact that the winning goal was scored by an Iraqi Sunni Muslim, the goal scorer was assisted by a pass from an Iraqi Kurd, and the lead was protected by an Iraqi Shiite Muslim goalkeeper would seem to have powerful symbolic significance, since these three ethnic groups were fighting with each other in the war raging in their country. The respite from war was only temporary, though. Despite the excitement and pride felt by many Iraqis after the championship victory, the fragile Iraqi government was unable to use the residue of these feelings to stop the war, internal ethnic conflicts, or suicide bombings and create political stability and peace.

Sports contests may suggest the possibilities of social and national integration, but they cannot by themselves overcome deep ethnic divisions or enduring political conflicts that governments cannot resolve. They might convey what change could look like but cannot by themselves produce enduring political changes in a country or the world. However, a structural functionalist perspective at least enables us to see that sport may provide brief respites from political turmoil.

Symbolic interactionists offer another way to look at politics and sport. Through the eyes of a symbolic interactionist, we are able, for example, to gain a deeper understanding of how the golden triangle creates political images and meanings in sport. Patriotic anthems and displays, flags, and other political symbols are frequently part of sport, and symbolic interactionists draw our attention to the meanings and implications of these patriotic symbols and displays in sport. We can see how their orchestrated presence in the sports arena publicly ties sport to dominant cultural values and established institutions in the larger society and nation. We recall that a major theme of the Dominant American Sports Creed expressed this connection in the idea that sport promotes patriotism.

A symbolic interactionist perspective can also help us understand why political struggles have arisen between sports traditionalists and Indian and feminist activists who have tried to rid sport of widely recognized symbols they have perceived as offensive and degrading, such as Indian mascots, team names, and logos and gendered team names such as "Lady Tigers" or the oxymoronic "Lady Rams." Symbols can be powerful means of defining a group's status or identity in society. They may be perceived as demeaning, racist, or sexist, or they may be seen as a source of pride or allegiance. These power struggles over ethnic and gender symbols have involved people with very strong views on both sides of these issues who have constructed very different meanings of these symbols.

Conflict and critical theories emphasize how social and political inequalities in society reinforce each other and how political struggles about issues such as sexism, racism, and exploitation can surface in sport and highlight the inequalities in both sport and society. The *political economy* perspective is a critical perspective for understanding how political power and capitalism combine in sport and shape how sports are organized and used by powerful people and organizations (Nixon and Frey 1996:32–33). Political economy particularly emphasizes network ties linking sports, media, and corporate elites in the golden triangle to government elites. These relationships involve golden triangles using governments for their economic purposes and governments using sports for their political purposes. For example, legislative, judicial, and administrative decisions by governments have often created a favorable economic environment for sports investors and sports bodies to make money. Similarly, even in the United States, where the federal government has had relatively little direct control over sports, government officials and elected politicians have used sports and athletes to try to increase their popularity among voters and as a means to conduct foreign policy.

The political economy perspective enables us to see complex connections linking the golden triangle to government and politics. For example, the Chinese government cooperated with the media and corporate sponsors in its hosting of the 2008 Beijing Olympics. In turn, Olympic officials, the media covering the Games, and corporate sponsors overlooked protests against the Chinese government for its human rights violations, just as officials, the media, and sponsors largely overlooked the Russian government's legislative crackdown on gays prior to the 2014 Sochi Games. The payoff of these ties to host governments for businesses in the golden triangle is the chance to expand markets and increase profits.

The ways in which business enterprises in the golden triangle try to exploit ties to government and politics for commercial gain illustrate *corporate nationalism*. Corporate nationalism has taken a number of different forms involving sport (e.g., see Silk, Andrews, and Cole 2005a), but it generally involves exploiting nationalistic and patriotic feelings within nations and localities by associating global brands with these feelings. Sport and the media have helped spawn these feelings in their emphasis on competitions between nations in global mega-events such as the Olympics and the FIFA World Cup. Corporate nationalism often involves a process of economic globalization that overlaps with national identities in global mega-events of sport. This process creates a paradox. The paradox in these cases is that as the cultural economy of sport in the golden triangle has become more globalized, national and even local identities have become more significant (Silk, Andrews, and Cole 2005b).

Nike and Under Armour are two prominent examples of how corporate nationalism manifests itself in golden triangle business enterprises. On its website, Nike calls itself "the world's leading innovator in athletic footwear, apparel, equipment, and accessories." It is an example of how corporate nationalism and glocalization became linked with the Nike advertising campaign in Asia that tied its brand to "the nation" (Kobayashi 2012). Nike used Brazilian star Ronaldinho, who was the top soccer player in the world at the time, in its "Where is the Next?" marketing campaign in Asia. He was seen as a global or transnational athlete, much like Michael Jordan, David Beckham, and Yao Ming before him. The campaign was inaugurated at the time of the 2007 Asian Cup and targeted at the major national markets of Australia, China, Japan, and South Korea. It challenged aspiring young soccer players to become the next Ronaldinho. Thus, Nike's strategy of corporate nationalism was to use local media outlets to glocalize its advertising message to make it seem relevant to potential consumers in different markets in Asia. These messages were glocalized by utilizing different national symbols to evoke feelings of the local relevance of the global message in different national markets.

When Under Armour was launched in the late 1990s, Nike was well established as the dominant player in the global sports footwear and apparel market. Under Armour began with its own original brand of sports performance apparel and then branched out into manufacturing sports bras, cleats, running shoes, and accessories. In 2014, it became the second-biggest sportswear brand in the United States (Germano 2014). In its approach to corporate nationalism, the company devised a marketing campaign in the post-9/11 era in the United States that played to patriotic feelings (Weedon 2012). The company's "protect this house" slogan associated the brand with defending the nation in the post-9/11 period. But it also carried over to the athletic realm in its relevance to defending or protecting a team's turf. Thus, the message is part-nationalistic, part-militaristic, part-masculine stereotype, and easily tied to sport. Under Armour made its ties to the nation and military explicit in its Freedom campaign that it inaugurated in 2010. It was meant to be patriotic in the company's show of support for the armed forces and public safety officers. The challenge for Under Armour was to find a way to expand its message globally, without undermining the pro-US message that enabled it to grow in the United States. That is, it needed to try to emulate the Nike model of corporate nationalism. Of course, Nike's globalization path was bumpy at times, as we will see in the discussion of the anti-globalization movement against Nike.

Political economy and corporate nationalism are among various ways to think about the politics of sport. Houlihan (2000) offered another useful conceptual approach. He distinguished between politics *and* sport and politics *in* sport. *Politics and sport* mainly refers to how governments exercise power over or through sports in the public domain for their political ends. For example, governments may decide to use public funds to host an Olympics or build a stadium. *Politics in sport* concerns how various individuals and organizations outside government and inside and outside sport use power to pursue their own political, economic, or social interests in ways that affect sport. Examples of this perspective include public pressure on sports officials to increase access to sport for women or minorities, anti-sweatshop boycotts of Nike products, and advocacy to get sports to be more environmentally responsible or to get nations to treat access to sports for people with disabilities as a human rights issue. Corporate nationalism illustrates how politics and sport and politics in sport can overlap. For example, Olympic host governments establish corporate ties to further their national interests, and media and other business enterprises in the golden triangle pursue their commercial ends by trying to link their brands to symbols that evoke local, state, or national sensibilities.

We have seen that in the United States, major sports in the golden triangle have generally tried to avoid government interference but have welcomed court decisions and legislation that made it easier to pursue their commercial interests. Elsewhere in the world, sports have been regulated and run by government agencies. In the Olympics, officials have long held the view that politics do not belong in their arena. But reality has frequently contradicted this expressed desire. In the rest of this chapter, we will see the relevance of both the politics and sport and politics in sport perspectives in national and international sports contexts. We will also see how the interplay of governments, political power, and economic forces in the golden triangle have shaped sport at the global level, especially in the Olympic arena.

Governments and Political Uses of Sport

Governments have tried to control, use, or otherwise intervene in sports for political purposes in a number of different ways (e.g., see Houlihan 2000:215–220; Nixon and Frey 1996:273–288). One type of intervention has involved the regulatory role of government. For example, the Swedish government banned boxing due to its extreme violence as a "blood sport." In Italy, government officials barred spectators from soccer stadiums that could not meet safety and security standards following the death of a police-man during an episode of spectator violence. In the United States, a stronger internal regulatory body for college athletics, new rules, and innovations in the game curtailed violence in college football and averted a government ban of the sport in the early twentieth century. The effects of Title IX legislation on sport were probably not fully anticipated when the law was passed. It was not initially seen as a means of achieving gender equity in high school and college sports. But despite oppositional politics and court challenges, it has profoundly affected sports opportunities for female students in those two realms. At the state level in the United States, legislatures have occasionally played a controversial regulatory role in sports, as when Texas legislators approved the "no pass, no play" law, which prohibited high school athletes and band members with failing grades from participating in these extracurricular activities.

The US Government and Sport

Sports officials in the United States have often been reluctant to encourage government intervention in their sports when they have seen government involvement as a threat to their control. This has been true in issues ranging from doping to blackout policies. In college sports, NCAA officials have tried to make the case that their business practices should be exempt from government regulation. But there have been times when sports bodies in the United States and elsewhere have cooperated with governments to deal with troubling and intractable problems. For example, Houlihan (2000) noted that the success of International Olympic Committee (IOC) and World Anti-Doping Agency (WADA) efforts to fight doping in Olympic sports depended on the cooperation of governments. In North America, professional sports leagues cooperated under duress. Congressional pressure and its threatened intervention spurred the leagues to establish tougher anti-doping policies and drug enforcement procedures.

The United States has been different from most other countries in the relative amount of government detachment from big-time sports. For example, it has not had a centralized federal sports authority to regulate and sponsor Olympic sports. This reflects a political ideology of limited government and a belief in private individual initiative as well as a tradition of strong and independent national governing bodies (NGBs) of Olympic sports in the United States (Coakley 2009:379–380). However, federal involvement in Olympic sports increased in the United States in the late 1970s after a period of declining US performance in international competition and conflicts among major amateur sports organizations, including the NCAA, the US Olympic Committee (USOC), and the Amateur Athletic Union (AAU). In 1978, the US Congress, with the backing of the president, passed the Amateur Sports Act. It made USOC the major coordinating body for US amateur sports, which are now usually called Olympic sports because of the growing element of professionalism in these sports. The government also authorized a one-time appropriation to fund three Olympic training centers (Nixon and Frey 1996:275).

Probe 9.1: Resisting USOC Control over Amateur and Olympic Sports in the United States

Despite its designated central role in amateur and Olympic sports in the United States, the USOC has existed in the shadow of the NCAA. The USOC was supposed to coordinate the NGBs of sports not under the auspices of the NCAA, but it has been much weaker than the NCAA in its regulatory role because the NGBs it was supposed to coordinate have fought hard to maintain their autonomy. These individual governing bodies have been unwilling to yield much control over either the athletes or the flow of resources in their sports. In the US tradition of commercialism in the sports marketplace, these bodies have raised their own money to support athletes, training, and events and have not wanted to share the revenue their sports have generated. Thus, limited government intervention and limited subsidies in the United States have opened the door for these Olympic sports, as well as the NCAA, to pursue their sports and economic interests through ties with the golden triangle.

The amount of autonomy given to amateur and Olympic sports bodies by the US government is relatively unusual globally. A combination of political expediency, political values, and the traditional power of the sports establishment probably explains much of this autonomy. Other nations typically take a more active role in sports, with federal sports ministries or agencies overseeing all national sports bodies, formulating policies for them, and providing government subsidies. Having control over sport has enabled government leaders to manipulate or exploit sports and athletes for their political purposes. For example, government-sponsored sports academies and training programs have been used to socialize athletes to embrace a national political ideology or culture, as in the political education of athletes in the Soviet Union (Riordan 1980) and other communist nations. The role of government leaders in this kind of political socialization is more subtle in democratic nations such as the United States, where the rhetoric of the American Dream in politics and sport asserts the superiority of the US way of life.

Government and Sport: Cuba versus the United States

In her study of ideology, politics, and market forces in Cuban baseball, Baird (2005) showed how baseball in Cuba differed from MLB as a result of being in a state-run, rather than a market-driven, system. Cuban government officials have characterized US professional sports as a "capitalist perversion of athletics" that exploited players and the public (Jamail 2000:49). In Cuba, baseball is a national passion (O'Brien 2010). For longtime Cuban leader Fidel Castro, it was a special delight to be good at a game invented by his enemy, the United States, and the Cubans were very good at the sport. The Cuban national team was runner-up in the first World Baseball Classic in 2006 and has had great success over the years in global competitions.

In Castro's socialist model, baseball teams were "owned" by the government, which paid players minimal salaries. According to official policy, players earned about the same amount, which was about $12–$16 per month in 2010 and was equivalent to what most of the Cuban workforce earned (O'Brien

2010). Players played for the team in their region and did not move between teams. There were no wealthy teams to buy the best players, since there was no market to make some teams wealthier than others. The government placed players on teams in the regions where they lived. Advertising did not exist in the stadium or in media coverage, and games cost nothing to attend before 1994. When financial hard times occurred in Cuba, it became necessary to charge a small price for admission to games, but the aim was to keep game tickets inexpensive to allow ordinary people to attend.

As Baird pointed out, Cuban baseball and the Cuban sports system in general were managed to serve the interests of the Cuban people as a whole and not individuals. This emphasis on the public good is a basic socialist principle derived from Karl Marx, and it contrasts with the preeminence of private interests in a capitalist marketplace. Under socialism, the government articulated and represented the public interest. In this model of sport, there was no place for market forces or the golden triangle. There was no market to create economic inequalities among teams or players, since the government controlled the economics of the sport.

Despite government support of their sport, many Cuban players have been disgruntled about the restrictions on their careers and economic opportunities imposed by the government. They were prohibited from playing overseas, were compelled to finish their careers with their assigned teams, and then were reassigned to other employment by the government after their sports careers ended. In addition, they were paid a paltry amount compared with players with equivalent talent in the United States, Japan, Italy, and Latin America. For these reasons, many Cuban players have defected to play overseas since the early 1990s, even though they were officially viewed as traitors. To the frustration of the Cuban government, Cuban fans continued to follow the careers of these players when they played in foreign leagues.

Disgruntled players, embarrassing defections of star players, and a chronically distressed economy and need for hard currency led Cuban leaders to make periodic compromises of their egalitarian socialist principles. In 1995, they began a pattern of loosening and tightening restrictions on player movement and compensation. When players were permitted to play overseas and earn foreign salaries, the Cuban government took as much as 80 percent of these earnings. Frustrated with the ongoing loss of top players, the Cuban government introduced new regulations in 2013 that removed the upper limit on salaries and allowed players to sign with foreign teams without having to give up their citizenship. By that point, it had already lost a number of its biggest stars to the lure of MLB fame and fortune. They included Aroldis Chapman, Yoenis Cespédes, Yasiel Puig, and Jose Abreu, who signed contracts ranging from $30 million to $68 million (Watts 2013).

It was nearly impossible for Cuba's socialist model to compete with the golden triangle. As Baird (2005) observed, Cuban leaders kept a tight rein on the sport and players to project a socialist example, but then faced various problems that pushed them to resort to capitalistic practices. They could not simultaneously keep players and fans happy, maintain a competitive balance among regionally based teams in the Cuban League, deal with their economic problems, and uphold their socialist principles. Their political compromises and strategic flip-flops highlighted the dilemma posed by baseball for Cuban officials. Socialist principles and a managed economy were difficult to sustain in the management of sport when the country faced severe economic problems caused in part by its political ideology. As Baird observed, trying to regulate baseball to demonstrate the superiority of a political ideology was ultimately very costly for those from whom the Cuban regime most wanted support, the stars of its athletic system and the people, who loved their sports stars.

Although Cuba and the United States represent opposite ends of the continuum of centralized government control over sports, there are some surprising similarities in their sport systems. In Cuba, the government has tried to limit marketplace influences and the compensation and freedom of athletes. In the United States, the federal government has historically done very little to limit antitrust practices or to ensure the economic and legal freedom of athletes at the professional and big-time college levels. Except for occasional instances such as the passage of the Amateur Sports Act and the boycott of the 1980 Moscow Olympics, it has also generally tried to avoid direct involvement in sports to clean up organizational feuds, improve the performance of US sports teams, or make a political point through sports. On the other hand, big-time college sports and professional sports leagues in the United States have operated as virtual cartels to restrict economic competition and the economic and legal rights of athletes. In addition, revenue-sharing policies in college athletic conferences and in professional sports leagues have seemed to conform more to socialist principles than to capitalist principles of the free market. Thus, the similarities between the sports systems in the two countries have resulted from the actions of the Cuban government on the one hand and the inaction of the US government to control antitrust practices on the other hand.

The Cuban and American cases illustrate how difficult it can be to generalize about the relationship between types of governments and types of sports systems. In Cuba, government leaders tried to construct a sports system that mirrored their political ideology, but found it necessary to make compromises. In the United States, government leaders have generally tried to stay clear of sports, but sports have imposed their own rules to restrict economic free-market practices. Sports systems in many democratic countries have been less restrictive than those in communist countries such as Cuba but more restrictive than the US system. For example, in Canada, the United Kingdom, and Australia, the national government has funded NGBs, shaped their policies, and regulated their organizational practices. In these countries, there have been histories of government funding, policy, and regulation that often made elite sports development and performance the highest priority (Green 2004; Green and Houlihan 2006). The cases of North Korea (officially the Democratic People's Republic of Korea [DPRK]) and China (officially called the People's Republic of China [PRC]) have shown that communist countries may differ in how they approach golden triangle influences in the global sports system.

Contrasting Communist Approaches to the Golden Triangle: North Korea and the PRC

North Korea's approach to international relations and sport has seemed to be closer to that of China in the years after its revolution than to contemporary China. Lee and Bairner (2009) argued that in the early twenty-first century, North Korea and Cuba were the highest-profile Marxist-Leninist regimes of the post–Cold War period. Like Cuba, North Korea was largely isolated in international relations and in the global economy. However, as in Cuba, sport was one of the few areas where the North Korean people could make contact with the outside world. North Korea's political ideology of self-reliant socialism has generally isolated it from globalization and global capitalism. North Korean leaders have viewed globalization as closely tied to American imperialism. They have seen it as a reactionary threat to the worldwide expansion of socialist ideology and practices. Of course, the dominant influence on global sports has been the golden triangle, which is similarly aligned with "reactionary" capitalism. Thus, North Korea's desire to raise its international status by competing in largely commercialized global sports has meant that it has had to place its nationalistic goals ahead of its communist political goals and its distinctive socialist ideology. This is like Cuba's concessions to the golden triangle to preserve its domestic sports system, which has been a source of national pride for the Cuban government and people.

The PRC has followed a different path than that of North Korea and Cuba in aggressively pursuing capitalism while also trying to retain its communist political system. Its desire to be respected as a major global player was an important motivating factor in rejoining the Olympic movement in 1980 and hosting the 2008 Beijing Olympics (Manzenreiter 2010). However, the story of China in international relations and in sports has been the story of two Chinas. A major objective of PRC state policy has been to pursue the absorption of Taiwan as a province, which meant incorporating Taiwanese sports organizations and the Taiwanese population under the control of the PRC central government (Bairner and Hwang 2011). Taiwan identifies itself as the independent democratic state of the Republic of China (ROC) and has asserted its national sovereignty in defiance of efforts by the PRC to get it under its jurisdiction.

The China conflict carried over into sports, with sports policy being an extension of broader political objectives in both countries. After initially excluding the PRC in 1949, the IOC adopted its "two Chinas" policy prior to the 1956 Olympics. However, seeing itself as the only legitimate government of China, the PRC withdrew from the 1956 Olympic Games and did not return for over twenty years (Xiao 2004). In 1979, the IOC admitted the PRC's Olympic committee as the "Chinese Olympic Committee." It relegated the Taiwanese committee to the status of the "Chinese Taipei Olympic Committee" and directed the committee to use a different anthem and flag distinguishing it from the PRC. Since then, the ROC has had to compete in the Olympics under conditions strongly influenced by the PRC (Bairner and Hwang 2011). It currently competes as "Chinese Taipei," although the PRC would like it to be designated as "China Taipei," making it equivalent to the province of "China Hong Kong." However, by whatever name, the opportunity for the ROC to compete in mega-events such as the Olympics has been a way for it to continue to assert its own national identity and distinguish itself from the PRC.

By the beginning of the twenty-first century, the PRC had established itself as a major player in the world economy, and it was also gaining prestige in the world of sport and was a popular tourist destination. However, it still faced many questions about its abuses of human rights, its treatment of Tibet, its environmental policy, and its support for repressive regimes in countries such as North Korea and Sudan. It hoped that hosting the 2008 Olympics in Beijing would give it a chance to demonstrate to the world that it was a worthy, proud, responsible, and hospitable member of the world community. However, public opinion polls showed that despite the spectacular show it put on for the Olympics, it was unable to change the skeptical minds of a majority of the people in Western nations (Bairner and Hwang 2011; Manzenreiter 2010). Its treatment of its own dissidents before the staging of the Games was at odds with the more principled values in the Olympic rhetoric, which reinforced prior negative attitudes.

Building National Identity through Sport: Slovenia and South Africa

Slovenia is one of seven countries that achieved independence from the former Soviet state of Yugoslavia. As a small fledgling nation created in 1991, it had to convince both the world and its own citizens of its legitimacy as an emerging democratic nation-state. It achieved some stability and respectability when it joined the European Union in 2004. But its national identity was still a work in progress, as it seemed to be drifting away from its goal of becoming a Western-style democracy at the end of the first decade of the twenty-first century (Zgaga 2009).

Dominant performances by its athletes or teams in global sports mega-events such as the Olympics and FIFA World Cup have the potential to transcend ethnic differences and make people proud to be Slovenians. Although it has done relatively well for a tiny nation, Slovenia has not yet had enough global sports success to generate this kind of international recognition or national pride. Topič and Coakley (2010) considered a number of factors likely to affect the relationship between sport and perceptions of national identity in struggling young nations such as Slovenia in the post-Soviet era.

It will take time for Slovenia to establish a reputation as a sporting power, and it has to achieve a distinctive national identity in a context where the European Union and UEFA may be promoting pan-European identity ahead of national identity. In addition, it is difficult for relative newcomers to achieve a distinctive and prominent status in a crowded golden triangle dominated by elite leagues and teams. Thus, Slovenes have many fewer opportunities for performances that can capture their continent's and the world's attention and bring pride to the nation. We have seen how difficult it has been to break into the mediascapes of the core European golden triangle and earn the amount of media revenue that could propel Slovenia's teams and athletes into the limelight. Slovenia faces competition not only from the established sporting nations but also from other emerging nations wanting to make their mark on the global sports terrain and boost their national image and identity. These emerging nations also face the challenge of finding enough resources to support national sports while they invest in critical economic development, social programs, and political infrastructure.

Sports success might burnish a nation's image and strengthen its sense of national identity at least for a while after getting a burst of publicity from its success. But the case of Slovenia reminds us that the strength of the relationship between sport and national identity can vary a great deal across nations, especially when the aim is to gain more international recognition. However, sport might have a bigger political payoff when it is used as a means of trying to achieve national solidarity or integration in nations split by political and ethnic or racial differences. For example, as noted in Chapter 3, nation seemed to trump race during a time of virulent racism when Jesse Owens and

Joe Louis vanquished opponents who were despised as representatives of Nazi Germany. Their victories earned them worldwide acclaim as *American* athletes. Of course, their victories did not extinguish racism in the United States. More recently, sport seemed to play an important role in uniting the new South African democracy in the period after apartheid.

Probe 9.2: Invictus and the Role of Rugby in Uniting South Africa

The story of sport and national integration in South Africa was captured in the film *Invictus*. Nelson Mandela was not a rugby fan and had reason to loathe the national team, the Springboks, as a symbol of the oppressive white apartheid regime that had kept him imprisoned for decades for his political resistance. However, he believed that sport had the capacity to unite a nation and saw a chance to promote national unity through this nearly all-white team (Carlin 2008). The new president mounted a promotional campaign to get the blacks and nonwhites in his country behind the Springboks as they competed in the 1995 Rugby World Cup in his country. In dramatic fashion, South Africa defeated New Zealand in extra time, and Mandela awarded the trophy dressed in a green Springbok jersey. The crowd was 95 percent white, but he was cheered by the crowd and the victory was celebrated as South African. Mandela believed that a threatened civil war and right-wing terrorism were averted because whites, blacks, and nonwhites were able to share in this major national sporting success. The game was also a step in the direction of the multiracial society he sought in the aftermath of the vicious racism of apartheid. Nelson Mandela's faith in sport as a nation builder seemed to be justified. Although other government leaders have seen mixed results from their involvement in sport, governments still tend to believe that sport can serve their political purposes.

Sport, Diplomacy, and International Hostility

Diplomacy is another example of a political use of sport. One of the most famous and consequential cases of sports diplomacy involved the United States, the PRC, and table tennis. The governments of the United States and the PRC used a series of table tennis matches between the US national Ping-Pong team and the world champion PRC team in the early 1970s as a first step in establishing broader relations between the nations. The PRC issued a surprise invitation to the US team to visit China when it was competing at the World Table Tennis Championship in Japan in 1971. The Chinese premier Chou En-lai welcomed the American team as diplomats who were ushering in a new period of friendship between nations that had a very chilly relationship since the communist takeover of China in 1949 (PBS 1999). The premier also encouraged more US journalists to visit his country. This diplomacy through sport, known as "ping-pong diplomacy," also prompted the US government to drop a trade embargo of Chinese goods that had been in effect for twenty years. A visit to the United States by the Chinese team followed. These sporting contacts were a crucial first step in China's emergence from isolation and more active involvement in international relations and the global economy.

A case of "beisbol diplomacy" involved two exhibition games in Cuba and in Baltimore in 1999 between the Baltimore Orioles and a Cuban all-star team. This case was distinctive because it was the initiative of a private citizen, Orioles owner Peter Angelos, and occurred outside formal diplomatic channels. As with China, the United States had a long-standing embargo against Cuba from the early days of Fidel Castro's communist regime. Formal diplomatic ties did not exist and other kinds of ties were severely restricted. Thus, Angelos had to obtain approval from his own and the Cuban government as well as from MLB to play the games he planned. He and his team served as a surrogate for the US State Department and government in broaching relations with Cuba. The games were possible because US president Bill Clinton had begun to relax restrictions on communications and travel between the two countries (Knowlton 1999). On the surface, the two games between the Orioles and the Cuban all-star team in 1999 might appear simply to be a gesture of goodwill aimed at thawing relations between two hostile countries. However, a closer look at the political context and implications of these games reveals a much more complex picture.

Clinton wanted to use the games as a humanitarian means to gain the sympathy of the Cuban people, but he was not interested in bolstering Castro's regime (Knowlton 1999). This may be why the Justice Department responded to political pressure to investigate the Orioles after the games were over. Mutual antagonism between the governments and hostility toward Castro from Cuban exiles and anticommunist politicians in the United States were part of the political landscape of this experiment in baseball diplomacy. They help explain why political controversy swirled around the games in the United States and raised security concerns (Chass 1999). The game in Baltimore was not disrupted by protest, but it caused bitter feelings among those virulently opposed to Castro and spawned conflicts with those seeking rapprochement with Cuba and other US enemies in the interests of international cooperation and world peace. Peter Angelos's baseball diplomacy may have ignited some political fires, but it ultimately had little immediate effect on US-Cuba relations. However, a failed effort at politics in sport through baseball diplomacy allowed the governments of the countries involved to back away without a loss of face domestically or internationally. Much more political capital is expended when even informal government-to-government contacts are involved, as in the case of ping-pong diplomacy.

Probe 9.3: Using Youth Sports to Achieve Peace

A number of non-governmental organizations (NGOs) have used youth sports programs as a means to achieve reconciliation and restore social order in areas torn apart by terrorism, civil war, and international conflict. They can be seen as a form of "humanitarian intervention" to address the humanitarian crises often produced by these kinds of political violence (Rookwood and Palmer 2011). Soccer has frequently been used as the humanitarian or peacemaking vehicle. For example, the Open Fun Football Schools (OFFS) project in the Balkans has brought together youths from different ethnic background in a context of reconciliation. The Football for Peace (F4P) program is a British universities project that has tried to intervene at the grassroots level of the sporting culture of Israel and Palestine. It has tried to overcome a history of violence, mistrust, and segregation by nurturing peaceful integration through values-based coaching. In programs such as the STAR project (emphasizing self-discipline, truthfulness, appreciation, and respect) in Liberia, the aim is to turn child soldiers into peacemakers in the aftermath of bloody civil wars. While sympathetic to the goals of these programs, Rookwood and Palmer (2011) raised questions about the appropriateness of "invasion games" such as soccer for achieving their goal of a lasting peace or even a respite from violence. Soccer was characterized this way because they saw it based more on aggressive principles of invasion than on actions meant to achieve reconciliation, cooperation, or peace. In fact, it could be a means of acting out internalized hostility. They suggest the importance of thinking carefully about the conditions under which youths exposed to racism, violence, and exploitation are thrust together to encourage them to get along better with each other. Their competitive structure and the opportunity for aggressive physical contact may make many sports counterproductive vehicles for teaching about reconciliation and peace.

Hostile nations often have no interest in diplomacy or peacemaking. Sport may even serve as a surrogate for military conflict in a "war without weapons" (Goodhart and Chataway 1968). In this sense, athletic competition is a symbolic substitute for the bloodier and more costly conflict of a war. A nation can trumpet its wins on the athletic field instead of its conquests on the battlefield as an indication of its national superiority. During the Cold War, competition between US and Soviet teams could be seen as wars without weapons. Another kind of war without weapons involved the use of sports boycotts by governments to protest the actions of other countries or express hostility toward them. There is a long history of these kinds of boycotts in the Olympics. For example, in 1980, the United States boycotted the Moscow Summer Olympic Games to punish the Soviets for their occupation of Afghanistan. In 1984, the Soviets and their allies boycotted the Los Angeles Summer Olympics, ostensibly because of concerns about the safety of their athletes and anti-Soviet feelings in the United States but perhaps more importantly as retaliation against the US boycott in 1980 and because the Soviets perceived the 1984 Games as the "Capitalist Olympics" (Nixon 1988).

The boycott of South Africa and of nations having sporting contacts with South Africa to end South Africa's racist apartheid system may be the most prominent and effective example of this kind of war without weapons. The international sports boycott was followed by an international economic boycott, which ultimately led to the end of apartheid in 1993 (Nixon and Frey 1996:288–289). The antiapartheid movement is also an example of a case of effective political pressure on Olympic sports officials, who banned apartheid South Africa from the Olympic Movement for nearly three decades.

Sometimes sports competition between hostile nations escalates from a war without weapons to violence and a war *with* weapons. For example, in 1969 during a World Cup qualifying competition, a long-standing border dispute between El Salvador and Honduras erupted into violence between spectators in a San Salvador soccer stadium. El Salvador won the game and its strong nationalistic sentiments led to the burning of Honduran flags on the field and attacks on Honduran spectators as they fled the stadium. This violence precipitated a protest from the Honduran government, a counterprotest by the government of El Salvador about mistreatment of Salvadoran immigrants and refugees by Honduras, the severing of diplomatic relations by El Salvador, and, a month later, a five-day armed conflict, which has been called the "soccer war" (Morello 1997). Although historical tension between the nations was the underlying cause of this international conflict, a soccer match provided a trigger for the conflict.

Political Activism and the Golden Triangle

Nike became a target of a global anti-sweatshop movement that opposed both the practices of specific transnational corporations and the broader processes of economic globalization and global capitalist expansion. Nike has been a major player in the golden triangle for several decades. It has turned sports stars into icons to sell its footwear, apparel, and equipment products. It has had a significant influence on the global culture and cultural economy of sport. It has also become very wealthy as a result of its sports business. We have seen that it has developed clever glocalized approaches to expand its global reach. It is the best-known brand among sporting goods manufacturers, and its pursuit of corporate nationalism has made it a dominant player in its sector of the golden triangle. According to the investment tracking company MarketWatch, Nike earned $27.8 billion in revenue and had a net income of $2.7 billion for the fiscal year ending in May 2014. These numbers represented huge jumps of 46 percent in revenue and 42 percent in net income since 2010. Nike visibility and success very likely contributed to its becoming a major target of activists in the anti-sweatshop movement in the 1990s.

Nike and other transnational corporations were criticized for operations in low-income countries. Like many major corporations today, Nike moved its factories from a wealthy capitalist nation, the United States, with its relatively expensive labor force and cost of operations, to parts of the world where wages were low and the political climate was favorable to its manufacturing, export, and profit-making aims. By 1998, approximately 450,000 workers at over 450 factories were making sporting goods for Nike in Southeast Asia in countries such as Indonesia, Vietnam, and China. It became a focus of the emerging *antiglobalization* and *anti-sweatshop* movements when evidence began to surface that Nike paid its workers in these countries less than $1 per day. This was less than was needed for basic subsistence. It also was criticized for employing children and subjecting workers to oppressive management and working conditions and long hours (Sage 2005).

Sage (1999) constructed a case study of the Nike Transactional Advocacy Network, which was organized to protest Nike's behavior and try to get it to change its manufacturing practices in low-income nations. The network was spearheaded by activists who specifically opposed Nike for its labor practices. But it also opposed the general patterns of economic globalization, in which workers in poor nations were exploited in the manufacturing of products for sale in richer nations. Its protests were aimed at the global expansion of capitalism for profit and the government economic policies that allowed transnational corporations to operate virtually without constraint in many parts of the world.

The anti-Nike social movement was strengthened by its ties to labor organizations, religious organizations, human rights organizations, individual activists, and students. Students organized United Students Against Sweat-shops (USAS) in 1998. The movement against Nike was the first global social movement to make extensive use of the Internet, and its political tactics included demonstrations, protests, editorial columns in newspapers, TV adver-tisements, sit-ins, and marches. It also urged consumers and sports organi-zations buying Nike products to boycott the company. Activists wanted Nike to pay workers a subsistence wage, provide safe working conditions, allow workers to organize, and respect the human rights of its workers. They hoped that their efforts would damage Nike's brand name and reputation enough to compel it to change its practices (Sage 1999, 2005).

According to Sage (2010:123), the anti-Nike movement became so effective that the Nike logo was associated with sweatshops and unfair labor practices for many consumers. The protests seemed to contribute to a sharp decline in Nike's earnings. Nike was also hurt by a dip in several Asian economies in the late 1990s, which reduced the earnings of many transnational corporations doing business in Asia at that time. As a result of the combination of the ongo-ing protests and declining profits, Nike executives began to change conditions in production facilities. They increased the minimum age of factory workers, adopted US Occupational Safety and Health Administration (OSHA) standards, expanded educational programs for workers, and increased monitoring of fac-tory conditions. As a result of the protests, Nike also found that negotiations with some of its high-visibility customers had changed. USAS organized chap-ters at over two hundred universities by 2003, and student activists were able to persuade administrators at their schools and corporations to provide full disclosure of locations and labor practices of factories manufacturing products used by their university's sports teams and sold with its institutional logo. USAS also got commitments that manufacturers would adhere to a code of conduct for their workers and that universities would expect manufacturers to honor this commitment (Sage 2010:118–126).

The Nike case shows that extensive and well-organized oppositional net-works with a lot of resources are needed to influence large and wealthy transnational corporations in the golden triangle and in the global economy. Recent record-breaking revenue and income reports for Nike demonstrate the capacity of powerful transnational corporations in the golden triangle to recover from damage to their prestige and profits from opposition movements. Although the anti-Nike movement was able to achieve some improvements in the lives of the workers who made Nike products, big corporations such as Nike tend to remain more committed to their bottom line than to the welfare of their workers. As in the case of Nike, company executives make public statements about concerns for workers in their overseas factories and say they will make improvements. However, it is not clear whether this is merely public relations rhetoric and a marketing strategy or a real commitment to reform. Nike and other companies in its industry continue to operate in countries where wages are low and manufacturers can make huge profits (see Sage 2010:125–126).

The major corporate sponsors in the golden triangle tend to retain the loyalty of the athletes who endorse their products, despite political protests against these companies. For example, the anti-Nike movement could not enlist the public support of famous athletes such as Michael Jordan, who endorsed Nike products. Star athletes have been loyal to the companies whose products they endorse because these companies have helped make them rich and famous, and they have not wanted to risk losing the support of their sports-consuming fans by taking a controversial political stand.

These athletes have generally tried to remain "apolitical," even though their failure to take a position on social issues or political candidates clearly reflects their political values. Michael Jordan took a political position when he failed to speak out against Nike sweatshops. When LeBron James was a rising NBA star, he was also a "Nike star." Like Michael Jordan, he took a political position when he did not sign a petition that was signed by nearly all his teammates calling for China to support a United Nations action to defuse the genocidal violence in Darfur (Leitch 2007). Both Jordan and James chose to make commercial values and their business interests a higher priority than human rights. It is noteworthy that after Michael Jordan became an NBA owner and LeBron James became an established NBA superstar, they took strong stands against owner Donald Sterling for the racist remarks that ultimately led to Sterling's ban from the league and the sale of his team (Frizell 2014). It was not difficult for them to become "political" on this issue because the remarks had already been strongly condemned by many other public figures, including President Obama, and by NBA icon Magic Johnson, who was named in Sterling's comments. The NBA commissioner also took strong action against Sterling, and none of the major players in the NBA's golden triangle was likely to side with Sterling.

Michael Jordan's reticence about expressing his political opinions during his playing career was common among players of his generation and afterward (Agyemang 2012). Having become a global icon "without color," he avoided political statements that could risk his widespread popularity. As noted earlier, this was a result of trying to preserve his endorsement value in the golden triangle. However, there is a history of black athletes challenging the status quo and taking political stands when racism was more rampant and such stands were potentially more damaging to their careers.

Early in the twentieth century, boxing champion Jack Johnson was unapologetic about his controversial lifestyle that involved interracial relationships. Brilliant and multitalented football star, singer, and actor Paul Robeson was outspoken about social injustice around the world, but became a victim of McCarthyism and Cold War politics when he made comments sympathetic to the Soviets after World War II. Bill Russell was a rising NBA star for the Boston Celtics when he spoke and wrote about the racism that existed in sports and in the United States during his career. It was a kind of racism that relegated black stars to second-class citizenship both on the road with their team and in the community. Runners Tommie Smith and John Carlos were banished from the Olympic movement and lost their medals after making quiet and dignified black-gloved protests of racial injustice during the medal ceremonies at the 1968 Mexico City Summer Olympics. Basketball star Kareem Abdul-Jabbar was an outspoken advocate of social justice and opponent of racism in sport and society, beginning during the turbulent years of the 1960s in the United States and continuing through his sports career and life. Tennis star Arthur Ashe became an articulate spokesperson and activist for social and racial equality and wrote a multivolume history of African Americans in sport.

Perhaps even better known for speaking out than all of these people was Muhammad Ali. He sacrificed the prime years of his boxing career by taking a position against the Vietnam War, in which he refused to serve for religious reasons. He had converted to Islam, which had made him unpopular among segments of the white population. However, like his activist predecessors, Ali was respected by many whites and was a hero to many African Americans. Like Robeson, he also was widely respected around the world. These people were polarizing figures, though, because they were outspoken or defiant black men who refused to accommodate to the mainstream, to established patterns of race, or to the political currents of their time.

Iconic photo of black-gloved victory stand demonstration protesting racism in the US Gold medalist Tommie Smith and bronze medalist John Carlos in 200-meter run at Mexico City Olympics in 1968 were both banned from the Olympics and sent home after their protest; silver medalist Peter Norman received criticism in his native Australian press for supporting Smith and Carlos. (AP Photo)

With the powerful influence and incentives of the golden triangle, both white and black athletes in more recent decades have become acutely sensitive to the damage to their endorsement potential that could come from offending major brands in the golden triangle. During his career Michael Jordan steered away from the sweatshop issue, but engaged in a kind of "politics of brands." He was paid very well by Nike and was unwilling to risk his relationship with the company by criticizing its business practices. He was willing, however, to show his support for Nike when he played for the 1992 Olympic "Dream Team." He refused to appear on the victory stand wearing the red, white, and blue US warm-up suit with the logo of official Olympic sponsor Reebok, a competitor of Nike. He compromised by wearing the team clothing but covering its logo with the US flag. He drew some harsh criticism from the press for being more concerned about representing Nike than his country, but he asserted, "I do not believe in endorsing my competition. . . . I feel strongly about loyalty to my own company" (quoted in LaFeber 2002:100).

The world in which Nike, star athletes, and others in the golden triangle operate and prosper is described by Barber's (2006) term "McWorld." He coined the term to refer to the globalization of politics through forces such as the McDonaldization of organizations and culture and the influence of the market imperatives of capitalism. This world is focused on profits and expanding markets, and according to Barber, "Human rights are needed to a degree [in McWorld], but not citizenship or participation—and no more social justice and equality than are necessary to promote efficient economic production and consumption" (2006:456).

As capitalist enterprises, Nike and the other dominant actors in the golden triangle are obligated to respond to the interests and wishes of owners or stockholders, which usually involve maximizing stock values, profits, and dividends. The star athletes they hire to endorse their products are generally loyal to them and the commercial values of McWorld, while being reluctant to question their sponsors' political actions. By pursuing their own economic and political interests, the most powerful and famous actors in the golden triangle may ignore or blatantly disregard values of social responsibility. Governments can constrain corporations and compel them to comply with laws and regulations that make them act more socially responsible. However, in a climate of neoliberalism, which gives capitalists and corporations considerable freedom, governments are not inclined to do much to constrain them. In addition, since they operate across national borders, transnational enterprises are difficult for governments to monitor or control, which is why global social movements and global NGOs may be more likely than governments to monitor these transnational corporations and hold them responsible for their actions.

Politics and the Political Economy of the Olympics

Olympic officials and organizing committees hosting Olympic Games have openly and aggressively pursued relationships in the golden triangle to fund, stage, and televise the Games. However, officials of the IOC and national Olympic committees have steadfastly expressed their desire to keep politics out of the Olympics. Of course, Olympic history has long been influenced by politics as well as economics. It is difficult to envision the absence of politics in a competition of the magnitude of the Olympics involving athletes and teams from nations around the world. The Olympic Games have frequently been the site of political displays and actions because they are arguably the most prestigious venue where the nations of the world gather to compete in sport and because they attract worldwide attention. The meeting of nations in a highly publicized global sports mega-event creates conditions highly conducive to politics. In this section, we will explore the often-political nature of the Olympics and the role of political economy in the Olympic Games.

The Olympic Games were reborn as the Modern Olympics in 1896, and their history has been marked by a pattern of politics, even though the rhetoric of the Olympics and the Olympic ideals disavow political purposes for the Games. We will consider the inconsistencies between Olympic ideals and political realities after briefly summarizing the ideals that inspired the rebirth of the Olympics at the end of the nineteenth century. The original goals and ideals of the Modern Olympics were espoused by a French nobleman, Baron Pierre de Coubertin, who is generally considered the founder of the Modern Games (Nixon and Frey 1996:289–294). The original Olympic ideals were amateurism, the preeminence of athletes as individuals unaffiliated with government or commercial sponsors or professional clubs, sportsmanship, and international understanding. Olympic athletes were supposed to compete in friendly competition and build ties across national borders and cultures in competition and in the Olympic Village. According to the Olympic charter, Olympic competitions were also supposed to be hosted and funded by cities and not by national governments or private corporations. All of these ideals and organizing principles have been violated at various times in the history of the Modern Olympics.

Probe 9.4: The Elitism of Amateurism and the Hypocrisy of Shamateurism in the Olympics

If the Olympics fully embodied its original amateur ideal, it would be an event restricted only to the elite. This ideal was supposed to glorify the idea of sport for its own sake. But in prohibiting financial subsidies for athletes, it made it difficult or impossible for athletes of modest means to compete in this global sports festival as pure amateurs. Only the wealthy could afford the serious training, coaching, competitive experience, and travel needed to compete successfully at an international level. However, the Olympics could only attract global interest and investment from the golden triangle if it featured top athletes from around the world in its various sports. This was only possible when athletes and nations resisted or ignored the Olympic ideal of amateurism. *Shamateurism* was what happened when athletes and nations bent to the realities of trying to compete at a global level without officially being allowed to rely on financial subsidies. Olympic shamateurism included under-the-table payments by corporate sponsors to athletes and government subsidizing of athletes. Critics decried the hypocrisy of shamateurism because so much money was being made from sponsors and the media in capitalistic sports systems and because so many athletes and teams were being subsidized by their governments. Olympic officials occasionally and arbitrarily punished athletes for their professionalism, which kept payments to athletes under the table. In addition, Olympic officials were not inclined to question the well-established practices of nations supporting their Olympic teams and athletes. As a result, Olympic officials danced around the issue of shamateurism for decades. However, as the twenty-first century approached, Olympic officials finally bowed to the realities of global sports in the golden triangle and gave up their rhetoric and pretense of amateurism.

The commercialization and global media attention that contributed to the global growth of sport and the Olympics made it inevitable that professionalism would be found in the Olympic arena, first illegally and then openly. The golden triangle became the financial backbone of the Olympics, and its desire to expand markets and commercial opportunities by showcasing the world's best athletic talent ultimately overcame the anachronistic, elitist, and frequently abused ideal of amateurism. Thus, the economic power of the golden triangle reshaped the official culture of the Olympic Games, and Olympic officials then promulgated a policy that permitted NGBs and national Olympic committees to embrace professionalism openly and select professional athletes to compete in the Olympics.

The ideals of the Olympics have been violated for political purposes in sometimes subtle and sometimes very public ways. In fact, some historians have proposed that the founding of the Modern Olympics by Baron Pierre de Coubertin was colored by his political motives. He wanted to use international sports competition to inspire French men to higher levels of physical fitness and military preparedness after the disappointing performance of French soldiers during the Franco-Prussian War in 1870–1871 (Nixon and Frey 1996:289). At the same time, he seemed genuinely committed to establishing a relatively informal sports competition between amateur athletes at the international level that embodied the principles of international understanding and world peace. Yet from the beginning of the Olympic Games in 1896, national affiliations of athletes and teams were emphasized, as athletes displayed flags and wore clothing representing their nation. A parade of nations became a highlight of the opening ceremony, the playing of the national anthem of victorious athletes became a hallowed ritual of the Games, and the media have routinely published unofficial medal rankings of the nations. Athletes realized that they were not competing for themselves. They represented the pride of their nation.

As the Modern Olympic Games have evolved, national governments, protest groups, and terrorists have used the Olympic stage for their political purposes (Senn 1999). In 1936, Hitler used his "Nazi Olympics" in Berlin as a propaganda vehicle. He wanted the Olympics to help him build popular support in Germany for his extremely nationalistic and fascist Nazi ideology and regime and to demonstrate the superiority of the Aryan race. According to historian Richard Mandell (1971), Hitler also used the Olympics to distract the world from his aggressive militaristic plans to conquer neighboring countries and extend his international influence. IOC officials disregarded international concerns about Hitler and Germany's exploitation of the Games for their political ends because the Germans assured them that the Games would adhere to Olympic standards. They adopted a position of ignoring internal politics of members and host nations as long as the Games met their sporting expectations. This became a consistent pattern in the actions of Olympic officials.

Politics again visited the Olympics in Germany in the 1972 Munich Games, when the Olympic Village became a venue for terrorism. The Black September Movement was a little-known militant Palestinian rights organization. In an Olympic setting where security was relatively lax and in a world in which there was a history of ongoing political tension in the Middle East, eight members of Black September scaled a fence and invaded the Olympic Village in a carefully planned early-morning guerrilla operation (Time 1972). They took nine members of the Israeli Olympic team as hostages, killed two others, and captured world attention as their siege continued over the next twenty hours. Their

Adolf Hitler opens the 1936 Berlin Olympics, flanked by leading members of his regime Rudolf Hess, Joseph Goebbels, and Hermann Goering. Known as the "Nazi Olympics," these Games represented the use of sport for political purposes. (© Austrian Archives/Corbis)

political aims were to gain freedom for two hundred Arab prisoners in Israeli jails and, more broadly, to get international attention for their Palestinian cause. However, their actions caused outrage in many parts of the world and provoked Israeli retaliatory military strikes against suspected guerrilla bases in neighboring Arab countries.

This violent invasion of the Games embarrassed the German Olympic hosts, who were trying to use this event to create a positive national image that would put the memory of the 1936 Olympics and Nazism out of people's minds. The tragic episode ended with the deaths of the Israeli hostages and five of the terrorists and the surrender of the remaining terrorists in a gun battle as the terrorists were en route to a plane that was supposed to be their means of escape. The response of Olympic officials was consistent with a past history of trying to sustain an image of the Games as apolitical. The IOC president at the time, Avery Brundage, had a long history of his own with the Games that included ardently supporting US participation in the 1936 Olympics in Germany as president of the US Olympic organization. In 1972, he acknowledged the tragedy of the massacre but still asserted that "the Games must go on," leaving virtually no time for the Israelis to mourn their dead team members.

The well-orchestrated propaganda of the Nazi Olympics in 1936 and the dramatic and deadly terrorism in 1972 have been major events in the political history of the Olympic Games. This history has also included victory stand protests such as the demonstrations against racial injustice by US athletes in 1968 and 1972 and boycotts such as the efforts to isolate South Africa from the sporting world, to put pressure on the Soviet Union to withdraw from Afghanistan, and to retaliate against the United States for boycotting the Moscow Games. Threatened and actual boycotts have spanned several decades of Olympic history, and the IOC officially banned apartheid South Africa from the Games for thirty years. In addition, the IOC became entangled in the tensions between the PRC and the ROC, which led to the IOC's "two Chinas" policy.

Economics has been as much a part of Olympic history as politics. The dependence of host city organizing committees and the IOC on the golden triangle has put marketing and money in a prominent place in the Olympics. According to the IOC's website, in 2014, revenue generated by the IOC and organizing committees was from four major sources: broadcast (47 percent), sponsorships (45 percent), ticketing (5 percent), and licensing (3 percent). There has been a pattern of steep increases in revenue from these sources over the past several decades, with media and sponsorship revenue increasing the most. For example, broadcast revenue from the Summer Games increased from $1.2 million in 1960, to $88 million in 1980, to $1.3 billion in 2000, to $2.6 billion in 2012 (Statista 2014a). With over $800 million in additional income from marketing, investment, and other sources, total revenue for the 2012 London Summer Games was more than $3.4 billion. This was over $1 billion more than total revenue for the 2008 Beijing Summer Games (Mickle 2013). Broadcast revenues for the Winter Games jumped from $50,000 in 1960, to $20.7 million in 1980, to $738 million in 2002, to $1.26 billion in 2014 (Fung 2014; Statista 2014b). The Sochi broadcast revenue was down slightly from Vancouver's $1.28 billion in 2010. NBC accounted for a disproportionate amount of Olympic media revenue in recent Olympics. It was one of more than twenty media companies involved in broadcasting the Games (Fung 2014).

Probe 9.5: Spending, Making Money, and Competing in the Olympic Golden Triangle

The British sports market news and data service Sportcal (2012) reported that the IOC would set a record in 2012 of over $8 billion in commercial revenue for the four-year cycle including the 2010 Vancouver Winter Games and 2012 London Summer Games. This was an estimated 47 percent higher than the revenue amount for the previous 2006/2008 cycle. The media revenue in this cycle was up 52 percent, and revenue from The Olympic Partner (TOP) program of major commercial sponsors of $957 million was up 10.5 percent from the previous cycle. In 2012, TOP sponsors paid up to $100 million each for their elite ties to the IOC and its Games. The names of most of these global corporations are familiar to most people, especially those in the investment world. They included Acer, Atos Origin (IT), Coca-Cola, Dow Chemical, General Electric, McDonald's, Omega, Panasonic, Procter & Gamble, Samsung, and Visa. There are other tiers of sponsors that paid from $15 million to about $63 million in 2012 for the right to have their brand associated with the Olympic rings (Guardian 2012).

The value of these expensive investments was somewhat diminished by "ambush marketing" campaigns. Corporate competitors of some sponsors did not pay for the right to be an official Olympic sponsor but were still able to get substantial visibility for their brands by clever product placement in and around the Olympic arena. Nike was known as the "king of ambush marketing" (Minato 2012). An example cited earlier involved Michael Jordan's attempt to deflect attention from official Olympic sponsor Reebok to his own brand Nike. Another example was in 1996 when Nike gave US runner Michael Johnson gold shoes to drape around his neck to display with his gold medals. Nike also erected a billboard over Olympic Park in Atlanta in 1996. Firmly entrenched in the golden triangle, major corporations find various official and unofficial ways to display their brand and try to make money from visibility at mega-events.

Olympic revenue figures show that the Olympic Games have become a multibillion dollar mega-event. This is thanks to the increasing media coverage and increasing investment by corporate partners and sponsors in the golden triangle. However, these figures mask a difficult reality for Olympic hosts. There are unfulfilled expectations of money, enhanced global reputation, and infrastructure improvements (Newman 2014; New York Times 2009). In regard to money, local organizing committees often run deficits. For example, the 1976 Montreal Olympics saddled the city with a debt of $2.7 billion that took nearly thirty years to pay off. Athens budgeted $1.6 billion for its Olympics in 2004. The final cost was estimated to be $16 billion. This was an open sore a few years later when Greece plunged into a virtual economic depression. Despite great hopes, host cities rarely are able to cover their costs. Los Angeles is often cited as the major exception (Low 2014). Facing a shortage of host bids, the IOC allowed the 1984 Los Angeles Summer Games to be organized by a private corporation, which kept tight control over expenses. It generated a surplus of over $230 million by renovating existing facilities, building less extravagant temporary facilities, relying heavily on volunteers, and keeping operating costs at a minimum. Many taxpayers felt they were misled because they were told they needed to pay for security costs of approximately $100 million to keep the budget balanced and then learned the Games had generated a substantial surplus that made the public investment unnecessary (Nixon 1988; Nixon and Frey 1996:292).

In regard to local and national pride, exposing the world to the attractions of an Olympic city has sometimes made the city more of a tourist destination. It also may have encouraged some corporations to consider doing more business there. However, the afterglow from hosting an Olympics can have a short shelf life. Hosting an Olympics does not make social problems or political unrest that existed before disappear. Beijing and Sochi also discovered that being in the global public eye as an Olympic host can bring unwanted world media scrutiny to sensitive public issues such as human rights, environmental quality, and gay rights. This is similar to the controversy surrounding Brazil's hosting of the 2014 World Cup and Rio's hosting of the 2016 Olympics. The striking contrast between the "two Brazils"—that is, the glistening new sports facilities and venues versus the severe poverty and woefully inadequate public facilities in poor neighborhoods—prompted public criticism and street protests (Wahl 2014). In addition, public spending on Olympic facilities, preparing the city for visitors, and police and security services have opportunity costs, since the money spent for these purposes is not spent on domestic priorities such as upgrading public schools or public housing or making the city safer for residents after the Games leave town.

In regard to infrastructure, there are cases of cities as different as Atlanta and Beijing that have gained infrastructure improvements such as highways, rail systems, airports, and new public spaces that have revitalized decaying urban centers. On the other hand, these improvements come at a great public cost. In addition, Olympic facilities often become white elephants that fail to meet the hoped-for public demand or need. They also burden host cities or nations with continuing costs of maintenance and debt service. This can be like the problem faced by cities that build new stadiums at public expense to attract a pro football franchise and then discover that they must build another new stadium after several years or risk losing the team.

The record cost of over $50 billion for the Sochi Olympics was said to be justified by the anticipated transformation of the Black Sea city into a major tourist and sporting destination (Pismennaya 2014). However, there was some concern about the multibillion dollar cost of maintaining the venues and other new infrastructure in the Sochi Olympic area in the years following the Olympics. Furthermore, Russia's optimism about the post-Olympic prospects for Sochi might have been tempered somewhat by the experience of Greece. It had turned a former airport into its Olympic Sports Complex with several venues for the Games, but the area remained undeveloped years after its Olympic flame was extinguished. Its inability to generate revenue from this investment both resulted from and compounded Greece's economic woes. Russia's ambitious plans for Sochi also might have been adversely affected by the political controversy and economic sanctions resulting from its aggressive actions to help pro-Russian separatists in Ukraine. Thus, government and private-sector plans to benefit from the Olympics can be upset by economic and political events and actions outside the sports arena.

Critics of the Olympics (e.g., Boykoff 2014; Lenskyj 2000) have emphasized the self-serving behavior of Olympic organizers and officials, their excessive and extravagant spending, their unresponsiveness to local community needs, the financial and political scandals, and the instances of racism, sexism, and class elitism that have diluted or distorted the Olympic ideals. While recognizing these problems, others have pointed to the capacity of these Games *as games* to capture our attention and have special significance for those who compete in them. For example, Cantelon wrote that a reason why the media are especially interested in the Olympics is because of "the authentic sense of enchantment embedded in Olympic competition" (2002:104). This sense of enchantment must be most embedded in the spectacles of the opening and closing ceremonies because they tend to be the most watched Olympic broadcasts.

The skillful blending of politics, economics, and enchanting symbols with sports entertainment has made the Olympics a global mega-event. The essential paradox of the Olympics is that both the mythical ideals and the crasser realities of politics, commerce, and the golden triangle coexist in the Games and contribute to their success. The golden triangle uses the myths to market the Olympics and compete for its share of the increasingly crowded and competitive global sports marketplace. In doing so, it sells its products, including its telecasts of the Olympics, official Olympic merchandise, and products advertised by "official Olympic sponsors," and it also sells the ideology of consumer capitalism.

Political Violence and Sport

It would be nice to conclude this chapter and the book with an acknowledgment that sport seems to be able to maintain an illusion for many that it can rise above politics, economics, and the mundane to be something special that grabs our attention and even inspires our passion. The reality is that the world is often messy, turbulent, and dangerous. As much as sports organizers might try to insulate their sports from these influences, the less pleasant aspects of the real world eventually intrude into sport. The fundamental insight of this book as an application of sociology is that sport is part of society and mirrors many of its desirable *and* undesirable aspects.

We have seen that sports officials have confronted or been involved in a variety of forms of social deviance and social problems, ranging from social injustice to crime, corruption, doping, and violence inside and outside sport. The most menacing threat they face today may be political violence because it can be so disruptive, can lead to deaths, and is difficult to control.

In addition, the threat of political violence can discourage investment from the golden triangle, on which commercialized sports depend for their success. Although the term "political violence" has been defined in various ways, it generally refers to the intentional use of physical force to achieve political ends by people acting outside the norms and legitimate authority of government (e.g., O'Neil 2012:ch. 7). It can involve protests, strikes, riots, guerilla warfare, revolutions, and terrorism. Although all forms of political violence are a threat to major political, economic, and social institutions, we will focus on terrorism in this section because it often targets core nations and institutions in the world capitalist system. The major sports, media, and corporations of these nations dominate the global golden triangle. Thus, terrorism is a potential threat to popular commercialized sports and major corporate actors in the golden triangle (Hassan 2012).

People in the United States had little concern about terrorism on its soil before the 9/11 bombings. People in other parts of the world were much more familiar with its dangers. Terrorism may be the new form of warfare in international conflicts in the new world order that emerged after the fall of the Soviet Union. It pits relatively small numbers of attackers willing to die for their cause against governments with large armies and stockpiles of weapons. Terrorists use fear as a tactic and may cause democracies to rethink their constitutional commitments to protect themselves. Democracies such as the United States have abandoned historical commitments to political liberty, privacy, and due process to combat the lawlessness of terrorists.

The Palestinian Black September invasion of the Olympic Village at the 1972 Munich Olympics put the IOC and governments and sports officials around the world on notice that the safety of athletes and spectators at their sports events could not be ensured. Sports mega-events were potential targets because they symbolized the perceived excesses of capitalism to terrorists, but they were also vulnerable to attack because the golden triangle had made them so popular (see Giulianotti and Klauser 2012). This irony of success now means that event organizers have to include big security budgets in their plans, and that athletes must be virtually quarantined in the Olympic Village or special housing to protect them from potential threats. This also means

An Arab terrorist extends his hand as he talks with another terrorist, leaning from an upper window, during discussions with Munich chief of police Manfred Schreiber, far left, and West German Interior Minister Hans-Dietrich Genscher on September 5, 1972. They were outside the building of the Munich Olympic Village where thirteen Israeli team members were being held hostage by the Arab terrorists of the Black September movement. Nine of the Israeli hostages, five terrorists, and a German police officer died in a shoot-out at the airport when the terrorists tried to escape by plane. Two other members of the Israeli team died before the hostages were taken from the Olympic Village. This incident is known as the "Munich massacre." (AP Photo)

that the atmosphere at events such as the Olympics has been significantly transformed. Athletes can no longer mingle with family, friends, and fans between competitions.

Events such as marathons are especially vulnerable to attacks because they occur outside the enclosed spaces of arenas and stadiums along routes covering long distances where it is difficult to ensure safety at every point. The terrorist bombing at the finish line of the Boston Marathon in 2013 demonstrated the challenge of preventing the placement of bombs in thickly crowded areas where people are thinking more about the competition than their own safety (CNN 2014c). We also are reminded by this act that innocent victims who are considered "collateral damage" in wars are actually intended targets of terrorist violence, as terrorists strive for fear, panic, and disorder.

Probe 9.6: Sports Mega-Events as Targets of Terrorists

A list of ten major terrorist attacks and threats in sport spans the Black September attack at the 1972 Munich Olympics and the withdrawal of many athletes from the 2010 Commonwealth Games in Delhi (Benammar 2013). A warning of the "high threat of terrorism throughout India" caused the withdrawals from the Commonwealth Games. Although the event occurred without incident, the perceived possibility of terrorism had left its imprint on the Games. The bombing in Centennial Olympic Park during the Atlanta Olympics in 1996 was prominent among the other events on the terrorism list. Two people were killed and one hundred were injured. The bomber said he targeted the Olympics because the event "promoted the values of global socialism" (cited in Benammar 2013), which is ironic in light of the usual criticism of the Olympics being too capitalistic. In another terrorist act, a car bombing occurred in Madrid in 2002 close to the stadium where Real Madrid and Barcelona were to play. Seventeen people were injured, but the game proceeded after UEFA was reassured that security at the stadium was adequate. On other occasions between 2002 and 2009, athletes, sports officials, police, and spectators were victimized by suicide bombs, armed attacks, and kidnappings in Pakistan, Iraq, and Sri Lanka at venues for sports including cricket, taekwondo, and a marathon. These various attacks resulted in the deaths or disappearance of over fifty people and injuries to nearly one hundred. We can add the Boston Marathon bombing to the list. It left 3 dead and over 170 injured. In general, sports mega-events draw large crowds and extensive publicity, which are major reasons they are potential targets for terrorists. The politics of sports terrorism is about exploiting sport for political purposes, which is an ironic twist of the political uses of sport by governments.

A terrorist attack on Togo's national soccer team in Angola in 2010 illustrates the complex ways that politics and sports become intertwined and deadly (Economist 2010). The soccer team was ambushed by well-armed separatist guerrillas during a bus trip from their training site to Angola to compete in the Africa Cup of Nations tournament. The terrorists killed the assistant coach, the team spokesman, and the bus driver and injured nine other people, including the reserve goalkeeper. The Front for the Liberation of Cabinda (FLEC) claimed responsibility and threatened more if Angola and the Confederation of African Football (CAF) continued to hold soccer tournaments in the disputed Cabinda province. Togo pulled its team from the tournament, even though a separatist leader claimed the attack on the Togo team was not intentional. Three other African national teams agreed to stay and compete when they were assured of extra security by the Angolan government.

Selliaas (2012) concluded that international and national security got tighter after the terrorist acts in Munich (1972) and in Atlanta (1996) and prior to the Games in Athens (2004) and in Beijing (2008) to prevent threatened terrorism. The Olympics in Munich, Atlanta, and Athens had contributed to the development of national antiterrorism units, more interagency cooperation within nations, and cooperative international antiterrorism networks. Selliaas proposed that by the time of the lead-up to the Beijing Games, an "Olympic Stress Syndrome" had emerged. It prompted a concentration of more international attention and resources on antiterrorism and even fostered cooperation between democratic and authoritarian governments to combat this threat.

At the same time, though, security costs continued to escalate and concerns about democratic and human rights seemed to diminish. That is, the increasingly sophisticated and tight security measures that made the Games appear safer for Olympic officials, teams, spectators, and media and corporate investors also might have made the Games too expensive for some prospective hosts and also may have made cracking down on minorities and dissidents easier to justify for hosts such as the PRC in 2008, Russia in 2014, and perhaps Brazil in the run-up to the 2016 Games.

Atkinson and Young (2012) raised the question of whether organizers of mega-events such as the Olympics might inflate or "fabricate" risk and threat levels to serve the political purpose of greater control over the event and their population. In a parallel analysis, Schimmel (2012) argued that the NFL has developed increasingly close relationships with government institutions and agencies from local police to the Department of Homeland Security (DHS) to keep its venues safe. She further argued that these were mutually beneficial relationships in which the threat of violence enabled both the league and the government to increase security measures. Schimmel proposed that in addition to providing heightened security, the NFL was able to protect its status and profitability and the DHS was able to increase public support for its ongoing "war on terror."

The special status of the NFL and its premier event, the Super Bowl, is reflected in the fact that the first Super Bowl after 9/11 was the first sports event and the twelfth event overall to be treated as a "National Security Special Event." This designation put it in a category that included presidential inaugurations, national political conventions, and United Nations assemblies. It also meant that a number of special security technologies and practices were introduced at Super Bowls, from biometric scanning devices, encrypted video cameras, and hazardous duty robots to sophisticated "pat downs" of spectators. Military and investigative agencies benefited from experimentation at Super Bowl sites before implementing these technologies and practices for their own purposes. Super Bowl security also became a justification for dragnets to locate illegal immigrants and travel restrictions to keep out potential threats in the vicinity of games near the Canadian and Mexican borders. US and local security and law enforcement agencies were able to use devices and employ practices that might have otherwise been controversial if not associated with the most popular sports event in the United States. By providing this protection for ostensible security reasons, government agencies were serving their own interests. They also were protecting major sports investments by global corporations in the golden triangle. This intertwining of government and economic interests with sport is what the political economy of sport implies. We also see a new interpretation of corporate nationalism.

Contemporary Forces of Change and the Future of Sport

Terrorism and civil unrest are serious issues in the contemporary world that should not be underestimated. But the ways they are approached in sport reveals a great deal about the priorities and interests of major actors in the golden triangle. Safety and order are surely concerns. However, sports, the media, and businesses in the golden triangle generally cooperate with government in ways that reinforce existing institutions and people in power. It is not about partisan politics. It is about protecting the value of sports and corporate brands and making profits by associating sports with evocative and compelling national symbols such as the flag, the national anthem, and the military. While fans love sports *because they are sports*, popular commercialized sports in the golden triangle also serve other purposes for governments, for the businesses that invest in them, and even for sports officials and owners.

In a rapidly changing world, sport and the golden triangle must adopt the latest technologies and be sensitive to the currents of social and cultural change or risk becoming irrelevant. We have seen throughout this book the various ways that sports in the golden triangle have responded to threats and change. Sports officials have confronted issues of inequality, injustice, diversity, globalization, evolving media, crime and corruption, and political threats and government influence. They have done so at the many levels of sport in golden triangles, from youth, high school, and college sports to the professional and Olympic levels. However, sport has typically stayed at least slightly behind the curve of societal change. Sport and its major partners in the golden triangle are embedded in the institutional structure of society and typically change their basic structural commitments and patterns slowly or reluctantly. However, as the asteroid theory implied in our discussion of college sports reform, when the people who run sports fail to make changes that respond to powerful forces of change within their institution or to major changes in society, they may find themselves suddenly disrupted by forces that they had not anticipated and that are not under their control.

The golden triangle overall has seemed to adapt fairly well to the changing world, if we use increasing media coverage, expanding markets, and bigger profits as major indicators of its success. Certainly, these are the measuring sticks the dominant players in the golden triangle use, since they are driven by capitalist, market-oriented, McWorld goals. Recall that in Barber's (2006) conception, "McWorld" refers to the globalization of politics through forces such as McDonaldization and the market imperatives of capitalism. McWorld seeks to make the world a single commercially and culturally unified global marketplace tied together by modern markets, communication, and technology. In McWorld, national borders and identities are meaningless.

In the political environment of contemporary sports that has been shaped by McWorld, terrorism is such a major threat because it is so violent, but also because it often represents a fundamentally antithetical vision of the world and the future. Barber called this antithetical vision or force for change "Jihad," and he theorized that the *clash between McWorld and Jihad* would reveal the future direction of global change. By implication, this clash could also tell us how the most popular contemporary commercialized sports will fare in the future.

The term "jihad" literally means holy war or hostile acts against an enemy, and it has been used in recent years to refer to the militant actions by radical Muslims in defense of a fundamentalist and politicized form of Islam. Barber used the term to represent the forces in the contemporary world that are diametrically opposed to the forces of globalization represented by McWorld. He proposed that the forces of Jihad are aimed at dividing or "retribalizing" large parts of the world by nationality, ethnicity, or religion, and they have used war and terrorism to accomplish their divisive aims. They use historical differences in territory, ethnicity, and culture to cultivate animosity and hostility. Jihadists want to transform the world into one dominated by their strictly defined idea of traditional religious culture in Islamic states. Jihad has targeted the United States in various ways in recent decades. For example, there have been shouts of "Death to America" from agitated mobs on the street, references to the United States as the "Great Satan," the trampling and burning of US flags, and attacks on embassies, military installations, personnel, and symbols of the US power such as the Pentagon and the twin towers of the World Trade Center near Wall Street. These words and actions targeted the United States and its assets and people at least in part because the United States represented McWorld to its enemies.

Along with the United States, popular contemporary commercialized sports around the world and their golden triangles are also so intertwined with the forces of McWorld that they, too, are logical sites for jihadist attacks. The sports of the golden triangle embody the modern Western influences that jihadists seek to destroy: the global cultural economy of consumer capitalism, domination by major transnational corporations, and their global expansion. The ideology and actions of Jihad are a threat to the power, cultural legitimacy, and economic and organizational rationale of the golden triangle and, more generally, are a threat to the legitimacy of modern sport as a rational, corporate, and highly commercialized enterprise. The tactics of jihadists have been displayed in sport in the various acts of terrorism we have discussed in this chapter. Sports mega-events are convenient venues for playing out jihadist politics and for engaging in aggression against nations and corporations associated with McWorld. By drawing attention to themselves with their actions and threats, militant jihadists and other terrorists have accomplished the important goal of publicity for their cause. Although evidence suggests that organizers of sports mega-events may be overreacting to these threats or using them for their political or commercial purposes, the uncertainty and potential damage of acts of terror make it necessary to include them in planning agendas and budgets. This is the nature of global sports in this unsettled contemporary era.

According to Barber, McWorld is like Jihad in one noteworthy respect. It is not focused on making the world more democratic. Neither Jihad nor McWorld needs democracy and neither seeks it. Jihad has little interest in cooperation or compromise with its enemies. McWorld operates according to a corporate bureaucratic and capitalist model oriented to rational decision making and the pursuit of profit, which leaves little room for democratic values or participatory decision making. In fact, transnational corporations often find it more expedient and profitable to do business with autocratic rather than democratic political leaders because they do not have to worry about building popular consensus for their business activities (Barber 2006:456). This explains the apparent ease with which Olympic officials and others in the Olympic golden triangle dismissed the political controversies surrounding the Games in Beijing and Sochi. It also might be a reason for maintaining an official policy of the Games "not being political."

The reality is that Olympic and other sports officials have been unable to keep politics out of their arenas because sport is part of society and politics is also part of society. They have also been willing to accommodate to politics when it has served their interests. Their primary interest has been to keep teams and athletes on the field competing, which has sustained the flow of golden triangle resources. It has not always been possible to keep sports open for business.

There have been occasions during the history of sports when political events such as world wars caused the cancellation of global mega-events such as the Olympics and terrorist attacks such as 9/11 caused postponements of games in professional and college sports in the United States. Internal politics has also interfered with play on a number of occasions. All of the Big Four leagues in North America have had work stoppages due to strikes and lockouts, and professional soccer leagues in Europe and other parts of the world have had to deal with player strikes. In general, though, leagues have tried to avoid politically related stoppages of play. At times they have made highly controversial decisions to continue play in the face of compelling reasons that would seem to require suspension of competition. For example, they have hired replacement players and referees a few times during strikes, despite the objections of player and referee unions and fans. More seriously, Olympic officials ignored the looming Nazi threat and allowed the 1936 Olympics to be played in Berlin. They decided against canceling the remaining competition after the killing of Israeli athletes by terrorists in 1972 in Munich. In 1963, the NFL decided not to suspend play after the assassination of the US president, while the rival American Football League decided not to play.

Sports officials have had difficult decisions brought about by political events and influences, and they have not been completely insensitive to the complexities of political issues and influences. Surely, it was not easy to decide whether to keep playing when a president or athletes have been killed. However, there are powerful incentives for the games to go on, even under the most difficult or controversial political circumstances. After all, sports lose attention and money when they are not played. As a result, sports officials have either put aside politics or made political accommodations to make it possible for their games or events to take place. We have considered how controversial political issues were overlooked prior to the Olympics in Beijing and Sochi. The "two Chinas" policy was adopted by the IOC in the 1950s as a compromise to try to disentangle itself from the conflict between the PRC and the ROC. The IOC responded to political pressure when it banned apartheid South Africa from the Games for three decades. In choosing a host for the 1984 Summer Games, IOC officials ignored their own rule requiring cities to be Olympic hosts because their only viable option was a private corporation. In 1994, the IOC bowed to environmental politics in Norway and made accommodations that led to the Winter Olympics in Lillehammer becoming the "Green Games" (Cantelon and Letters 2000; Lesjø 2000). Activists were able to get organizers to employ protective environmental measures in the location of venues and in construction projects. The IOC embraced the idea of the Green Games when it saw the possibility of favorable media attention from this approach. Its embrace was a "light green," which was meant to convey an *image* of social responsibility without offending corporate investors who were not known as paragons of environmental consciousness.

There may have been a time when the IOC and other sports organizations made decisions primarily to protect the integrity of sport and the quality of competition. But as the golden triangle has become more important and more influential, decisions have seemed to be guided increasingly by the desire to protect brands, markets, and revenue streams. There has been little desire to change structures or cultures that have made sports popular and commercially successful. However, MLB found that adverse publicity forced it to adopt more stringent drug policies. NCAA officials realized that they had to make some changes in anticipation of a future in the courtroom trying to preserve legally and educationally dubious policies of ostensible amateurism at its most commercialized level.

The NFL apparently spent many years trying to suppress damaging evidence linking concussions in the sport to serious memory problems later in life. It also felt compelled to act in response to a revealing video of domestic abuse by one of its stars, running back Ray Rice of the Baltimore Ravens. When it belatedly came up with a policy to punish him and future abusers, it was criticized for not being tough enough. When a second and more damning video surfaced, the team released him from his contract and the league suspended him indefinitely. There was little doubt among many in the press and public that the commissioner's actions fit a pattern of acting first to protect the league's image and second to right a wrong. This pattern of making protection of the brand the top priority also applied to the Penn State cover-up case (Rhoden 2014a). Media criticism of the NFL's handling of domestic abuse put other leagues on notice regarding their domestic abuse policies (Crouse 2014).

The NBA has often seemed to be more progressive in its handling of social issues than other sports leagues have been. Although it may have ultimately been a politically astute decision, the decisiveness displayed by the new commissioner in 2014 to dismiss an owner from the league for his blatant racism was applauded for being the right thing to do. This suggests that sports officials can make politically smart and morally sensitive decisions. However, for most of those with power in sports, the priority is making decisions that keep their sport popular and profitable and that keep it in the good graces of powerful politicians whom they hope will not interfere. Sports officials have to be careful, though. Becoming dependent on the media and commercial partners in the golden triangle and trying to cultivate politicians carry risks. The media and businesses in the golden triangle turn sports into commodities that they exploit for their economic purposes, and government leaders may try to exploit sports for their political purposes.

While sport can be an entertaining escape or even a passion for fans, it is also a commercial enterprise that turns athletes into commodities, fans into consumers, and events into products in the marketplace. Mega-events are special opportunities for sponsors to market and sell their products. Sports officials try to maximize the special symbolic qualities of sport and minimize the crass commercialism, political influences, and troubling realities that make sport too much like everyday life. We have seen, though, that major social issues, problems, and conflicts of society penetrate the sports arena as reminders of reality. In this real world, the major social forces that transform societies around the globe are also at play. Sport tends not to lead the way as much as it tries to keep up and be responsive to social tastes and trends that keep it popular.

Seven years after the publication of the first edition of this book, I have no reason to think that the influence of the golden triangle will diminish in popular commercialized sports in North America or around the globe. We have not tired of watching sports, and talented athletes have continued to push and sacrifice their bodies in pursuit of fulfillment, fame, and money. Even though the golden triangle has been able to depend on sports fans, consumers, and athletes, it may see increasing challenges from critics, activists, and opponents in local, national, and global political arenas in the future. The business practices and social policies of popular commercialized sports and their treatment of fans, the public, and athletes are likely to face increasing scrutiny. In addition, we have seen that the people who run these sports have not been able to deflect attention from themselves or their sport when athletes, coaches, or spectators misbehave. They have become especially vulnerable in the age of social media.

The sports, media, and businesses of the golden triangle may find they are ultimately most threatened, directly or indirectly, by the forces of Jihad. The unfriendly nations and terrorist groups of Jihad could disrupt the stability of world financial markets, free trade, the free flow of communication, and democratic institutions that allow the golden triangle to pursue growth and profits without interference. They could also engage in violence in the sports arena and threaten the safety of spectators and athletes. Jihadists are like the asteroids we considered in relation to college sports in their unpredictability and potential effects on existing institutions in sport. But they are far more deadly when they turn their threats into violence. In a world shaped by conflicts between Jihad and McWorld, we will find in the sports of the golden triangle a complex and dynamic interplay of sport, politics, and economics on the global level that should provide useful clues about how society will change in the future. Thus, sport in a changing world is ultimately about how the world is changing.

Stop and Think Questions

1. How does the concept of political economy apply to sports in the golden triangle, and what is an example of corporate nationalism in the golden triangle that demonstrates the political economy perspective?

2. Why has Nike been such a powerful player in the business sector of the golden triangle, what has been the greatest threat to its status in the golden triangle, and why was it able to rebound successfully from this threat?

3. What is the difference between the politics *and* sport and the politics *in* sport perspectives, and in what ways have both perspectives applied to the Olympic Games?

4. How have governments used sports effectively, and ineffectively, for their political purposes, and why was ping-pong diplomacy successful while beisbol diplomacy was not?

5. How has the Cuban sports system been similar to, and different from, the sports systems of the twenty-first century PRC and the United States?

6. Why are sports mega-events logical targets for terrorists, and how might the terrorism threat be abused by sports officials and public officials?

7. How do the tensions between Jihad and McWorld relate to the golden triangle, and which forces of social and cultural change seem most likely to turn into asteroids for officials of the most popular sports in the golden triangle in North America and Europe in the coming decade?

References

Acosta, R. Vivian, and Linda Jean Carpenter. 2012. "Women in Intercollegiate Sport. A Longitudinal, National Study, Thirty-Five Year Update. 1977–2012." Unpublished manuscript, January. Available for downloading at www.acostacarpenter.org.

Adams, Mary Louise. 2011. *Artistic Impressions: Figure Skating, Masculinity, and the Limits of Sport.* Toronto: University of Toronto Press.

Adler, Lindsey. 2014. "52 NBA Players Who Make More Money Than Every Player in the WNBA Combined." *Buzz Feed*, May 19. Retrieved July 31, 2014 (www.buzzfeed.com).

Adler, Patricia A., and Peter Adler. 1991. *Backboards and Blackboards: College Athletes and Role Engulfment.* New York: Columbia University Press.

Agyemang, Kwame JA. 2012. "Black Male Athlete Activism and the Link to Michael Jordan: A Transformational Leadership and Social Cognitive Theory Analysis." *International Review for the Sociology of Sport* 47:433–445.

Al Jazeera. 2013. "Iran Urged to End Ban on Female Football Fans." *AP*, November 7. Retrieved April 4, 2014 (www.aljazeera.com).

Alsever, Jennifer. 2006. "A New Competitive Sport: Grooming the Child Athlete." *New York Times*, June 25. Retrieved October 1, 2006 (www.nytimes.com).

Amani, Aslan. 2013. "Football in Turkey: A Force for Liberalisation and Modernity?" *openDemocracy*, July 19. Retrieved April 4, 2014 (www.opendemocracy.net).

Amdur, Neil. 1971. *The Fifth Down: Democracy and the Football Revolution.* New York: Delta.

Anderson, Denise. 2009. "Adolescent Girls' Involvement in Disability Sport: Implications for Identity Development." *Journal of Sport & Social Issues* 33:427–449.

Anderson, Elijah. 1999. *The Code of the Street: Decency, Violence, and the Moral Life of the Inner City.* New York: W.W. Norton.

Andreff, Wladimir. 2011. "Some Comparative Economics of the Organization of Sports Competition and Regulation in North American vs. European Professional Team Sports Leagues." *European Journal of Comparative Economics* 8:3–27.

Andrews, David L. 1996. "The Fact(s) of Michael Jordan's Blackness: Excavating a Floating Racial Signifier." *Sociology of Sport Journal* 13:125–158.

Andrews, David L. 2000. "Posting Up: French Post-Structuralism and the Critical Analysis of Contemporary Sporting Culture." Pp. 106–137 in *Handbook of Sports Studies*, edited by J. Coakley and E. Dunning. London: Sage Publications.

Andrews, David L., Ben Carrington, Steven L. Jackson, and Zbigniew Mazur. 1996. "Jordanscapes: A Preliminary Analysis of the Global Popular." *Sociology of Sport Journal* 13:428–457.

AP. 2014. "Study: Premier League Season Ticket Prices Highest in Europe." *Fox Soccer*, October 14. Retrieved January 13, 2015 (www.foxsports.com).

Appadurai, Arjun. 1996. *Modernity at Large: Cultural Dimensions of Globalization.* Minneapolis: University of Minnesota Press.

Araton, Harvey. 2014. "Collins Finds Spot Again, Moving the NBA Forward." *New York Times*, February 23. Retrieved February 24, 2014 (www.nytimes.com).

Aris, Stephen. 1990. *Sportsbiz: Inside the Sports Business.* London: Hutchinson.

Armour, Nancy. 2012. "As Title IX Turns 40, Legacy Goes beyond Numbers." *AP. The Big Story*, June 21. Retrieved March 3, 2014 (bigstory.ap.org).

Armour, Nancy. 2014. "NFL Should Be Rattled by Budweiser Statement." *USA Today*, September 17. Retrieved September 23, 2014 (www.usatoday.com).

Arms, Robert L., Gordon W. Russell, and Mark L. Sandilands. 1987. "Effects on Hostility of Spectators of Viewing Aggressive Sports." Pp. 259–263 in *Sport Sociology: Contemporary Themes*, 3rd ed., edited by A. Yiannakis, T. D. McIntyre, M. Melnick, and D. P. Hart. Dubuque, IA: Kendall/Hunt.

Assael, Shaun. 2011. "Why Do Fans Riot?" *ESPN.com*, August 1. Retrieved May 27, 2014 (espn.go.com).

Associated Press. 2012. "Tim Tebow Prevails in Trademarking 'Tebowing.'" *USA Today*, October 19. Retrieved April 17, 2014 (www.usatoday.com).

Associated Press. 2013. "Chancellor Holden Thorp Leaving UNC." *ESPN.com*, June 6. Retrieved July 15, 2014 (espn.go.com).

Atkinson, Michael, and Kevin Young. 2012. "Shadowed by the Corpse of War: Sport Spectacles and the Spirit of Terrorism." *International Review for the Sociology of Sport* 37:286–306.

Badenhausen, Kurt. 2013. "Real Madrid Tops the World's Most Valuable Sports Teams." *Forbes*, July 15. Retrieved January 15, 2015 (www.forbes.com).

Badenhausen, Kurt. 2014. "The Most Valuable Nascar Teams." *Forbes*, February 20. Retrieved July 27, 2014 (www.forbes.com).

Baird, Katherine E. 2005. "Cuban Baseball: Ideology, Politics, and Market Forces." *Journal of Sport & Social Issues* 29:164–183.

Bairner, Alan, and Dong-Jhy Hwang. 2011. "Repressing Taiwan: International Sport, Ethnicity and National Identity in the Republic of China." *International Review for the Sociology of Sport* 46:231–248.

Ball, Donald. 1976. "Failure in Sport." *American Sociological Review* 41:726–739.

Barber, Bernard. 2006. "Jihad vs. McWorld." Pp. 449–459 in *Readings for Sociology*, 5th ed., edited by G. Massey. New York: W.W. Norton.

Barker, Jeff. 2014. "O's-Nats Dispute Could End Up in Court." *Baltimore Sun*, July 31, pp. D1, D7.

Battista, Judy. 2012. "Saints Coach Is Suspended for a Year over Bounties." *New York Times*, March 21. Retrieved May 15, 2014 (www.nytimes.com).

BBC. 2000. "The Heysel Disaster." *BBC News*, May 29. Retrieved January 19, 2007 (news.bbc.co.uk).

BBC. 2013. "Egypt Football: Death Sentences over Port Said Stadium Violence." *BBC News Middle East*, January 26. Retrieved May 19, 2014 (www.bbc.com).

Bègue, Laurent, and Sebastian Roché. 2009. "Multidimensional Social Control Variables as a Predictor of Drunkenness among French Adolescents." *Journal of Adolescence* 32:171–191.

Bell, Jarrett. 2012. "Study Shows NFL Players Live Longer." *USA Today*, May 9. Retrieved August 14, 2014 (www.usatoday.com).

Bell, Jarrett. 2014. "Bell Tolls: A Key to Goodell's NFL Survival Is Player Relationships." *USA Today*, September 20. Retrieved September 24, 2014 (www.usatoday.com).

Bellah, Robert, Richard Madsen, William M. Sullivan, Ann Swidler, and Steven M. Tipton. 1985. *Habits of the Heart: Individualism and Commitment in American Life.* Berkeley: University of California Press.

Belson, Ken. 2010. "As Stadiums Vanish, Their Debt Lives On." *New York Times*, September 7. Retrieved September 8, 2010 (www.nytimes.com).

Belson, Ken. 2014a. "Goodell's Pay of $44.2 Million in 2012 Puts Him in the Big Leagues." *New York Times*, February 14. Retrieved February 15, 2014 (www.nytimes.com).

Belson, Ken. 2014b. "Brain Trauma to Affect One in Three Players, N.F.L. Agrees." *New York Times*, September 12. Retrieved September 13, 2014 (www.nytimes.com).

Benammar, Emily. 2013. "10 Sporting Events Marred by Terrorism." *Australian Broadcasting Corporation (ABC) News*, April 16. Retrieved June 28, 2013 (news.yahoo.com).

Benedict, Jeff, and Armen Keteyian. 2011. "Special Report on Gangs and Sport: Straight Outta Compton." *Sports Illustrated*, December 5, pp. 82–90.

Benedict, Jeff, and Armen Keteyian. 2013. *The System: The Glory and Scandal of Big-Time College Football.* New York: Doubleday.

Bennett, Brian. 2014. "B1G Ranks High for Thriving College Teams." *ESPN.com*, May 1. Retrieved May 5, 2014 (espn.go.com).

Berger, Peter. 1963. *Invitation to Sociology: A Humanistic Perspective.* New York: Random House/Doubleday.

Berkowitz, Steve. 2014. "Nick Saban to Make $6.9 Million as Part of New Contract." *USA Today*, June 3. Retrieved June 4, 2014 (www.usatoday.com).

Berkowitz, Steve, Jodi Upton, and Erik Brady. 2013. "Most NCAA Division I Athletic Departments Take Subsidies." *USA Today*, July 1. Retrieved March 31, 2014 (www.usatoday.com).

Betts, John Rickards. 1974. *America's Sporting Heritage: 1850–1950.* Reading, MA: Addison-Wesley.

Blythe, Anne. 2014. "Mary Willingham Files Suit against UNC-Chapel Hill." *Charlotte Observer*, July 1. Retrieved July 16, 2014 (www.charlotteobserver.com).

Bogdanich, Walt. 2014. "A Star Player Accused, and a Flawed Rape Investigation." *New York Times*, April 16. Retrieved April 17, 2014 (www.nytimes.com).

Bois, Jon. 2011. "Major Cities without a Major Pro Team, and Their Likelihood of Ever Landing One." *SB Nation*, December 8. Retrieved August 2, 2014 (www.sbnation.com).

Bok, Derek. 2003. *Universities in the Marketplace: The Commercialization of Higher Education.* Princeton, NJ: Princeton University Press.

Boorstin, Daniel J. 1962. *The Image, or What Happened to the American Dream.* New York: Atheneum.

Boorstin, Daniel J. 1964. *The Image: A Guide to Pseudo-Events in America.* New York: Harper and Row. Republication of *The Image, or What Happened to the American Dream.*

Borden, Sam. 2013. "Police Call Match-Fixing Widespread in Soccer." *New York Times*, February 5. Retrieved February 11, 2013 (www.nytimes.com).

Borden, Sam. 2014. "Home League, National Goal." *New York Times*, March 7. Retrieved March 8, 2014 (www.nytimes.com).

Bostock, Mike, Shan Carter, and Kevin Quealy. 2013. "Tracing the History of N.C.A.A. Conferences." *New York Times*, November 30. Retrieved July 8, 2014 (www.nytimes.com).

Boston Globe. 2006. "Kids in a Money Machine." *Boston Globe* Editorial, July 29. Retrieved August 11, 2006 (www.boston.com/sports).

Boykoff, Jules. 2014. *Celebration Capitalism and the Olympic Games.* London and New York: Routledge.

Bradley, Bill. 1976. *Life on the Run.* New York: Quadrangle.

Brady, Erik, and Mary Beth Marklein. 2006. "A Perfect Storm: Explosive Convergence Helps Lacrosse Scandal Resonate." *USA Today*, April 26. Retrieved January 25, 2007 (www.usatoday.com).

Branch, John. 2013. "In San Francisco, It's Rich Club, Poor Club." *New York Times*, September 4. Retrieved September 5, 2013 (www.nytimes.com).

Branch, John. 2014. "N.B.A. Bars Clippers Owner Donald Sterling for Life." *New York Times*, April 29. Retrieved April 30, 2014 (www.nytimes.com).

Branch, Taylor. 2011. "The Shame of College Sports." *The Atlantic*, October. Retrieved September 14, 2011 (www.theatlantic.com).

Brandmeyer, Gerard A., and Luella K. Alexander. 1983. "Private Life in the Public Domain: The Vicarious Career of the Baseball Wife." Presented at the annual conference of the North American Society for the Sociology of Sport, November, St. Louis, MO.

Brewer, Benjamin. 2002. "Commercialization in Professional Cycling 1950–2001: Institutional Transformations and the Rationalizations of 'Doping.'" *Sociology of Sport Journal* 19:276–301.

Brown, Marni, Erin Ruel, and Stephanie Medley-Rath. 2011. "High School Students' Attitudes toward Providing Girls' Opportunities to Participate in Sport." *Sociology of Sport Journal* 28:239–253.

Brown, Maury. 2014a. "MLB's Billion Dollar TV Deals, Free Agency, and Why Robinson Cano's Deal with the Mariners Isn't 'Crazy.'" *Forbes*, January 7. Retrieved July 26, 2014 (www.forbes.com).

Brown, Maury. 2014b. "Super Bowl Most-Watched U.S. TV Event of All-Time with 111.5 Million Viewers." *Forbes*, February 3. Retrieved February 19, 2014 (www.forbes.com).

Buffington, Daniel. 2012. "Us and Them: U.S. Ambivalence toward the World Cup and American Nationalism." *Journal of Sport & Social Issues* 36:135–154.

Burdsey, Daniel. 2010. "British Muslim Experiences in English First-Class Cricket." *International Review for the Sociology of Sport* 45:315–334.

Busfield, Steve. 2014. "Biogenesis Owner Says He Injected PEDs into Alex Rodriguez." *The Guardian*, January 12. Retrieved May 14, 2014 (www.theguardian.com).

Buzinski, Jim. 2012. "23 Openly Gay and Lesbian Athletes at the 2012 London Summer Olympics." *SB Nation Outsports*, July 18. Retrieved March 13, 2014 (www.outsports.com).

Byrne, Julie. 2005. "Remembering Immaculata during This Year's NCAA Women's Basketball Tournament." *Duke University News & Communications*, March 18. Retrieved April 20, 2007 (today.duke.edu).

Calcaterra, Craig. 2014. "The Nationals and Orioles Dispute over TV Money is about to Explode." *NBC Sports*, July 29. Retrieved July 30, 2014 (hardballtalk.nbcsports.com).

Campbell, Rook. 2011. "Staging Globalization for National Projects: Global Sport Markets and Elite Athletic Transnational Labour in Qatar." *International Review for the Sociology of Sport* 46:45–60.

Cantelon, Hart. 2002. "Book Review: Helen Jefferson Lenskyj's *Inside the Olympic Industry: Power, Politics, and Activism*." *International Review for the Sociology of Sport* 37:103–106.

Cantelon, Hart, and Michael Letters. 2000. "The Making of the IOC Environmental Policy as the Third Dimension of the Olympic Movement." *International Review for the Sociology of Sport* 35:294–308.

Carlin, John. 2008. "The Full Nelson." *Sports Illustrated*, August 18, pp. 20–21.

Carlson, Deven, Leslie Scott, Michael Planty, and Jennifer Thompson. 2005. "Statistics in Brief: What Is the Status of High School Athletes 8 Years after Their Senior Year?" National Center for Education Statistics, September. Washington, DC: U.S. Department of Education Institute of Education Sciences.

Carmin, Mike. 2014. "Big Ten Projects Next TV Deal to Pay More Than $40M per School." *USA Today*, April 26. Retrieved July 7, 2014 (www.usatoday.com).

Cashmore, Ellis, and Jamie Cleland. 2011. "Glasswing Butterflies: Gay Professional Football Players and Their Culture." *Journal of Sport & Social Issues* 35:420–436.

Cavalier, Elizabeth S. 2011. "Men at Sport: Gay Men's Experiences in the Sport Workplace." *Journal of Homosexuality* 58:626–646.

CBS Miami. 2014. "Bowl Games Are Not Always Winners for Schools." *CBS Miami*, January 2. Retrieved July 17, 2014 (miami.cbslocal.com).

Chass, Murray. 1999. "Major Leagues Have Security Concerns over Orioles' Proposal to Play Cuba." *New York Times*, January 5. Retrieved July 15, 2007 (www.nytimes.com).

Cho, Younghan, Charles Leary, Steven J. Jackson. 2012. "Glocalization and Sports in Asia." *Sociology of Sport Journal* 29:421–432.

Clarey, Christopher. 2014. "Slopestyle Asks, When Is a Risky Sport Too Dangerous?" *New York Times*, April 18. Retrieved April 19, 2014 (www.nytimes.com).

Claringbould, Inge, and Annelies Knoppers. 2012. "Paradoxical Practices of Gender in Sports-Related Organizations." *Journal of Sport Management* 26:404–416.

Clotfelter, Charles T. 2011. *Big-Time Sports in American Universities.* New York: Cambridge University Press.

CNBC. 2012. "High School Sports Have Turned Into Big Business." *CNBC.com*, December 9. Retrieved June 28, 2014 (www.cnbc.com).

CNN. 2007. "Duke Lacrosse Prosecutor Disbarred." *CNN.com*, June 17. Retrieved May 29, 2014 (www.cnn.com).

CNN. 2014a. "Oscar Pistorius Fast Facts." *CNN Library*, March 5. Retrieved March 24, 2014 (www.cnn.com).

CNN. 2014b. "Performance Enhancing Drugs in Sports Fast Facts." *CNN Library*, March 6. Retrieved May 8, 2014 (www.cnn.com).

CNN. 2014c. "Boston Marathon Terror Attack Fast Facts." *CNN Library*, August 28. Retrieved September 4, 2014 (www.cnn.com).

Coakley, Jay. 2009. *Sports in Society: Issues and Controversies*, 10th ed. Boston: McGraw-Hill.

Collins, Jason, with Franz Lidz. 2013. "I'm a 34-Year-Old NBA Center. I'm Black. And I'm Gay." *Sports Illustrated*, May 6, pp. 34–41.

Cook, Bob. 2012. "Will 'Pay to Play' Become a Permanent Part of School Sports?" *Forbes.com*, August 22. Retrieved February 11, 2014 (www.forbes.com).

Cooky, Cheryl, and Shari L. Dworkin. 2013. "Policing the Boundaries of Sex: A Critical Examination of Gender Verification and the Caster Semenya Controversy." *Journal of Sex Research* 50(2):103–111.

Cooky, Cheryl, Michael A. Messner, and Robin H. Hextrum. 2013. "Women Play Sport, but Not on TV: A Longitudinal Study of Televised News Media." *Communication & Sport*, April 4. Retrieved August 20, 2013 (www.sagepub.com).

Cooley, Will. 2010. "'Vanilla Thrillas': Modern Boxing and White-Ethnic Masculinity." *Journal of Sport & Social Issues* 34:418–437.

Corben, Billy. 2012. "Broke. Sometimes You Play the Game. Sometimes It Plays You." *30 for 30*, ESPN Films, October 2.

Corrigan, Dermot. 2013. "Platini: Spanish 'Socio' System Ideal." *ESPNFC*, December 12. Retrieved August 4, 2014 (www.espnfc.com).

Coser, Lewis A. 1974. *Greedy Institutions: Patterns of Undivided Commitment.* New York: Free Press.

Coté, John. 2013. "America's Cup Put San Francisco $5.5 Million in the Red." *San Francisco Chronicle*, December 10. Retrieved February 11, 2014 (www.sfgate.com).

Coté, John. 2014. "America's Cup Cost to S.F. More Than Doubles." *San Francisco Chronicle*, February 10. Retrieved February 13, 2014 (www.sfgate.com).

Crouse, Karen. 2014. "Ray Rice Is an Outlier: Most Domestic Abuse Suspects Play On." *New York Times*, September 11. Retrieved September 12, 2014 (www.nytimes.com).

Cunningham, George B. 2010. "Predictors of Sexual Orientation Diversity in Intercollegiate Athletics Departments." *Journal of Intercollegiate Sport* 3:256–269.

Daily Telegraph. 2014. "Racism in United Kingdom Soccer under Fire." *Sport LIVE*, March 19. Retrieved March 20, 2014 (www.sportlive.co.za).

David, Ariel. 2006. "Sports Tribunal Demotes Juventus, Lazio, and Fiorentina for Match-Fixing." *USA Today*, July 14. Retrieved February 2, 2007 (www.usatoday.com).

Davis, Kingsley, and Wilbert E. Moore. 1945. "Some Principles of Stratification." *American Sociological Review* 10:242–249.

Davis, Rebecca. 2013. "Oscar Pistorius Dropped by Sponsors." *Guardian Africa Network*, February 20. Retrieved March 24, 2014 (www.theguardian.com).

Deford, Frank. 1976. "Religion in Sport." *Sports Illustrated*, April 19, 26, May 3, pp. 88–100; 55–56, 68, 69; 43–44, 57–60, respectively.

Deford, Frank. 2005. "America's Modern Peculiar Institution." Pp. 145–154 in *Declining by Degrees: Higher Education at Risk*, edited by R. H. Hersh and J. Merrow. New York: Palgrave Macmillan.

De Lench, Brooke. 2014. "Concussions in Sports: Does Gender Matter?" *MomsTeam. com*, August 26. Retrieved October 1, 2014 (www.momsteam.com).

Delsohn, Steve. 2014. "UNC's McCants: 'Just Show Up, Play.'" *ESPN.com*, June 6. Retrieved July 6, 2014 (espn.go.com).

DeMause, Neil. 2014. "Ditch the Owners." *Sports on Earth*, January 31. Retrieved August 2, 2014 (www.sportsonearth.com).

Derber, Charles. 2011. *The Wilding of America: Money, Mayhem, and the New American Dream*, 5th ed. New York: Worth Publishers.

DeSantis, Nick. 2013. "Football Players' Graduation Rates Continue to Lag Behind Male Peers'." *Chronicle of Higher Education*, September 26. Retrieved September 27, 2013 (chronicle.com).

DeSilver, Drew. 2013. "U.S. Income Inequality, on Rise for Decades, Is Now Highest since 1928." *Pew Research Center Fact Tank*, December 5. Retrieved February 3, 2014 (www.pewresearch.org).

Devereux, Edward C. 1976. "Backyard versus Little League Baseball: The Impoverishment of Children's Games." Pp. 37–76 in *Social Problems in Athletics*, edited by D. Landers. Champaign: University of Illinois Press.

Dickerson, John S. 2012. "The Decline of Evangelical America." *New York Times*, December 15. Retrieved April 18, 2014 (www.nytimes.com).

Dietl, Helmut, Martin Grossman, and Markus Lang. 2011. "Competitive Balance and Revenue Sharing in Sports Leagues with Utility-Maximizing Teams." *Journal of Sports Economics* 12:284–308.

DiMeglio, Steve. 2014. "Tiny Pre-Teen Golfer Big Attraction at U.S. Women's Open." *USA Today*, June 17. Retrieved June 18, 2014 (www.usatoday.com).

Dixon, Victor. 2013. "Why Is Soccer the Most Popular Sport in the World?" *Yahoo Contributor Network*, December 13. Retrieved February 19, 2014 (voices.yahoo.com).

Dodd, Dennis. 2014. "NCAA Class Warfare Closer." *CBSSports.com*, April 6. Retrieved April 7, 2014 (www.cbssports.com).

Dohrmann, George. 2008. "How Dreams Die." *Sports Illustrated*, June 30, pp. 54–60.

Dohrmann, George, and Thayer Evans. 2013. "SI Special Five-Part Report: The Dirty Game." *Sports Illustrated*, September 16, pp. 30–41.

Doley, Amrit. 2009. "Most Popular Team Sports: Soccer & Cricket, Basketball & Baseball???" *Bleacher Report*, May 7. Retrieved February 19, 2014 (bleacherreport.com).

Donaldson, Amy. 2013. "High School Sports: What It Really Costs to Play High School Football." *Deseret News*, September 2. Retrieved February 11, 2014 (www.deseretnews.com).

Donnelly, Peter. 2002. "George Herbert Mead and an Interpretive Sociology of Sport." Pp. 83–102 in *Theory, Sport & Society*, edited by J. Maguire and K. Young. Amsterdam: JAI/Elsevier Science Imprint.

Donnelly, Peter, Mark Norman, and Bruce Kidd. 2013. *Gender Equity in Canadian Sport: A Biennial Report (No.2)*. Centre for Sport Policy Studies Research Reports, December. Retrieved December 19, 2013 (www.sportpolicystudies.ca).

Dorsey, James. 2014a. "Saudi Soccer Debate Widens over Women's Rights and Nationalism." *FootballSpeak.com*, February 20. Retrieved April 4, 2014 (footballspeak.com/ post/2014/02/20/World-Football-Saudi-Arabia-Women.aspx).

Dorsey, James. 2014b. "Women's Right to Attend Sports Events at Centre of Iran's Culture Wars." *Turbulent World of Middle East Soccer Blog Post*, September 19. Retrieved September 19, 2014 (mideastsoccer.blogspot.com).

Drakos, Mark C., Benjamin Domb, Chad Starkey, Lisa Callahan, and Answorth A. Allen. 2010. "Injury in the National Basketball Association." *Sports Health* 2:284–290.

Duarte, Fernando, Jonathan Wilson, Shaun Walker, Paolo Bandini, and Paul Doyle. 2013. "Football Violence: A View from around the World." *The Guardian*, December 19. Retrieved May 19, 2014 (www.theguardian.com).

Dubner, Stephen J. 2006. "Put Down That Basketball! Sport Causes Crime!" *Freakonomics: The Hidden Side of Everything* (Website), October 30. Retrieved June 28, 2013 (www.freakonomics.com).

Durkheim, Emile. [1893] 1964. *The Division of Labor in Society*. New York: Free Press.

Durkheim, Emile. [1895] 1964. *The Rules of the Sociological Method*. New York: Free Press.

Dwyer, Brendan. 2011. "Divided Loyalty? An Analysis of Fantasy Football Involvement and Fan Loyalty to Individual National Football League (NFL) Teams." *Journal of Sport Management* 25:445–457.

Dwyer, Kelly. 2012. "The NBA Has Added Two Female Referees to Its Leaguewide Crew." *Yahoo! Sports*, November 5. Retrieved March 16, 2014 (sports.yahoo.com).

Easterbrook, Gregg. 2013. "How the NFL Fleeces Taxpayers." *The Atlantic*, September 18. Retrieved July 27, 2014 (www.theatlantic.com).

Eckholm, Erik. 2006. "Plight Deepens for Black Men, Studies Warn." *New York Times*, March 20. Retrieved March 20, 2006 (www.nytimes.com).

Economist. 2010. "Sport and Terrorism: A Deadly Game." *The Economist*, January 11. Retrieved June 28, 2013 (www.economist.com).

Economist. 2011. "Ranking Sports' Popularity: And the Silver Goes to . . ." *The Economist*, September 27. Retrieved February 19, 2014 (www.economist.com).

Edwards, Harry. 1973. *Sociology of Sport*. Homewood, IL: Dorsey Press.

Edwards, Harry. 1998. "An End to the Golden Age of Black Participation in Sport?" *Civil Rights Digest* 3 (Fall):19–24.

Eggerton, John. 2014. "Senators Push FCC Vote on Sports Blackout Rules." *Broadcasting & Cable*, June 4. Retrieved July 28, 2014 (www.broadcastingcable.com).

Eitle, Tamela McNulty, and David J. Eitle. 2002. "Race, Cultural Capital, and the Educational Effects of Participation in Sports." *Sociology of Education* 75:123–146.

Eitzen, D. Stanley, and George H. Sage. 1997. *Sociology of North American Sport*, 9th ed. Madison, WI: Brown and Benchmark.

Ekland, Jan. 2013. "Playing Too Many Matches Is Negative for Both Performance and Player Availability—Results from the On-Going UEFA Injury Study." *Jahrgang* 64(1):5–9.

Emmert, Mark. 2014. "NCAA President's Testimony on Value of College Model." Testimony to U.S. Senate Commerce Committee Hearing on "Promoting the Well-Being and Academic Success of College Athletes." *NCAA.org*, July 9. Retrieved July 12, 2014 (www.ncaa.org).

Engber, Daniel. 2012. "The Most Dangerous Game." *Slate*, August 20. Retrieved August 14, 2014 (www.slate.com).

Erhart, Itir. 2013. "Ladies of Besiktas: A Dismantling of Male Hegemony at Inönü Stadium." *International Review for the Sociology of Sport* 48:83–98.

Evans, Stephen. 2013. "German Football Model Is a League Apart." *BBC News*, May 23. Retrieved August 1, 2014 (www.bbc.com).

Fainaru-Wada, Mark, and Steve Fainaru. 2013a. "Head-On Collision." *ESPN The Magazine*, October 2. Retrieved October 4, 2013 (espn.go.com).

Fainaru-Wada, Mark, and Steve Fainaru. 2013b. *League of Denial: The NFL, Concussions, and the Battle for Truth*. New York: Crown Archetype.

Falcous, Mark, and Joseph Maguire. 2006. "Imagining 'America': The NBA and Local-Global Mediascapes." *International Review for the Sociology of Sport* 41:59–78.

Farhi, Paul. 2014. "In Coverage of the Olympics, NBC Has Largely Steered Clear of Controversy." *Washington Post*, February 21. Retrieved March 11, 2014 (www.washingtonpost.com).

Farnan-Kennedy, Catharine. 2011. "Concussion Matters in Girls' Basketball." Presented at the Brain Injury Association Conference of Pennsylvania, June, Lancaster, PA.

Farrell, Stephen, and Peter Gelling. 2007. "With Eyes Fixed on a Distant Soccer Field, Iraqis Leap at a Reason to Celebrate." *New York Times*, July 30. Retrieved July 30, 2007 (www.nytimes.com).

Farrey, Tom. 2013. "Preps at Greater Concussion Risk." *ESPN.com*, October 31. Retrieved November 4, 2013 (espn.go.com).

Feezell, Randolph. 2013. "Sport, Religious Belief, and Religious Diversity." *Journal of the Philosophy of Sport* 40:135–162.

FIFA. 2011. "Almost Half the World Tuned in at Home to Watch 2010 FIFA World Cup South Africa." *FIFA*, July 11. Retrieved February 20, 2014 (www.fifa.com).

FIFA. 2013. "Webb on Racism: Enough Is Enough." *FIFA*, March 2. Retrieved March 20, 2014 (www.fifa.com).

Fine, Gary Alan. 1987. *With the Boys: Little League Baseball and Preadolescent Culture.* Chicago: University of Chicago Press.

FIS-SKI. 2014. "Sochi 2014 Statistics." *FIS-SKI*, February 26. Retrieved March 3, 2014 (www.fis-ski.com/news-multimedia).

Fitzgerald, Tim. 2014. "Today's Coaches and Trainers Are Promoting Safety, Strength, and Conditioning to Protect Players from Disabling Injuries." *HealthDay*, March 11. Retrieved August 14, 2014 (consumer.healthday.com).

Fletcher, Thomas. 2012. "Who Do 'They' Cheer For? Cricket, Diaspora, Hybridity and Divided Loyalties amongst British Asians." *International Review for the Sociology of Sport* 47:612–631.

Florio, Mike. 2014. "Antitrust Exemption Limits NFL's Window for Saturday Games." *NBC Sports*, February 6. Retrieved July 29, 2014 (profootballtalk.nbcsports.com).

Forbes. 2013. "The World's Highest-Paid Athletes." *Forbes*, June 6 (pre-publication). Retrieved June 24, 2013 (www.forbes.com).

Forrest, David. 2012. "The Threat to Football from Betting-Related Corruption." *International Journal of Sport Finance* 7:99–116.

Foss, Mike, and Erik Brady. 2013. "Rogers Coming Back as First Openly Gay Player in MLS." *USA Today*, May 24. Retrieved May 25, 2013 (www.usatoday.com).

Frank, Andre Gundar. 1979. *Dependent Accumulation and Underdevelopment.* London: Macmillan.

Freeh, Louis. 2012. *Report of the Special Investigative Counsel Regarding the Actions of the Pennsylvania State University Related to the Child Sexual Abuse Committed by Gerald A. Sandusky,* July 12. Freeh Sporkin & Sullivan, LLP. Retrieved July 14, 2012 (progress.psu.edu/the-freeh-report).

Friedrichs, David O. 2010. *Trusted Criminals: White Collar Crime in Contemporary Society,* 4th ed. Belmont, CA: Wadsworth Cengage Learning.

Frizell, Sam. 2014. "Obama, LeBron Speak Out against Clippers Owner Donald Sterling." *Time*, April 27. Retrieved August 29, 2014 (time.com).

Fullinwider, Robert K. 2006. *Sports, Youth and Character: A Critical Survey.* Circle Working Paper 44. The Center for Information & Research on Civic Learning & Engagement. February. Retrieved September 2, 2006 (www.civicyouth.org).

Fung, Brian. 2014. "NBC Single-Handedly Pays for a Fifth of All Olympic Games." *Washington Post*, February 10. Retrieved September 2, 2014 (www.washingtonpost.com).

Gaines, Cork. 2014. "CHART: English Soccer Lags Way Behind Top American Sports in Revenue." *Business Insider*, March 18. Retrieved July 27, 2014 (www.businessinsider.com).

Ganim, Sara. 2014a. "CNN Analysis: Some College Athletes Play Like Adults, Read Like 5th-Graders." *CNN.com*, January 8. Retrieved January 28, 2014 (www.cnn.com).

Ganim, Sara. 2014b. "UConn Guard on Unions: I Go to Bed 'Starving.'" *CNN.com*, April 8. Retrieved July 13, 2014 (www.cnn.com).

Ganim, Sara. 2014c. "Charges Dropped in University of North Carolina 'Paper Classes' Case." *CNN.com*, July 3. Retrieved July 15, 2014 (www.cnn.com).

Gans, Herbert J. 1972. "The Positive Functions of the Undeserving Poor." *American Journal of Sociology* 78:275–288.

Ganucheau, Adam. 2013. "UM Students, Football Players Disrupt Play." *Daily Mississippian*, October 3. Retrieved March 11, 2014 (thedmonline.com/um-students-football-players-disrupt-play/).

Garcia, Borja. 2007. "The Independent European Sport Review: Half Full or Half Empty?" *Entertainment and Sports Law Journal*, January. Retrieved August 1, 2014 (go.warwick.ac.uk).

George, Rachel. 2012. "North Carolina Reputation Suffers with NCAA Violations." *USA Today*, October 10. Retrieved July 15, 2013 (www.usatoday.com).

Germano, Sara. 2014. "Adidas Slips Behind Under Armour in U.S." *Wall Street Journal*, September 5. Retrieved September 8, 2014 (online.wsj.com).

Gibson, Owen. 2013. "World Cup and Outbreak of Supporter Violence Link Brazil and Russia." *The Guardian*, December 19. Retrieved May 19, 2014 (www.theguardian.com).

Gibson, Owen. 2014. "FIFA Faces Calls to Quash Qatar World Cup Vote after Corruption Allegations." *The Guardian*, June 1. Retrieved June 3, 2014 (www.theguardian.com).

Gierer, Kathy. 2014. "Shannon Szabados Makes History as Goalie for Columbus Cottonmouths." *Columbus Ledger Enquirer*, March 15. Retrieved March 16, 2014 (www.ledger-enquirer.com).

Gilbert, Bill, and Nancy Williamson. 1973. "Three-Part Series on Women in Sport." *Sports Illustrated*, June 23, 30, July 7.

Gilmour, Callum, and David Rowe. 2012. "Sport in Malaysia: National Imperatives and Western Seductions." *Sociology of Sport Journal* 29:485–505.

Giulianotti, Richard. 2005. *Sport: A Critical Sociology*. Malden, MA: Polity Press.

Giulianotti, Richard, and Francisco Klauser. 2012. "Sport Mega-Events and 'Terrorism': A Critical Analysis." *International Review for the Sociology of Sport* 47:307–323.

Giulianotti, Richard, and Roland Robertson. 2012. "Glocalization and Sport in Asia: Diverse Perspectives and Future Possibilities." *Sociology of Sport Journal* 29:433–454.

Goffman, Erving. 1959. *The Presentation of Self in Everyday Life*. Garden City, NY: Doubleday/Anchor.

Goffman, Erving. 1967. *Interaction Ritual: Essays on Face-to-Face Behavior*. Garden City, NY: Doubleday/Anchor.

Gohir, Shaista. 2012. "Extraordinary Muslim Women at the Olympics: Past to Present." *HuffPost Sport United Kingdom*, February 8. Retrieved April 4, 2014 (www.huffingtonpost.co.uk).

Golliver, Ben. 2014a. "NBA Investigating Clippers Owner Donald Sterling for Alleged Racist Comments." *SI.com*, April 29. Retrieved April 29, 2014 (nba.si.com).

Golliver, Ben. 2014b. "Adam Silver Issues Lifetime Ban, $2.5 Million Fine to Clippers Owner Donald Sterling." *SI Extra*, April 29. Retrieved April 29, 2014 (www.si.com).

Golliver, Ben. 2014c. "Answering the Biggest Questions about the NBA's Record TV Deal." *SI.com*, October 6. Retrieved October 6, 2014 (www.si.com).

Goodhart, Philip, and Christopher John Chataway. 1968. *War without Weapons*. London: W.H. Allen.

Grasgreen, Allie, and Doug Lederman. 2014. "NLRB Office Backs Union for Northwestern Football Players." *Inside Higher Ed*, March 27. Retrieved July 12, 2014 (www.insidehighered.com).

Gray, Eliza. 2014. "Sexual Assault on Campus." *Time*, May 26, pp. 20–27.

Green, Mick. 2004. "Power, Policy, and Political Priorities: Elite Sport Development in Canada and the United Kingdom." *Sociology of Sport Journal* 21:376–396.

Green, Mick, and Barrie Houlihan. 2006. "Governmentality, Modernization, and the 'Disciplining' of National Sporting Organizations: Athletics in Australia and the United Kingdom." *Sociology of Sport Journal* 23:47–71.

Green Bay Packers. 2014. Official Website of the Green Bay Packers. *Packers.com*. Retrieved August 4, 2014 (www.packers.com).

Greenstone, Michael, Adam Looney, Jeremy Patashnik, and Muxin Yu. 2013. "Thirteen Economic Facts about Social Mobility and the Role of Education." *The*

Hamilton Project, June. The Brookings Institution. Retrieved February 11, 2014 (www. brookings.edu).

Gregory, Sean. 2012. "Can Roger Goodell Save Football?" *Time*, December 17, pp. 36–43.

Gregory, Sean. 2014. "It Didn't Cross My Mind That I Wouldn't See Him Come Off That Field: The Tragic Risks of an American Obsession." *Time*, September 29, pp. 32–39.

Groves, Roger. 2013. "Why the NBA Will Have Better Profit Growth Than the NFL." *Forbes*, October 21. Retrieved August 8, 2014 (www.forbes.com).

Guardian. 2010. "Zinedine Zidane 'Would Rather Die' Than Apologise to Marco Materazzi." *The Guardian*, March 1. Retrieved April 14, 2014 (www.theguardian.com).

Guardian. 2012. "London 2012 Olympic Sponsors List: Who Are They and What Have They Paid?" *The Guardian*, July 19. Retrieved September 3, 2014 (www.theguardian. com).

Guttmann, Allen. 1978. *From Ritual to Record: The Nature of Modern Sports*. New York: Columbia University Press.

Guttmann, Allen. 2000. "The Development of Modern Sports." Pp. 248–259 in *Handbook of Sports Studies*, edited by J. Coakley and E. Dunning. London: Sage Publications.

Halberstam, David. 1991. "A Hero for the Wired World." *Sports Illustrated*, December 23, pp. 76–81.

Haley, A. J., and Brian S. Johnston. 1998. "Menaces to Management: A Developmental View of British Soccer Hooligans, 1961–1986." *The Sport Journal* 1(1). Retrieved January 19, 2007 (www.thesportjournal.org).

Halkidis, Anna. 2012. "Women Tackle College Discrimination with Title IX." *Forbes Women's eNews*, September 4. Retrieved March 3, 2014 (www.forbes.com).

Halley, Jim. 2013. "Should High School Football Be Televised?" *USA Today*, August 22. Retrieved August 22, 2013 (www.usatoday.com).

Hamil, Sean, Geoff Walters, and Lee Watson. 2010. "The Model of Governance at FC Barcelona: Balancing Member Democracy, Commercial Strategy, Corporate Social Responsibility and Sporting Performance." *Soccer & Society* 11(4):475–504.

Harris, Craig. 2011. "Trips to BCS Bowl Games Can Cost Some Schools Big Money." *USA Today*, September 28. Retrieved July 17, 2014 (www.usatoday.com).

Harris, Nick. 2013. "New Research: Foreign Players at Record Levels across European Football." *Sporting Intelligence*, January 21. Retrieved August 9, 2014 (www. sportingintelligence.com).

Harvey, Jean, Alan Law, and Michael Cantelon. 2001. "North American Professional Team Sport Franchise Ownership Patterns and Global Entertainment Conglomerations." *Sociology of Sport Journal* 18:435–457.

Harvey, Jean, Geneviève Rail, and Lucie Thibault. 1996. "Globalization and Sport: Sketching a Theoretical Model for Empirical Analyses." *Journal of Sport & Social Issues* 20:258–277.

Hassan, David. 2012. "Sport and Terrorism: Two of Modern Life's Most Prevalent Themes." *International Review for the Sociology of Sport* 47:263–267.

Healy, Michelle. 2013. "1.35 Million Youths a Year Have Serious Sports Injuries." *USA Today*, August 6. Retrieved August 6, 2013 (www.usatoday.com).

Heino, Rebecca. 2000. "New Sports: What Is So Punk about Snowboarding?" *Journal of Sport & Social Issues* 24:176–191.

Henderson, Amy. 1999. "From Barnum to 'Bling': The Changing Face of Celebrity Culture." *Hedgehog Review*, Fall. Retrieved August 12, 2005 (www.virginia.edu).

Herranz, Alejandra. 2014. "Real Madrid's Ownership and Sense of Belonging." *Footy News24*, January 4. Retrieved August 2, 2014 (www.footynews24.com).

Higgs, Robert. 1995. *God in the Stadium: Sports and Religion in America*. Lexington: University of Kentucky Press.

Highkin, Sean. 2013. "Formerly Homophobic NBA Star Joins Marriage-Equality Campaign." *USA Today*, July 3. Retrieved July 4, 2013 (ftw.usatoday.com).

Hildebrandt, Amber. 2014. "Sochi Paralympics: Corporate Sponsorship the 'Last Barrier' for Athletes." *CBC News Canada*, March 12. Retrieved March 24, 2014 (www.cbc.ca).

Hill, Declan. 2010. "A Critical Mass of Corruption: Why Some Football Leagues Have More Match-Fixing Than Others." *International Journal of Sports Marketing & Sponsorship* 11(April):221–235.

Hill, Declan, and Jeré Longman. 2014. "Fixed Soccer Matches Cast Shadow over World Cup." *New York Times*, May 31. Retrieved June 1, 2014 (www.nytimes.com).

Hinch, Jim. 2014. "Where Are the People?" *The American Scholar*, Winter. Retrieved April 18, 2014 (theamericanscholar.org/where-are-the-people).

Hirschi, Travis. 1969. *Causes of Delinquency*. Berkeley: University of California Press.

Hoberman, John M. 1992. *Mortal Engines: The Science of Performance and the Dehumanization of Sport*. New York: Free Press.

Hohler, Bob. 2006a. "$neaker War: Ethical Questions Raised as Amateur Basketball Recruiters Engage in a High-Stakes Battle for Blue-Chip Recruits." *Boston Globe*, July 23. Retrieved August 11, 2006 (www.boston.com).

Hohler, Bob. 2006b. "$neaker War: Wading in Cesspool." *Boston Globe*, July 24. Retrieved August 11, 2006 (www.boston.com).

Hohler, Bob. 2006c. "$neaker War: Are You Kidding?" *Boston Globe*, July 25. Retrieved August 11, 2006 (www.boston.com).

Holder, Larry. 2013. "New Orleans Saints' Bounty Scandal Timeline as Sean Payton Prepares for Return." *Times-Picayune*, August 30. Retrieved May 15, 2014 (www.nola.com/saints).

Hooper, John. 2014. "Coppa Italia Officials and Police Accused of Capitulating to Football Hooliganism." *The Guardian*, May 4. Retrieved May 19, 2014 (www.theguardian.com).

Horne, John, and Wolfram Manzenreiter, eds. 2006. *Sports Mega-Events: Social Scientific Analyses of a Global Phenomenon*. Malden, MA: Blackwell Publishing.

Hosick, Michelle Brutlag. 2005. "The Hidden Hazards of Hazing." *NCAA News Archive*, September 26. Retrieved October 5, 2005 (www.ncaa.org).

Houlihan, Barrie. 2000. "Politics and Sport." Pp. 213–227 in *Handbook of Sports Studies*, edited by J. Coakley and E. Dunning. London: Sage Publications.

Hruby, Patrick. 2013. "The Sports Cable Bubble." *Sports on Earth*, July 12. Retrieved August 6, 2014 (www.sportsonearth.com).

Huffington Post. 2014. "Fan Violence." *Huffington Post* (collection of articles from September 18, 2012, to January 23, 2014). Retrieved May 27, 2014 (www.huffingtonpost.com).

Hughes, Rob. 2012. "An Ugly and Violent Month for Soccer." *New York Times*, October 23. Retrieved May 19, 2014 (www.nytimes.com).

Hughes, Rob, and Eric Pfanner. 2009. "Raids Expose Soccer Fixing across Europe." *New York Times*, November 21. Retrieved November 22, 2009 (www.nytimes.com).

Hughes, Robert, and Jay Coakley. 1991. "Positive Deviance among Athletes: The Implications of Overconformity to the Sport Ethic." *Sociology of Sport Journal* 8:307–325.

Hyman, Mark. 2009. "The Kids Aren't Alright." *Sports Illustrated*, April 13, pp. 14–15.

IBNLive. 2013. "English Premier League: Clubs and Owners." *IBNLive Sports*, July 16. Retrieved July 30, 2014 (ibnlive.in.com).

IOC. 2013. "Factsheet: Women in the Olympic Movement Update 2013." *International Olympic Committee*, November 6. Retrieved March 3, 2014 (www.olympic.org).

IPC. 2014. "History of the Paralympic Movement." *The IPC—Who We Are* (IPC website). Retrieved March 25, 2014 (www.paralympic.org).

Irwin, Neil. 2014. "What the Numbers Show about N.F.L. Player Arrests." *New York Times*, September 12. Retrieved September 22, 2014 (www.nytimes.com).

Jamail, Milton H. 2000. *Full Count: Inside Cuban Baseball*. Carbondale: Southern Illinois University Press.

Janis, Irving L. 1972. *Victims of Groupthink*. Boston: Houghton Mifflin.

Jenkins, Lee. 2014. "Adam Silver." *Sports Illustrated*, May 26, pp. 66–74.

Jenkins, Sally. 2007. "History of Women's Basketball." *WNBA.com*. Retrieved April 20, 2007 (www.nba.com).

Jenkins, Sally, and Rick Maese. 2013. "NFL Medical Standards, Practices Are Different Than Almost Anywhere Else." *Washington Post*, March 16. Retrieved August 14, 2014 (www.washingtonpost.com).

Jenkins, Sally, Rick Maese, and Scott Clement. 2013. "Do No Harm: Retired NFL Players Endure a Lifetime of Hurt." *Washington Post*, May 16. Retrieved August 14, 2014 (www.washingtonpost.com).

Jennings, Andrew. 2011. "Investigating Corruption in Corporate Sport: The IOC and FIFA." *International Review for the Sociology of Sport* 46:387–398.

Jessop, Alicia. 2013. "The Economics of College Football: A Look at the Top-25 Teams' Revenues and Expenses." *Forbes*, August 31. Retrieved July 7, 2014 (www.forbes.com).

Jessop, Alicia. 2014. "The NCAA Approves Unlimited Meals for Division I Athletes after Shabazz Napier Complains of Going Hungry: The Lesson for Other College Athletes." *Forbes*, April 15. Retrieved July 14, 2014 (www.forbes.com).

Johnson, K. C. 2006. "The Academy and the Duke Case." *insidehighered.com*, December 28. Retrieved December 28, 2006 (www.insidehighered.com).

Johnson, Thomas. 2014. "The Largest Transfers of the World Cup." *Washington Post*, July 15. Retrieved July 28, 2014 (www.washingtonpost.com).

Kacsmar, Scott. 2013. "Where Does NFL Talent Come From?" *Bleacher Report*, May 16. Retrieved August 8, 2014 (bleacherreport.com).

Kaestner, Robert, and Xin Xu. 2010. "Title IX, Girls' Sports Participation, and Adult Female Physical Activity and Weight." *Evaluation Review* 34:52–78.

Kapadia, Anush. 2014. "What German Football Has Done Right." *NDTV*, July 13. Retrieved August 1, 2014 (www.ndtv.com).

Katz, Daniel, and Floyd H. Allport. 1931. *Student Attitudes*. Syracuse, NY: Craftsman.

Keh, Andrew. 2014. "Views on Race again Prompt an N.B.A. Sale." *New York Times*, September 7. Retrieved September 18, 2014 (www.nytimes.com).

Kelley, Bruce, and Carl Carchia. 2013. "Hey, Data Data—Swing!" *ESPN The Magazine*, July 11. Retrieved July 13, 2013 (espn.go.com).

Kelley, Margaret S., and Jan Sokol-Katz. 2011. "Examining Participation in School Sports and Patterns of Delinquency Using the National Longitudinal Study of Adolescent Health." *Sociological Focus* 44:81–101.

Kennedy, Kostya, Mark Bechtel, and Stephen Cannella. 2007. "Goodbye to All That." *Sports Illustrated*, August 20, p. 28.

Kerasidis, Harry. 2014. "Brain Trauma." *Psychology Today*, August 19. Retrieved September 30, 2014 (www.psychologytoday.com).

Késenne, Stefan, and Wilfried Pauwels. 2006. "Club Objectives and Ticket Pricing in Professional Team Sports." *Eastern Economic Journal* 32:549–560.

Kim, Janine Young, and Matthew J. Parlow. 2009. "Off-Court Misbehavior: Sports Leagues and Private Punishment." *Journal of Criminal Law and Criminology* 99(3): 573–597.

King, Peter. 2012. "Way Out of Bounds." *Sports Illustrated*, March 12, pp. 34–41.

Kivisto, Peter. 2004. *Key Ideas in Sociology*, 2nd ed. Thousand Oaks, CA: Pine Forge Press.

Klein, Alan. 2006. *Growing the Game: The Globalization of Major League Baseball*. New Haven, CT: Yale University Press.

Klemko, Robert. 2013. "Brad Johnson Paying Physical Price for Long NFL Career." *USA Today*, April 24. Retrieved April 24, 2013 (www.usatoday.com).

Klis, Mike. 2003. "Fewer Blacks Step Up to the Plate in Pro Baseball." *Denver Post*, May 11, pp. 1A, 14A–15A.

Knight Commission. 2006. *Public Poll: Americans Are Concerned about College Sports*. Executive Summary, January. Knight Commission on Intercollegiate Athletics. Retrieved May 26, 2007 (www.knightcommission.org).

Knowlton, Brian. 1999. "Expanding Ties, Clinton Extends a Hand to Cuba." *International Herald Tribune*, January 6. Retrieved July 15, 2007 (www.iht.com).

Kobayashi, Koji. 2012. "Corporate Nationalism and Glocalization of Nike Advertising in 'Asia': Production and Representation Practices of Cultural Intermediaries." *Sociology of Sport Journal* 29:42–61.

Kohut, Andrew. 2013. *The Global Divide on Homosexuality*. Pew Research Center, June 4. Retrieved March 11, 2014 (www.pewglobal.org).

Krattenmaker, Tom. 2010. *Onward Christian Athletes: Turning Ballparks into Pulpits and Players into Preachers*. Lanham, MD: Rowman and Littlefield.

Kuriloff, Aaron. 2012. "Stadiums Cost Taxpayers Extra $10 Billion, Harvard's Long Finds." *Bloomberg.com*, November 6. Retrieved August 7, 2014 (www.bloomberg.com).

LaFeber, Walter. 2002. *Michael Jordan and the New Global Capitalism*. New York: W.W. Norton.

Lamberti, Chris. 2013. "Rich Man's Game: Rising Ticket Prices in Taxpayer Funded Facilities." *Chicago Sport & Society*, May 9. Retrieved August 6, 2014 (www.chicago-sportandsociety.com).

Lanter, Jason R. 2011. "Spectator Identification with the Team and Participation in Celebratory Violence." *Journal of Sport Behavior* 34:268–280.

Lapchick, Richard, with Robert Agusta and Nate Kinkopf. 2013. "The 2013 Women's National Basketball Association Racial and Gender Report Card." *The Institute for Diversity and Ethics in Sport (TIDES)*, October 9. Retrieved March 20, 2014 (www. tidesport.org).

Lapchick, Richard, with Robert Agusta, Nathaniel Kinkopf, and Frank McPhee. 2013. "The 2012 Racial and Gender Report Card: College Sport." *The Institute for Diversity and Ethics in Sport (TIDES)*, July 10. Retrieved March 3, 2014 (www.tidesport.org).

Lapchick, Richard, with Devin Beahm, Giomar Nunes, and Stephanie Rivera-Casiano. 2013. "The 2012 Racial and Gender Report Card: National Football League." *The Institute for Diversity and Ethics in Sport (TIDES)*, October 22. Retrieved March 20, 2014 (www.tidesport.org).

Lapchick, Richard, with Cory Bernstine, Giomar Nunes, Nicole Okolo, Deidre Snively, and Curtis Walker. 2013. "The 2013 Racial and Gender Report Card: Major League Baseball." *The Institute for Diversity and Ethics in Sport (TIDES)*, May 21. Retrieved March 19, 2014 (www.tidesport.org).

Lapchick, Richard, with Andrew Hippert and Cory Bernstine. 2013. "The 2013 Racial and Gender Report Card: Major League Soccer." *The Institute for Diversity and Ethics in Sport (TIDES)*, November 21. Retrieved March 19, 2014 (www.tidesport.org).

Lapchick, Richard, with Andrew Hippert, Stephanie Rivera, and Jason Robinson. 2013. "The 2013 Racial and Gender Report Card: National Basketball Association." *The Institute for Diversity and Ethics in Sport (TIDES)*, June 25. Retrieved March 19, 2014 (www.tidesport.org).

Larmer, Brook. 2005. "The Center of the World." *Foreign Policy*, September/October, pp. 66–74.

Lasch, Christopher. 1979. *The Culture of Narcissism: American Life in an Age of Diminishing Expectations*. New York: Warner Books.

Lavigne, Paula. 2014. "College Sports Thrive amid Downturn." *ESPN.com*, May 1. Retrieved May 5, 2014 (espn.go.com).

LaVoi, Nicole M. 2014. *Head Coaches of Women's Collegiate Teams: A Report on Select NCAA Division-I FBS Institutions 2013–2014*. Minneapolis, MN: Tucker Center for Research on Girls and Women in Sport. January. Retrieved March 7, 2014 (www. TuckerCenter.org).

Layden, Tim. 2012. "Intimidation Rules." *Sports Illustrated*, March 12, p. 41.

Lee, Jason W., and Jeffrey C. Lee, eds. 2009. *Sport and Criminal Behavior*. Durham, NC: Carolina Academic Press.

Lee, Jung Woo, and Alan Bairner. 2009. "The Difficult Dialogue: Communism, Nationalism, and Political Propaganda in North Korean Sport." *Journal of Sport & Social Issues* 33:390–410.

Lefton, Terry, and John Ourand. 2013. "ESPN Signs Six-Year Extension with WNBA That Is Worth $12 M per Year." *Sports Business Journal*, March 28. Retrieved July 31, 2014 (www.sportsbusinessdaily.com).

Leitch, Will. 2007. "In Brand We Trust." *New York Times Play*, July 12. Retrieved December 1, 2007 (www.nytimes.com).

Lenskyj, Helen Jefferson. 2000. *Inside the Olympic Industry: Power, Politics, and Activism.* Albany: State University of New York Press.

Leonard, David J. 2007. "Innocent until Proven Innocent: In Defense of Duke Lacrosse and White Power (and against Menacing Black Student-Athletes, a Black Stripper, Activists, and the Jewish Media)." *Journal of Sport & Social Issues* 31:25–44.

Leonard, David J. 2009. "New Media and Global Sporting Cultures: Moving Beyond the Clichés and Binaries." *Sociology of Sport Journal* 26:1–16.

Lesjø, Jon Helge. 2000. "Lillehammer 1994." *International Review for the Sociology of Sport* 35:282–293.

Levitt, Steven D., and Stephen J. Dubner. 2005. *Freakonomics: A Rogue Economist Explores the Hidden Side of Everything.* New York: HarperCollins.

Lewis, Michael. 2007. "Serfs of the Turf." *New York Times*, November 11. Retrieved July 15, 2014 (www.nytimes.com).

Liberty Mutual. 2013. "Parents and Coaches Express Conflicting Opinions Regarding Priorities in Youth Sports." *Liberty Mutual Insurance ResponsibleSports*, September 17. Retrieved June 20, 2014 (responsible-sports.libertymutual.com).

Lipka, Sara. 2007. "North Carolina Attorney General Exonerates Duke Lacrosse Players." *Chronicle of Higher Education*, April 12. Retrieved April 12, 2007 (www.chronicle.com).

Lipsyte, Robert. 1996. "Little Girls in a Staged Spectacle for Big Bucks? That's Sportainment!" *New York Times*, August 4, p. 28.

Lipsyte, Robert. 2005. "Outraged over the Steroids Outrage." *USA Today*, March 21. Retrieved January 28, 2007 (www.usatoday.com).

Long, Judith Grant. 2012. *Public/Private Partnerships for Major League Sports Facilities.* New York: Routledge.

Longman, Jeré. 2013. "Outrage over an Antigay Law Does Not Spread to Olympic Officials." *New York Times*, August 6. Retrieved August 7, 2013 (www.nytimes.com).

Low, Tobin. 2014. "Hosting the Olympics and Coming Away with a Profit? Imagine That. Three Cities That Bucked the Trend." *Marketplace*, May 29. Retrieved May 29, 2014 (www.marketplace.org).

Lowe, Maria R. 1998. *Women of Steel: Female Bodybuilders and the Struggle for Self-Definition.* New York: New York University Press.

Lowrey, Annie. 2013. "Household Incomes Remain Flat Despite Improving Economy." *New York Times*, September 17. Retrieved February 7, 2014 (www.nytimes.com).

MacGregor, Roy. 2014. "The True Cost of Injuries to NHL Players: $218 Million Each Season." *Globe and Mail*, January 20. Retrieved August 14, 2014 (www.theglobeandmail.com).

Madden, Paul. 2012. "Fan Welfare Maximization as a Club Objective in a Professional Sports League." *European Economic Review* 56:560–578.

Madkour, Abraham D. 2013. "50 Most Influential People in Sports Business." *Sports Business Journal*, December 9. Retrieved February 18, 2014 (www.sportsbusinessdaily.com).

Maguire, Joseph. 1999. *Global Sport.* Cambridge, UK: Polity Press.

Malcolm, Dominic, Alan Bairner, and Graham Curry. 2010. "'Woolmergate': Cricket and the Representation of Islam and Muslims in the British Press." *Journal of Sport & Social Issues* 34:215–235.

Mandel, Stewart. 2014. "The Long Play." *Sports Illustrated*, June 23, pp. 52–56.

Mandelaro, Jim. 2014. "Hazing Continues Despite Efforts to Change." *Rochester (NY) Democrat and Chronicle*, January 12. Retrieved January 13, 2014 (www.democratandchronicle.com).

Mandell, Richard D. 1971. *The Nazi Olympics*. New York: Macmillan.

Manzenreiter, Wolfram. 2010. "The Beijing Games in the Western Imagination of China: The Weak Power of Soft Power." *Journal of Sport & Social Issues* 34:29–48.

Markovits, Andrei S. 2010. "The Global and the Local in Our Contemporary Sports Cultures." *Society* 47:503–509.

Markovits, Andrei S., and Steven L. Hellerman. 2001. *Offside: Soccer and American Exceptionalism*. Princeton, NJ: Princeton University Press.

Martel, Brett. 2013. "Oregon's Schimmel Sisters Showcase 'Rez Ball' for Louisville." *KATU.com*, April 9. Retrieved April 10, 2013 (www.katu.com).

Martens, Rainer, and James A. Peterson. 1971. "Group Cohesiveness as a Determinant of Success and Member Satisfaction in Team Performance." *International Review of Sport Sociology* 6:49–59.

Marx, Karl, and Friedrich Engels. 1978. "Manifesto of the Communist Party." Pp. 473–478 in *The Marx-Engels Reader*, 2nd ed., translated by R. C. Tucker. New York: W.W. Norton.

Mascaro, Chris. 2014. "ESPN Survey: Eighty-Six Percent of NFL Players OK with Gay Teammate." *Sports Illustrated SI Wire*, February 17. Retrieved March 11, 2014 (tracking.si.com).

Masters, James. 2014. "And the Richest Soccer League in the World Is . . ." *CNN.com*, June 5. Retrieved July 27, 2014 (edition.cnn.com).

McCann, Allison. 2014. "Low Pay Limits Player Experience in National Women's Soccer League." *FiveThirtyEight*, March 24. Retrieved July 31, 2014 (fivethirtyeight.com).

McCann, Michael. 2014a. "O'Bannon v. NCAA: With Trial Over, What Comes Next?" *SI.com*, June 30. Retrieved July 11, 2014 (www.si.com).

McCann, Michael. 2014b. "Next Steps in O'Bannon Case: Both NCAA and the Plaintiffs Could Appeal." *SI.com*, August 11. Retrieved August 12, 2014 (www.si.com).

McFadden, Tatyana. 2014. "Equity in Sports." *Tatyana McFadden Website*. Retrieved March 26, 2014 (www.tatyanamcfadden.com).

McGrath, Shelly A., and Ruth A. Chananie-Hill. 2009. "'Big Freaky-Looking Women': Normalizing Gender Transgressing through Bodybuilding." *Sociology of Sport Journal* 26:235–254.

McLaughlin, Elliott C. 2010. "Super Bowl Is King at Home but Struggles on World Stage." *CNN*, February 4. Retrieved February 20, 2014 (www.cnn.com).

Mellgren, Doug. 2006. "America's Cup a Lesson in Team Diversity." *Chicago Sun Times*, July 2. Retrieved July 10, 2006 (www.suntimes.com).

Mellman Group. 2007. "Memo to 'Interested Parties.' Re: Title IX." *The Mellman Group*, June 14. For the National Women's Law Center. Retrieved March 3, 2014 (www.nwlc.org).

Mennesson, Christine. 2000. "'Hard' Women and 'Soft' Women: The Social Construction of Identities among Women Boxers." *International Review for the Sociology of Sport* 35:21–33.

Merkel, Udo. 2012. "Sport and Physical Culture in North Korea: Resisting, Recognizing and Relishing Globalization." *Sociology of Sport Journal* 29:506–525.

Merton, Robert K. 1938. "Social Structure and Anomie." *American Sociological Review* 3:672–682.

Merton, Robert K. 1957. *Social Theory and Social Structure*. Glencoe, IL: Free Press.

Messner, Michael A. 1990. "Boyhood, Organized Sports, and the Construction of Masculinities." *Journal of Contemporary Ethnography* 18:416–444.

Messner, Michael A. 1992. *Power at Play: Sports and the Problem of Masculinity*. Boston: Beacon Press.

Messner, Michael A., Cheryl Cooky, and Robin H. Hextrum. 2010. *Gender in Televised Sports: News & Highlights Shows, 1989–2009*. Los Angeles: University of Southern California, Center for Feminist Research. Retrieved January 16, 2014 (dornsife.usc.edu).

Messner, Michael A., Michele Dunbar, and Darnell Hunt. 2000. "The Televised Sports Manhood Formula." *Journal of Sport & Social Issues* 24:380–394.

Messner, Michael A., and Michaela Musto. 2014. "Where Are the Kids?" *Sociology of Sport Journal* 31:102–122.

Mickle, Tripp. 2013. "TV Rights Push IOC Revenue to Record." *Sport Business Journal*, August 26. Retrieved September 2, 2014 (www.sportsbusinessdaily.com).

Mihoces, Gary. 2013. "Dolphins Players Defend Incognito, Question Martin in Bullying Case." *USA Today*, November 6. Retrieved November 7, 2013 (www.usatoday.com).

Miller, Kathleen E., Merrill J. Melnick, Grace M. Barnes, Michael P. Farrell, and Don Sabo. 2005. "Untangling the Links among Athletic Involvement, Gender, Race, and Adolescent Academic Outcomes." *Sociology of Sport Journal* 22:178–193.

Mills, C. Wright. 1956. *The Power Elite*. New York: Oxford University Press.

Mills, C. Wright. (1959) 2000. *The Sociological Imagination*. New York: Oxford University Press.

Minato, Charlie. 2012. "Ingenious Ambush Campaigns from Nike, Samsung and BMW Make Official Sponsorships Look Like a Waste." *Business Insider*, June 14. Retrieved September 3, 2014 (www.businessinsider.com).

Moltz, David. 2011. "Rich Get Richer in Athletics." *Inside Higher Ed*, June 16. Retrieved July 18, 2014 (www.insidehighered.com).

Moody's. 2013. *Eye on the Ball: Big-Time Sports Pose Growing Risks for Universities*. Moody's Investor Service, October 10. Retrieved July 16, 2014 (www.insidehighered.com).

Moore, Molly. 2006. "Zidane Says 'Harsh' Insults by Italian Led to Head Butt." *Washington Post*, July 13. Retrieved July 13, 2006 (www.washingtonpost.com).

Morello, Danielle. 1997. "Soccer War." *Inventory of Conflict and Environment (ICE) Case Studies*, Case Study #32/35. Retrieved July 7, 2007 (www.american.edu).

Morgan, Glennisha. 2013. "Brittney Griner Says Baylor Coach Wanted Lesbian Players to Keep Quiet about Sexuality." *Huffington Post*, May 20. Retrieved March 12, 2014 (www.huffingtonpost.com).

Morris, Benjamin. 2014. "Comparing the WWF's Death Rate to the NFL's and Other Pro Leagues'." *FiveThirtyEight*, April 24. Retrieved August 14, 2014 (fivethirtyeight.com).

Morrison, L. Leotus. 1993. "The AIAW: Governance by Women for Women." Pp. 59–66 in *Women in Sport: Issues and Controversies*, edited by G. L. Cohen. Newbury Park, CA: Sage Publications.

Mravic, Mark. 2010. "Soccer's Ugly Eastern Front." *Sports Illustrated Scorecard*, October 25, p. 21.

MSNBC. 2007. "Tim Hardaway Says He Wants 'Second Chance.'" *MSNBC News Service*, March 14. Retrieved May 13, 2007 (www.msnbc.msn.com).

Munson, Lester. 2008. "Donaghy's Claims Serious, Troubling for NBA." *ESPN.com*, June 11. Retrieved May 14, 2014 (www.espn.go.com).

Murphy, Chris. 2013. "Tackling Racism in the Beautiful Game." *CNN World Sport Presents Documentary*, May 31. Retrieved March 20, 2014 (edition.cnn.com).

Myerberg, Paul. 2012. "Ohio State Freshman Takes the 'Student' Out of Student-Athlete." *USA Today*, October 5. Retrieved July 14, 2014 (www.usatoday.com).

Myrdal, Gunnar. 1944. *An American Dilemma: The Negro Problem and American Democracy*. New York: Harper Brothers.

NASBE. 2004. *Athletics and Achievement: The Report of the NASBE Commission on High School Athletics in an Era of Reform*. Alexandria, VA: National Association of State Boards of Education.

National Football Foundation. 2014. "Intense Interest in College Football Continues," April 9. Posted in *College Athletics Clips*. Retrieved April 28, 2014 (www.college athleticsclips.com).

NBC Sports. 2013. "NBC Universal to Provide Unprecedented Coverage of 2014 Sochi Olympics." *NBC Sports.com*, December 19. Retrieved March 23, 2014 (nbcsports grouppressbox.com).

NCAA. 2012. "Estimated Probability of Competing in Athletics beyond the High School Interscholastic Level." *NCAA*, September 17. Retrieved February 5, 2014 (www.ncaa.org).

NCAA. 2014. "NCAA College Athletics Statistics." Reported in *Statistic Brain*, April 26. Retrieved July 7, 2014 (www.statisticbrain.com).

Nelson, Jeff. 2013. "Penn State Continues Strong Home Football Attendance; Ranks No. 5 Nationally." *Penn State*, November 25. Retrieved May 15, 2014 (news.psu.edu).

New, Jake. 2014a. "Senate Committee Grills NCAA President about College Athlete Rights." *Inside Higher Ed*, July 10. Retrieved July 10, 2014 (www.insidehighered.com).

New, Jake. 2014b. "With Autonomy Granted, 'Rocky Road' Still Ahead for Five Richest NCAA Conferences." *Inside Higher Ed*, October 3. Retrieved October 3, 2014 (www.insidehighered.com).

New York Times. 2009. "Do Olympic Host Cities Ever Win?" *New York Times*, October 2. Retrieved September 3, 2014 (roomfordebate.blogs.nytimes.com).

Newberry, Paul. 2002/2005. "NASCAR: A Big Money Machine." Pp. 227–233 in *Sport in Contemporary Society: An Anthology*, 7th ed., edited by D. S. Eitzen. Boulder, CO: Paradigm Publishers.

Newman, Cathy. 2014. "Olympic Games: Legacy or Money Pit?" *National Geographic News*, February 21. Retrieved September 3, 2014 (news.nationalgeographic.com).

Newman, Jonah. 2014. "Coaches, Not Presidents, Top Public-College Pay List." *Chronicle of Higher Education*, May 16. Retrieved May 16, 2014 (chronicle.com).

Newman, Joshua I., and Adam S. Beissel. 2009. "The Limits to 'NASCAR Nation': Sport and the 'Recovery Movement' in Disjunctural Times." *Sociology of Sport Journal* 26:517–539.

Newport, Frank. 2010. "Near-Record High See Religion Losing Influence in America." *Gallup*, December 29. Retrieved April 18, 2014 (www.gallup.com/poll).

NFL. 2012. "NFL Says Saints Created 'Bounty' Program from 2009 to 2011." *NFL.com*, March 2. Retrieved May 15, 2014 (www.nfl.com).

Nielsen. 2013. "Tops of 2013: TV and Social Media." *Nielsen*, December 17. Retrieved February 19, 2014 (www.nielsen.com).

Nightengale, Bob. 2012. "Growing Number of Injuries Gives MLB Pause." *USA Today*, August 17. Retrieved August 14, 2014 (www.usatoday.com).

Nilsson, Jeff. 2014. "Top 5 Highest Average Ticket Prices for the NASCAR Sprint Cup." *The Richest*, February 18. Retrieved August 6, 2014 (www.therichest.com).

Nixon, Howard L. II. 1976. "Team Orientations, Interpersonal Relations, and Team Success." *Research Quarterly* 47:429–435.

Nixon, Howard L. II. 1977. "Reinforcement Effects of Sports Team Success on Cohesiveness-Related Factors." *International Review of Sport Sociology* 4(12):17–38.

Nixon, Howard L. II. 1984. *Sport and the American Dream*. Champaign, IL: Leisure Press Imprint/Human Kinetics.

Nixon, Howard L. II. 1988. "The Background, Nature, and Implications of the Organization of the 'Capitalist Olympics.'" Pp. 237–251 in *The Olympic Games in Transition*, edited by J. O. Segrave and D. Chu. Champaign, IL: Human Kinetics.

Nixon, Howard L. II. 1993. "Accepting the Risks of Pain and Injury in Sport: Mediated Cultural Influences on Playing Hurt." *Sociology of Sport Journal* 10:183–196.

Nixon, Howard L. II. 2002. "Studying Sport from a Social Network Approach." Pp. 267–291 in *Theory, Sport and Society*, edited by J. Maguire and K. Young. Amsterdam: JAI/ Elsevier Science Imprint.

Nixon, Howard L. II. 2004. "Cultural, Structural and Status Dimensions of Pain and Injury Experiences in Sport." Pp. 81–97 in *Sporting Bodies, Damaged Selves: Sociological Studies of Sports-Related Injury*, edited by K. Young. Amsterdam: Elsevier.

Nixon, Howard L. II. 2007. "Constructing Diverse Sport Opportunities for People with Disabilities." *Journal of Sport & Social Issues* 31:417–433.

Nixon, Howard L. II. 2008. *Sport in a Changing World*. Boulder, CO: Paradigm Publishers.

Nixon, Howard L. II. 2011. "Engagement of People with Disabilities in Sport across the Life Span." Pp. 111–121 in *Lifelong Engagement in Sport and Physical Activity: Participation and Performance across the Lifespan*, edited by N. L. Holt and M. Talbot. London and New York: Routledge.

Nixon, Howard L. II. 2014. *The Athletic Trap: How College Sports Corrupted the Academy.* Baltimore: Johns Hopkins University Press.

Nixon, Howard L. II., and James H. Frey. 1996. *A Sociology of Sport.* Belmont, CA: Wadsworth.

Norlander, Matt. 2014. "NCAA Will Re-open Academic Fraud Investigation at North Carolina." *CBSSports.com*, June 30. Retrieved July 15, 2014 (www.cbssports.com).

Novak, Michael. 1976. *The Joy of Sport.* New York: Basic Books.

O'Brien, Kat. 2010. "Passion, Shame Fills Cuban Baseball." *Cincinnati Enquirer*, April 6. Retrieved August 28, 2014 (archive.cincinnati.com).

Office for Civil Rights. 2013. "Dear Colleague Letter: Students with Disabilities in Extra-Curricular Athletics." *United States Department of Education Office for Civil Rights*, January 25. Letter from Acting Assistant Secretary for Civil Rights. Retrieved March 26, 2014 (www2.ed.gov).

ONE News. 2011. "Team NZ Defends Government Funding." *TVNZ*, April 21. Retrieved February 11, 2014 (tvnz.co.nz).

O'Neil, Patrick H. 2012. *Essentials of Comparative Politics*, 4th ed. New York: W.W. Norton.

Onishi, Norimitsu. 2013. "When Billionaire Sets Rules, It's an Exclusive Race." *New York Times*, June 3. Retrieved February 11, 2014 (www.nytimes.com).

Ozanian, Mike. 2013. "The Forbes Fab 40: The World's Most Valuable Sports Brands 2013." *Forbes*, October 11. Retrieved February 19, 2014 (www.forbes.com).

Panja, Tariq. 2013. "Top Soccer Leagues Get 25% Rise in TV Rights Sales, Report Says." *Bloomberg News*, November 10. Retrieved July 26, 2014 (www.bloomberg.com).

Pappa, Evdokia, and Eileen Kennedy. 2013. "'It Was My Thought . . . He Made It a Reality': Normalization and Responsibility in Athletes' Accounts of Performance-Enhancing Drug Use." *International Review for the Sociology of Sport* 48:277–294.

Parker, Graham. 2013. "Can MLS Escape the Violent Side of Soccer's Globalization?" *The Guardian*, April 17. Retrieved May 27, 2014 (www.theguardian.com).

Parker-Pope, Tara. 2010. "As Girls Become Women, Sports Pay Dividends." *New York Times*, February 16. Retrieved February 16, 2014 (well.blogs.nytimes.com).

Pathe, Simone. 2013. "Law Enables Students with Disabilities to Play Sports." PBS NewsHour Extra, February 18. Retrieved March 26, 2014 (www.pbs.org).

PBS. 1999. "Nixon's China Game: Ping-Pong Diplomacy (April 6–17, 1971)." Documentary Film. *PBS American Experience Series.* Retrieved August 29, 2014 (www.pbs.org).

Pearson, Demetrius W., and C. Allen Haney. 1999. "The Rodeo Cowboy: Cultural Icon, Athlete, or Entrepreneur." *Journal of Sport & Social Issues* 23:308–327.

Peers, Danielle. 2012. "Patients, Athletes, Freaks: Paralympism and the Reproduction of Disability." *Journal of Sport & Social Issues* 36:295–316.

Pelissero, Tom. 2013. "Stakes High for Jonathan Martin, Richie Incognito, Others in Dolphins Bullying Investigation." *USA Today*, November 15. Retrieved November 15, 2013 (www.usatoday.com).

Pelts, Jonathan, and Lizzie Haldane. 2014. "Keeping Score When It Counts: Academic Progress/Graduation Success Rate Study of 2014 NCAA Division I Men's and Women's Basketball Tournament Teams." *The Institute for Diversity and Ethics in Sport (TIDES)*, March 18. Retrieved July 16, 2014 (www.tidesport.org).

Pennington, Bill. 2014. "In a Hole, Golf Considers Digging a Wider One." *New York Times*, April 18. Retrieved April 19, 2014 (www.nytimes.com).

Pennington, Bill, and Steve Eder. 2014. "In Domestic Violence Cases, N.F.L. Has a History of Lenience." *New York Times*, September 19. Retrieved September 20, 2014 (www.nytimes.com).

Phillips, Angus. 2006. "The Best Boats Money Can Buy Are Ready for America's Cup." *Washington Post*, July 8. Retrieved July 10, 2006 (www.washingtonpost.com).

Pickett, Moneque Walker, Marvin P. Dawkins, and Jomills Henry Braddock. 2012. "Race and Gender Equity in Sports: Have White and African American Females Benefited Equally from Title IX?" *American Behavioral Scientist* 56:1581–1603.

Pilon, Mary. 2013. "Races End Fees to Top Runners, Drawing Outcry." *New York Times*, October 2. Retrieved October 3, 2013 (www.nytimes.com).

Pismennaya, Evgenia. 2014. "Putin Sochi Bill Seen Rising $7 Billion after Flame Dies." *Bloomberg*, February 13. Retrieved September 3, 2014 (www.bloomberg.com).

Pockrass, Bob. 2014a. "Danica Patrick Shrugs Off Criticism from Richard Petty." *Sporting News*, February 13. Retrieved March 16, 2014 (www.sportingnews.com).

Pockrass, Bob. 2014b. "What Is NASCAR's New Race Team Alliance Really After?" *Sporting News*, July 10. Retrieved August 6, 2014 (www.sportingnews.com).

Poli, Raffaele. 2010. "Understanding Globalization through Football: The New International Division of Labour, Migratory Channels, and Transnational Trade Circuits." *International Review for the Sociology of Sport* 45:491–506.

Porto, Brian, Gerald Gurney, Donna A. Lopiano, B. David Ridpath, Allen Sack, Mary Willingham, and Andrew Zimbalist. 2014. "The 'Big Five' Power Grab: The Real Threat to College Sports." *Chronicle of Higher Education*, June 19. Retrieved June 20, 2014 (chronicle.com).

Povoledo, Elisabetta. 2012. "After Scandal in Soccer, Italy's Leader Urges Break." *New York Times*, May 29. Retrieved May 30, 2012 (www.nytimes.com).

Prewitt, Alex. 2014. "Large Majority Opposes Paying NCAA Athletes, Washington Post-ABC News Poll Finds." *Washington Post*, March 23. Retrieved March 25, 2014 (www.washingtonpost.com).

Price, S. L. 2014. "Moment of Truth." *Sports Illustrated*, February 17, pp. 32–35.

Price, S. L., and Farrell Evans. 2006. "The Damage Done." *Sports Illustrated*, June 26, pp. 75–84.

Prisbell, Eric. 2014. "Blame Emerges Like Cracks in Texas High School Stadium." *USA Today*, June 10. Retrieved June 10, 2014 (www.usatoday.com).

Pronger, Brian. 2005. "Sport and Masculinity: The Estrangement of Gay Men." Pp. 332–345 in *Sport in Contemporary Society: An Anthology*, 7th ed., edited by D. S. Eitzen. Boulder, CO: Paradigm Publishers.

Pugmire, Jerome. 2006. "Zidane Ends World Cup Career with Head Butt, Red Card." *USA Today*, July 9. Retrieved July 9, 2006 (www.usatoday.com).

Putnam, Robert D. 2000. *Bowling Alone: The Collapse and Revival of American Community*. New York: Simon and Schuster.

Quinn, Ryan. 2014. "With Only 7 Openly Gay Athletes in Sochi, Those in Closet Are on the Wrong Side of History." *SB Nation Outsports*, January 30. Retrieved March 13, 2014 (www.outsports.com).

Quirk, James, and Rodney Fort. 1999. *Hard Ball: The Abuse of Power in Pro Team Sports*. Princeton, NJ: Princeton University Press.

RAM Financial Group. 2014. "Athlete Services." Retrieved February 5, 2014 (www.ramfg.com).

Raney, Arthur A. 2006. "Why We Watch and Enjoy Mediated Sports." Pp. 313–329 in *Handbook of Sports and Media*, edited by A. A. Raney and J. Bryant. Mahwah, NJ: Lawrence Erlbaum Associates.

Raney, Arthur A., and Jennings Bryant, eds. 2006. *Handbook of Sports and Media*. Mahwah, NJ: Lawrence Erlbaum Associates.

Rees, C. Roger, Wolf-Deitrich Brettschneider, and Hans Peter Brandl-Bredenbeck. 1998. "Globalization of Sports Activities and Sport Perceptions among Adolescents from Berlin and Suburban New York." *Sociology of Sport Journal* 15:216–230.

Rhoden, William C. 2012. "Breakout Stars Shine a Light on Those Left Out." *New York Times*, February 19. Retrieved February 20, 2012 (www.nytimes.com).

Rhoden, William C. 2013. "N.F.L. Protects the Pocket as Black Quarterbacks Transcend It." *New York Times*, September 29. Retrieved September 30, 2013 (www.nytimes.com).

Rhoden, William C. 2014a. "Pledging to Shield the N.F.L.'s Brand at All Costs." *New York Times*, September 9. Retrieved September 10, 2014 (www.nytimes.com).

Rhoden, William C. 2014b. "Vacillations on Discipline Put a Behemoth on Shaky Ground." *New York Times*, September 17. Retrieved September 18, 2014 (www. nytimes.com).

Rickman, Martin. 2014. "NCAA Announces $20M Settlement with Keller Plaintiffs over Video Game Claims." *SI.com*, June 9. Retrieved June 10, 2014 (www.si.com).

Riesman, David, and Reuel Denney. 1951. "Football in America: A Study in Cultural Diffusion." *American Quarterly* 3:309–319.

Rinehart, Robert, and Chris Grenfell. 2002. "BMX Spaces: Children's Grass Roots' Courses and Corporate-Sponsored Tracks." *Sociology of Sport Journal* 19:302–314.

Ring, Jennifer. 2013. "Invisible Women in America's Pastime . . . or, 'She's Good. It's History, Man.'" *Journal of Sport & Social Issues* 37(1):57–77.

Riordan, James. 1980. *Soviet Sport*. New York: New York University Press.

Ripley, Amanda. 2013. "The Case against High-School Sports." *The Atlantic*, September 18. Retrieved June 17, 2014 (www.theatlantic.com).

Ritzer, George. 2011. *The McDonaldization of Society 6*. Thousand Oaks, CA: Pine Forge Press.

Ritzer, George, and Todd Stillman. 2001. "The Postmodern Ballpark as a Leisure Setting: Enchantment and Simulated De-McDonaldization." *Leisure Sciences* 23:99–113.

Roberts, Daniel. 2013a. "Fortunate 50." *Sports Illustrated*, May 20. Retrieved February 7, 2014 (www.sportsillustrated.cnn.com).

Roberts, Daniel. 2013b. "2013 SI International 20." *Sports Illustrated*, May 20. Retrieved February 7, 2014 (www.sportsillustrated.cnn.com).

Roberts, Selena, and David Epstein. 2009. "Confronting A-Rod." *Sports Illustrated*, February 16, pp. 28–31.

Robinson, Mandrallius. 2014. "Freedom from Religion Foundation Files Complaint to Clemson." *Greenville News*, April 15. Retrieved April 18, 2014 (www.greenvilleonline.com).

Robson, Douglas. 2010. "Lana Lawless' Suit Puts Gender in Spotlight Again." *USA Today*, November 30. Retrieved November 30, 2010 (www.usatoday.com).

Roderick, Martin. 2012. "An Unpaid Labor of Love: Professional Footballers, Family Life, and the Problem of Job Relocation." *Journal of Sport & Social Issues* 36:317–338.

Rojek, Chris. 2001. *Celebrity*. London: Reaktion Books.

Rookwood, Joel, and Clive Palmer. 2011. "Invasion Games in War-Torn Nations: Can Football Help to Build Peace?" *Soccer & Society* 12:184–200.

Rookwood, Joel, and Geoff Pearson. 2012. "The Hoolifan: Positive Fan Attitudes to Football 'Hooliganism.'" *International Review for the Sociology of Sport* 47:149–164.

Roper, Emily A., and Erin Halloran. 2007. "Attitudes toward Gay Men and Lesbians among Heterosexual Male and Female Student-Athletes." *Sex Roles* 57:919–928.

Rovell, Darren. 2007. "Yahoo Buys Rivals.com: Is the Deal Worth It?" CNBC.com, June 21. Retrieved June 22, 2014 (www.cnbc.com).

Rovell, Darren. 2013. "Sports Owners Highlight U.S. 'Richest.'" *ESPN.com*, September 16. Retrieved September 16, 2013 (espn.go.com).

Rudolph, Frederick. 1962. *The American College and University*. New York: Random House Vintage Books.

Rushin, Steve. 2013. "The Kingdoms of Sport: The Power 50." *Sports Illustrated*, March 11, pp. 40–51.

Ryan, Nate. 2014. "Race Track Owner Blasts Race Team Alliance, Kauffman." *USA Today*, July 11. Retrieved August 6, 2014 (www.usatoday.com).

Sabo, Don. 2012. "High School Sports and Educational Benefits: What We Really Know and Don't Know." *LA84 Foundation*, November 8. Retrieved June 28, 2013 (www. la84.org).

Sabo, Don, and Philip Veliz. 2008. *Go Out and Play: Youth Sports in America.* East Meadow, NY: Women's Sports Foundation. October. Retrieved March 3, 2014 (www.ncys.org).

Sabo, Don, and Philip Veliz. 2011. *Progress without Equity: The Provision of High School Athletic Opportunity in the United States, by Gender 1993–94 through 2005–06.* November. East Meadow, NY: Women's Sports Foundation. Retrieved March 4, 2014 (www.ncys.org).

Sabo, Don, and Philip Veliz. 2012. *The Decade of Decline: Gender Equity in High School Sports.* October. Ann Arbor, MI: SHARP Center for Women and Girls. Retrieved January 15, 2015 (irwg.research.umich.edu/pdf/OCR.pdf).

Sabo, Don, Philip Veliz, and Lisa Rafalson. 2013. *More Than a Sport: Tennis, Education and Health.* White Plains, NY: USTA Serves.

Sacirbey, Omar. 2012. "Why Basketball Is Muslims' Favorite Sport." *Huff Post Religion,* May 21. Retrieved April 18, 2014 (www.huffingtonpost.com).

Sage, George H. 1998. *Power and Ideology in American Sport: A Critical Perspective,* 2nd ed. Champaign, IL: Human Kinetics.

Sage, George H. 1999. "Justice Do It! The Nike Transnational Advocacy Network: Organizations, Collective Actions, and Outcomes." *Sociology of Sport Journal* 16:206–235.

Sage, George H. 2005. "Corporate Globalization and Sporting Goods Manufacturing: The Case of Nike." Pp. 362–382 in *Sport in Contemporary Society: An Anthology,* 7th ed., edited by D. S. Eitzen. Boulder, CO: Paradigm Publishers.

Sage, George H. 2010. *Globalizing Sport: How Organizations, Corporations, Media, and Politics Are Changing Sports.* Boulder, CO: Paradigm Publishers.

Sage, George H., and D. Stanley Eitzen. 2013. *Sociology of North American Sport,* 9th ed. New York: Oxford University Press.

Sakurai, Joji. 2005. "Will French Riots Breed Islamic Jihadism." *Mail Guardian,* November 21. Retrieved June 18, 2014 (mg.co.za).

Sanchez, Ray. 2014. "Alex Rodriguez Drops Lawsuits, Accepts 162-Game Suspension." *CNN U.S.,* February 9. Retrieved April 15, 2014 (www.cnn.com).

Sandomir, Richard. 2013. "NBC Gets More Than It Expected." *New York Times,* September 25. Retrieved February 12, 2014 (www.nytimes.com).

Sandomir, Richard. 2014. "Deep-Pocketed Bayern Munich Is Open for Business in U.S." *New York Times,* July 31. Retrieved August 1, 2014 (www.nytimes.com).

Saslow, Eli. 2006a. "Turning Promise into a Commodity." *Washington Post,* January 29. Retrieved January 31, 2006 (www.washingtonpost.com).

Saslow, Eli. 2006b. "Opportunity Realized a World Away." *Washington Post,* January 30. Retrieved January 31, 2006 (www.washingtonpost.com).

Saslow, Eli. 2006c. "Trading Diamonds for Blue Chips." *Washington Post,* January 31. Retrieved January 31, 2006 (www.washingtonpost.com).

Saslow, Eli. 2006d. "Is There Such a Thing as a Perfect 10?" *Washington Post,* July 4. Retrieved July 4, 2006 (www.washingtonpost.com).

Saunders, Laura. 2012. "Are the Green Bay Packers the Worst Stock in America?" *Wall Street Journal,* January 13. Retrieved August 4, 2014 (blogs.wsj.com).

Savage, Howard J. 1929. *American College Athletics,* bulletin 23. New York: Carnegie Foundation for the Advancement of Teaching.

Scalia, Vincenzo. 2010. "Just a Few Rogues?" *International Review for the Sociology of Sport* 44:41–53.

Schaerlaeckens, Leander. 2013. "Battle against Racism Truly Alarming." *Fox Soccer Exclusive,* November 12. Retrieved March 20, 2014 (msn.foxsports.com).

Schell, Lea Ann "Beez," and Margaret Carlisle Duncan. 1999. "A Content Analysis of CBS's Coverage of the 1996 Paralympic Games." *Adapted Physical Activity Quarterly* 16:27–47.

Schimmel, Kimberly S. 2012. "Protecting the NFL/Militarizing the Homeland: Citizen Soldiers and Urban Resilience in Post-9/11 America." *International Review for the Sociology of Sport* 47:338–357.

Schinke, Robert J., Amy T. Blodgett, Hope E. Yungblut, Mark A. Eys, Randy C. Battochio, Mary Jo Wabano, Duke Peltier, Stephen Ritchie, Patricia Pickard, and Danielle Recollet-Saikonnen. 2010. "The Adaptation Challenges and Strategies of Adolescent Aboriginal Athletes Competing Off Reserve." *Journal of Sport & Social Issues* 34:438–456.

Schleifer, Yigal. 2009. "In Turkey, Women Playing Soccer View for Acceptance." *New York Times*, March 4. Retrieved March 4, 2014 (www.nytimes.com).

Schrotenboer, Brent. 2013a. "NFL Arrests Persist after Turbulent Offseason." *USA Today*, September 5. Retrieved September 24, 2014 (www.usatoday.com).

Schrotenboer, Brent. 2013b. "Richie Incognito's Bully Reputation Goes Back to 2002." *USA Today*, November 5. Retrieved November 7, 2013 (www.usatoday.com).

Schrotenboer, Brent. 2013c. "Black NFL Players Arrested Nearly 10 Times as Often as Whites." *USA Today*, November 29. Retrieved May 9, 2014 (www.usatoday.com).

Schrotenboer, Brent. 2014. "Ex-Players Clash on NFL Concussion Lawsuit Settlement." *USA Today*, August 19. Retrieved August 20, 2014 (www.usatoday.com).

Schwarz, Alan. 2014. "Uncertainty over Whether N.F.L. Settlement's Money Will Last." *New York Times*, January 29. Retrieved January 30, 2014 (www.nytimes.com).

Schwarz, Mark. 2002. "Will the Fans Strike Back?" *Outside the Lines (Show 123)*, August 4. Retrieved August 3, 2014 (espn.go.com).

Seattle PI. 2005. "WNBA Star Becomes Only Openly Gay Player Active in Pro Team Sports." *Seattle Post-Intelligencer*, October 26. Retrieved March 12, 2014 (www.seattlepi.com).

Segrave, Jeffrey O. 2000. "Sport as Escape." *Journal of Sport & Social Issues* 24:61–77.

Selliaas, Andreas. 2012. "From Olympic Massacre to the Olympic Stress Syndrome." *International Review for the Sociology of Sport* 47:379–396.

Senn, Albert Eric. 1999. *Power, Politics, and the Olympic Games*. Champaign, IL: Human Kinetics Publishers.

Sheinin, Dave. 2013. "You Gotta Play Hurt." *Sports Illustrated*, August 12, pp. 57–63.

SI.com. 2005. "Homosexuality and Sports." *SI.com*, April 12. Retrieved July 12, 2006 (sportsillustrated.cnn.com).

Silk, David. 1999. "Local/Global Flows and Altered Production Practices: Narrative Constructions at the 1995 Canada Cup of Soccer." *International Review for the Sociology of Sport* 34:113–123.

Silk, Michael, David L. Andrews, and C. L. Cole, eds. 2005a. *Sport and Corporate Nationalisms*. Oxford: Berg.

Silk, Michael, David L. Andrews, and C. L. Cole. 2005b. "Corporate Nationalism(s)? The Spatial Dimensions of Sporting Capital." Pp. 1–12 in *Sport and Corporate Nationalisms*, edited by M. Silk, D. L. Andrews, and C. L. Cole. Oxford: Berg.

Silva, Carla Filomena, and P. David Howe. 2012. "The (In)validity of Supercrip Representation of Paralympian Athletes." *Journal of Sport & Social Issues* 36:174–194.

Simon, David R. 2012. *Elite Deviance*, 10th ed. Upper Saddle River, NJ: Pearson.

Smart, Barry. 2005. *The Sport Star: Modern Sport and the Cultural Economy of Sporting Celebrity*. London: Sage Publications.

Smith, Chris. 2013a. "The Money behind the BCS National Championship." *Forbes*, January 7. Retrieved July 7, 2014 (www.forbes.com).

Smith, Chris. 2013b. "Major League Soccer's Most Valuable Teams." *Forbes*, November 20. Retrieved July 28, 2014 (www.forbes.com).

Smith, Gary. 2010. "Gareth Thomas . . . The Only Openly Gay Male Athlete." *Sports Illustrated*, May 3, pp. 54–62.

Smith, Stephanie. 2013. "NFL and Ex-Players Reach Deal in Concussion Lawsuit." *CNN.com*, August 30. Retrieved August 31, 2013 (www.cnn.com).

Snider, Mike. 1996. "Michael Jordan's Bigger Than Basketball; He's a Pop Icon." *USA Today*, July 19, p. 3D.

Sociology of Sport Journal. 2009. "Special Issue: New Media and Global Sporting Cultures." *Sociology of Sport Journal* 26(1).

Sokolove, Michael. 2007. "The Scold." *New York Times Magazine*, January 7. Retrieved January 28, 2007 (www.nytimes.com).

Solomon, Jon. 2014a. "NCAA Reaches $20 Million Settlement with Players in Video Game Suit." *CBSSports.com*, June 9. Retrieved July 11, 2014 (www.cbssports.com).

Solomon, Jon. 2014b. "NCAA's Next Big Lawsuit over Scholarships Comes into Focus." *CBSSports.com*, July 11. Retrieved July 12, 2014 (www.cbssports.com).

Sondheimer, Eric. 2012. "Playing in High School Is No Longer Vital for College Scholarship Seekers." *Los Angeles Times*, January 31. Retrieved June 5, 2014 (www.latimes.com).

Southall, Richard M., Mark S. Nagel, Eric D. Anderson, Fritz G. Polite, and Crystal Southall. 2009. "An Investigation of Male College Athletes' Attitudes toward Sexual-Orientation." Special issue, *Journal of Issues in Intercollegiate Athletics*: 62–77.

Southall, Richard M., Megan Sexton, and Ben Waring. 2014. "2014 Adjusted Graduation Gap Report: NCAA FBS Football." *College Sport Research Institute*, October 5. Retrieved October 6, 2014 (csri-sc.org).

Spencer, Nancy. 1997. "Once upon a Subculture: Professional Women's Tennis and the Meaning of Style, 1970–1974." *Journal of Sport & Social Issues* 21:363–378.

Sportcal. 2012. "Olympic Games Set to Break $8bn Revenues Barrier in Four-Year Cycle Ending with London 2012." *Sportcal*, July 19. Retrieved September 3, 2014 (www.sportcal.com).

Sports Illustrated. 2013. "Special Report on Oklahoma State Football: What It All Means." *SI.com*, September 16. Retrieved September 18, 2013 (www.si.com).

SportsBusiness Journal. 2006. "2006 SBJ/SBD Reader Survey." *SportsBusiness Journal*, December 3. Retrieved December 5, 2006 (www.sportsbusinessjournal.com).

Springer, Shira. 2012. "Female Muslim Olympians Try to Inspire, Bring More Progress." *Boston Globe*, August 9. Retrieved April 4, 2014 (www.bostonglobe.com).

Stancill, Jane. 2013. "In Moving On, Holden Thorp Will Leave Athletic Headaches Behind." *NewsObserver.com*, February 18. Retrieved July 15, 2014 (www.newsobserver.com).

Stankevitz, J. J. 2014. "The Most Expensive Ticket in College Football Is . . ." *NBC Sports.com*, June 3. Retrieved July 7, 2014 (collegefootballtalk.nbcsports.com).

Stanley, Alessandra. 2013. "Dispassionate End to a Crumbled American Romance." *New York Times*, January 18. Retrieved April 14, 2014 (www.nytimes.com).

Staples, Andy. 2011. "Youth Football Steadily Evolving into Mirror Image of AAU Hoops." *SI.com*, February 10. Retrieved February 14, 2011 (sportsillustrated.cnn.com).

Staples, Andy. 2012. "Full Cost-of-Attendance Scholarship Debate Breaks Up the FBS." *SI.com*, March 8. Retrieved March 14, 2012 (sportsillustrated.cnn.com).

Statista. 2014a. "Broadcast Revenue from the Summer Olympic Games from 1960 to 2012." *Statista: The Statistical Portal*. Retrieved September 2, 2014 (www.statista.com).

Statista. 2014b. "Broadcast Revenue from the Winter Olympic Games from 1960 to 2010." *Statista: The Statistical Portal*. Retrieved September 2, 2014 (www.statista.com).

Statistical Brain. 2013. "Professional Sports Average Salary/Revenue/Salary Cap." *Statistical Brain*. Retrieved February 7, 2014 (www.statisticbrain.com).

Steensland, Brian, Jerry Z. Park, Mark D. Regnerus, Lynn D. Robinson, W. Bradford Wilcox, and Robert D. Woodberry. 2000. "The Measure of American Religion: Toward Improving the State of the Art." *Social Forces* 79:291–318.

Stevenson, Betsey. 2009. "Beyond the Classroom: Using Title IX to Measure the Return to High School Sports." PSC Working Paper Series, PSC 10-03, July. University of Pennsylvania Scholarly Commons. Retrieved March 4, 2014 (repository.upenn.edu).

Strauss, Ben. 2014. "As Northwestern Players Pursue Unionization, Voice in the Wilderness Gains a Chorus." *New York Times*, February 8. Retrieved February 8, 2014 (www.nytimes.com).

Stripling, Jack. 2014. "At Chapel Hill, a Scandal That Won't Die." *Chronicle of Higher Education*, September 8. Retrieved September 8, 2014 (chronicle.com).

Sugden, John, and Alan Tomlinson. 1996. "What's Left When the Circus Leaves Town? An Evaluation of World Cup USA 1994." *Sociology of Sport Journal* 13:238–258.

Suggs, Welch. 2004. "Colleges' Expenditures on Athletics Can't Be Calculated, Panelists Tell Knight Commission." *Chronicle of Higher Education*, November 5. Retrieved March 21, 2005 (chronicle.com/weekly).

Supiano, Beckie. 2014. "Earnings Disparity Grows between Young Workers with and without Degrees." *Chronicle of Higher Education*, February 11. Retrieved February 16, 2014 (chronicle.com).

Swanson, Lisa. 2009a. "Complicating the 'Soccer Mom': The Cultural Politics of Forming Class-Based Identity, Distinction, and Necessity." *Research Quarterly for Exercise and Sport* 80:345–354.

Swanson, Lisa. 2009b. "Soccer Fields of Cultural [Re]Production: Creating 'Good Boys' in Suburban America." *Sociology of Sport Journal* 26:404–424.

Szymanski, Stefan. 2003. "Making Money out of Football." *Imperial College London, The Business School*, April. Retrieved July 30, 2014 (www1.imperial.ac.uk).

Thamel, Pete. 2013. "Wanted: 1.2 Billion Basketball Fans." *Sports Illustrated*, May 6, pp. 66–75.

Tharoor, Ishaan. 2012. "Port Said Stadium Disaster: What's behind Egyptian Soccer's Bloodiest Day?" *Time*, February 1. Retrieved May 19, 2014 (world.time.com).

Theberge, Nancy. 1981. "The World of Women's Professional Golf: Responses to Structured Uncertainty." Pp. 287–300 in *Sport in a Sociocultural Process*, edited by M. Hart and S. Birrell. Dubuque, IA: William C. Brown.

Theberge, Nancy. 2000. *Higher Goals: Women's Ice Hockey and the Politics of Gender*. Albany: State University of New York Press.

Thompson, Wright. 2013. "When the Beautiful Game Turns Ugly." *ESPNFC & ESPN The Magazine*, June 5. Retrieved March 20, 2014 (espn.go.com).

Time. 1972. "Horror and Death at the Olympics." *Time*, September 18. Retrieved July 8, 2007 (www.time.com).

Tippett, Krista. 2014. "Play, Spirit, and Character." Interview with Stuart Brown. *On Being*, June 21. Distributed by American Public Media to public radio stations. Retrieved June 22, 2014 (www.onbeing.org).

TNS Global. 2010. "TNS, ESPN Debut Sports Poll Europe Survey." *Market Research World*, March 3. Retrieved February 19, 2014 (www.marketresearchworld.net).

Tocqueville, Alexis de. (1853) 1969. *Democracy in America*, edited by J. P. Mayer. Garden City, NY: Doubleday.

Topič, Mojca Doupona, and Jay Coakley. 2010. "Complicating the Relationship between Sport and National Identity: The Case of Post-Socialist Slovenia." *Sociology of Sport Journal* 27:371–389.

Topping, Alexandra. 2013. "Paralympic Stars See Their Earning Potential Soar." *The Guardian*, September 7. Retrieved March 24, 2014 (www.theguardian.com).

Torre, Pablo S. 2009. "How (and Why) Athletes Go Broke." *Sports Illustrated (SI Vault)*, March 23. Retrieved February 11, 2014 (sportsillustrated.cnn.com).

Torre, Pablo S., and David Epstein. 2012. "The Transgender Athlete." *Sports Illustrated*, May 28, pp. 66–73.

Tracy, Marc. 2014. "N.C.A.A. Votes to Give Richest Conferences More Autonomy." *New York Times*, August 7. Retrieved August 8, 2014 (www.nytimes.com).

Trahan, Kevin. 2014. "Ranking College Football Coaches by Salary Earned per 2013 Win." *SB Nation*, June 30. Retrieved July 2, 2014 (www.sbnation.com).

Tramel, Jimmie. 2014. "SI Series Has Cost Oklahoma State More Than $100,000 So Far." *Tulsa World*, January 14. Retrieved July 17, 2014 (www.tulsaworld.com).

Trota, Brian, and Jay Johnson. 2004. "A Brief History of Hazing." Pp. x–xvi in *Making the Team: Inside the World of Sport Initiations and Hazing*, edited by J. Johnson and M. Holman. Toronto: Canadian Scholars' Press.

Tsitsos, William, and Howard L. Nixon II. 2012. "The Star Wars Arms Race in College Athletics: Coaches' Pay and Athletic Program Status." *Journal of Sport & Social Issues* 36:68–88.

Tucker, Tim. 2006. "Woods' Popularity Passes Jordan." *Atlanta Journal-Constitution*, June 11. Retrieved June 19, 2006 (www.ajc.com).

Turner, Elliott. 2014. "MLS vs. the Major Leagues: Can Soccer Compete When It Comes to Big Business?" *The Guardian*, March 12. Retrieved July 27, 2014 (www.the guardian.com).

UEFA. 2014. "Financial Fair Play: Everything You Need to Know." *Union of European Football Associations (UEFA)*, February 28. Retrieved July 30, 2014 (www.uefa.com).

USA Today. 2012. "NFLPA Cites 1996 Bounty Program Allowed by NFL." *USA Today*, October 18. Retrieved May 15, 2014 (www.usatoday.com).

USOC (United States Olympic Committee). 2014. "Television Schedule Set for Sochi 2014 Paralympic Winter Games." *TeamUSA.org*, February 19. Retrieved March 23, 2014 (www.teamusa.org).

Uthman, Daniel. 2014. "John Calipari, Kentucky Agree to $52 Million Contract Extension." *USA Today*, June 5. Retrieved June 6, 2014 (www.usatoday.com).

Van Natta, Don Jr. "Book: NFL Crusaded against Science." *ESPN.com*, September 29. Retrieved October 2, 2013 (espn.go.com).

Van Riper, Tom. 2014. "March Madness Ratings and Revenue Keep Reaching New Heights." *Forbes*, March 20. Retrieved July 7, 2014 (www.forbes.com).

Veblen, Thorstein. 1899. *Theory of the Leisure Class*. New York: Macmillan.

Veliz, Philip, and Sohaila Shakib. 2014. "Gender, Academics, and Interscholastic Sports Participation at the School Level: A Gender-Specific Analysis of the Relationship between Interscholastic Sports Participation and AP Enrollment." *Sociological Analysis* 47:101–120.

Voepel, Mechelle. 2014. "Stern Was 'Mastermind' behind WNBA." *ESPN.com*, January 31. Retrieved July 31, 2014 (espn.go.com).

Wahl, Grant. 2007. "What a Ball Can Do." *Sports Illustrated*, August 6, p. 25.

Wahl, Grant. 2011. "Sorry Soccer." *Sports Illustrated Scorecard*, May 23, p. 16.

Wahl, Grant. 2014. "The Two Brazils." *Sports Illustrated*, March 3, pp. 60–67.

Wahl, Grant, and L. Jon Wertheim. 2003. "A Rite Gone Terribly Wrong." *Sports Illustrated*, December 22, pp. 68–75.

Waldron, Travis. 2014. "F.C. Barcelona to Pay for $800 Million Stadium Upgrade with Private Finances." *ThinkProgress*, January 22. Retrieved August 5, 2014 (think progress.org).

Wallerstein, Immanuel. 1974. *The Modern World-System*. New York: Academic Press.

Walton, Theresa A. 2004. "Steve Prefontaine: From Rebel with a Cause to Hero with a Swoosh." *Sociology of Sport Journal* 21:61–83.

Wang, Chih-ming. 2004. "Capitalizing the Big Man: Yao Ming, Asian America, and the China Global." *Inter-Asia Cultural Studies* 5:263–278.

Warner, Brian. 2012. "Professional Athletes Who Have Gone Broke." *Celebrity Net Worth*, October 5. Retrieved February 4, 2014 (www.celebritynetworth.com).

Washington Post. 2013a. "NFL Football Poll: Playing through the Pain." *Washington Post NFL Retired Players Survey*, April 13. Retrieved August 18, 2014 (www.washingtonpost.com).

Washington Post. 2013b. "NFL Retirees Happy with Football Career Despite Lasting Pain." *Washington Post NFL Retired Players Survey*, May 17. Retrieved August 14, 2014 (www.washingtonpost.com).

Watts, Jonathan. 2013. "Cuba's Baseball Players Have Ceilings on Their Salaries Lifted and Can Play Abroad." *The Guardian*, December 18. Retrieved August 28, 2014 (www.theguardian.com).

Webb, Brant. 2012. "Unsportsmanlike Conduct: Curbing the Trend of Domestic Violence in the National Football League and Major League Baseball." *Journal of Gender, Social Policy & the Law* 20:741–761.

Weber, Bruce. 2011. "Al Davis, the Controversial and Combative Raiders Owner, Dies at 82." *New York Times*, October 8. Retrieved July 31, 2014 (www.nytimes.com).

Weber, Max. 1978. "Class, Status, and Party." Pp. 926–939 in *Economy and Society*, edited by G. Roth and C. Wittich, vol. 2. Berkeley: University of California Press.

Weedon, Gavin. 2012. "'I Will Protect This House': Under Armour, Corporate Nationalism and Post-9/11 Cultural Politics." *Sociology of Sport Journal* 29:265–282.

Weinstein, Arthur. 2013. "Top 10 Most Watched Sporting Events on U.S. Television." *Listosaur*, January 24. Retrieved February 19, 2014 (listosaur.com).

Weir, David R., James S. Jackson, and Amanda Sonnega. 2009. "Study of Retired NFL Players," Sponsored by the National Football League and the Player Care Foundation. University of Michigan Institute for Social Research (ISR), September 10. Retrieved August 17, 2014 (ns.umich.edu).

Weir, Tom. 2011. "Sports' First Openly Gay CEO Resigns from Suns." *USA Today*, September 9. Retrieved September 12, 2011 (www.usatoday.com).

Wertheim, L. Jon. 2005. "Gays in Sport: A Poll." *SI.com (Sports Illustrated)*, April 12. Retrieved July 12, 2006 (sportsillustrated.cnn.com).

Wertheim, L. Jon. 2010. "Did Yeardley Love Have to Die?" *Sports Illustrated*, May 17, pp. 28–34.

Wertheim, Jon. 2013. "A Reluctant Trailblazer, Navratilova Laid Groundwork for Collins." *SI.com*, April 30. Retrieved March 12, 2014 (sportsillustrated.cnn.com).

Wertheim, L. Jon, and George Dohrmann. 2006. "Going Big-Time." *Sports Illustrated*, March 13, pp. 62–69 .

White, Aaron, and Ralph Hingson. 2013. "The Burden of Alcohol Use: Excessive Alcohol Consumptions and Related Consequences among College Students." *Alcohol Research: Current Reviews*, NIH National Institute on Alcohol Abuse and Alcoholism 35(2):201–218. Retrieved May 29, 2014 (pubs.niaaa.nih.gov).

White, Philip, and William McTeer. 2012. "Socioeconomic Status and Sport Participation at Different Developmental Stages during Childhood and Youth: Multivariate Analyses Using Canadian National Survey Data." *Sociology of Sport Journal* 29:186–209.

Whiteside, Kelly. 2013. "NYC Marathon: Tatyana McFadden Completes Slam." *USA Today*, November 3. Retrieved April 1, 2014 (www.usatoday.com).

Wiedeman, Reeves. 2014. "In Search of the Next Andrew Wiggins." *New York Times Sunday Magazine*, August 3. Retrieved August 6, 2014 (www.nytimes.com).

Wieting, Stephen G. 2000. "Twilight of the Hero in the Tour de France." *International Review for the Sociology of Sport* 35:348–363.

Wiggins, David K. 2011. "Farewell to Sport: The Decline of the African American Athlete during the Age of the Collegiate Arms Race and Globalization." *Journal of Intercollegiate Sport* 3:32–37.

Williams, John-John IV. 2008. "A Salute to a Md. Athlete." *Baltimore Sun*, June 30. Retrieved April 1, 2014 (www.baltimoresun.com).

Williams, Sue. 2013. "Corruption in Sport—A 'Gold Rush' with the Law Left Behind." UNESCO, May 14. Retrieved May 13, 2014 (www.unesco.org).

Wilson, Brian, and Robert Sparks. 1996. "'It's Gotta Be the Shoes': Youth, Race, and Sneaker Commercials." *Sociology of Sport Journal* 13:398–427.

Wilson, William Julius. 1996. *When Work Disappears: The World of the New Urban Poor.* New York: Alfred A. Knopf.

Wilson, William Julius. 2011. "Being Poor, Black, and American." *American Educator* Spring: 10–25, 46. Retrieved April 1, 2014 (www.aft.org).

Withycombe, Jenny Lind. 2011. "Intersecting Selves: African American Female Athletes' Experiences of Sport." *Sociology of Sport Journal* 28:478–493.

Wolverton, Brad. 2006. "Duke Crisis Ripples through College Sports." *Chronicle of Higher Education*, April 21. Retrieved May 22, 2006 (chronicle.com).

Wolverton, Brad. 2010. "Arrests of College Athletes Are More Than Double Those of Pros." *Chronicle of Higher Education*, September 10. Retrieved September 11, 2010 (chronicle.com).

Wolverton, Brad. 2013a. "Ed O'Bannon: 'They're Going to Change the Game.'" *Chronicle of Higher Education*, November 13. Retrieved November 14, 2014 (chronicle.com).

Wolverton, Brad. 2013b. "With God on Our Side." *Chronicle of Higher Education*, November 24. Retrieved April 18, 2014 (chronicle.com).

Wolverton, Brad. 2014a. "Inside Colleges' Pursuit of a Future Star: The Courting of Marvin Clark." *Chronicle of Higher Education*, June 3. Retrieved June 3, 2014 (chronicle. com).

Wolverton, Brad. 2014b. "'I Was an Athlete Masquerading as a Student." *Chronicle of Higher Education*, June 10. Retrieved June 10, 2014 (chronicle.com).

Wolverton, Brad. 2014c. "Senate Committee Has Tough Questions for NCAA Leader." *Chronicle of Higher Education*, July 10. Retrieved July 10, 2014 (chronicle.com).

Wunderli, John. 1994. "Squeeze Play: The Game of Owners, Cities, Leagues and Congress." *Marquette Sports Law Review* 5:83–121.

Xiao, Li. 2004. "China and the Olympic Movement." *Getting Ready for the Games: Beijing 2008.* Retrieved July 9, 2007 (www.china.org.cn/english).

Yost, Mark. 2010. *Varsity Green: A Behind the Scenes Look at Culture and Corruption in College Athletics.* Palo Alto, CA: Stanford University Press.

Young, Kevin. 2000. "Sport and Violence." Pp. 382–407 in *Handbook of Sports Studies*, edited by J. Coakley and E. Dunning. London: Sage.

Young, Kevin, ed. 2004. *Sporting Bodies, Damaged Selves: Sociological Studies of Sports-Related Injury.* Amsterdam: Elsevier.

Yueh, Linda. 2014. "Why on Earth Buy a Football Club?" *BBC News*, February 27. Retrieved July 26, 2014 (www.bbc.com).

Zengerle, Jason. 2010. "Oracle of the Hardwood." *New York Magazine*, June 6. Retrieved June 22, 2014 (nymag.com).

Zgaga, Blaž. 2009. "Slovenia's Drift from Democracy." *The Guardian*, July 19. Retrieved August 28, 2014 (www.theguardian.com).

Zillgitt, Jeff. 2011. "NBA Fines Bulls' Joakim Noah $50,000 for Anti-Gay Slur." *USA Today*, May 23. Retrieved May 24, 2011 (www.usatoday.com).

Zimbalist, Andrew. 1999. *Unpaid Professionals: Commercialism and Big-Time College Sports.* Princeton, NJ: Princeton University Press.

Zirin, Dave. 2007. "Chief Concern." *SI.com*, October 30. Retrieved October 30, 2007 (sportsillustrated.cnn.com).

Index

Italicized page numbers refer to photo captions